'In this rich and vitally importan[t] ... most influential and creative write[rs] ... [brings] together an international group of widely respected analysts to address a broad landscape of contemporary psychoanalytic issues. This timely book is distinguished both by a level of clarity that reaches far beyond psychoanalytic tribalism and wise, discerning thought that will serve as a catalyst for further analytic progress.'

Michael J. Diamond, training and supervising analyst,
Los Angeles Institute and Society for Psychoanalytic Studies;
author, *Masculinity and Its Discontents* and *Ruptures in the
American Psyche: Containing Destructive Populism in Perilous Times*

'There are books that one has to pay attention to when reading them, and others that draw your attention. *Psychoanalysis at the Crossroads* belongs to this second class. In it, Fred Bush brings together prestigious colleagues from around the world who write about current issues that have to do with theoretical, clinical, and institutional concerns. There are multiple perspectives on each of the issues that makes it a book for real exchange. *Psychoanalysis at the Crossroads* is a symphonic work that shows the strength of our discipline and its continuous growth.'

Claudia Lucia Borensztejn, training analyst at the Argentine
Psychoanalytic Association (APA); ex-president of APA 2016–2020;
editor of *Diccionario de Psicoanálisis Argentino. Latinoamérican*; Board
representative in IPA 2021–2023

'Eloquent and compelling. With this new collection of essays, written by psychoanalysts from diverse and contradictory perspectives, Fred Busch challenges us to meet at this contemporary crossroads ... a current fork on the road ... to Thebes? ... and take it as an opportunity to rethink the psychoanalytic tapestry, not only by speaking in one's own direction, but also by listening to others. Otherwise, we are ineluctably doomed.'

Ellen Sparer, training analyst and director of Training of the
Paris Institute of Psychoanalysis, S.P.P.

Psychoanalysis at the Crossroads

In this clear and thoughtful book, an international group of distinguished authors explore the central issues and future directions facing psychoanalytic theory and practice.

The book explores four main questions in the development of psychoanalysis: what psychoanalysis is as an endeavour now and what it may be in the future; the effect of social issues on psychoanalysis and of psychoanalysis on social issues, such as race and gender; the importance of psychoanalytic institutes on shaping future psychoanalytic theory and practice; and the likely major issues that will be shaping psychoanalysis in years to come.

Including contributions from within every school of psychoanalytic thought, this book is essential reading for psychoanalysts, psychoanalytic psychotherapists and all who are curious about the future directions of the profession.

Fred Busch has published numerous articles on psychoanalytic technique and he has been invited to present papers and clinical workshops nationally and internationally. His last four books are *Creating a Psychoanalytic Mind* (2014); *The Analyst's Reveries: Explorations in Bion's Enigmatic Concept* (2019); *Dear Candidate* (2020); and *A Fresh Look at Psychoanalytic Technique* (2021).

Psychoanalysis at the Crossroads

An International Perspective

Edited by Fred Busch

Routledge
Taylor & Francis Group

LONDON AND NEW YORK

Cover image: fourleaflover, courtesy of Getty Images

First published 2023
by Routledge
4 Park Square, Milton Park, Abingdon, Oxon OX14 4RN

and by Routledge
605 Third Avenue, New York, NY 10158

Routledge is an imprint of the Taylor & Francis Group, an informa business

British Library Cataloguing-in-Publication Data
A catalog record has been requested for this book

Library of Congress Cataloging-in-Publication Data
Names: Busch, Fred, 1939– editor.
Title: Psychoanalysis at the crossroads: an international perspective / edited by Fred Busch.
Description: Milton Park, Abingdon, Oxon; New York, NY: Routledge, 2023. |
Includes bibliographical references and index. |
Identifiers: LCCN 2022039031 (print) | LCCN 2022039032 (ebook) |
ISBN 9781032375496 (hardback) | ISBN 9781032375502 (paperback) |
ISBN 9781003340744 (ebook)
Subjects: LCSH: Psychoanalysis.
Classification: LCC BF173 .P77529 2023 (print) | LCC BF173 (ebook) |
DDC 150.19/5–dc23/eng/20220906
LC record available at https://lccn.loc.gov/2022039031
LC ebook record available at https://lccn.loc.gov/2022039032

Every effort has been made to contact copyright-holders. Please advise the publisher of any errors or omissions, and these will be corrected in subsequent editions.

ISBN: 9781032375496 (hbk)
ISBN: 9781032375502 (pbk)
ISBN: 9781003340744 (ebk)

DOI: 10.4324/9781003340744

Typeset in Garamond
by Newgen Publishing UK

People wish to be settled: only as far as they are unsettled is there any hope for them.

Ralph Waldo Emerson

2, 11, 12, 14, 32, 43, 49, 77, 78, 82, 96, 112/113, 117, 118, 125, 131, 147/148, 163, 174, 206, 219, 242, 243, 281, 286, 287, 288, 292, 300,

Contents

Contributors

David Bell is a training and supervising analyst and a past president of the British Psychoanalytical Society. He retired in January 2021 from the Tavistock and Portman NHS Foundation Trust where he led the Fitzjohn's Unit – a service for the most complex and severe adult cases referred to the Trust. He also served two terms as the academic and clinical staff representative on the Tavistock Council of Governors. He lectures and publishes on a wide range of subjects including the development of psychoanalytic concepts, the work of Freud, Klein and Bion and the understanding of severe psychological disorder. Books include *Reason and Passion*; *Psychoanalysis and Culture: A Kleinian Perspective*; *Living on the Border*; *Turning the Tide* (on the work of the Fitzjohn's Unit); and one small book, *Paranoia*. He is a leading psychiatric expert in asylum/human rights.

Rachel Blass is a training and supervising analyst at the Israel Psychoanalytic Society, a member of the British Psychoanalytical Society and on the Board of the International Journal of Psychoanalysis where she is the editor of the 'Controversies' section. She was formerly a professor of psychoanalysis at universities both in Israel and England. She has published numerous papers and a book that elucidate the foundations of analytic thinking and practice, with a special focus on Kleinian psychoanalysis and its Freudian roots. Her writings have been translated into 15 languages. While she lives and practises in Jerusalem, via the internet she also teaches and supervises in the US, Australia and several countries in Europe and Asia.

Werner Bohleber is a psychoanalyst in private practice in Frankfurt am Main, a training and supervising analyst and a former president of the German Psychoanalytical Association (DPV). From 1997 to 2017 he was the main editor of the journal *PSYCHE*. In 2007 he received the Mary Sigourney Award. His research subjects and main publication themes are late adolescence and young adulthood; psychoanalytic theory; the history of psychoanalysis in Germany; transgenerational consequences of the Nazi period and the war on the second and third generation; nationalism, xenophobia and anti-Semitism; trauma; and religious fundamentalism and terrorism.

Stefano Bolognini is a psychiatrist and a training and supervising analyst of the Italian Psychoanalytic Society (SPI). He has served as president of SPI (2009–2013), was an IPA Board member (2002–2012) and was IPA president from 2013 to 2017. A member of the European Editorial Board of the *International Journal of Psychoanalysis* from 2002 to 2012, he was also the founder and chair of the *IPA Inter-Regional Encyclopedic Dictionary of Psychoanalysis (IRED)* from 2016 to 2021. He is an honorary member of the New York Contemporary Freudian Society (CFS) and of the Los Angeles Institute and Society for Psychoanalytic Studies (LAISPS), and a member of the Advisory Board of the International Psychoanalytic University of Berlin (IPU). He has published 260 psychoanalytic papers, and his books on empathy and on the inter-psychic dimension have been translated into several languages.

Fred Busch is a training and supervising analyst at the Boston Psychoanalytic Society and Institute. He has published over 70 articles in the psycho-analytic literature, and five books. His work has been translated into ten languages, and he has been invited to present over 180 papers and clinical workshops nationally and internationally. His last four books, published by Routledge, are as follows: *Creating a Psychoanalytic Mind* (2014); *The Analyst's Reveries: Explorations in Bion's Enigmatic Concept* (2019); *Dear Candidate: Analysts from Around the World Offer Personal Reflections on Psychoanalytic Training, Education, and the Profession* (2020); *A Fresh Look at Psychoanalytic Technique* (2021).

Roosevelt Cassorla is a psychoanalyst in Campinas, Brazil. He is a training analyst of the Brazilian Psychoanalytic Societies of São Paulo and Campinas, and has worked as a full professor in the Department of Medical Psychology at the State University of Campinas. He is a collabor-ator on the *IPA Encyclopedic Dictionary*. He co-ordinates the Working Party 'Microscopy of the Analytic Session' of the Brazilian and Latin-American Psychoanalytic Federations, and has published seven books including *The Psychoanalyst, the Theater of Dreams and the Clinic of Enactment* (Routledge). He received the 2017 Mary Sigourney Award for Outstanding Achievement in Psychoanalysis.

H. Shmuel Erlich is a former president and chair of the Training Committee of the Israel Psychoanalytic Society, and a training and supervising ana-lyst and faculty of the Israel Psychoanalytic Institute. He was professor of psychoanalysis (emeritus) and director of the Sigmund Freud Center at the Hebrew University of Jerusalem. He chaired the IPA Education Committee, served four terms as European Representative on the IPA Board, is currently chair of the IPA Institutional Issues Committee and has received the Sigourney Award. His publications span adolescent devel-opment and psychopathology, experiential dimensions of object relations, group and organizational processes, as well as two books: *The Couch in the Marketplace* and *Fed with Tears, Poisoned with Milk*. He is in private practice in Tel Aviv.

Abel Fainstein is a psychiatrist and master in psychoanalysis, as well as a former president of the Argentine Psychoanalytical Association (APA) and the Psychoanalytic Federation of Latin America (FEPAL). He has received the Konex Award in Psychoanalysis (2016), is a former member of the IPA Board and a former communications advisor of the IRED. In 2021 he was a judge for the first IPA Tyresias Award on Sexual and Gender Diversity, and in 2019 acted as co-editor of *On Training Analysis. Debates* (APA Editorial). His latest publications are as follows: *El poder en las instituciones psicoanalíticas*, en Acerca del Fanatismo, Carisma, Poder. Comp. J. Sahovaler (2022); *Transferencia, Contratransferencia y Encuadre*, Comp. F. Gomez (2021); *Dear Candidate*, Comp. F. Busch (2019); *Who Is Behind the Couch*, R. Winer and K. Malawista (2016).

Allannah Furlong, Psychologist, is a former president of the *Société psychanalytique de Montréal* and former member of the North American Editorial Board of the *International Journal of Psychoanalysis*. She has written about different aspects of the frame, including missed sessions, symbolic payments in state-covered health care, the notion of informed consent in psychoanalytic treatment, various aspects of confidentiality, and the issue of patient consent for the use of clinical material in publications and clinical presentations. She is also a co-editor of two interdisciplinary collections on confidentiality. Other articles have reflected on trauma and temporality in lovesickness and dehumanization as a shield against our helpless openness to the other. For the latter essay in 2013, she was the recipient of the JAPA prize for an original or significant contribution to the psychoanalytic literature.

Samuel Gerson is a founder and past president of the Northern California Society for Psychoanalytic Psychology (NCSPP) and of the Psychoanalytic Institute of Northern California (PINC) where he is a training and supervising analyst. Dr Gerson is an associate editor of *Psychoanalytic Dialogues*, and an editor for *Studies in Gender and Sexuality* and the *Psychoanalytic Quarterly*. He has written about aspects of intersubjectivity and psychopathology including the publications *Hysteria and Humiliation* (2011, *Psychoanalytic Dialogues*) and *The Relational Unconscious* (2004, *Psychoanalytic Quarterly*). In 2007 he received the Elise M. Hayman Award for the Study of Genocide and the Holocaust from the International Psychoanalytic Association for his paper *When the Third Is Dead: Memory, Mourning and Witnessing in the Aftermath of the Holocaust* (2009, *International Journal of Psychoanalysis*).

Arthur Leonoff is a psychologist and supervising and training analyst of the Canadian Psychoanalytic Society. He is an honorary member of the American Psychoanalytic Association, a former Board member of the International Psychoanalytic Association and current chair (2021–2025) of International New Groups. His most recent book is *When Divorces Fail: Disillusionment, Destructivity, and High-Conflict Divorce*.

Eric R. Marcus is a professor of Clinical Psychiatry at Columbia University College of Physicians and Surgeons, and a training and supervising analyst at the Columbia University Center for Psychoanalytic Training and Research, where he was the director for ten years. He is a distinguished life fellow of the American Psychiatric Association, and fellow of: the NY Academy of Medicine, the NY Psychiatric Society, the American Board of Psychoanalysis and the Center for Advanced Psychoanalytic Studies. He studies symbolic alterations of reality: their phenomenology, neurophysiology, psychic structure and adaptational uses by individuals and culture. He believes modern ego psychology is an umbrella meta-theory for psychoanalysis. Most recently, Eric authored *Psychosis and Near Psychosis: Ego Function, Symbol Structure, Treatment* (third edition; Routledge, 2017) and *Modern Ego Psychology and Human Sexual Experience: The Meaning of Treatment* (Routledge, 2023).

Jon Mills is a Canadian philosopher, psychoanalyst and retired clinical psychologist. He is Honorary Professor, Department of Psychosocial and Psychoanalytic Studies, University of Essex, Colchester; faculty member in the Postgraduate Programs in Psychoanalysis and Psychotherapy, Gordon F. Derner School of Psychology, Adelphi University, New York and the New School for Existential Psychoanalysis, California; and is Emeritus Professor of Psychology and Psychoanalysis, Adler Graduate Professional School, Toronto. He is the recipient of numerous awards for his scholarship, including four Gradiva Awards. He is also the author and/or editor of over 30 books in psychoanalysis, philosophy, psychology, and cultural studies. In 2015 he was given the Otto Weininger Memorial Award for Lifetime Achievement by the Canadian Psychological Association.

Cecilio Paniagua did his medical training at Universidad Complutense and Universidad Autónoma in Madrid, his hometown. With a Fulbright Scholarship, he did his psychiatric training at Philadelphia's Jefferson Medical College, and his psychoanalytic training at the Baltimore-Washington Institute. He became a teacher and training analyst at the Asociación Psicoanalítica de Madrid. He has authored over one hundred articles, chapters, prologues and translations in Spanish and English, and two books: *Técnica Psicoanalítica: Aportaciones de la Psicología del Yo* and *Visiones de España: Reflexiones de un Psicoanalista*.

Cordelia Schmidt-Hellerau is a training and supervising analyst and in the faculty of the Boston Psychoanalytic Society and Institute as well as of the Swiss Psychoanalytic Society. Her area of expertise is metapsychology, in particular drive theory. She has published numerous papers and three books on theoretical and clinical psychoanalysis. Her 2018 publication of *Driven to Survive* (IPBooks) was a finalist of the American Board and Academy of Psychoanalysis Book Prize. She published her first novel, *Rousseaus Traum*, in 2019 in German and her second novel, *Memory's Eyes*, in 2020 (IPBooks). Since 2017 she has been the chair of the IPA in Culture Committee and works in private practice in Chestnut Hill near Boston.

Harvey Schwartz is a training and supervising analyst at the Psychoanalytic Association of New York and the Psychoanalytic Center of Philadelphia. He currently is the co-chair of the IPA in Health Committee and the book series editor of IPA in the Community and the World. He has contributed to and edited six volumes, most recently, *The Jewish Thought and Psychoanalysis Lectures* and *Applying Psychoanalysis in Medical Care*. He is the producer and host of the IPA podcast Psychoanalysis on and off the Couch.

Alan Sugarman is a training and supervising psychoanalyst and a supervising child and adolescent psychoanalyst at the San Diego Psychoanalytic Center. He is also a clinical professor of Psychiatry at the University of California, San Diego. Dr Sugarman is the former and founding head of the APsaA Department of Psychoanalytic Education. He serves on the editorial Boards of *Psychoanalytic Psychology*, the *Psychoanalytic Quarterly* and the *Journal of the American Psychoanalytic Association*.

David Tuckett is a fellow and training analyst of the British Psychoanalytic Society, and Emeritus Professor of Decision-Making at UCL and a senior research fellow at the Blavatnik School of Government, University of Oxford. He founded the New Library of Psychoanalysis (1987), was editor-in-chief of the *International Journal of Psychoanalysis* (1988–2001) and president of the European Psychoanalytic Federation (1999–2004). The author of books and journal articles in psychoanalysis, economics, finance and sociology, he received the IPA Training Award (2004) and the Sigourney Award for distinguished contributions to the field of psychoanalysis once in 2007 and again (as a CEO of Psychoanalytic Electronic Publishing [PEP]) in 2018. He is also in private practice.

Virginia Ungar is a training analyst at the Buenos Aires Psychoanalytic Association. She has taught at the Institute of Psychoanalysis of her society and in other societies in Argentina and abroad such as Brazil, Chile, USA and Europe. She has published numerous articles in psychoanalytic journals and book chapters. She was the former chair of the IPA's Child and Adolescent Psychoanalysis Committee (COCAP) and of the IPA Committee for Integrated Training. She was given the Platinum Konex

Award, for the most outstanding personality of the last decade in the discipline of psychoanalysis, in 2016. She is the former president of the IPA (in the period 2017–2021), the first woman to be elected to that position since the IPA's inception.

Harriet Wolfe is President of the International Psychoanalytical Association, past president of the American Psychoanalytic Association, clinical professor of Psychiatry and Behavioral Sciences at the University of California, San Francisco and training and supervising analyst at the San Francisco Center for Psychoanalysis. Her scholarly interests include clinical applications of psychoanalytic research, organizational processes, female development and therapeutic action. She has co-authored a number of psychoanalytically informed guided activity workbooks for children, parents and teachers to help children cope with natural and man-made disasters. She has a private practice of psychoanalysis, and individuals' and couples' psychoanalytic psychotherapy in San Francisco.

Introduction

Fred Busch

Yogi Berra, an American baseball player, was well known for his malapropisms. One saying of his came to mind when thinking about this book ... "When you come to a fork in the road, take it".[1] It is my impression that, over the years, there have been many forks in the road that psychoanalysis faced, without any consensus on which direction to take. Some believe this is a good thing, concluding that ferment leads to creativity, which can be true. Still, over the last twenty years, I have grown concerned with what seems to me an increasing feeling of ennui that has taken over what I thought was central to psychoanalysis ... i.e., the psychoanalytic method and the goals of psychoanalysis, issues that I consider crucial to the legitimacy of our profession. At this point we have multiple perspectives of what *is* psychoanalytic technique, often in conflict with each other, with little attempt to resolve differences. Not an easy task, but I fear that within our field too many of us have come to favor the comfort of conviction over the discomfort of doubt. We listen to opinions that make us feel good, instead of ideas that make us think hard. We see disagreement as a threat to our convictions and our egos, rather than an opportunity to learn. We surround ourselves with people who agree with our conclusions, when we should be gravitating towards those who challenge our thought process. One example is the increasing number of themed journals, where primarily those of a particular theoretic persuasion publish, quoting those of the same ilk, without bothering to incorporate or even know of contradictory positions. Further, it was my belief that we hadn't confronted certain issues for political reasons, and that we were drifting towards others without rigorous discussion. This was my concern, but in discussions with colleagues I realized there were many issues that others considered crucial.

It is from this perspective that I asked a number of internationally well-known psychoanalysts if they would be interested in contributing to a book on psychoanalytic crossroads. I hoped to capture their current thinking about a broad landscape of psychoanalytic issues. I suggested they could write about the profession, psychoanalytic technique, psychoanalytic theory, or any psychoanalytic issue that they believed was important for psychoanalysts to consider at this point in time. There was a lot of eagerness to join this project.

DOI: 10.4324/9781003340744-1

Contributing to this project are psychoanalysts well known to most everyone, either through their roles as a current President or past Presidents of the International Psychoanalytic Association, those writing on key topics, and some who may not be so well known, but who I've come to know in my involvement with the International Psychoanalytic Association and whose careful thinking I've appreciated.

I didn't know what to expect from the contributors, and therefore was surprised and pleased that their responses clustered around a few key topics ... i.e., what is psychoanalysis as a treatment and profession, what are the pluses and minuses of psychoanalysts delving into the social issues of our time, institute and organizational functioning, and new ways of looking at certain basic psychoanalytic concepts. I think you will find the chapters thoughtful, clear, and well argued.

The book starts with several chapters on what is basic to psychoanalysis, and the theory behind it. Cordelia Schmidt-Hellerau believes that the neglect of our theoretical foundation is pervasive, especially when it comes to the drives. Additionally, she describes the reasons why Freud's leaving behind the self-preservative drives led to confusion, especially when it came to the aggressive drive. Stefano Bolognini describes the changed conditions in the work of contemporary analysts, who are increasingly dealing with patients' difficulty and reluctance in accepting their basic dependence inside the object relationship. Commitment, the rhythm of the sessions, contractual obligation, and the perception of the complexity and depth of the analytic relationship today much more than in the past arouse their mistrust towards their engagement with psychoanalysis. David Tuckett then wonders if we've lost sight of basic foundational concepts addressed by Freud. He believes that the focus on unconscious mental processes, as in resistances, and the unconscious beliefs driving the transference-countertransference are central to any treatment called psychoanalysis. He believes the "relational turn" ignores what he considers fundamental. Samuel Gerson presents a comprehensive review of relational psychoanalysis, which questions many foundational principles. I then suggest that a number of theories about psychoanalytic treatment and the curative process have been built in opposition to basic Freudian principles rather than as additions, when a more comprehensive view would make for more complex, nuanced theory. Rachel Blass' chapter takes up these issues from a different perspective, while Arthur Leonoff argues that fealty to Freud's view of the destiny of psychoanalysis can inhibit the field. Allanah Furlong wonders about the future role of neuoropsychoanalysis' impact on psychoanalytic thinking. Finally, we have Cecilio Paniagua's masterful description of psychoanalytic technique based on Freud's second *topique* (structural model).

The next cluster of chapters presents various ways of thinking about psychoanalysts' involvement in the social, political, and real-world problems of today. Harriet Wolfe begins with a view of psychoanalysis as a necessary contributor to understanding these issues, followed by a chapter from Roosevelt Cassorla that demonstrates how a deep understanding of psychoanalysis contributes to comprehending one of the most important issues of our time … i.e., what exists and what is true. David Bell's moving chapter delves into how social-political pressures can interfere with a psychoanalytic approach to treating a patient. Jon Mills then explores in detail how a paper appearing in a psychoanalytic journal, seemingly having gone through the usual review process (but didn't), tries to explain white racism based on what Mills believes are dubious ideas.

The next four chapters (Marcus, Sugarman, Erlich, and Fainstein) delve into the functioning of institutes, and describe very different ideas, and in this way present the reader with more crossroads. The last three chapters bring fresh ideas to understanding dreams (Bolognini), trauma (Bohleber), as well as feminism and the infantile (Ungar).

In summary, the contributors raised many fundamental issues for psychoanalysts and psychoanalysis to ponder at this important time. I'm someone who prefers we don't drift into going one way or the other when we reach the crossroads. Lively debate of these issues, I believe, is our main task. It is my hope this book serves as a catalyst for further discussions.

Note

1 Scott, N. (2019) The 50 greatest Yogi Berra quotes. *USA Today Sports*.

Part I

What is basic in psychoanalytic technique and theory?

Chapter 1

Waking a sleeping beauty

Cordelia Schmidt-Hellerau

Once in a while on our long journey in psychoanalysis we come to a crossroad where it makes sense to pause and look around. Where have we gone, and how do we want to proceed? With a keen sense of the current psychoanalytic climate, one of our senior leaders, Fred Busch, invites us to reflect: What have we gained or lost? What do we want to achieve? What are the challenges we have to face? In its roughly 120 years psychoanalysis has grown in depth and width. It has refined its understanding of the development of mental processes and severe psychopathology, and it has disseminated its organization and attracted members all over the world. In this process of geoscientific expansion different cultures of thinking emerged and had their impact on the articulation and application of psychoanalysis in clinical practice. On and off, these differences have ignited excitement and the zest for conquering new territory mostly in our younger members, while our senior members were raising concern over guarding what is essential to psychoanalysis. Whatever the mood of the moment was, I never doubted that psychoanalysis will prevail. To this very day psychoanalysis, its controversial discussions notwithstanding, provides the most detailed understanding of psychic functioning, is capable of learning from criticism, disposed to integrating new research results, and reflective with regard to its effects on clinical practice and social as well as cultural trends. With this in mind I want to address, first, what I believe has been marginalized over time and needs to be refocused on and, second, what we can and should develop as we go into the future.

A theory of the mind

It is my contention that all of Freud's research activities from his 1895 *Project for a Scientific Psychology* till his 1938 *An Out-line of Psycho-Analysis* were geared towards understanding and conceptualizing how the mind works. The specific dynamic that propelled his work to further and deeper insight is characterized by a pendulum motion back and forth between clinical work and theoretical formulation. As he progressed he reconsidered, revised, and refined his

DOI: 10.4324/9781003340744-3

concepts many times, recognizing errors and shortcomings and trying out various solutions for persistent problems, as he strived for greater clarity in his theory of mental functioning. Still, it is indisputable that Freud's work left us with many contradictions and inconsistencies. This actually isn't a bad thing, because what puzzles us keeps us thinking. Thus, following Freud's passing, over the decades many of the loose ends in his metapsychology have been picked up and knitted into a tapestry of conceptions that theoretically and clinically comprehend certain phenomena in a more sophisticated way. The best example for such progress is Freud's concept of narcissism: introduced in 1914 with a short essay of barely thirty pages, the literature on it nowadays extends to thousands of papers and books from many different psychoanalytic vantage points.

While such progress certainly proves the vitality of psychoanalysis (Busch, 2015), it has to be recognized that some of these developments (e.g., Kohut's concept of narcissism) ended up opposing or even trying to replace Freud's basic assumptions. The problem I see with this tendency is certainly not one of fidelity. We don't need to worship Freud nor preach his ideas and arguments. Good criticism has always been integral to Freud's intellectual approach. However, it should be evident by now that starting early on with Jung, Rank, and Adler, efforts to replace Freud's metapsychology with the one or other new concept always lead to an impoverished conception of our theory of mental functioning. Freud's model of the mind was concerned with elaborating the minutiae of processes like cathexes and inhibitions, thresholds and their facilitations, the principles of homeostasis, the formation of structure (representation) through associations of memory traces, perception, and information processing, as well as the conditions and working principles of conscious, preconscious, and unconscious thought processes. Jung's *analytical psychology* by contrast was based on global ideas like individuation, archetypes, or the collective unconscious; Adler's *individual psychology* centered on the inferiority complex; and Rank traced most psychic difficulties back to the patient's birth trauma. These ideas could have contributed to Freud's psychoanalysis; however – following the clashes of personalities, the politics of groups, and the ensuing splits in the psychoanalytic community, all of which I won't get into here – they finally were taken as a new paradigm that led the adherers of these ideas away from those who continued to work with Freud's concepts. Even highly developed psychoanalytic schools, like the Kleinians, whose thinking tackles the dynamics between the paranoid-schizoid and the depressive positions with projective identification as a major mechanism of defense, or Winfried Bion's followers, who organize their work with regard to the ideas of alpha and beta functions in a container-contained model, exist somewhat apart from and competitive with the Freudians under the big tent of the International Psychoanalytical Association (IPA). Group dynamics aside, the reason or necessity for this separateness of schools is obvious: their concepts can only partially be integrated in or compared with those of Freud's metapsychology. As we may note when we listen to panel discussions, it is not so much the clinical outcome or understanding of a patient's material that divides these schools, it is their basic concepts, their theories of mental functioning, that are incompatible. They all – Winnicott's Middle School or Relational Analysis included – do make use of some of Freud's ideas and concepts and then sprout out using them within their own framework, differently from the context and function these concepts were originally created for and contingent on. Evidently, these schools have done valuable clinical work, enabled new insight, and produced interesting literature. However, they abandoned Freud's carefully built *psychic apparatus*. Thus, we may ask, does psychoanalysis still need metapsychology if productive schools can refrain from referring to it? Originally built on the basis of neuronal and cerebral functioning, Freud's model of the mind has always been best suited to be developed further in correspondence to the growing body of brain science (Fotopoulou, Pfaff, and Conway, 2012). Maybe this link seems of minor importance to the clinician. But if we don't subscribe to an esoteric or spiritual idea of the psyche, if we understand that body and mind are two sides of the same coin (Schmidt-Hellerau, 2019), and if we want to keep up with the progress of natural and communication sciences, we better don't lose sight of metapsychology.

In fact, the neglect of our theoretical foundations is pervasive. Psychoanalytic candidates still have to read and discuss Freud's papers on metapsychology and the seventh chapter of *The Interpretation of Dreams*. However, this often seems to degenerate into a matter of duty – to be forgotten almost immediately thereafter. Concededly, it is not easy to elucidate the clinical material based on theoretical conceptions. We tend to be swayed by the *content* of the patient's communications, hence by its conscious portion, and even the idea that this latter is only the currently admissible derivative of an unconscious fantasy easily fades from our consideration. However, already the simple question *why does this come up now?* can lead us to a deeper reflection about the psychic processes at play. For example, the most common notions we hear about during clinical presentations are *identification* with a parental figure, *repetition* of early interactions, *trauma*, and *superego punishment*. While these are important concepts, taken as such without a more detailed reflection on whether the identification is a primary or secondary one and what purpose it may serve, what unconscious fantasy may be enacted in a repetition, in trauma and in superego punishment, what specific defenses are employed therein to keep the psyche balanced and the threat level bearable – just to mention a few possibilities – often seems beyond the presenter's grasp. And it is these detailed reflections based on our *theory of mental functioning* that would deepen our understanding of a patient's inner world.

Metapsychology is a complex theory. It's hard but not impossible[1] to find one's way through the jungle of Freud's statements, assumptions, speculations, and hypotheses. And certainly, this difficulty with getting a clear idea of the various concepts makes it tempting to push theoretical considerations aside. For a while now we've been told that the times of comprehensive theories of the mind are over. Are they really? Freud's ingenious undertaking, his relentless quest to understand *how the mind works*, rewarded him with an abundance of insights into many dimensions of psychic life in the individual as well as in society and culture. I believe, without grounding our work in a basic theory of the mind, we won't make the lasting progress we may want to strive for.

The offense: humans are animals

It wasn't always like this, it's where we arrived at, and it's also Freud's fault! Despite the elegance, freedom, and boldness of his theoretical formulations, reaching some crossroads in his thinking, Freud did muddle up his concepts. What had fit together and made sense before a certain juncture, became contradictory and left the reader baffled thereafter. As is well known, one such point of confusion arose in 1914 with the introduction of narcissism, another in 1920 with his revision of drive theory, and a third in 1923 with his introduction of the structural model – three important expansions of his theory, but not fully mastered. Instead, everything became rather confusing, pitting adherers of Freud's earlier theories against followers of his later formulations. Lacking a comprehensive integration of all different parts of Freud's theory, over time psychoanalysts turned away from metapsychology in general and from drive theory in particular. This temptation was always at hand. The drives represent the most offensive and provocative part in Freud's theory, because they root our highest mental operations in the primordial demands of our body.

> However jealously we usually defend the independence of psychology from every other science, here we stood in the shadow of the unshakable biological fact that the living individual organism is at the command of two intentions, self-preservation, and the preservation of the species, which seem to be independent of each other, which, so far as we know at present, have no common origin and whose interests are often in conflict in animal life. Actually what we are talking now is biological psychology, we are studying the psychical accompaniments of biological processes.
>
> (Freud, 1933, p. 95f)

Freud's assertion that our thinking, our feelings, and perceptions are not only driven by something unconscious (which romanticism could cast in the favorable terms of something *mysterious*), but that they are generated by primitive forces, the drives, aligns us squarely with the animalistic nature of any other living creature. This notion has remained hard to swallow. In 2000 the world reacted with amazement when Craig Venter announced the results of the genome analysis, revealing that humans and chimpanzees share 98.8 %

of their DNA. We are after all not as superior to the brute as we may like to fancy ourselves. Freud would not have been surprised.

To delude ourselves about the animalistic foundation of our mental operations by trying to split drives from wishes (Holt, 1976) and metapsychology from clinical theory (Klein, 1973) has major consequences. Freud's theory of the mind is carefully built with only two axiomatic concepts, namely drive and structure. The drives, representing the body's demands on the mind (Freud, 1915), provide the energies and keep us moving towards the object. The structures (associated memory traces of experiences) organize and balance (homeostasis) these energies and direct our moves by representing the object. We could say, structures are like light bulbs: they only shine when they are activated by electrical (drive) energy; thus, "without drives we'd be stuck in the dark" (Schmidt-Hellerau, 2018, p. 8). This was Freud's position from his earliest (Freud, 1900) to his latest (see above, Freud, 1933) formulations:

> But all the complicated thought activity which is spun out from the mnemic image to the moment at which the perceptual identity is established by the external world – all this activity of thought merely constitutes a roundabout path to wish-fulfilment which has been made necessary by experience. *Thought is after all nothing but a substitute for a hallucinatory wish*; and it is self-evident that dreams must be wish-fulfilments, since *nothing but a wish can set our mental apparatus at work*.
>
> (Freud, 1900, p. 566f, my italics)

Nothing but a wish can move us. A wish is a more complex concept than the drive, because it associates a drive's need with the representations of the required object and the specific actions that lead to satisfaction. But it's always the drive energy that activates the wish. No drive – no wish – no thought – and no psychoanalysis.

This tight synopsis shows that the concept of the drives connects the body with the mind and the subject with the object. Freud's metapsychology is a psychoanalytic object-relations theory rooted in human physiology that informs the intricate ways in which our psychic worlds are mapped out. Take away the drives, and the whole model collapses.

A sleeping beauty

To recapture the value of drive theory in our thinking, we need to straighten out its ruptures and understand how its first version can be integrated into the second. Over the years I have done extensive research in metapsychology and the multi-faceted discussions about it (Schmidt-Hellerau, 2001; 2018), of which I can only offer a brief summary here.

Freud, influenced by Darwin, started out with positing a self-preservative and a sexual drive, declaring both as antagonists, which is the basis for his psychoanalytic conflict theory. Within this framework he viewed aggression as the drives' capacities to enforce their strivings for satisfaction should they be met with resistance or obstacles. Most of his theoretical developments are based on this conception. In 1920 he changed the denomination and definition of the drives, now postulating a life and a death drive (aimed at reaching an earlier state of being[2]). While the sexual drive easily fit to the notion of a life drive, the self-preservative drive seemed to contradict its integration into the concept of a death drive. Thus, Freud assigned both, the self-preservative and the sexual drives, to the life drive (with libido as the energy term for both), and declared aggression or destruction as the representative of the death drive. To be sure, Freud wasn't all too convinced about this solution, but he didn't succeed in finding a better one. His contemporaries first grumbled about the idea of a death drive, but soon happily agreed with aggression now being elevated into the rank of a primary drive. Ever since that move psychoanalysts work with sexuality and aggression as the two basic drives in mental life.

Many problems arose from Freud's 1920 turn, not the least of which was that the self-preservative drive, now outfitted with libidinal energy, almost completely faded behind Freud's habitual focus on the sexual drives and his newly established aggressive drives. Till the end of his life and work, Freud held on to his concept of a self-preservative drive, but he never focused enough on it to fully grasp its importance and potential. For a hundred years it remained in the shadows of our theoretical discussions: one hundred years, a sleeping beauty waiting to be woken. It always seemed quite amazing to me that psychoanalysis wouldn't recognize the driven nature of self- and object-preservation, which inform a good part of our mental life in health and peril, in reality and fantasy. We are driven to survive and to keep our objects alive – keep them and us from slipping towards disease and death. The preservative drives, their ideas and fantasies about caretaking, healing, and rescuing, their functions, deviations, and pathologies in individuals, groups, societies, and the environment, occupy substantial areas in mental life, and yet they are an almost unknown continent in psychoanalysis still open for discovery.

In order to start this exploration, we first need to redifferentiate what got muddled in 1920. Here is a short sketch of how I revised Freud's drive theory. For reasons that will become clear in the course of the following, let's start out with the notion of two antagonistic drives as primary forces in mental life, called a life and a death drive. We can say: for the newborn, everything is a matter of life and death. We can't know what an infant experiences; however, when hunger comes up, the sense of starvation may feel like a threat, a move, a drive racing towards death – a death drive. The infant cries, mother comes and nurses the baby, satisfaction ensues. The constant repetition of this feeding experience will establish memory traces, a representation of the satisfying interaction, which then will be activated/cathected ("light up") whenever hunger arises: the baby "knows" she is hungry and can "hallucinate" for a while the upcoming nursing scene. The physiological hunger tension is associated with and will elicit the mental representation of being nursed and satisfied. Thus, it is the repeated intervention of the nursing object that stops this surge towards death and establishes a first structure and idea of self-preservation. Now the infant is no longer driven towards death but towards being nursed, towards survival. Other structures around self-preservation will form, built upon bodily needs (digestion, breath, warmth, sleep, comfort, etc.) tended to and in interaction with the caretaking object. These structures will coalesce and build preservative screens that are more or less capable of containing the drives' urges, activating their specific meaning and directing the moves towards satisfaction. The death drive insofar as it aims at and cathects the representations/screens of self-preservation can now be called a self-preservative drive. However, when the drive pressure is stronger than the screen's capacity to hold it, a surge will reach beyond these representations into an area of disease (which requires intensified care), and finally towards death. This trajectory shows how the preservative drive can be conceptualized as the first and highly structured part of the death drive. For instance, a glass of wine may be good for your health, too much alcohol will make you sick, and *if you can't stop drinking*, and your addiction isn't taken care of, you may eventually die. It is the stability of the preservative screens that keeps the dangers of the death drives at bay by allowing the individual to invest in the tasks of self-preservation. Further development will structurally differentiate between the representations of self and object, both of which can be cathected with *lethe*,[3] the energy of the preservative and death drives. We notice this representational differentiation when the baby not only wants to be fed but also wants to feed the mother; self- and object-preservation (to eat and to feed) will become represented separately.

Reorganizing Freud's drive theory, as sketched above, shows how the self-preservative drive can be understood as part of the death drive – a semantic contradiction that Freud couldn't dissolve. It basically says: if you don't limit the strivings of the death drive, if you don't protect yourself with the measures of self-preservation, you will die. It's not that the death drive kills or wants to kill you, it's that you cannot survive the extreme one-sided strivings of the death drive unless you learn to preserve yourself. This conception allows an integration of Freud's sexual and self-preservative drives into his second antagonism of life and death drives. On both sides it is the object that structures the drives, thereby introducing the needs of self- and object-preservation as well as the desires of self- and object-love. Behind the safety of good self- and object-preservation final death is lurking; and beyond the pleasures of narcissistic and sexual gratification there is the promise of eternal life (in fame, art, science, etc.). Freud's 1920 conception wanted to broaden the perspective from the immediate everyday concerns of the individuum (sex and survival) to his/her strivings for a place within society and culture (framed by life and death).

Reconceptualizing aggression

Finally, this revision of drive theory compels us to rethink aggression. In Freud's 1920 formulation aggression became a primary drive with the aim to destroy for the sake of its own satisfaction. Accordingly, aggression would need to be tamed and sublimated like the sexual drives. This conception is apparent in clinical discussions when the question is raised: What about the patient's aggression? Here, aggression is viewed as a thing in itself, needing to be addressed. However, if we view the (death and) preservative and the (life and) sexual drives as primary, how do we understand aggression? In 1909 Freud had it right when he rejected the idea of "a special aggressive drive alongside of the familiar drives of self-preservation and of sex" and instead held on to his previous conception, which "leaves each drive its own power of becoming aggressive" (Freud 1909, p. 140f). *This power of both primary drives to become aggressive is solely about being effective, succeeding in reaching satisfaction.*

It still makes sense. When you or your object is experienced as endangered, when your narcissism is wounded or your love is interfered with, your efforts increase, more energy is activated, your drives' urges intensify, you fight for what is essential to you – you become aggressive. Obviously then, aggression is about asserting your need and/or desire. We may call it healthy aggression and won't take issue with it if one defends against an attacker. However, transference feelings and perceptions can interfuse reality testing to such an extent that your assertion grows neurotically disproportionate.[4] That's where pointing out aggression won't help. Aggression needs to be *analyzed* in relation to the needs and desires that seem to be endangered to our patient. What are the underlying unconscious fantasies and fears that result in aggressive or destructive thoughts and actions? Once such ideation is understood, reality testing can follow. Are the dangers real? Has the patient reached the object, made his/her point clear to me? These are the questions aggression calls for. The second drive theory lost Freud's previous understanding that aggression comes up as a backup when the goals of the preservative or sexual drives are endangered, when their satisfaction is interfered with or prevented. This correction of our view of aggression seems to me as important as the resumption and development of the preservative drives. *Aggression is the intensified expression of the preservative needs or sexual desires; it is the individual's way of asserting him/herself.*

The way forward

My revision of drive theory is rooted in Freud's 1915 definition of the drive "as a measure of the demand made upon the mind for work in consequence of its connection with the body" (Freud, 1915, p. 122); and it is consistent with his view that the function of the drive is solely to reach satisfaction. Once satisfied, the urge subsides. In line with our physiology, the primary drives have to serve our self-preservation and our sexuality; and aggression is the necessary backup, an energetic drive increase in order to assert their needs and desires.

I suggest reorganizing our thinking according to this revised drive theory. It would be a meaningful shift. I'm not saying that psychoanalysis has not analyzed fantasies related to aggression or has ignored issues of caretaking. However, to consider the *driven nature* of self- and object-preservation and their at times aggressive assertions will deepen our analysis and reconnect our thinking to metapsychology, which will lead us to a more detailed, sophisticated understanding of mental processes.

There are many areas to be rethought and explored on the basis of what we have already understood now in connection with an expanded view of the developmental steps and the pathological derailments of self- and object-preservation, their neglect or aggressive pursuit. It may shed new light on, e.g., greed, eating disorders, addictions, exploitation, hypochondria, or obsessive-compulsive behaviors – just to name a few. To understand that there are powerful drives of a basically animalistic nature at the root of these pathologies will not only deepen our psychoanalytic work with our patients, but may also give us far-reaching insight into the troubles of our times. Still, at the beginning of the twenty-first century, we are called upon to provide some applied psychoanalysis of, e.g., the throwaway mentality of the Western world, the litter pollution of the environment, the lack of climate protection and the denial of the disasters it causes, the exploitation of natural resources in third world countries, and the disregard of the ensuing human catastrophes. In all of these the lack of object-preservation is glaring. Psychoanalysis could provide a deeper understanding of it.

Notes

1   I have offered a formalized, consistent model of Freud's metapsychology in Schmidt-Hellerau, 2001.

2   While Freud's first drive theory is directly linked to the body's demands, his second is formulated in teleological terms. As I have previously elaborated in detail, to define a drive as "an urge inherent in organic life to restore an earlier state of things" (Freud, 1920, p. 36) casts the drives in the role of "intelligent entities that know what they want and remember what has been" (Schmidt-Hellerau, 2001, p. 182). However, "a system's memory consists in its structures, and not in its drives" (ibid.). Obviously, Freud's second drive definition confuses the notion of drives as unidirectional forces or "freely mobile [nervous] processes which press towards discharge" (Freud, 1920, p. 36) with the notion of structure. The drives' only function is to drive until satisfaction is reached, while the structure's function is to organize, balance, and remember *where* satisfaction can be reached.

3   Freud never found a fitting energy term neither for his self-preservative drive nor for his death or aggressive drive. I have suggested to call the energy of the death and preservative drives *lethe* (borrowed from Greek mythology, which names the

river that flows from the land of the living to the land of the death *Lethe*; to drink of it leads to forgetting).

4   For a detailed elaboration of aggression see Schmidt-Hellerau (2002).

References

Busch, F. (2015) Our vital profession. *International Journal of Psychoanalysis*. 96: 533–568.

Fotopoulou, A., Pfaff, D., and Conway, M.A. (2012) *From the Couch to the Lab: Trends in Psychodynamic Neuroscience*. New York: Oxford University Press.

Freud, S. (1900) The interpretation of dreams. *The Standard Edition of the Complete Psychological Works of Sigmund Freud*. 4–5: 1–627.

Freud, S. (1909) Analysis of a phobia in a five-year-old boy ("Little Hans"). *The Standard Edition of the Complete Psychological Works of Sigmund Freud*. 10: 3–149.

Freud, S. (1915) Instincts and their vicissitudes. *The Standard Edition of the Complete Psychological Works of Sigmund Freud*. 14: 109–140.

Freud, S. (1920) Beyond the pleasure principle. *The Standard Edition of the Complete Psychological Works of Sigmund Freud*. 18: 3–64.

Freud, S. (1933) New introductory lectures on psycho-analysis. *The Standard Edition of the Complete Psychological Works of Sigmund Freud*. 22: 3–182.

Holt, R. (1976) Drive or wish? A reconsideration of the psychoanalytic theory of motivation. In: M. Gill and P.S. Holzman (editors) *Psychology versus Metapsychology. Psychoanalytic Essays in Memory of George S. Klein*. New York: International Universities Press, pp. 158–197.

Klein, G.S. (1973) Two theories or one? *Bulletin of the Menninger Clinic*. 37: 102–132.

Schmidt-Hellerau, C. (2001 [1995]) *Life Drive & Death Drive, Libido & Lethe: A Formalized Consistent Model of Psychoanalytic Drive and Structure Theory*. New York: Other Press.

Schmidt-Hellerau, C. (2002) Why aggression? Metapsychological, clinical and technical considerations. *International Journal of Psychoanalysis*. 83(6): 1269–1289.

Schmidt-Hellerau, C. (2018) *Driven to Survive: Selected Papers on Psychoanalysis*. New York: International Psychoanalytic Books.

Schmidt-Hellerau, C. (2019) Body and mind: two sides of one coin. *The Scandinavian Psychoanalytic Review*. 42: 93–102.

Chapter 2

New forms of psychopathology in a changing world

A challenge for psychoanalysis in the twenty-first century[1]

Stefano Bolognini

In order to gain a broad overview of such a vast and complex topic, we can imagine a communal mental process for which a large global organisation (in this case, the IPA) represents and works through – as far as it can – the epochal macro-changes occurring in the context with which its members are concerned: for our purposes, that of individual psychic pathologies and dysfunctions.

This is the sphere in which psychoanalysis has investigated, theorised, and operated for 120 years: in other words, more than enough time for the creation of living and working conditions that are profoundly different from those of the era in which it began.

It is not by chance that the 2015 IPA Congress held in Boston was significantly and succinctly entitled "Psychoanalysis in a changing world".

When I suggested this topic to the IPA Board, I received an immediate positive response because it does indeed give a voice to an experience undergone by almost all the analysts who, in this body (the genuine "parliament" of the global analytic community), represent the experiences, professional situations, and movements in the field in Europe, North America, and Latin America.

However, such a broad title could sound perilously generic: the word "change", as we know, has become something of a stereotype in the titles of many scientific books and papers, and could be understood as intentionally innocuous, vague, and undefined. That was most definitely not the reason why I chose it.

And so, specifically in order to avoid a perilous abstractness and a theoretical generalisation detached from reality, I will here explore the topic of change in contemporary forms of pathology, starting from some important signals that come directly from the field of analytic practice and its transformations.

Having had the opportunity to travel over the years from one society to another across the world, questioning colleagues on the de facto state and developments of psychoanalysis in their countries (I asked about everything: training, setting, fees, average number of sessions, types of patient,

DOI: 10.4324/9781003340744-4

contributions and interference from insurance services, both public and private, varying from nation to nation, etc.), I had received direct confirmations of real, important changes in the way our profession is practised today.

The most striking datum was the drop in intensive, frequent analytic treatments despite the fact that analysts are receiving an ever-higher demand for help; what was causing difficulties in the majority of cases was the number of sessions.

Of course, within the general picture there are specific features and unexpected differences between different geographical and cultural areas which stand out: for example, in countries where psychoanalysis has developed most recently (as in some Eastern European countries or in China, in a more or less advanced re-emergence from strongly de-subjectivising regimes), the difficulties encountered by colleagues in getting their patients to accept therapeutic contracts with a high level of frequency and continuous relational dependency seem surprisingly fewer than in nations where psychoanalysis has been practised for many years, where the mean income is higher, and where the collective mentality has apparently evolved further and become more liberal. This had made me highly suspicious of the presumed fundamental (and, for some people, only) relevance of economic factors as an explanation of the phenomenon.

However, it was undeniable that many colleagues were complaining about difficulties that had not been so present in previous decades; paradoxically, almost all of them had found it easier in the years from the seventies to the nineties to offer a true, classical analysis, rather than one that is adjusted on a case-by-case basis; what is more, this happened regardless of how much personal experience and theoretical-clinical competence they had built up, and no matter how firmly established a societal structure they had trained and developed in.

Not being satisfied with the hasty and simplistic explanation based on economic factors – which is contradicted by, among other things, the common observation that it is often in the wealthiest patients that we encounter the greatest reluctance to accept the rhythms and discipline of analytic treatment – I had begun to gather other observations and to work through them with my own reflections.

I was also taking into account the accusation – a very weighty one, admittedly – that was being levelled by some representatives of more conservative centres, often with a rather self-righteous air, about what was really responsible for the phenomenon: according to them, it was a simple matter of a deplorable deterioration in the state of psychoanalytic practice caused by "poor introjection" of the true nature of the analytic method by the new generations of analysts, and almost certainly connected to a certain sloppiness in the training offered by psychoanalytic societies with a lax and superficial style.

The slogan was, "The patients haven't changed, it's the analysts who've changed!" and the complacent and insinuating manner with which this

perspective was loftily inculcated by the speaker very often produced immediate assent in the listener for fear of being included in the category of "second-
class" analysts with a culpable tendency towards a decline in quality.

Though I was initially impressed by these *ex-cathedra* formulations, I went
ahead nonetheless with my informal inquiries in the various countries, and
began to suspect that these epochal changes, strongly imbued with much
more substantial psychosocial and cultural changes, were meeting the same
denialist resistance from the traditionalist sectors I just mentioned as some
British colleagues, coordinated by Sally Weintrobe (2012), had confirmed and
analysed as a collective response to the global phenomenon of climate change;
the focus was different, but the defensive phenomenon seemed surprisingly
similar, and was based alternately on negation and outright denial.

Acknowledging the change in a significant proportion of the
psychopathologies presented today by our patients, and at the same time
reflecting on the changes in technique connected to this (and to a large
extent determined by it), still seems to be a difficult task for our scientific-
professional community, struggling between attachment to rooted schemata
and models that are reassuring for the sense of identity and the acknowledgement of the new realities which entail (and indeed determine) a consequent
theoretical–technical adaptation.

I would add that the extent of the socio-cultural changes is so great that it
may not perhaps be possible for an individual mind to represent, contain, and
comprehend their complexity; an integrated and well-coordinated interdisciplinary approach would be helpful in describing it, putting many minds to
work in a regime of calm, reflective cooperation.

Finally, I will conclude this introduction to the topic by formulating a
hypothesis which may trouble more than one colleague: I suspect that an
investigation of this kind may also stir up a deep anxiety, generated by the
quantity and quality of the disturbing and uncontrollable factors which
characterise our age (fears connected to the identity crises caused by mass
migrations, the proliferation of substance abuse, to ecological disasters caused
by the multiplication of consumers, to the disorienting plurality of knowledge, etc.) and which could in the end constitute an enormously significant
problem for the future of humanity.

In the past, Italian psychoanalysis has made an illustrious contribution to
describing the progressive historical changes in the forms of the psychopathology observed by analysts during the last century: at the beginning of the
eighties, Eugenio Gaddini did not confine himself to describing changes in
psychopathology as abstract, free-standing forms, but made in in-depth study
of their interconnections with major historical events on the one hand, and
with progress in practice and theory on the other.

In "Se e come sono cambiati i nostri pazienti fino ai nostri giorni" [Whether
and how our patients have changed up to the present time] (1984), Gaddini
made a detailed resumé of observations offered by previous studies in various

socio-geographical contexts, beginning with Freud after the First World War, bringing them together into a synoptic view of his time:

> What we can deduce from looking back seems quite explicit: the preva-
> lent forms seem to be progressively more serious. The objective test,
> determined not by psychoanalysts but by exceptional external events,
> indicated that the prevalent forms were, in the first instance, hysteria;
> then in a second phase, character disturbances; and in a third phase, bor-
> derline and narcissistic personalities, at intervals of twenty/twenty-five
> years: if all this were true, as it seems to be, we would have to conclude
> that it is like sailing, against our will and with increasing speed, towards
> the edge of a waterfall.
>
> (pp. 660–661)

It must be emphasised that in his work, Gaddini was already taking into consideration the fact that not only was the object of investigation (psychopathology) changing, but also the observational instrument (psychoanalysis), and
that this might contribute to a different understanding of the phenomenon
being observed.

I will add that some favourable factors have actually widened the field of
observation: for example, the broadening of the socio-cultural range of those
who use psychoanalysis, related to an increased awareness of the social function
of psychoanalysis (Bolognini, 2013), especially in the countries of Latin America
and Southern Europe; the development of new perspectives, especially in the
treatment of children, adolescents, couples, and families; and the undeniable
progress in the sphere of analytic treatment of severe pathologies, albeit often
in a scenario of conflict with broad swathes of contemporary psychiatry.

But let's go back to how the psychoanalytic community, always via the IPA,
which is its principal agency, is proceeding in representing and transforming
itself in the face of the great changes in the context in which it operates.

Here, I will extract a substantial passage from the opening speech to the
plenary of the 2015 Boston Congress (which, I mention in passing, later had
an influence on the IPA's subsequent decision about the Eitingon Variation
in training):

> I believe that the changing world in which we live is undeniably affecting
> our work, and that – as far as the sphere of human relationships is
> concerned – it is impossible to insist categorically that "human beings
> are always the same"; this may be true for the most part, yes, but in some
> specific aspects this is no longer the case.
>
> *Many patients today, in fact, reject the idea of depending openly and intensively
> on someone.*
>
> For complex, but not necessarily mysterious, reasons they seem to bear
> the signs of a substantial distrust and/or disaccustoming with regard to

the presence and the constancy of the object, its substantial reliability and the consequent dependence on it.

In an ideal line connecting the subject to the object, the investment center of gravity seems in many cases today to remain pre-emptively and implicitly shifted toward the subject itself, which is careful not to put its own libidinal and narcissistic capital in the hands of the other, at least until the other has (with time) overcome the barriers of mistrust and Self-protection that we presume were built up early on.

If we think of the necessary primary fusionality between mother and child and of the subsequent need for a strong continuity in the family organization, we might ask ourselves – fully aware of the risks of such a potentially "politically incorrect" question ... whether analysts are not inheriting in their consulting rooms at least some of the consequences of a series of circumstances typical of our contemporaneity: the early inter-ruption of maternàge for professional reasons, where mothers are called straight back to work by legislation and excessively demanding corporate environments; the confusing fallback on a rotation of private and insti-tutional caregivers in bringing up very young children, in "nuclear" families without grandparents, who often live very far away; ubiquitous family ruptures owing to separations and divorces, especially where a new family member enters the scene who "must" be accepted, sometimes in an atmosphere of rejection or at least denial of the difficulties involved; nar-cissistic self-centered parenting organizations, favored by contemporary, and largely individualistic, cultural models; the loss of the large container of "extended families", and in general all those circumstances that influ-ence the psychic environment in a child's growth today, better now than in the past from the point of view of food, but probably less so from the point of view of real, genuine relationships.

We no longer have – at least for now – massive and devastating world wars: what we have instead are countless micro-fractures in the initial mother–infant dyad and in the family that may instinctively deter the subject from "surrendering to the relationship"; and here I cannot but mention the extreme and emblematic clinical case of that child, treated by one of my Italian colleagues, who moved away from the other children he was playing with to hug and kiss the TV.

Let me be clear: I am not saying here that mothers should not return to work, or that families should live with grandparents, or that unhappy couples should not be able to separate, and so on. I am saying that psychoanalysts should not deny the momentous consequences of these huge changes, and neither should they be surprised by their impact on the relational styles and possibilities of this new humanity, when a patient who hears the phrase "four sessions a week" vanishes right away without any negotiation.

(Bolognini, 2015)

What would I add to these notes today to give a clearer picture of the changes that have occurred in psychopathology and the technical modifications devised by analysts in a rather Lamarckian process ("it is the function which creates the organ")?

Here are some further possible annotations on the macro-factors in play.

The progressive loss of trust in the social, cultural, political, and religious equivalents of the parental figures

Today, the merest glimpse of anything with a hint of the Superego tends to be rejected or avoided, not only as dangerous and frightening, but also as unacceptable and offensive to one's sense of narcissistic sovereignty.

Also excluded in this way from individual intrapsychic play are the sane and necessary components of the Superego, those with a nutritive and protective function: to be clear, the fact that parents prevent their small child from sticking his fingers in the electrical socket is not a despotic and repressive attack on learning from experience and creativity, just as protecting adolescents from alcoholism or substance abuse is not repression; and even more naturally, accepting the formative dependency on someone who knows more than us is not a humiliating infantilisation but a precious opportunity (and here we enter the vast field of the paternal code, which has also in recent decades been predominantly considered in its possible negative or tyrannical aspects); and yet, for a long time, this has been the widespread pseudo-cultural meta-message which – perhaps in reaction to previous cultures and social systems of an opposite stamp – has characterised an important part of our era.

We could claim that until fifty years ago a traditional historic task of psychoanalysis (modifying the power relations between a crushing Superego and an Ego and a Self that are often weak and hypotrophic) has partly been transformed into the opposite – and not less arduous – task required by the treatment of "boundary pathologies" correlated to regulation-deficit, the narcissistic preservation of omnipotent illusions, anti-object autonomism, and also to another contemporary innovation: the clearly detectable shortening of the duration and functions of the latency period through a ubiquitous, premature, and insistent exposure to excitatory sexual stimuli.

Paradoxically, the preliminary narcissistic stance of not wanting to depend on the analyst and on analysis is actually flaunted with a certain pride in the initial consultations by many potential patients as if they felt that, just by being there, they were halfway to regaining their health.

The temporary and maturational dependency on analysis is not only feared, but also egosyntonically disdained with a full feeling of self-legitimation, the subject being evidently unaware of her own profound needs and the problematic state of her relationship with the object.

The widespread experience of relativity and "fluid playability" in every kind of affective investment

As a direct consequence of this narcissistic and primordially defensive orientation, which is later organised and structured in a stable and self-confirmatory way, many individuals develop a great capacity for not linking to the object in multiple settings: amorous, work, and parental/filial.

However much the term is abused, it cannot be denied that contemporary society is tending towards real "liquidity", in various senses, allowing highly unstable libidinal and narcissistic "provisioning" which guarantees a sense of freedom from the link with the object.

Understandably, many of the children born and raised in this unstable relational environment later implicitly defend themselves with similar anti-binding countermeasures: from the media – when not from direct experience – they absorb a pervasive sensation of precariousness in family links, from the manifest ease with which parental couples break up and recombine in various ways, and this has effects on the unconscious and implicit (unthought) defensive organisation of the children.

In essence, the initial, profound, and narcissistic devalorising experience is, "I feel I'm not a valid and sufficient reason for my family/'team' to stay united". Obviously, a thought like this is absolutely contestable at the level of logic, rationality, culture, ethics, and even common sense, which is why it would be immediately rejected by the environment as unacceptable; the problem is that none of this stops it being "felt" by the subject, whereas it does stop the thought being formulated, and even thought.

A not dissimilar sensation is probably also transmitted by other contexts equivalent and subsequent to the family context: for example, in the field of public psychiatry there has been very little work done on service users' basic need for constancy in the "caring object". On the contrary, for decades the alternation and rotation of therapeutic figures (doctors, psychologists, and nurses), who are the equivalent of caregivers in infancy, has been presented with ideological pride as a qualitive benefit.

Today, analysts instantly – or even in advance – "inherit" this ready-made relational disposition in the transference when they offer themselves as an object onto which discouraging and dissuasive fantasies about linking are immediately projected, with the result that their first task, when these patients attend for a preliminary assessment, seems in many cases to be that of offering them some kind of initially bearable contact, while looking ahead to a more substantial project which may allow them to open an "analytic workshop" that can be organised over time.

This puts me in mind of the famous advice given by the fox in *The Little Prince* by Saint-Exupéry (1943):

> You must be very patient ... First you will sit down at a little distance from me – like that – in the grass. I shall look at you out of the corner of my

eye, and you will say nothing. Words are the source of misunderstandings. But you will sit a little closer to me, every day.

In my opinion, this psychosocial macro-phenomenon of new defences organised against dependency on the fundamental object at least partly explains – much more than the unreliable hypothesis about "failed introjection of a model" – the ever more widespread clinical phenomenon of a low-level attachment which is scarcely avoidable at first, but then gradually becomes more intensive as the therapeutic relationship is tolerated and finally accepted (and in some cases requested) as the patient gains in trust and then confidence.

In a certain sense, it could be said that many patients have to be "trained" or "retrained" in psycho-emotional coexistence and in interdependent analytic cooperation: it is a matter of testing the terrain, in many cases surveying it *tout court*, and of laying the foundations before building the house.

On the institutional level, all this has coincided, as a large-scale collateral phenomenon, with a certain difficulty that candidates have in finding patients who are immediately available at the necessary frequency for a training supervision, and this has had the consequence of correspondingly lengthening the average time taken for the training of new analysts (thus contributing to the cumulative phenomenon of ageing in many psychoanalytic societies).

In essence, it seems today that "constructing the analytic patient" has in many cases become a virtually inescapable intermediate stage before embarking on a genuine analysis based in reality.

The sense of trans-individual omnipotence induced by the Internet

Beside its marvellous usefulness, the Internet narcissistically deceives subjects into believing that they can do without the real object (examples: the frequent replacement of medical consultation by online self-diagnosis, the unlimited offer of online sexual excitement with the avoidance of real relationships, the megalomaniac illusion of cognitive control of global reality by newsfeeds, etc.).

As Gabbard and Crisp (2019) neatly sum up: "Online culture has fueled a particular form of narcissistic desire that can circumvent the complications of mutuality in real-life relationships and gratify the viewer without having to think about anyone else's needs or wishes" (p. 30). Similarly, the non-stop and now paroxysmal use of mobile phones has accustomed individuals to an experience of non-separation, a sort of "absence of the absence of the object".

With her setting and contractual obligations which imply separateness, something being held back, the analyst is an anomaly to these relational regimes, and hence configured as a dangerous object for many patients' habitual defensive systems.

The cultural (in a broad sense) valorisation of narcissistic ideals and dispositions in the media, and generally in the current mentality

Collective admiration is awarded to the concrete success obtained for the most part by markedly exhibitionist figures, while the real parents and their subsequent equivalents are often bypassed as being disappointing to the narcissistic ideal.

This is the case with the status of teachers, for example, the natural equivalent of parents, who are greatly undervalued today in many countries. We are a very long way from the atmosphere thick with transferential admiration described by Freud (1914) in *Some Reflections on Schoolboy Psychology*! And analysts too, after decades during which the myth of psychoanalysis as an omnipotent mystery has been downgraded, are likewise suffering this drop in narcissistic prestige and consequently in patients' capacity for devoting themselves *ab initio* to subjective emotional investment.

What's more, it is not rare for the analyst to be the final link in a chain of healthcare professionals previously consulted without success, a sort of last-ditch attempt made *obtorto collo*, following drug treatments that have either had minimal efficacy or been rejected in their turn: "I definitely don't want to end up being dependent on drugs!" is often the conscious, egosyntonic motive for requesting a consultation.

The increase in narcissistic pathologies is furthered by fashions and mass tendencies that are offered as generically liberating and provide individuals with standardised, anti-subjectivating formulae based on an easy and reassuring homologation: a conformist and imitative pseudo-socialisation which Gaddini himself called "an eclipse of the social" (op. cit., p. 652).

Twenge and Campbell (2009) have described the overload of pathological narcissism as a "generational epidemic": those born after 1982 (the millennials), who have grown up in a self-referential network of "likes" (a quantitative tool for building up self-esteem), were the most filmed and photographed children of all time, raised with the idea of being special and with the conviction that everything is owed to them by right, as a result of which, when they fail to achieve the objectives they thought were within their reach, they lapse into a crisis. The fact is that their readiness for a real object relation is inferior to that of previous generations.

According to the same authors, young people of the next generation (generation *iGen*), who became adults after the arrival of the iPhone (2007), would be yet more subject to anxiety and depression of a narcissistic kind, fostered by the constant, compulsive comparison with others.

The recent, massive phenomenon of tattooing, concretely transcribing onto the skin traumatic elements that have not been worked through – an ever more widespread practice at all levels (whereas it used to characterise those sections of society who really had been exposed to extreme traumas of separation or aggression, such as sailors and long-term prisoners) – seems to have achieved a status of complacent, narcissistic aestheticisation which makes it especially difficult, outside analytic work, to reconnect with experiences of suffering: a trendy aestheticising status which, as we know, has ended up celebrating and consolidating to an impressive extent, through fashion and its idealised icons, the omnipotent, sadistic-tyrannical control by narcissistic-destructive components which stamp themselves outwardly on the bodily Self and often attack its basic libidinal needs.

I believe this to be a very special transformation of contemporary psycho-pathology: whereas in the past we would have seen sadness, grief, desolation, the impoverished sense of an injured and mortified self, today we come into contact with a strong narcissistic investment, contentedly on display, of those very features that denote a serious underlying suffering.

The proud and confrontational autonomism against object relations and against the painful perception of the true state of one's own Self is consolidated by a valorising narcissistic veneer which is supposed to refute the basic suffering.

Analysts today are dramatically confronted by these fundamentally anti-object internal organisations where the conflict between life and death is coated in this striking narcissistic veneer, intensely invested and often resistant for a long time to the usual techniques of psychological treatment.

The de facto legitimising of substance abuse

Even though psychoanalytic articles make quite sparing reference to this pervasive macro-phenomenon, today a growing number of potential young patients present themselves at their first consultations admitting to substance abuse, sometimes habitual and sometimes apparently occasional (which is often not true: as analysts we know how drug use rises and falls in reaction to pain and as a substitute for reality-testing).

One part of these patients runs away from the idea of dependency on a human being, while others accept a connection, though hardly ever whole-heartedly. The difficulty encountered by analysts in treating these ever more widespread pathologies is historically testified by the fact that only in June 2016 did the IPA set up an "Addiction Sub-Committee of the Psychoanalysis and Mental Health Field Committee", which began its work at the Buenos Aires IPA Congress in 2017.

In the same light, recourse to a psychoanalytic treatment is regarded most of the time as a "last resort" and is usually requested when the processes of addiction to this kind of satisfaction and defence have become deeply rooted.

This requires the analyst to place an additional trust in the method, a tol-erance of frustration at the slowness in achieving therapeutic results, and settling for a compromise, "one does what one can", not always in line with either the clients' expectations or the residual unconscious megalomaniac ideals of the analyst himself.

The distancing of vast sectors of psychiatry from psychoanalysis

As is well known, following historical periods when psychiatry has held psychoanalysis in high esteem, progress in psychopharmacology and an increasing closure of university departments and health services to analysis in many countries have not only reduced the number of referrals, but have given weight to alternative forms of psychotherapy (especially the behavioural type) that are presented by many medical practitioners as more "scientific" and less likely to stir up fantasies of dependence.

Despite this quite powerful dissuasion against psychoanalysis, recourse to analytic help by patients in the general sphere of psychosis has not diminished at all, which is in line with the unsatisfactory level of psychiatric assistance in almost all countries. Thus, analysts have progressively become equipped for specific therapeutic relationships suitable for treating patients with higher levels of difficulty in separation, often with highly disturbed Ego functioning and enormous fragility, weakness, and fragmentation of the sense of Self.

In these cases more than in others, analysts are tested by constant experiences of the primary levels of relationship and with very powerful regressive transferences which engage the therapist countertransferentially at very deep levels, sometimes with weighty consequences for the everyday psychic metabolism of the analyst himself.

In fact, the ever-widening field of intervention by analysts in the serious pathologies is also the result of two factors that, in themselves, are positive: one is increased technical competence fostered by a now extensive and well-established analytic literature on the subject, and especially by the sometimes enthusiastic contributions of great Teachers who have opened up new theoretical-clinical paths in the treatment of the psychoses; the other has been a different "political" (in a broad sense) stance in some countries about the social function of psychoanalysis (Bolognini, 2013) with a much wider remit than in the past, aimed at caring for socio-cultural clusters of the population who used to be excluded for diagnostic or economic reasons.

Paradoxically, and simultaneously, many psychiatrists in private practice and almost all neurologists are conversely tending to appropriate cases in the area of neurosis, which is apparently easier to manage with symptomatic pharmacological treatments, and thus they are draining a significant part of the psychopathological sector which used to be the province of psychoanalysis; and of course this is accompanied by the growing phenomenon of therapists calling themselves "psychoanalysts" without having undergone appropriate training, and polluting the popular image of psychoanalysis, presenting it as a practice with a setting and method that can be modulated according to taste, with serious consequences for properly trained psychoanalysts.

The "creeping assimilation" of psychoanalysis into contemporary pseudo-culture

This subtle and pervasive phenomenon, which Sacerdoti (1987) has described as "projective assimilation", derives from the fact that many patients who consult a psychoanalyst have a tamed, defensively preformed and grossly standardised image of the analytic experience in mind, one largely based on the illusion of being able to control and dominate the treatment; the implicit fantasy is that of a treatment focused on "self-empowerment" and the confirmation of their narcissistic desires, having projected into the object (in this case, psychoanalytic treatment) an idea of it that conforms to their narcissistic desires.

This idea, aimed at forestalling the dangers of dependency and change, runs into a crisis as soon as the analytic method and the non-manipulability of the analyst become clear. The complexity and profundity of the method soon conflict with the illusion of an experience that is intended, from the perspective of the pleasure principle, to be shaped and resolved according to the formula proposed by Asclepiades of Bithynia (130 B.C.E.–60 B.C.E.): that the doctor should cure the patient *cito, tuto et iucunde*, quickly, with a guaranteed outcome and no suffering; whereas the reality of a long and challenging treatment is often unacceptable for many patients who, in life in general and in their educational history, have been unaccustomed to protracted and taxing effort.

The "assimilation" therefore consists in the reduction of psychoanalysis, at least as it is often presented in the media, to a treatment that in the end is "very like" most of the less challenging psychotherapies, a version of itself that has been pre-digested and neutralised by its possible users with regard to both its potential and its difficulty.

Of course, this distortion/falsification of the image of psychoanalysis is exacerbated by all those unqualified professionals who call their therapies "psychoanalysis", and by all those sources of information which present analysis as if it were a course of meditation or wellness or general building up of self-esteem, etc.

Conclusion

The narcissistic Ego Ideal, reinforced by the withdrawal of the subject's relational centre of gravity along the subject–object axis because of the complex of factors described above, seems progressively to have replaced the Superego as an inner persecutory element in many configurations of the personality, with a consequent influence on psychoanalytic technique, especially in the early phases of negotiation and intake.

At the same time, the narcissistic wound connected to seeking help and accepting the commitment, dependency, and rules of analytic work today seems in many cases to be the greatest factor obstructing immediate access to traditional ongoing analytic work, just as – on a much wider scale, in real life – it prevents the achievement of stable, in-depth object relations invested with value and based on a sufficient mutual trust.

It could be said, in my opinion, that psychoanalysis is once again being challenged or avoided for exactly the reasons why the contemporary individual needs it so much.

The rejection/terror of interdependence is transferentially manifested in precisely that initial reluctance towards the intensity and frequency of analysis, and analysts find themselves facing ever longer preliminary phases for retraining the patient in contact, cooperation, and intimacy, both with the object and with the patient's own Self. It is not by chance that we talk more and more often today about "constructing the analytic patient" (Ogden, 1994; Bolognini, 2015; Romano, 2019), with a view to work on the internal world which may actually go beyond hyper-rational and controlled exchanges on the level of the Ego which do not substantially touch the internal areas of the Self.

I have tried to point out some possible factors of contemporary significance connected to the changes in the modes of child-rearing, family structures, shifts in values, and in the general conditions of people's psychic life in the new millennium, which may have a far from occasional function in the organisation of the mind and styles of relationship with the object.

However much it may disturb us as psychoanalysts (it is not humanly possible for this to be otherwise) in our traditionally constituted identities, we have to acknowledge that psychoanalysis is changing in step with the world in which it operates; and our scientific-professional community has the task and the opportunity to work through this process, distinguishing as far as it can the actually denaturing and deteriorating aspects from the developmental ones in which changes of technique are reasonable and appropriate and the psychoanalytic essence is essentially maintained intact.

Note

1   This chapter first appeared in the "Italian Psychoanalytical Annual" (2020), *Rivista di psicoanalisi*, Journal of the Italian Psychoanalytic Society, 14, Raffaello Cortina Editore, and is here republished by kind permission of the journal's editor, Alfredo Lombardozzi.

References

Bolognini, S. (2013) Die institutionelle und die innere Familie des Analytikers. *Forum der Psychoanalyse.* 29(3): 357–372.

Bolognini, S. (2015) Psychoanalysis in a changing world. President's Opening Speech at the 2015 IPA Congress, Boston.

Freud, S. (1914) Some reflections on schoolboy psychology. *The Standard Edition of the Complete Psychological Works of Sigmund Freud*. 13.

Gabbard, O.G. and Crisp, H. (2019) *Narcissism and its Discontents: Diagnostic Dilemmas and Treatment Strategies with Narcissistic Patients*. Washington, DC: American Psychiatric Association Publishing.

Gaddini, E. (1984) Se e come sono cambiati i nostri pazienti fino ai nostri giorni. *Rivista di psicoanalisi*. 30: 560–580.

Ogden, T. (1994) The analytic third. Working with intersubjective clinical facts. *International Journal of Psychoanalysis*. 75: 3–19.

Romano, R. (2019) Etica della psicoanalisi. Presented at the SPI Scientific Study Day on Training, Rome.

Sacerdoti, G. (1987) Ebraismo e psicoanalisi davanti all'assimilazione. In: *Giorgio Sacerdoti, Scritti psicoanalitici*. Rome: Borla.

Saint-Exupéry A. (1943) *Le Petit Prince*. New York: Reynal & Hitchcock.

Twenge, J.M. and Campbell, W.K. (2009) *The Narcissism Epidemic: Living in the Age of Entitlement*. New York: Free Press.

Weintrobe, S. (2012) *Engaging with Climate Change: Psychoanalytic and Interdisciplinary Perspectives*. *The New Library of Psychoanalysis*. London: Routledge.

Chapter 3

A turn towards or a turn away?

Why and how resistance to unbearable ideas evoked in the analyst's presence must be the cornerstone of psychoanalytic work

David Tuckett

> The assumption that there are unconscious mental processes, the recognition of the theory of resistance and repression, the appreciation of the importance of sexuality and of the Oedipus complex—these constitute the principal subject-matter of psycho-analysis and the foundations of its theory. No one who cannot accept them all should count himself a psycho-analyst.
>
> (Sigmund Freud, 1923, p. 247)

The purpose of this chapter is to ask questions about the direction psycho-analysis has been taking. It will focus specifically on its "relational turn", which is a specifically North American phenomenon, but has much wider generalisability. It is a preliminary effort to ask whether psychoanalysts have lost sight of the fundamental contributions of their founder. Have they inadvertently stepped away from a principal somewhat passive focus on being "analysts" into the more active role of becoming life coaches or counsellors, evading the central challenge that follows from the assumptions that Freud named as the cornerstone of his discoveries in the quotation above? If so, with what consequences?

Briefly, Freud wrote to explain why he named his new approach "psycho-analysis" in 1923.

> Psycho-Analysis is the name (1) of a procedure for the investigation of mental processes which *are almost inaccessible in any other way*, and (2) of a method (based upon that investigation) for the treatment of neurotic disorders.[1]
>
> (Freud, 1023, p 235, emphasis added)

Further down in the article, in the quotation above, is the core proposition on which he built psychoanalytic *theory* – the assumption that there are *unconscious mental processes*. Specifically, he had in mind ideas (beliefs about the world and our situation) built up from childhood experience that are *inaccessible and*

DOI: 10.4324/9781003340744-5

kept unknown to us, because we are resistant to their felt implications. Such ideas are held unconscious. It is to our detriment because, as we live our lives and situations evoke them, they dominate our responses. In other words, the central problem with unconscious beliefs is that they are necessarily experienced as facts, not hypotheses to be examined and perhaps modified.[2] Crucially, Freud's realisation *emerged* specifically from his own imperfect efforts to investigate issues within himself through the analysis of his dream thoughts using a technique with two crucial components: free association and evenly suspended attention. As I elaborate below, both components involve passive observation of experience prior to active construction of meaning.

Investigation, that is, implementing curiosity no matter the potential for unwelcome conclusions, lies at the heart of Freud's opus. He built the idea that psychoanalysis is a treatment on a core proposition sometimes known as the *Junktim*. It is the idea that therapeutic work operates in conjunction with the main products of the investigative work: in other words, signs of resistance to emerging ideas and more specifically from transference, i.e. the ideas about the analyst and what he or she was doing that he thought Dora and his other patients were betraying. Freud thought that the investigation revealed that the same ideas that dominated patients' experience, thinking and behaviour with their analysts in sessions, were also the ones dominating their experience in their lived lives.

Of course, later Freud extended the idea to emphasise that it is not only patients to whom transference applies. Countertransference is the term he coined to take account of the *unwelcome* clinical observation that the analyst is not immune to being drawn in. Sometimes, in response to their patients, ideas inaccessible to the analyst will betray themselves as dominating their experience, thinking and behaviour in sessions. Freud worried about it and its impact on the investigation a great deal, as did Melanie Klein. But, as we know, later Heiman, Racker, Bion and Baranger, particularly, showed how it was both unavoidable and useful. My argument in this chapter is that these two core propositions – (1) unconscious mental processes signified by resistance and (2) transference-countertransference understood as unconscious beliefs about the other in the therapeutic couple and their intentions – are fundamental to any treatment called psychoanalysis. At the same time, I want to argue that major trends in modern psychoanalysis, particularly the "relational turn", are now tending to evade both propositions.

To make my argument, I will begin with a summary of some core features of the "relational turn" and then explore them in terms of four essential suppositions that I argue every psychoanalyst *must make*, whether known explicitly or not, when conducting psychoanalytic treatment. The relational turn in psychoanalysis, like similar developments elsewhere, may have brought psychoanalysis to a crossroads. There are, I will suggest, several paths available which can make use of the constructivist challenge relational analysts have introduced. Some could bring psychoanalysis back towards Freud's core propositions, others could take it further away. To understand the choice requires clarification of the underlying suppositions.

The relational turn

Davies (2018) outlined what she saw as the three basic questions that gave rise to the evolution of the relational perspective, as well as what she termed the resulting theoretical assumptions that underlie many of the more technical shifts within this perspective.

Her first question concerns what she calls the constructivist challenge and the role of the analyst's subjectivity. The second is about the nature of mind and psychic structure. The third concerns therapeutic action and the relation between interpretation and self-experience. To clarify her thinking, Davies provides clinical examples to support her understanding of each point, as indeed she has often done in a series of papers published over the last thirty years.

What this careful argument brings out is that at the heart of the relational turn is a central question: how does the analyst claim (to herself and her patients) to know what she thinks she knows?

> If one takes the constructivist challenge seriously—that all experience is inherently ambiguous and that we each construct, out of that experience, our own idiosyncratic sets of meanings influenced by our own conscious and unconscious psychic processes and our own unique set of internalized object relations—where do we find the *inherently objectivist basis* for the traditional understanding of therapeutic action, that is, the analyst's interpretation of the patient's unconscious process? Of what good is *traditional interpretation* as the central mode of therapeutic action if it is constructed idiosyncratically, by each given analyst, out of his own unconscious psychic process? What, indeed, constitutes *insight* if the patient's basic conflicts might be viewed differently by any given analyst based on his own unique, unconscious, conflicts, organizing principles and assumptions? Problematic as well is the ineluctable nature of the analyst's limited vision. To the extent that we all possess an unconscious, our understanding of the meaning, motivation, and impact of our own behavior is limited. The analyst is not only impacted by his own unconscious process in the formulation of any interpretation, not only a full participant in any analytic enactment, but partially blind to the role he plays in helping the patient to understand both of these processes. To put it more simply, relational psychoanalysis takes quite seriously Freud's basic dictum that the countertransference is by definition unconscious. *There is no training analysis in the world that rids the analyst of his own unconscious.* Analyst and patient alike engage with each other in a multiplicity of ways that exist outside of awareness.
>
> (p. 654, emphasis added)

I have underlined three terms in this excerpt – inherent objectivist bias, traditional interpretation and insight – and the whole sentence about however successful a training analysis it cannot rid the analyst of his or her unconscious.

What Davies does with these insights is to outline the changes in technique that she thinks follow. She writes:

> It is in this context and based primarily on this [Constructivist] challenge that relational analysts have *moved the essential data of therapeutic work away* from the patient's free associations and toward enactments and reenactments in the intersubjective field [Benjamin, 1990] between the patient's conscious and unconscious processes and those of the analyst's. The analyst as a now *"flawed" interpretive instrument* can no longer be relied upon to *decipher the unconscious codified meaning* hidden in the patient's purely linguistic and nonverbal productions, and so, instead, both the *analyst and the patient, together, become interpreters of the unbidden relational processes* that unfold between them as the transference–countertransference configurations—always linked—unfold.
>
> (pp. 654–655, emphasis added)

In this excerpt I have underlined four passages – emphasising the move away from free association towards analyst and patient as mutual interpreters of their relationship. The idea, expressed in Davies words, is that although once "'accurate' interpretation of an oedipally derived transference neurosis was the sine quo non of analytic process", now, "relational analysts stress the ambiguity of meaning and the multiple possible interpretations of any given piece of analytic data" (p. 650).

The clinical examples that Davies and other relational analysts provide (e.g. Aron, 1996; Benjamin, 2004; Hoffman, 1983; Stern, 2019) illustrate this new approach. The sessions they report often deal with overcoming impasse or the difficulties in the relationship when direct (conscious) and intensely emotional comments are made by patients to analysts (and sometimes analysts to patients). The sessions look like conversations on a topic with analyst and patient taking turns to speak. Moreover, analysts make many interventions in sessions. They seem mostly to be conversations around topics in their relationship and sometimes the relationships the patient has with others – who might desire who, feel disappointed by who, be jealous of who, dislike an aspect of who, etc. The patient is also often reported as in a chair facing the analyst. Few silences or slips of the tongue (etc.) are reported and usually the dialogue is intelligible and easy to follow. In short, sessions are not unlike the exchanges of ideas and feelings about each other and people who are not present of the kind that are common in a more or less intimate relationship between friends. They usually have a powerful affective relational context.

The "traditional" model

As noted, relational psychoanalysts, like Davies above, make a point of differentiating their technique from traditional (North American) approaches. The latter are described as using free association by the patient to create an understanding on the part of the analyst. The analyst's interpretation is then designed to give (authoritative) insight into unconscious (i.e. not known to the patient) Oedipal and other infantile wishes and conflicts in the patient's life.

For an outsider it is not always easy to judge exactly what traditional analysts did or do or, indeed, are believed to do. Whereas relational analysts, like the intersubjective analysts influenced by Kohut's thinking who evolved in parallel (e.g. Fosshage, 1990), publish significant amounts of detailed clinical material showing the dialogue between them and their patients. The traditional psychoanalysts with whom they are debating often did not.

A useful exception is Kurt Eissler (1953). His original analytic training had been in pre-war Vienna and at the time he wrote he was widely considered the magisterial voice of psychoanalytic orthodoxy in the US.[3] Although his paper may be something of a "straw man", it is useful for its tone and for its account of clinical situations and the rather "authoritative" guidance he offers as to the "proper" way to do psychoanalysis. It starts from the basic rule:

> The patient is informed of the *basic rule* and of his obligation to follow it. He adheres to it to the best of his ability, which is quite sufficient for the task of achieving recovery. The tool with which the analyst can accomplish this task *is interpretation*, and the goal of interpretation is to provide the patient with *insight*. Insight will remove the obstacles which have so far delayed the ego in attaining its full development. The problem here is only when and what to interpret; for in the ideal case the analyst's activity is limited to interpretation; no other tool becomes necessary.
>
> (Emphasis added)

The words interpretation and insight appeared pejoratively in Davies' description of traditional technique. In fact, both Davies and Eissler seem to be using the word *interpretation* in a similar way – both as the process of inferring the unconscious meaning of free association and as the primary form of the intervention when speaking to the patient in the treatment. Eissler certainly does phrase his paper in an "authoritative manner" leaving little room for doubt – emphasising that the term interpretation, as intervention, always presupposes "the proper use of this technique", stressing that "it would be foolish to suggest that just any kind of interpretation, or the mere act of interpreting, will do". In any case, what is useful for my purposes is that he also provides a condensed but rather precise clinical example, to show us how he works.

> A patient of superior intelligence … filled long stretches of his analysis with *repetitive complaints* about trivial matters regarding his wife. He did not show any understanding of the obvious fact that the discrepancy between the intensity of his complaints and the triviality of their content required a discussion and explanation. One day he reported, somewhat abruptly, that he enjoyed his wife's doing the very things he had always complained of and that he knew how secretly to manipulate situations in such a way as to make his wife act the way he had considered so obnoxious, and which *gave him occasion to be cold and unfriendly to her*.
>
> (pp. 138–139, emphasis added)

Eissler explains how what he is struck by from these associations, what he uses to infer unconscious meaning, is the vivid picture provided of his patient's hidden sadistic, aggressive impulse to be unfriendly and cold to his wife. Based on this inference (a translation of meaning) and his idea that the situation would continue to repeat because the patient gained unconscious sadistic pleasure from it without feeling guilty, Eissler then intervened to give him "insight". He "explained", that is, he shared his insight with his patient, about what the patient was doing with his wife.

Apparently, Eissler's patient acknowledged this "interpretation". Moreover, in further associations, the patient then volunteered that he had known this for a long time and, according to Eissler, now "showed some understanding of the uncanny sadistic technique with which he maneuvered his wife into the situation of a helpless victim without giving her an opportunity of defending herself" (p. 139). By this point, therefore, Eissler thought he knew enough to infer a broader diagnosis of the repetitive causal dynamics of the patient's problem in his marriage.

However, when he conveyed his construction[4] to his patient the response was what he called "resistance". The patient could agree that he was behaving in the way he did towards his wife, but he was also convinced this was entirely justified. He "tried to prove to himself", Eissler writes, "and to the analyst that he was not cruel, but that he deserved pity owing to his wife's deficiencies".

Resistance here apparently has the meaning of a patient disagreeing with an analyst's construction. As Schafer (1973) observed, that makes it hard to distinguish it from a countertransference response of frustration.

Eissler goes on to indicate how faced with this response from his patient he understood it using a further construction. His patient's response, his resistance, he thought, could be understood by *assuming* that the problem was that his patient could not cope with the guilt feelings that would necessarily accompany being conscious of the meaning of his activity with his wife and, therefore, he was refusing to recognise his reasons for behaving as he was. His solution was to try to give him the insight that his *"incessant complaining"* about being a victim of the situation in reality served the purpose of assuaging his feelings of guilt.[5] Eissler summarises the situation by writing that "the more successful he was in gratifying his sadism in the camouflaged way he used so expertly, the more he had to present himself the next day as injured and unjustly treated by fate in being married to an allegedly unsatisfactory partner" (p. 139).

The problem was that this further constriction was not accepted by the patient. "He could not understand it; he could not follow me; and he insisted upon the validity of his complaints, although he had just agreed that he himself secretly induced his wife to behave in the manner about which he habitually complained to me the following day" (p. 139).

In the published paper, written to illustrate resistance, we do not learn more about the outcome of the ensuing struggle between patient and analyst as to who "knew". From what Eissler writes, it seems there was something of an impasse. He had not "come to a point when he would more readily forego the sadistic gratification and acquire mastery over this force than he would sacrifice the feeling of being unjustly treated by fate" (p. 140).

How typical of traditional North American practice Eissler's practice really was is a matter for debate, particularly due to the dearth of detailed material about what they did. For example, the classic paper on technique at this time by Loewenstein (1951) is frugal. Six clinical situations are mentioned to illustrate points about the need for tact,[6] the difficulty of finding the right words for an interpretation, how talking about a wish to be loved by his analyst was a married man's defence against attractions to other women, and so on. None provide any indication of the exchange between analyst and patient, nor of the processes through which unconscious content was inferred.

Insofar as Eissler's example is a useful excerpt, its tone of certainty (and the lack of any described attention to alternative ways of thinking about the patient's response or the part the analyst might unconsciously be playing in provoking it) may help to illustrate why subsequent relational analysts might have wanted to question the analyst's authority and his or her claims to knowledge.

To take us further, in the next section I want to discuss four suppositions every analyst must make when conducting an analysis. I will explore differences in these suppositions to compare the position Eissler and relational analysts seem to take with those I derive from Freud.

Four suppositions

For many psychoanalysts in Europe and those calling themselves North American Freudians (e.g. colleagues like Abend, Busch, Tuch, Hanly), psychoanalysis can be considered a meeting between two people and their subjectivities, traditionally with one on a couch[7] and the other in a chair. But to decide what else it is that specifically makes a meeting a psychoanalysis session requires theories of how psychoanalysis *should* be done.[8]

A great deal of research carried out with colleagues over the last twenty years[9] suggests to me, no matter the apparent divergences in what they do, that four theories are always in play. They are enacted in what the psychoanalyst does,[10] whether they are explicit or not, and, of course, they interact with the patient. The theories address:

1. **Unconscious inference**. An analyst's suppositions about how to investigate or claim to know the inaccessible (i.e. the unconscious ideas that evoke resistance to knowing).
2. **Unconscious repetition**. An analyst's suppositions about how what is inaccessible to a patient repetitively generates the patient's problems.
3. **The analytic situation**. An analyst's suppositions about the inaccessible dynamics of the situation between the two people in the investigation (i.e. theories of transference and countertransference).
4. **Furthering the process**. An analyst's suppositions about how sessions produce change and what should be done to produce this change in each one.

Unconscious inference

> We have learnt from psycho-analysis that the essence of the process of repression lies, not in putting an end to, in annihilating, the idea which represents a drive but in preventing it from becoming conscious. When this happens we say of the idea that it is in a state of being unconscious and we can produce good evidence to show that even when it is unconscious it can produce effects, even including some which finally reach consciousness.
>
> (Freud, 1915, p. 166)

Here, Freud hints at the process through which ideas attached to wishes are kept out of consciousness. Later, in 1923, in the encyclopaedia articles already mentioned, he rather precisely describes "free association" as the basis of the method for inferring unconscious ideas, before using the term "fundamental rule".

> The treatment is begun by the patient being required to put himself in the position of an attentive and dispassionate self-observer, merely to read off all the time the surface of his consciousness, and on the one hand to make a duty of the most complete honesty while on the other not to hold back any idea from communication, even if (1) he feels that it is too disagreeable or if (2) he judges that it is nonsensical or (3) too unimportant or (4) irrelevant to what is being looked for. It is uniformly found that precisely those ideas which provoke these last-mentioned reactions are of particular value in discovering the forgotten material.

He then adds a corollary about the analyst's role:

> experience soon showed that the attitude which the analytic physician could most advantageously adopt was to surrender himself to his own unconscious mental activity, in a state of evenly suspended attention ["gleichschwebende Aufmerksamkeit"], to avoid so far as possible reflection and the construction of conscious expectations, not to try to fix anything that he heard particularly in his memory, and by these means to catch the drift of the patient's unconscious with his own unconscious.
>
> (Freud, 1923, p. 237)

These two procedural attitudes, free association for the patient and evenly suspended attention for the analyst, highlight Freud's ideas about unconscious inference and in doing so transform the epistemological status of the content of sessions.

Ideas inaccessible to a patient are enabled to turn up because in free association they are (betrayed, *verraten*) via signs of resistance and this then allows them to be guessed (*erraten*).[11] In other words, resistance indicates the existence of unconscious ideas. Construction (guessing) allows the inference of their content. The crucial point is that in his thinking Freud is not claiming that the analyst can translate unconscious to conscious in a consistent or reliable way, such as when a physician takes a blood pressure reading to draw conclusions about a patient's health. But what can be done reliably is to observe signs of the presence of unconscious ideation – "a psychical force in the patients which was opposed to the pathogenic ideas becoming conscious" (Freud, 1893, p. 268). It works, he writes, because an analyst can recognise

> a universal characteristic of such ideas: they were all of a distressing nature, calculated to arouse the affects of shame, of self-reproach and of psychical pain, and the feeling of being harmed; they were all of a kind that one would prefer not to have experienced, that one would rather forget.
>
> (Freud, 1893, pp. 268–269)

In other words, as Bion (1976) was later to remark,

> feeling is one of the few things which analysts have the luxury of being able to regard as a fact … If patients are feeling angry, or frightened, or sexual, or whatever it is, at least we can suppose that this is a fact; but when they embark on theories or hearsay we cannot distinguish fact from fiction.
>
> (p. 132)

The point about unconscious ideas, by this definition, is that they are not bearable to the one holding them, which means that any claim an analyst makes to be an authoritative translator of the meaning of free association is fraught with difficulty – as we saw with Eissler's example, it raises the significant epistemic challenges and issues about countertransference and the potential misuse of power that Schafer (1973) and the relational analysts have exposed.

It is also quite apparent that when Freud tried to translate his patients' associations into unconscious ideas, as in his description of both the Dora and the "Rat Man" treatments, he clearly ran into trouble. One reason was that although he invented the term transference, he did not yet fully appreciate it's overwhelming importance, particularly in its counter-transferential mutual enactment form (Diercks, 2018). For this reason, Freud's distinction between the analyst's reliable ability to recognise signs of an unconscious idea being present (i.e. resistance) and his or her much less certain ability reliably to achieve the task of constructing what these ideas actually are, is crucial. To my way of thinking, it provides a more supportable and ultimately more defensible position.

The point is that resistance to ideas turning up in a patent's (or indeed an analyst's) mind can be defined and recognised via affects, slips of the tongue, hesitation, somatic occurrences, silence, collapse into incoherence, switches of mood, etc. Such signs are emotionally palpable. Construction, interpreting the meaning of the patient's utterances in a particular way, on the other hand, must be uncertain. It is what it claims to be – conjectural reason. The point is that whatever his practice, it is an error to suppose that Freud's theoretical approach to the nature of an analyst's knowledge is grounded in claims to reliable authority.

It is in this context that we need to understand that Freud's approach mixes free association with evenly suspended attention (*Gleichschwebende Aufmerksamkeit*). His use of the German word Gleich to describe the analytic stance has the connotation that attention should hover "in equal measure". The idea is not that an analyst can or will be objective or able to claim certain knowledge. Rather, it is to make it normative that analysts *should aspire to* adopt a *neutral attitude* towards the words and other material patients bring and to the feelings and thoughts this induces in their analysts. The aspiration is there to provide a vantage point to notice such shifts in the analyst's attention when they occur.

Additionally and quite crucially, both the German phrases *freier Einfall* (free association) and *Gleichschwebende Aufmerksamkeit* (evenly suspended attention) imply that the normative stance for both patient and analyst is passive, or receptive.[12] Their task is not to make interpretations and meanings but, so to speak, to notice the one being made and to consider them. In other words, for both the necessity is to try to notice what thoughts and feelings come to their minds so that new meanings can emerge conjecturally. The patient reports, the analyst notices and sometimes, via construction, there is a conjecture about unconscious meaning. Although either party may eschew curiosity to treat conjecture as fact, this model of unconscious inference is far away from the idea either of an omniscient analyst or patient or of an all-knowing couple.

Organised in this way, it is mistaken to take the fundamental rule as one designed to support the analyst's objective authority. Below, Freud is succinct in how he sets up the setting with his patients and it is not as a normal conversation with turn-taking and logically conscious sequences and themes:

> One more thing before you start. What you tell me must differ in one respect from an ordinary conversation. Ordinarily you rightly try to keep a connecting thread running through your remarks and you exclude any intrusive ideas that may occur to you and any side-issues, so as not to wander too far from the point. But in this case you must proceed differently. You will notice that as you relate things various thoughts will occur to you which you would like to put aside on the ground of certain criticisms and objections. You will be tempted to say to yourself that this or that is irrelevant here, or is quite unimportant, or nonsensical, so that there is no need to say it. You must never give in to these criticisms, but must say it in spite of them—indeed, you must say it precisely because you feel an aversion to doing so. Later on you will find out and learn to understand the reason for this injunction, which is really the only one you have to follow. So say whatever goes through your mind. Act as though, for instance, you were a traveller sitting next to the window of a railway carriage and describing to someone inside the carriage the changing views which you see outside. Finally, never forget that you have promised to be absolutely honest, and never leave anything out because, for some reason or other, it is unpleasant to tell it.
>
> (Freud, 1913, pp. 134–135)

Such a setting allowed Freud to sense resistance and intuit latent content in much the same way as Bion (1967) tried to formulate the need for an analyst to proceed without memory and desire. As Parthenope Bion Talamo, his daughter, pointed out, he was essentially restating Freud's recommendations as to how to make unconscious inference (Bion Talamo, 1997). Bion's distinction between "selected fact" and "overvalued idea" rests on the same conjectural uncertainty as did Freud's.

My experience on and behind the couch also leads me to emphasise that implementing free association and evenly suspended attention in the context of sensing resistance radically transforms the epistemological status of the content of sessions. A metaphor I use to incorporate this approach is the window. With it I argue that, although the events and remembered happenings the patient describes from life outside the window in the sessions are undoubtedly expressions of lived reality, their epistemological relevance in the session is that they are a response to unconscious experience evoked in the session on the couch in my consulting room (Tuckett, 2011).

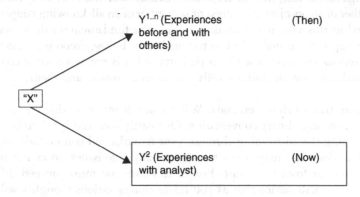

$Y^{1..n}$ (Experiences before and with others)   (Then)

"X"

Y^2 (Experiences with analyst)   (Now)

Figure 3.1 Transference as an unconscious causal template
Source: From Tuckett (2019)

The window metaphor captures the idea that when free associating, a patient has at the moment s/he is doing it, a sequence of experience (Y^1 in Figure 3.1 below). The conscious representations (memories, thoughts, stories, dreams, feelings, etc.) s/he formulates are stimulated here and now by this experience, which is reflexive and dynamic – each thought and feeling evoking further thoughts and feelings. In this way, associations can be treated as latent experiences transformed in the patient's mind into manifest thoughts, at the moment they are spoken – inside the window. Likewise, as the analyst listens to the patient (in evenly suspended attention) s/he also has a dynamic experience, which s/he also transforms into thoughts, images, etc., of which she becomes conscious.

From these viewpoints, it is hard to see how either a deliberate abandonment of the fundamental rule and evenly suspended attention or claims to be able to arrive at unconscious meaning infallibly in a one-person psychology model, or to do so interactively via an exchange of ideas and meanings, can capture ideas inaccessible to consciousness in Freud's sense.

Unconscious repetition

Unconscious ideas, which are beliefs, produce effects. If I think you are being cruel to me, it colours my response to you. In other words, applied to the perception and interpretation of the world, unconscious beliefs are simply experienced facts.

If I have a history of associating feeling guilty (or shameful or belittled or left out) to the belief someone is attacking or taking advantage of me, then, as I experience these feelings in future, my beliefs are evoked. I expect a perpetrator. Insofar as feelings like guilt, or other social emotions encountered as life goes on, are inevitable, I am caught in a repetitive vicious circle of belief in persecutors as fact, from which there is no exit.

Freud's suppositions about how what is inaccessible to a patient repetitively generates the patient's problems is of the essential form just suggested. The issue is not what happened once upon a time, which may well been cruel or traumatic, but how it goes on happening when the situation is unconsciously evoked.

Freud based his principal understanding of the cause of mental difficulty as the attempt to apply repetitive solutions to repetitively perceived internal conflicts — continuously evoking inaccessible conflicts originally experienced in managing infantile sexual impulses. From this viewpoint, the Oedipal configuration built up from infancy is not central to modern theory because we all concretely go on wanting to sleep with or kill our mothers or fathers (or are stuck in old-fashioned concepts of male and female, etc.). Rather, it matters because so much of human life evokes modern versions of the issues we first encountered in infancy:

- Feelings when we recognise our **difference** from those of the opposite sex and **sameness** with those of the same sex.
- **Rivalrous feelings** and ambivalence (hatred and love) towards the parent of the same sex and ambivalence or feelings of lack towards the parent of the opposite sex and guilt or shame about those feelings.
- Hatred and guilt about hatred at the recognition of the existence of time or **bigness and smallness**, or in other words, of generational difference and capacity.
- Hatred at the recognition of **exclusion from the parent's relationship**, or in other words, the primal scene causing difficulties with the third position.

In Freud's classical view, the conflicts, and the feelings they generate, are inevitably evoked in infancy and the solutions (understandings) perpetuate as a template throughout life. The ways we have unconsciously managed them are repeated. If repressed, the underlying ideas are inaccessible. But this is because they have been made inaccessible, not because the conflicts never took place.

In this theory of repetition, the primary driver is the evocation throughout life of new situations unconsciously experienced in old ways and so subject to old solutions. It will be precisely such repetitions, therefore, that will turn up in the analytic situation — for both patient and analyst.

The analytic situation

I have already mentioned how Freud realised early on that the way patients thought about and treated their psychoanalysts was important. As discussed above, he first identified what he thought of as resistance to ideas and then, as he realised that signs of resistance provided the route to unconscious inference, coined the term transference. He first used it in the clinical situation to explain his patient Dora's premature termination. But gradually he evolved the view that resistance in free association is resistance to repressed theories about the analyst and his or her intentions, derived from experiencing the analyst through a set of unconscious beliefs fossilised from past efforts to explain experience and now drawn on automatically in the present.

Freud invented the terms "transference" and then "countertransference" to explain what he observed in his sessions or those of others (and to suggest the underlying mechanisms brought pathological repetitions into the sessions so they could be recognised and interpreted). But he did not plumb their depths, nor apply them in detail to any of his own work that he described, leaving them implicit.

Figure 3.1 represents my view of the logic of Freud's transference theory as we can now understand it. The idea is that affects and beliefs in evidence in free associations in sessions derive from an unconscious internal template "X". It becomes manifest in sessional experience with an analyst, as in all other relationships of emotional significance.

Transference theory of this kind amounts to the proposition that the same unconscious internal template for understanding and acting on the world, "X," built in unconscious iterations from infancy, influences experience here and now in sessions (Y^1) as well as in past and present experience in the world ($Y^{2...n}$). Life generally and life in sessions, therefore, repetitively enacts and evokes affects and beliefs (unconscious phantasy meanings) built up and modelled from infancy and still treated as fact. If we add countertransference to this model, then what we are adding is the analyst's internal template. It is logical to suppose that it is that which activates unconscious "mutual enactment" between patient and analyst which, potentially, can eventually be recognised by the analyst or not.

In this theory of the analytic situation, it is an unconscious dynamic field. Whatever takes place between analyst and patient is influenced by it. So, for example, just as it becomes possible to imagine Freud mutually enacting the transference with Dora and the Rat Man, so might it have been happening to Eissler. The main problem with Eissler's technical theory, perhaps, was not its basis in an all-knowing analyst. Rather, the problem was that he took a theoretical position in which outside the action he could easily migrate unconsciously to enactment – enacting with his patent the very sado-masochistic process the patient was believed to be enacting with his wife. It also seems unlikely that relational analysts will escape the pull of unconscious enactment any more easily.

Furthering the process

Although Freud provided us with examples of his therapeutic approach at various stages of his development, as well as numerous comments scattered throughout his work, he nonetheless left a great deal of latitude around what it is in psychoanalysis that produces change and how to proceed to achieve it. Critical in this respect are the suppositions any analyst has about the meaning of the word "interpret" and Freud's ideas about *Junktim* already mentioned – the idea that in psychoanalysis the therapeutic work operates in conjunction with the investigative work, to such an extent that the concept of investigation is contained in that of technique.

A noticeable feature of both Eissler's case example and the approach taken by relational analysts is that that they rely on interpretations which are constructions – in some form or other explaining links between the patient's feelings and their thoughts here and now or outside or in the past. In fact, as the constructivist challenge highlights, we cannot know if Eissler's inferences and constructions about his patient's unconscious ideas were right. They may have been. Or not. The same is in fact true of all interpretation of this sort, even if agreed by the patient and analysts together.

The use or misuse of authority that relational analysts have focused on, however important, in my view is not the main point. Rather, the epistemological problem, if we accept the Freudian unconscious, is that we do not know if *any* conscious construction is valid. In Bion's terms we may have a "selected fact" but it may be an "overvalued idea" serving a defensive function. We can conjecture explanations and perhaps refute them, but we can't know them.

Freud's idea is that what is knowable, under conditions of free association and evenly suspended attention, are signs of unbearable unconscious ideas possessed by patient or analyst (betrayed, *verraten*) via instances of resistance. The underlying ideas can then be guessed (*erraten*) but not known. In other words, although resistance indicates the existence of unconscious ideas, construction (guessing) allows inferences about their content, but with no certainty.

Vassalli (2001) argued that the necessity of "guessing" leads to a different sort of knowing than the sort built up in medical or social science. This knowing cannot be a claim to know "what happened" (whether outside the window of the consulting room or in the patient's past or current relationships). It is a conjecture about the possible ideas (unconscious templates in terms of Figure 3.1) that seems to dominate a patient's reality at a moment.

To pick up the earlier discussion, Freud stressed that interpretations *always* remain provisional[13] until the problem the analyst and patient are trying to grasp has disappeared. What is important about this deferred effect is that it means that the analyst should not encourage the patient to believe in him or her as a superior omniscient figure. Rather, conviction should come from repeated own experience (Vassalli, 2001). As Freud put it, "One must allow the patient time to become more conversant with this resistance with which he has now become acquainted" (1914, p. 155).

All this causes me to suppose that the guessed knowledge implicit in the idea of interpretation as construction might usually best remain with the analyst

Table 3.1 Types of interpretation

	Desigation	Construction
Implicit	x	x
Explicit	x	x

until and unless the underlying situation (usually a transference experience) is so deeply felt by that intervention to designate it becomes essential.

Table 3.1 uses these points to make some rather gross oversimplifications. First, I distinguish between interventions in which psychoanalysts either *construct* ideas to explain what is going on or to simply *designate* their presence. Second, I distinguish whether they either designate or construct explicitly in relation to *here and now descriptions* of the analytic situation, or implicitly and more generally, for instance in relation to past relationships, including those with the analyst.

By *construction*, I refer to any interpretations an analyst makes claiming that hitherto unconscious links are apparent. It might be this is done via what amounts to conscious reasoning in some approaches, or via unconscious association in others. Here are three examples:

1. An analyst might construct to a patient how he or she feels frightened in a session – perhaps because they have attacked their analyst's work and then projected their destructive wishes into the analyst.
2. An analyst might show a patient that the behaviour he describes with his wife is exactly the behaviour he exhibited with his mother – apparently because unconsciously they evoke one and the same feelings.
3. An analyst might simply make a comment like "a big voracious mouth", an implicit construction, potentially stimulating in the patient further unconscious chains of thoughts to emerge.

The crucial point about all three is they suggest connections to the patient which are made in the analyst's mind. They are constructions between things picked out by the analyst. So, the first one connects comments that the patient has made about experiences with the analyst (Y^2) to defences the patient is inferred to have and suggests a causal connection. This is, perhaps, a strong claim. The second connects behaviour at Y^1 and Y^2 to suggest the causal influence of X – also a strong claim. The third simply seeks to enhance an associational chain – an inference but not a strong claim about connections.

By *designation*, I refer to statements about the patient's direct experience. The analyst picks out something to which to draw attention, but it is something that can easily be shared. It is usually done explicitly but not always.

4. "It looks like you are now *having* to stop your thoughts and are terrified not just about what is in your mind but about my reaction to your thoughts."
5. "A pause!"
6. "You stopped just then! Just as you were talking about your feelings."

(4) is an interpretation that "designates" the emotional situation between patient and analyst – using a shared observation to suggest how the patient unconsciously experiences the analyst. (5) points to a moment of apparent resistance with no further comment. (6) comments on a moment of resistance and specifies it, as apparent when talking about feelings.

A mutual evasion?

The suppositions psychoanalysts make both about what I have termed unconscious repetition and unconscious inference tend also to have consequences, not always intended, for those they make about both the analytic situation and furthering the process.

Relational analysts set out to correct what they saw as the hidden suppositions about unconscious inference made in classical North American technique – objecting to the implicit distribution of "who knows" in the consulting room by introducing suppositions from British and Latin American writers about the nature of the analytic situation as formed by the unconscious interaction of both participants in the session. Their main target was the supposition that anyone can reliably infer unconscious processes from a position of neutrality, but they do not seem to have considered this might not have been Freud's position.

In any case, for them it followed that the supposition that furthering the process by offering "accurate" interpretations that explain their patients' repetitive behaviours would be deeply flawed. So, in place of the classical suppositions about how to derive unconscious inference and further the process through accurate interpretation, a dialogic method evolved. Patient and analyst would now share constructions of the effect of each other's behaviour on each other and perhaps construct their possible origins in the other's needs or desires and how they suppose they had been met or frustrated in their history.

However, these "relational" suppositions, intended to liberate the patient from a potentially domineering analyst, necessarily create an active setting. A possibly unintended consequence is that these suppositions are entirely at odds with the method Freud called psychoanalysis, which I have argued he specifically created to allow him to infer unconscious ideas – via passive repetitive observation of discomfort and conjectural inference rather than via interpersonal action and mutual sense-*making*.

Relational suppositions are supported by new theories of early infancy, such as attachment theory, as well as by long-established evidence of the value of relationships. But is what has necessarily gone missing in the relational turn, as others have also argued,[14] the core of psychoanalysis – namely the previously pivotal supposition Freud made about unconscious repetition? His theory was that the repetitive disadvantage that patients suffer (their symptoms) are the product of their repressed ideas, however it is that they may have come to internalise them. If so, then the relational turn necessarily leads psychoanalysis away from Freud's core discovery of psychoanalysis as a method to identify the *unwelcome* ideas, repressed from consciousness, that repetitively create our troubles. Indeed, many of the troubles the patients of relational analysts seem to have often turn out to result not from the intrinsic conflicts thrown up by the Oedipal configuration but from conflict with their environment.

Because I do think the relational turn dramatically alters Freud's core suppositions about unconscious inference and unconscious repetition, I do think it tends to take psychoanalysis away from itself. However, I think this development is far from unique – a product in fact of a general difficulty transposing Freud's ideas, particularly as they have been interpreted by key European and Latin American writers (like Klein, Heimann, Winnicott, Bion, Racker and Baranger) into a North American classical context (and other contexts influenced by it).

The two core suppositions that make me argue on these lines refer to differences in how to understand the analytic situation and the primary role of construction as the vehicle of therapeutic effort. To clarify, let me use my position as a straw man:

1. We cannot reliably "know" another person's unconscious ideas, but we can reason conjecturally (*erraten*) to infer them by guesswork in a specific context based on attending to situations where they betray (*verraten*) signs of discomfort and different ideas come together in our mind. When this happens, it may constitute a "selected fact" but it can also result in an "overvalued idea". Only time and repetition or a shift in a patient's freedom to associate (less frequent discomfort in similar situations) will tell.

2. The only place where we can securely observe these betrayals is when we are with the patient – in other words, in a session. It will be much easier to do this in a parsimonious environment such as if the patient is provided with the fundamental rule and the analyst sets out to adopt *evenly* suspended attention aiming him or her passively to notice configurations and generally to be parsimonious as to when and what he speaks about (Tuckett, 2019).

3. I understand the analytic situation, if set up by the fundamental rule and evenly suspended attention, as *inevitably* and continuously evoking transference and countertransference, meaning that it is always evoking ambivalent affects and unconscious mental processes that are understood

and enacted in terms of the patient and analyst's internal template (Figure 3.1). The patient and analyst may at times think they are talking about the world "outside the window" or believe they are tending towards objectivity but in fact they can never "know" they have escaped the transference – i.e. their unconscious ambivalent ideas about each other and their intentions towards each other. Freud was very clear (a) that what he called pathogenic complexes cannot be addressed "*in absentia*" or "*in effigie*" (1913, p. 108), and (b) that the essence of transference was ambivalence between positive and negative wishes or ideas to the other (1912, p. 105[15]).

4. The furthering of the analytic progress primarily takes place via the set-up of the investigation (the fundamental rule and evenly suspended attention) and the analyst's ability to designate transference resistance – i.e. moments in sessions when the patient betrays discomfort and therefore the presence of *unconscious ambivalent ideas about the analyst and his or her intentions and attitudes to the patient* approaching the surface of consciousness. Construction as to what these ideas are beyond the feelings they evidently produce (e.g. anxiety, excitement, guilt, loss, triumph) and where they come from is possible and can help, but (a) is always only conjectural and provisional, and (b) essentially rests on a foundation of accurate designation. It is this process of furthering the investigation rather than the arrival at "correct" interpretation of the patient's mental complexes – however interesting and brilliant – that is at the heart of psychoanalysis as a therapeutic method.

Four features of my position may be useful to spell out in relation to the arguments that have gone on, particularly in the US, but elsewhere. They are around neutrality, transference, resistance and interpretation.

First, the fundamental rule and evenly suspended attention are adopted not from a belief that an analyst will be or can be consistently neutral. That is a mistaken supposition.[16] Objective neutrality is impossible in practice. "Evenly" suspended attention is an attribute of a theoretical model of practice only. In practice, the idea can be used to help the analyst note his or her hidden preconceptions and responses. In this way it's a device to help surface attention shifts and resistances in the analyst's mind. In other words, by accepting the need to aspire to neutrality, an analyst can better become an observer of herself.

Second, I suppose transference to be a process, deriving from the patient's unconscious mental life (i.e. ideas) evoked in the session. The patient builds up and expresses ambivalent pictures (imagos) of the analyst as chains of thought in the associations emerge and the analyst responds.[17] Theoretically, of course, we may think of the picture of the analyst as built from an internal template (X) via projective and introjective processes. But that is theory – a construction of psychoanalysis. The patient's experience, as discussed above, is simply that the analyst is felt to be whatever he or she is felt to be.

Third, I limit the term resistance. I *suppose*, following Freud's original idea, that all interruptions to free association derive from ideas inaccessible to (i.e. repressed by) patients, as they seek to follow the fundamental rule. The latter, like "evenly" suspended attention (neutrality), is a model-based rule. No one who has been in analysis believes they said everything that came to their mind. In practice, we forget, explain away, etc., as Freud eloquently described in his original formulation of the rule. The purpose of modelling the funda-mental rule is that a normative framework is set up *in the analyst's mind*. As discomfort with the framework emerges, it is not a patient's opposition to the analyst or his or her ideas, nor opposition to the treatment or negative thera-peutic reaction, etc., that is being expressed, whatever it may feel like. Rather, underlying unconscious ideas are being caught as they are being repressed, *in flagrante*, as Freud might have said. It is these ideas that are causing resistance, not the conscious rationalisations. From this viewpoint, it does not matter at all what the patient "chooses" to say and nor can there be more or less interesting or free association. That's countertransference. Instead, there is associating and resisting. It is to be expected so long as bothersome *unconscious* ideas are around.

Fourth, interpretation and construction. Freud and those that followed gave us fascinating accounts of their interpretive work. They elaborated compelling reasons to suppose symptoms and transference to be a product of repressed ideas in patients' unconscious minds (perhaps such as the secret satisfaction gained by Eissler's patient in the way he treated his wife). But such interpretations can only be conjectures. So, I suppose that while very tempting to make and useful to relate to those interested in psychoanalysis to show how unconscious ideas work *in general*, constructions of what a patient is really thinking or doing (etc.) are mostly a distraction from everyday work. Often, constructions become overvalued ideas – in whichever of the psycho-analytic traditions they are proposed.

An important and somewhat unexpected corollary to my suppositions is caution about the concepts of working through[18] and resistance to treatment. As these terms were used by Loewenstein and many others since, they seem to me to be dangerous if used alongside suppositions that construction is *the* tool for furthering the process, particularly if suppositions about the analytic situation allow the analyst to escape having to recognise that at all times he or she, necessarily, must be experienced and so represented in the patient's mind as a profoundly ambivalent object. Loewenstein's (1958; 1963) review of numerous delineations of "resistances" and aids to "working through", including the use of "tact" to try to get over them, or Greenson's (1970) ideas about the need for the patient to trust the analyst (a therapeutic alliance), seem to me to side-step these issues. Similarly, although Kohut's (1984) stress on empathy with the patient's viewpoint may seem desirable, it becomes prob-lematic if the patient's internal template creates ambivalence. Similarly, while classical ideas on technique from Fenichel (1939) which advocate care in the ordering of interpretations, or Busch's (1995) argument for close focus on interpreting the meaning of signs of resistance before progressing to deeper fantasies, make sense, they will remain problematic so long as the essential idea behind interpretation is construction.

Many contributions since the 1950s (see, for example, Alexander, 1956; Jacobs, 1990, Kohut, 1971; 1977; Loewald, 1978) have questioned the role of interpretation to argue that what really matters is the relationship. Indeed, in one sense the relational turn, albeit in an extreme way, fits into this evolution. Most other approaches ultimately suppose that the analyst must get to the construction because the patient cannot be conscious. The relational turn asks the patient to join in. Neither solve the problem as to how to proceed if unconscious ideas cannot be known and only (seriously) guessed at from the analytic situation. My supposition is that although unconscious ideas are central to psychoanalysis in general, they are unknowable in any case. The foundation of psychoanalytic treatment, therefore, rests on designation.

In conclusion, the relational turn has taken psychoanalysis directly to a crossroads that could be faced more explicitly in psychoanalytic technique in North America and far beyond. Accepting that unconscious ideas cannot be imposed on patients via authoritative construction, is psychoanalysis ready to "return" rigorously to an analytic setting of free association and evenly suspended attention, focused on designating the discomfort the patient feels being with the psychoanalyst and guessing at the underlying ideas, or is it to proceed rather blindly along its present lines as a kind of Freudian-informed life coaching? The crossroads exists as much in the various European and Latin American techniques as it does in North America, although perhaps it is more hidden.

Notes

1 It was also "(3) a collection of psychological information obtained along those lines, which is gradually being accumulated into a new scientific discipline".

2 "Initially in our development we treat beliefs as facts, and it is only with emancipation from an inner certainty that we can see our beliefs as requiring reality testing" (Britton, 2009, p. 924).

3 "For most analysts at that time, Eissler's paper was seen as setting the standard for what might properly be called analysis" Cooper, 2008, p. 105.

4 "I tried to show the patient that his incessant complaining had also served the purpose of assuaging his feelings of guilt. The more successful he was in gratifying his sadism in the camouflaged way he used so expertly, the more he had to present himself the next day as injured and unjustly treated by fate in being married to an allegedly unsatisfactory partner" (p. 139).

5 Eissler uses this example to demonstrate what he called secondary resistance from the superego.

6 The example is actually about a patient who coughed to awaken the analyst who had fallen asleep. To the patient's observation that he had been asleep, the analyst replied: "You always want everybody's attention". Loewenstein writes that "This was true of the patient; but said at that moment, it could hardly have had a beneficial effect, first of all, because an analytic patient is entitled to have the attention of his analyst; but also because the analyst misused the correct observation in order to displace the guilt about having been asleep onto his patient. Had he made this remark at another time, it might have increased the patient's insight" (Loewenstein, 1951, pp. 8–9). There is no discussion of the transference-countertransference field that might have "produced" this interchange.

7 In fact, relational analysts like Jodie Davies appear to have abandoned the couch for chairs.

8 In fact, two sets of theories, of course, originating with each participant and then dynamically interacting. In other words, to be a psychoanalysis sets role limits for patient and analyst.

9 The work has been done in the European Working Party on Comparative Clinical Methods (Tuckett et al., forthcoming).

10 Arlow (1995) has also drawn out connections between "working concepts" psychoanalysts may have and their interpretations – for example, between their theories of pathogenesis (our term, unconscious repetition) and what and how they interpret (our term, furthering).

11 See Vassalli, 2001.

12 My colleague Michael Diercks (personal communication) relates this to Bion's "container". It is, of course, typically labelled as a feminine position.

13 "It will all become clear in the course of future developments" (Freud, 1914, p. 265), in the words of Nestroy's manservant, whom Freud quotes in this connection.

14 E.g. Busch (2001), Eagle (2003), Hanly (1999), Sugarman and Wilson (1995).

15 "We find in the end that we cannot understand the employment of transference as resistance so long as we think simply of 'transference'. We must make up our minds to distinguish a 'positive' transference from a 'negative' one, the transference of affectionate feelings from that of hostile ones, and to treat the two sorts of transference to the doctor separately ... Bleuler has coined the excellent term 'ambivalence' to describe this phenomenon" (Freud, 1912, pp. 104–106).

16 My second supervisor, Paul Heimann, was often eloquent on this point, as was a later supervisor and colleague, Betty Joseph.

17 "If now we follow a pathogenic complex from its representation in the conscious (whether this is an obvious one in the form of a symptom or something quite inconspicuous) to its root in the unconscious, we shall soon enter a region in which the resistance makes itself felt so clearly that the next association must take account of it and appear as a compromise between its demands and those of the work of investigation. It is at this point, on the evidence of our experience, that transference enters on the scene" (Freud, 1912, p. 103).

18 Busch (2013) notes that it isn't widely appreciated that Freud used the term "working through" sparingly, and only in regard to "resistances".

References

Alexander, F. (1956) *Psychoanalysis and Psychotherapy*. New York: Norton.

Arlow, J.A. (1995) Stilted listening: psychoanalysis as discourse. *Psychoanalytic Quarterly*. 64: 215–233.

Aron, L. (1996) *A Meeting of Minds: Mutuality in Psychoanalysis*. Hillsdale, NJ: The Analytic Press.

Benjamin, J. (1990) An outline of intersubjectivity: the development of recognition. *Psychoanalytic Psychology*. 7: 33–46.

Benjamin, J. (2004) Beyond doer and done to: an intersubjective view of thirdness. *Psychoanalytic Quarterly*. 73: 5–46.

Bion, W.R. (1967) Notes on memory and desire. *The Psychoanalytic Forum*. 2: 272–273, 279–280.

Bion, W.R. (1976) Evidence. In: *Four Papers in Volume 10 of The Complete Works of W. R. Bion* (edited by F. Bion and C. Mawson). London: Taylor and Francis.

Bion Talamo, P. (1997) Bion: a Freudian innovator. *British Journal of Psychotherapy*. 14: 47–59.

Britton, R. (2009) Religion und Fanatismus. *Psyche – Zeitschrift für Psychoanalyse*. 63: 907–924.

Busch, F. (1995) Do actions speak louder than words? A query into an enigma in analytic theory and technique. *Journal of the American Psychoanalytic Association*. 43: 61–82.

Busch, F. (2001) Are we losing our mind? *Journal of the American Psychoanalytic Association*. 49: 739–751.

Busch, F. (2013) L'analyse des résistances: Analyse de la résistance et perlaboration. Un domaine négligé de l'élaboration psychanalytique quotidienne. *Revue française de psychanalyse*. 77: 781–798.

Cooper, A.M. (2008) Commentary on Greenson's "The Working Alliance and the Transference Neurosis". *Psychoanalytic Quarterly*. 77: 103–119.

Davies, J.M. (2018) The "rituals" of the relational perspective: theoretical shifts and clinical implications. *Psychoanalytic Dialogues*. 28: 651–669.

Diercks, M. (2018) Freud's "transference": clinical technique in the "rat man" case and theoretical conceptualization compared. *International Journal of Psychoanalysis*. 99: 58–81.

Eagle, M.N. (2003) The postmodern turn in psychoanalysis: a critique. *Psychoanalytic Psychology*. 20: 411–424.

Eissler, K.R. (1953) The effect of the structure of the ego on psychoanalytic technique. *Journal of the American Psychoanalytic Association*. 1: 104–143.

Fenichel, O. (1939) Problems of psychoanalytic technique. *Psychoanalytic Quarterly*. 8: 57–87.

Fosshage, J.L. (1990) The analyst's response. *Psychoanalytic Inquiry*. 10: 601–622.

Freud, S. (1893) The psychotherapy of hysteria from studies on hysteria. *The Standard Edition of the Complete Psychological Works of Sigmund Freud*. 2: 253–305.

Freud, S. (1912) The dynamics of transference. *The Standard Edition of the Complete Psychological Works of Sigmund Freud*. 12: 97–108.

Freud, S. (1913) On beginning the treatment (further recommendations on the technique of psycho-analysis I). *The Standard Edition of the Complete Psychological Works of Sigmund Freud*. 12: 121–144.

Freud, S. (1914) Remembering, repeating and working-through (further recommendations on the technique of psycho-analysis II). *The Standard Edition of the Complete Psychological Works of Sigmund Freud*. 12: 145–156.

Freud, S. (1915) The unconscious. *The Standard Edition of the Complete Psychological Works of Sigmund Freud*. 14: 159–215.

Freud, S. (1923) Two encyclopaedia articles. *The Standard Edition of the Complete Psychological Works of Sigmund Freud*. 18: 233–260.

Greenson, R.R. (1970) The exceptional position of the dream in psychoanalytic practice. *Psychoanalytic Quarterly*. 39: 519–549.

Hanly, C. (1999) On subjectivity and objectivity in psychoanalysis. *Journal of the American Psychoanalytic Association*. 47: 427–444.

Hoffman, I.Z. (1983) The patient as interpreter of the analyst's experience. *Contemporary Psychoanalysis*. 9: 389–422.

Jacobs, T.J. (1990) The corrective emotional experience – its place in current technique. *Psychoanalytic Inquiry*. 10: 433–454.

Kohut, H. (1971) *The Analysis of the Self*. New York: International Universities Press.

Kohut, H. (1977) *The Restoration of the Self*. New York: International Universities Press.

Kohut, H. (1984) *How Does Psychoanalysis Cure?* Chicago: University of Chicago Press.

Loewald, H.W. (1978) Instinct theory, object relations, and psychic-structure formation. *Journal of the American Psychoanalytic Association*. 26: 493–506.

Loewenstein, R.M. (1951) The problem of interpretation. *Psychoanalytic Quarterly*. 20: 1–14.

Loewenstein, R.M. (1958) Remarks on some variations in psycho-analytic technique. *International Journal of Psychoanalysis*. 39: 202–210.

Loewenstein, R.M. (1963) Some considerations on free association. *Journal of the American Psychoanalytic Association*. 11: 451–473.

Schafer, R. (1973) The idea of resistance. *International Journal of Psychoanalysis*. 54: 259–285.

Stern, D.B. (2019) How I work with unconscious process: a case example. *Contemporary Psychoanalysis*. 55: 336–348.

Sugarman, A. and Wilson, A. (1995) Introduction to the section: contemporary structural analysts critique relational theories. *Psychoanalytic Psychology*. 12: 1–8.

Tuckett, D. (2011) Inside and outside the window: some fundamental elements in the theory of psychoanalytic technique. *International Journal of Psycho-Analysis*. 92: 1367–1390.

Tuckett, D. (2019) Transference and transference interpretation revisited: why a parsimonious model of practice may be useful. *The International Journal of Psychoanalysis*, 100(5): 852–876.

Tuckett, D., Allison, E., Bonard, O., Bronstein, A., Bruns, G., Christopoulous, A., Diercks, M., Hinze, E., Linardos, M., Rudden, M., and Sebek, M. (Forthcoming) Knowing what psychoanalysts do and doing what psychoanalysts know: a report on the Comparative Clinical Methods Project.

Vassalli, G. (2001) The birth of psychoanalysis from the spirit of technique: what have we learned? How can we apply it? *International Journal of Psychoanalysis.* 82: 3–25.

Chapter 4

The relational unconscious

A core element of intersubjectivity, thirdness, and clinical process

Samuel Gerson

Introduction

It may have taken the field of psychoanalysis eighty years to take full note of the "third" so evident to Eliot's (1922) poetic vision, yet it seems that having only recently broadened our purview from a singular focus on the patient, our gaze now moves urgently past the engagements of the dyad and into an opaque space beyond identifiable subjects. For some, this something called the "third" that transcends individualities is thought of as a product of an interaction between persons; others speak of it as a context that originates apart from us even as it binds us together; and there are some for whom the third is a developmental achievement that creates a location permitting reflective observation of lived experience. These multiple meanings indicate the need for concepts to contain and further the abundant new observations that have stimulated us as we have evolved into a theoretically pluralistic discipline tied to contemporary developments in related fields of study.

In this chapter, I hope to further this project by rethinking some of the foundational concepts that originated within an exclusive intrapsychic orientation and extending them from an intersubjective perspective.[1] After briefly considering some premises that inform a relational view of the mind, I will elaborate on these elements of intersubjectivity, with three purposes in mind. The first is to extend the concept of the unconscious and its processes in a manner consistent with intersubjective views of human development and communication of knowledge. In this regard, I will suggest that the concept of the relational unconscious best captures the theoretical and clinical implications of intersubjectivity. Second, I will contrast the concept of the relational unconscious with those that involve notions of thirdness, and in this effort I will delineate three different usages of the concept of thirdness— namely, the developmental third, the cultural third, and the relational third. My third aim is to draw attention to the operations of the relational unconscious within psychoanalytic practice. Here, I examine two clinical vignettes in which the work is temporarily stagnant as a consequence of intersubjective resistances; I suggest that the unraveling of such resistances alters both the

DOI: 10.4324/9781003340744-6

structures of each individual's unconscious and the patterning of their relational unconscious. I conclude with the view that clinical progress is regularly
characterized by analytic discourse that creates the dual therapeutic action of
affecting both the individual and relational unconscious of both participants
in the analytic dyad.

In 1994, the International Journal of Psychoanalysis published a 75th anni-
versary issue entitled "The Conceptualization and Communication of Clinical
Facts in Psychoanalysis." In a paper surveying and summarizing the content
of the articles of that issue, Mayer (1996) wrote:

> Almost every contributor makes a point of emphasizing how crucial and
> basic is the relational, intersubjective and subjective nature of a psycho-
> analytic clinical fact ... Clinical facts are not about how, in the context
> of one person's mind, the unconscious becomes conscious or structural
> change happens. Unconscious fantasy and genetic reconstruction do not
> themselves constitute clinical facts; they simply do not exist as discern-
> ible facts outside the subjectivity and intersubjectivity of the analytic
> relationship.
>
> (p. 710)

This broad movement within psychoanalysis to embrace relationally based
conceptions of developmental and clinical processes represents a significant
departure from the debates that marked the emergence of the intersubjective
perspective (roughly from the mid-1980s to the mid-90s). Often framed
as a debate between one-person and two-person psychologies, these controversies reflected a false dichotomy between intrapsychic (one-person) and
intersubjective (two-person) conceptions of the analytic interaction. More
recent contributions have attempted to transcend the initial polarizations by
revisioning psychoanalytic theory in a manner that seeks to describe the always
intertwined and necessary contributions of each viewpoint (Green, 2000).

In addition to general attempts to reconcile the intersubjective and
intrapsychic, the current focus has shifted to specific aspects of theory and
technique that require elaboration from within the emergent integrative perspective. Fundamental concepts that form the theoretical base for analytic
practice are currently being rethought from within the enriched perspective
of a relational model that is fully informed by intrapsychic phenomena.[2] These
efforts are part of an evolution that seeks to refashion psychoanalytic theory
and principles of technique by assimilating newer modes of thought into
prior understandings in a way that enables both continuity and innovation.

The intersubjective creation of meaning

I introduce this section with a very brief vignette, one that occurred twenty-
five years ago, yet only recently returned as a memory and now informs my

thinking about intersubjectivity and the clinical process. Early in my career, a man came to see me hoping that I might help him reach some decision about how to proceed in his professional life. His frustration was palpable, and while I sensed that he wished that I might advise him and rescue him from his interminable dilemma, he downplayed this idea and said he wanted only to figure out his own mind.

One day, in the midst of his reflections about how he would know when the right choice presented itself, he said, "I'm thinking about that question that's asked in all introductory philosophy courses, the question of 'If a tree falls in the forest and there is no one to hear it, does it make any sound?'" He went on to say, "Well, neither of the two choices makes any sense to me. It seems to me that in order for a tree to make a sound, there has to be more than one person to hear it. If I were alone in the woods and a tree fell, I would need to turn to someone and ask, 'Did you hear that?' Without someone else's response, how could I be certain about what had happened?"

I have come to believe that this man's novel solution to the "If a tree falls in the forest" question can be heard as an allegory about the communal origins of knowledge—a rendering that contains essential truths about human development, as well as about the analytic process. His reflections about the familiar philosophical puzzle contain the belief that our sense of the world around us, and of our position in that world, is forever contextualized in an intersubjective matrix of perception, speech, and signification.

His solution also captures two foundational elements of an intersubjective orientation to psychoanalysis. First is the premise that all subjectivity exists as a fluid state in which there is continuous movement from evanescent perceptions toward stability of meanings. This core aspect of mental activity involves processes of finding ways to represent our inner states to ourselves in a manner whereby experience achieves a sense of coherence. In this process, subjectivity tends toward its own transformation into objectivity via processes that aim to anchor the internal in external realities (e.g., projection and theories of causation). In these fundamental endeavors, we are perpetually engaged with the task of organizing internal experience in ways that allow us to discover and create external realities that provide reflections and justifications for our affective states. As clinicians, we articulate this understanding in our efforts to demonstrate to our patients how their feelings may be transformed into "facts." Elusive as it may be, subjectivity always seeks to locate itself in the ground of objectivity. Lear (1990) spoke to this issue when he noted that "Subjectivity is upwardly mobile. The meanings and memories that shape a person's outlook on the world do not lie dormant in the soul; they are striving for expression" (p. 29).

A second premise of an intersubjective psychoanalysis is that the organization of meaning in one mind is always embedded in processes of reciprocal influence with other minds similarly engaged in processes of altering subjective sensibilities into seemingly objective realities. The emphasis here is that the maintenance, transformation, and/or creation of organizations of meaning in one person rely on an active engagement with others (internally and/or externally) for realization. The journey of subjectivity toward its expression occurs via systems that originate beyond the individual and, through their use by the individual, inform and transform subjectivity itself. This developmentally progressive, or "upwardly mobile," movement of subjectivity follows a trajectory from the internal, unique, and private domain toward external, shared, and communal worlds; it is a dynamic process wherein context infiltrates internal experience and saturates private fantasy with meanings that are publicly comprehensible. As each person strives to transform private sensation into symbolic communication, he or she also traces the route by which all individual minds become both the creator and the expression of culture. Implicit here is the inherent quality of mind to utilize systems of meanings external to itself in the service of transforming inchoate impression into a communicable form while simultaneously preserving the idiosyncratic truth of experience.

Bollas (1992) illustrates this fundamental dynamic to when he describes how we are continuously involved in attempts to utilize elements of the environment as opportunities for "thinking ourselves out." As he noted, "Without giving it much thought at all, we consecrate the world with our own subjectivity, investing people, places, things, and events with a kind of idiomatic significance" (p. 3). Objects that can contain the projection of our idioms and play them back in a way that neither destroys nor mystifies our experience best allow us to articulate our sensibilities. In this benign and creative process, that which has been felt but not reflectively organized becomes available for our consideration and use. A major implication of the idea that minds are always engaged in procuring opportunities to know themselves and to be known is that the entirety of one's psychological content is not already organized, but rather, that some contents achieve coherence only in acts of communication and recognition.

From this vantage point, the unconscious is not only the receptacle of repressed material driven underground to protect one from conflict-induced anxieties; it is also a holding area whose contents await birth at a receptive moment in the contingencies of evolving experience. Stern (1989) outlined this perspective when he described the nature of unformulated experience: "Unconscious contents can no longer be conceived of as concrete or literal, but must instead be understood as potential mental activity: thoughts not yet thought, connections not yet made, memories one does not yet have the resources or the willingness to construct" (p. 12].

The concept of unformulated experience is of a similar order to Bollas's (1987) "unthought known", Bion's (1962) "beta elements", and Mitrani's (1995) unmentalized experience—each notion refers to experience that eludes consciousness due to absences of a resonant interpersonal environment. These theories of mental organization describe an unconscious that fashions the forms of individual subjectivity, even while its contents await elaboration and the possibility of self-knowledge through external experience with another. Together, they highlight the necessity of another mind capable of receiving, containing, and expressively elaborating one's experience, if that experience is to become a vital element of one's consciousness.

These fundamental processes constitute, according to Spezzano (1995), a "theory of mind that posits an unconscious psyche constantly driven to bring its contents into consciousness. Consciousness, in turn, is viewed as, inherently, the creation of minds in interaction" (p. 24). Similarly, Cavell (1988) has written that "since meaning is understood to be intrinsically social, so in an important sense is mind" (p. 859). Both these authors point toward the postulate that the development and transformation of the unconscious is part of a continuous process that is rooted in the always evolving dialectics of private and social experience, and therefore cannot progress as an act of one mind in solitude. Rather, the presence of another mind is required for the registration, recognition, and articulation of the unconscious elements of the first. It is this necessary presence of the other that establishes knowledge as an intersubjective creation and renders that which is knowable as socially determined.

All intersubjective theorization exists in opposition to "the myth of the isolated mind" (Stolorow and Atwood, 1992, p. 7), and thereby issues a fundamental challenge to contemporary views about the privacy, unity, and primacy of the self (Blatt and Blass, 1990; Cushman, 1995). The intersubjective focus highlights those modes of experience wherein the sharp distinctions between inner and outer, between self and other, are replaced by fluid boundaries that surround rather than separate individuals. As such, this jointly constituted area may be most fruitfully thought of as an entity of its own, rather than as a site of exchange between bounded individual selves. Winnicott (1953) captured the radical implications of this perspective in his formulation of an intermediate area of experience.

Throughout these literatures, we are reminded that our sensibilities are formed and reformed by the presence of the other, and that our seemingly autonomous selves are social constructions, containing what Vygotsky (1978) aptly referred to as a culturally embedded "loan of consciousness," while constituting individuals as containing "a consciousness of two" (p. 88).

The relational unconscious

I propose that this reciprocal and mutual influence of unconscious minds upon one another creates a relational unconscious. The uniqueness of each relationship is in large part due to its singular mix of the permitted and prohibited, a mix that is formed from, yet transcends, the individual conscious and unconscious elements of each partner. Imagine the relationship as the offspring of the two individuals, constituted by each of their unconscious material, and, as in the mix of genetic material, having features both recognizable and novel and always containing marks of mysterious origin. The jointly developed relational unconscious affords each participant novel opportunities for the expression of previously unactualized, as well as repressed, elements of subjectivity and experience, even as it contains limitations and prohibitions unique to the dyad, which culminate in a variety of mutually supported defensive processes.

The relational unconscious, as a jointly constructed process maintained by each individual in the relation, is not simply a projection of one person's unconscious self and object representations and interactional schemas onto the other, nor is it constituted by a series of such reciprocal projections and introjections between two people. Rather, as used here, the relational unconscious is the unrecognized bond that wraps each relationship, infusing the expression and constriction of each partner's subjectivity and individual unconscious within that particular relation. In this regard, the relational unconscious is a concept that allows the joining of psychoanalytic thought about intrapsychic and intersubjective phenomena within a theoretical framework that contains each perspective and elaborates their inherent interconnectedness. Green (2000) has made a similar point. "We need to consider that it is more enriching to think of the relation between the two poles than to think of each pole (the intrapsychic and the intersubjective) separately, as these do not remain the same in the context of their mutual relations" (p.21).

The relational unconscious may be thought of as that which is, in Green's (2000) words, "beyond the two poles," and as the unseen bridge that "eludes the observation of their relations." It is by dint of its existence in and between both minds that the concept of the relational unconscious described here differs from other recent usages of the term, each of which has addressed the content of an individual unconscious, rather than the bond made between the two individuals while going beyond each. Davies's (1996) conception of the relational unconscious delineated a set of individually held experiences of unacceptable object-related wishes or fantasies, and incompatible self-experiences in relation to the other. These experiences, while relational in nature, are nonetheless viewed as aspects of each person's psyche and not as a mutually constructed and maintained unconscious. Similarly, Rucker and Lombardi's (1997) ideas about the "related unconscious" described a region of "undifferentiated" experience within the individual. They referred to interactions that occur on this plane as "subject-relations" and identified this level of interaction as one in which "two individuals experience their sameness and indivisibility rather than their individuality" (p. 20). In their model, the unconscious is related as an inherent product of its own organizing activity, and not as a result of the actual modes of engagement and separation created by two people in their relationship.

Recently, the concept of a relational unconscious has been fruitfully utilized by clinical scholars, who attempted to understand therapeutic processes from the vantage point of mutually constituted and maintained forms of regulation (Lyons-Ruth, 1999; Zeddies, 2000). The increasing emphasis on the reciprocal and reverberating influences of analyst and analysand upon each other has found expression in the concept of enactment, and I will consider this phenomenon in a subsequent section of this chapter. Suffice to say here that even the enactment literature contains scant reference to a jointly created unconscious; rather, the formulations offered typically involve how two distinct unconsciouses affect each other. Here in the rich field of the transference-countertransference matrix, as in the great majority of psychoanalytic scholarship, the unconscious is represented almost exclusively as a property of each individual in interaction with an other's similarly bounded, even if responsive, unconscious.

The basic psychoanalytic premise that all human groupings are characterized by both conscious and unconscious domains of experience and belief leads us to think of each individual's unconscious life as existing in a continuous relation with the unconscious life of all other persons and groupings in which his or her life is lived. A full description of any individual's unconscious life in relation to the unconsciouses of all human individuals and groupings in that person's life would be of immense complexity, inevitably beyond two-dimensional renderings. Nonetheless, I would like to offer a few imaginary structures to explicate the concept of the relational unconscious. First, visualize a triangular structure wherein the individual unconscious forms the apex and rests upon multiple dyadic relational unconsciouses. The relational unconsciouses (one for every relationship) may be thought of, in turn, as resting upon a series of ever more inclusive group unconsciouses (e.g., memberships in sexual, professional, political, national, religious, and cultural groupings). All these layers exist simultaneously and are more or less energized at any time, depending on the groupings with which the individual is actively engaged at any moment. Similarly, one might imagine that each relational unconscious is like the point of intersection on a Venn diagram between one's individual unconscious and that of one's partner, and that this relational unconscious is itself intersected by an ever more inclusive set of human groupings to which each member of the relationship belongs, with some of these groupings shifting from foreground to background, yet all represented unconsciously.

The visual metaphor of a triangular structure or of a nested series of overlapping circles does not, of course, capture the complexities created by the multidimensional interweavings of each layer or circle as it evolves from relationship to relationship. Yet I hope that in these imaginary configurations, the breadth of unconscious life finds representation and may shed light on how, in our existence as individuals, our seemingly most private unconscious is always being shaped by the multiple forces and contexts in which we are embedded and through which we are constituted.

Thirdness

The widespread recognition that analytic practice involves processes and phenomena that transcend the boundaries of a single mind has led to a variety of attempts to conceptualize, name, and explore that which exists beyond the individual psyches of analyst and analysand. Many of these attempts have invoked structures, positions, or locations that occupy a space apart from the minds of the participants themselves. In recent years, the concept of thirdness has been increasingly utilized to speak of a realm that transcends the subjectivities of the two participants. In what follows, I highlight some of the usages of the concept of the third and of related terms, and contrast these with the concept of the relational unconscious put forth in the previous section. Thirdness, or the concept of the third, like the concept of intersubjectivity itself (Levine and Friedman, 2000), has no singular, agreed-upon definition. Nonetheless, a review reveals three primary usages of the term, each of which describes a different (even if overlapping) domain of experience and set of conceptual concerns. I will call these three usages the "developmental third", the "cultural third", and the "relational third", and will briefly explicate each.

The numerical connotation of the third as occurring along a sequential order is embodied in those usages of the term that seek to name a stage in a developmental progression from individual and dyadic concerns and capabilities to recognition of the independence of another person. The prime exemplar of the developmental third is found in the application of the concept of thirdness to refer to Oedipal processes. Here, Oedipal conflicts are thought of as a third force that (potentially) moves the individual from a narcissistic form of relating and toward an acceptance of relating to needed others, while recognizing that others have needs of their own. Developmental thirdness is represented in the work of Britton (1998), for whom the third position always invokes an Oedipal constellation, as it represents a third entity (be it person, institution, symbol) that disrupts the dyadic. The intrusion into the cloistered twoness creates a psychic spaciousness that Britton refers to as triangular space (1998, 2004), a positioning that allows the mental freedom of independence of mind, as well as a vantage point from which to observe oneself and one's interactions with others. Britton writes that "in all analyses, the basic Oedipus situation exists whenever the analyst exercises his or her mind independently of the intersubjective relationship of patient and analyst" (1998, p. 44). Of note here is that, for Britton, the "intersubjective" is a dyadic configuration that, by force of its fusion of subjects, limits independence of mind. The third for Britton represents a third entity (parental relations) and, as such, it is not a quality of the intersubjective relation itself. Rather, in Britton's usage, the third position could be considered an intrapsychic achievement, born in the recognition of separateness, that permits reflection about separation. From this perspective, the third position—and the triangular space it creates—lies beyond, and perhaps even stands in opposition to, the intersubjective.

Britton's view of thirdness as a developmental achievement bears an affinity to what I am referring to as "cultural thirdness," since both usages of thirdness emphasize the third as existing beyond and intruding upon the dyad. The cultural third, as represented in the work of Chasseguet-Smirgel (1974) and Lacan (1977), also refers to a non-intersubjective form of thirdness; that is, a form of thirdness that does not arise from the subjectivities of the individuals in the dyad, but rather one that envelops, intrudes upon, and shapes the interactions of the dyad, as well as the subjectivities of each member of the dyad. Exemplars of the cultural third are such forces as the incest taboo, language, and professional standards (Aron, 1999; Crastnopol, 1999; Spezzano, 1998), with each representing a codification, both legal and semiotic (Peirce, 1972), of the possible and the prohibited.

Cavell (1998) positions the third as an entity beyond the dyad and language, yet one that serves as a point in a triangular structure that includes as well as organizes the intersubjective relation of the dyad. In her view, the third creates a triangulation that permits experiences that arise within the dyad to be reflectively organized through shared as well as external realities. In this regard, Cavell's cultural third is a necessary constituent of intersubjectivity, rather than a disjunctive force.

The notion of thirdness as arising from within the dyad is, I believe, best described as the "relational third," and it is this usage of the concept of thirdness that is most frequently associated with an intersubjective perspective. Early references to the concept of a relational third did not invoke nomenclature of the third, yet spoke to the same phenomenon that would later be placed under this rubric. We see this in contributions from Green (1975), Baranger (1993), and, of course, Ogden (1994a).

While each of these authors evocatively articulates the notion that analysis occurs within a third arena, which is formed by individual subjectivities even as it alters them, I suggest that it is advantageous to think of an intersubjectively defined relation not as a third entity, but rather as constituting the relational unconscious of the dyad. Perhaps the most basic benefit of this terminology is that it allows us to utilize our already developed and richly nuanced ideas about the nature of unconscious processes to study the formation, regulation, and communication of relational processes. In addition to its abundant historical linkages, the concept of the relational unconscious is, I believe, preferable to that of concepts invoking thirdness because it signifies a dynamic process that belongs fully to the human participants, whose hopes and fears silently combine in ways that may eventuate in creative, as well as destructive, engagement. The relational unconscious is not an object, a third, a triad, a field, or a space. Each of these renderings connotes—even if it is not the intention of the author to do so—an entity that can be separated from the two subjectivities that combine to create it. Intersubjectivity and the relational unconscious are better thought of as processes through which individuals communicate with each other without awareness about their wishes and fears, and in so doing, structure the relation according to both mutually regulated concealments and searches for recognition and expression of their individual subjectivities.

The mind of the other is both the location of another subjectively organized unconscious, with its own archaic modes of operating and its own repository of experience striving for expression, and an interactive system buffeted by the unconscious forces in the interpersonal and cultural surround. Bollas (1992) captured the elemental power of the interaction of multiply located and structured unconscious processes when he wrote that:

The relational unconscious, intersubjective resistance, and clinical process

> To communicate with one another is to evoke each other, and in that moment, to be distorted by the laws of unconscious work. To be touched by the other's unconscious is to be scattered by the winds of the primary process to faraway associations and elaborations, reached through the private links of one's own subjectivity.
>
> (p. 45)

These thoughts echo Freud's (1912; 1913; 1915) descriptions of unconscious processes in interpersonal communication, wherein he consistently pointed out that one's unconscious is inevitably and indispensably involved in receiving and learning about the hidden mental lives of others. Freud (1913) noted that "everyone possesses in his own unconscious an instrument with which he can interpret the utterances of the unconscious of other people" (p. 320). In a further elaboration of the process of unconscious transmission and transformation of meaning, Freud (1915) noted that "it is a very remarkable thing that the Unconscious of one human being can react upon that of another, without passing through the Conscious" (p. 194). These observations about unconscious communication were, however, at least as much a source of concern for Freud as they were his routes toward psychoanalytic understanding, to be valued and explored. Freud's (1912) recommendation that the analyst "must turn his own unconscious like a receptive organ toward the transmitting unconscious of the patient" (p. 115) was intended to suggest that the analyst's unconscious could receive the patient's unconscious communications without distortion, and that the analyst could then proceed to decode and reconstruct the meanings hidden in the patient's message. In his very next paragraph, however, Freud implied that the analyst's knowledge of the patient always contains mixtures and residues of the analyst's own unconscious. Freud assumed that these admixtures would inevitably be detrimental to the task of understanding the patient, and therefore must be filtered out by means of the analyst's undergoing his or her own "psychoanalytic purification" (1912, p. 116).

Advances in our understanding of analytic processes and our contemporary postmodern sensibilities render us unable to endorse Freud's early optimism about the possibilities of psychic purification. Rather, we are compelled to take account of the fact that the conscious meanings we develop about the patient, and the conscious intentions we maintain when we offer these meanings as interpretations, simultaneously reflect and obscure how we have received and processed the unconscious elements of the patient's mind via our own unconscious. As participants in a continuous mix of unconscious mental life, we can never be simply receivers or containers of the patient's affects and meanings; rather, we always saturate elements of the patient's subjectivity with our own, producing the novel admixture of a relational unconscious that makes each analysis unique.

Earlier, I noted that a basic premise of an intersubjective orientation is that we are all motivated to utilize elements from the environment to help cohere internal experience, as well as to creatively transform it. As Ogden (1994b) put it: "Human beings have a need as deep as hunger and thirst to establish intersubjective constructions (including projective identifications) in order to find an exit from unending, futile wanderings in their own internal object world" (p. 105). It is this movement toward enlivenment in the presence and through the medium of another's subjectivity that creates the analytic process. Furthermore, it is the intersubjective nature of the interaction that both enables the evolution of the particular transference-countertransference dynamic of the analytic dyad, and creates the conditions for its resolution—a resolution in which the subjectivity of each participant is altered as it lives through its archaic expression in the other and within the dyad's unique relational unconscious.

Perhaps the most frequently described clinical phenomena that indicate the presence of relationally embedded and structured forms of unconscious engagement is the configuration known as enactment. Enactments may be thought of as a manifest content of the relational unconscious, for it is in these moments that transference and countertransference become mutually stimulating forces, unconsciously driving toward an expression that could not be consciously known and articulated between the individuals and within the relationship. Enactments are indicators of an intersubjective process that is not yet available for active reflection, and as such, are derivatives in action of the relational unconscious of the analytic dyad. Enactments have often been treated ambivalently in our literature, with some authors suggesting that while enactments may be inevitable, they nonetheless indicate an untoward or less than adequately processed countertransference. For others, however, enactments are not only inevitable, but also a major medium through which all analyses progress. Renik (1997) succinctly articulates this view in his statement that enactments are "the required text for the analysis of the transference" (p. 10). It is through the process of recognizing and working through enactments that the analyst gains access to the relational unconscious that structures the analytic work, and can thereby begin to alter its repetitive and constraining hold on him or her, as well as on the patient.

At those times when the relational unconscious includes contents that do not permit or yield to attempts at conscious reflection, the transference and countertransference matrix may evolve into enmeshments in stagnant or destructive forms of interaction. In an earlier communication (Gerson, 1996), I referred to such states as signifying

> a joint project designed to suspend the development of new modes of affecting and imagining the other and the relation. Such mutually and reciprocally motivated states can be thought of as intersubjective resistances, as they are sustained by each participant's efforts to maintain the other in the familiar transference-countertransference configuration. Intersubjective resistances and enmeshments are formed by the reciprocal influence upon each other of patient's and analyst's unconscious motivations and are a constituent of the relational unconscious of the analytic pair.
>
> (p. 362)

This view of resistance as an intersubjective creation elaborates Boesky's (1990) oft-noted statement that "the manifest form of a resistance is even sometimes unconsciously negotiated by both patient and analyst" (p. 572). It also reflects an earlier understanding by Bird (1972) of the analyst's contribution to an impasse in the treatment: "a stalemate in the analysis, an implacable resistance, an unchanging negative therapeutic reaction—anything of this kind should be suspected of consisting of a silent, secret, but actual destructive act engaged in by both patient and analyst" (p. 294).

What I wish to emphasize here is that, while moments of enactment and impasse often reveal in dramatic fashion specific dynamic constraints to what is knowable, the relationship itself is continuously being patterned in more subtle ways that embody and elaborate a reciprocally constructed, intersubjective dynamic. In this perpetual process, enactments are like disruptive events that indicate "fault lines" between the analyst's and patient's dynamic trajectories, yet they do not describe the configurations that result from the interaction of these individual forms. Before, during, and after the drama of enactment captures our attention, the continuously operating relational unconscious is silently configuring the landscape. An important implication of linking intersubjective resistances to content within the broader framework of the structuring functions of the relational unconscious is that we may then observe how the unraveling of resistances not only reveals hidden conflicts in each person, but also alters the unconsciously maintained patterning of the relationship. As a result of the successful working through of a conflicted area of functioning, there is an increased range of possibilities in each mind and in the relationship itself. These wider arcs of possibility create a virtuous chain wherein individual and relational growth mutually and reciprocally reinforce each other.

An example of an approach that furthers our understanding of the operations of the relational unconscious within the analytic setting can be found in the work of the Boston Change Study Process Group (2002). In a series of papers, these clinicians and developmentalists have suggested that therapy progresses via changes in the patient's implicit relational knowing, and that this level of knowledge is unconsciously held as a form of procedural knowing (Bucci, 2001). The BCSPG investigators maintain that implicit relational knowledge shifts in moments of meeting that are often constituted by relational moves—the small, interactive units wherein the intentionality of each partner to affect the other may be gauged. It is believed that these relational moves are all formed within a context in which "each partner is not only putting forth actions and inferring intentions, but also having an effect on shaping the actions and intentions of the other as they emerge" (Boston Change Study Process Group 2002, p. 1058). As such, "what has been created belongs to both, becoming part of the implicit relational knowing of each" (p. 1058). Here they are referring to an emergent and fluid set of procedural moves and knowledge that are intersubjectively created. Lyons-Ruth (1999; Lyons-Ruth and Boston Change Study Process Group, 1998) elaborated on this process:

> If representational change involves not only cognition or "insight" but also changes in affectively rich "ways of being with," a shift in organization must also involve a reorganization of the analyst's and patient's ways of being together. Therefore, moments of reorganization must involve a new "opening" in the interpersonal space, allowing both participants to become agents toward one another in a new way ... This new organization is not simply a product of the individual patient's intrapsychic work, however, but of the working out of new relational possibilities with the analyst.
>
> (Lyons-Ruth, 1999, pp. 611–612)

The BCSPG's work resonates with the idea that the therapeutic action of psychoanalysis is formed on a dual basis, consisting of a restructuring of both the individual unconscious of the analysand and the relational unconscious of the analysand and analyst. In addition, the concept of the relational unconscious contains the fundamental systems, or "field," notion that change in one member of the analytic dyad inevitably involves and invokes shifts in the other and in their relationship. Another way of conceptualizing this is that a shift in an individual transference presumes shifts in the countertransference aspect of the matrix, and thereby results in mutually reinforcing movement in the individual unconsciouses of analyst and analysand and in their relational unconscious. This multifaceted perspective on the dynamics of change

highlights how our contemporary recognition of the patternings of unconscious processes within structures of relating permits us to broaden the psychoanalytic project of making the unconscious conscious, such that it includes
working through those aspects of the relational unconscious that limit knowledge and creative development.

Conclusion

The increasingly commonplace understanding of change as involving relational processes that are beyond insight has often left the analytic clinician
grappling with questions about what modes of intervention best serve the
analytic process. We generally agree that the analyst's "irreducible subjectivity" (Renik, 1993) has been draped over the tattered remains of the classical
blank screen, yet when we enter the consulting room, intersubjective theory
is confronted by, and yields to, modes of practice shaped by the objectivist
orientation of our theoretical heritage. Here we encounter the oft-noted lag
between innovations in our theory and their application to clinical practice.
It has been my aim in this work to suggest that the concept of the relational unconscious can serve us well as a bridging structure that is at once
firmly rooted in the historical insights and terminology of traditional psychoanalysis, even as it incorporates our contemporary theoretical and clinical understandings and sensibilities. We are left with substantial and vexing
questions of how best to work with the broadened concept of the unconscious
that we inhabit with our analysands, and of whether the principles of technique that we apply to understand the individual unconscious will serve us as
well to understand the relational unconscious.

There is always a preexisting blueprint of experience in the minds of the
analyst and analysand. Yet a new and more livable architecture of knowledge
is built through their discourse about how they use and respond to each
other's subjectivity as they construct their unique relationship. Knowledge
that carries the conviction of being lived is created in dialogical moments
in which traces of each participant's private meanings provide a marker for
the other's expression, until a pattern that fits both of their experiences and
imaginings is created. Much as we agree about the arrangement of stars to
form constellations, the mutual creation of coherence alters the private and
dark unknown of the individual unconscious into a shared geography of
meaning.

Notes

1   For overviews of the intersubjective and relational perspectives, see Aron, 1996;
    Benjamin, 1995; Frie and Reis, 2001; Hoffman, 1998; Mitchell, 1997; 1998;
    Momigliano and Robutti, 1992; Renik, 1998; Spezzano, 1996; Stern, 1997; and
    Stolorow, Atwood, and Brandchaft, 1994.

2 See, for example, the concepts of drive and object (Green, 2000), empathy (Fishman, 1999), enactment (Friedman and Natterson, 1999), holding (Ginot, 2001), neutrality (Gerson, 1996; Hoffman, 1983; Renik, 1996), self-disclosure (Crastnopol, 1997; Ehrenberg, 1992; Gerson, 1996; Jacobs, 1999; Maroda, 1991; Meissner, 2002; Renik, 1995; 1999), and supervision (Berman, 2000).

References

Aron, L. (1996) *A Meeting of Minds: Mutuality in Psychoanalysis*. Hillsdale, NJ: Analytic Press.

Aron, L. (1999) Clinical choices and the relational matrix. *Psychoanalytic Dialogues*, 9: 1–29.

Baranger, M. (1993) The mind of the analyst: from listening to interpretation. *International Journal of Psychoanalysis*, 74: 15–24.

Benjamin, J. (1995) *Like Subjects, Love Objects*. New Haven, CT: Yale University Press.

Berman, E. (2000) Psychoanalytic supervision: the intersubjective development. *International Journal of Psychoanalysis*. 81: 273–290.

Bion, W. (1962) *Learning from Experience*. London: Karnac.

Bird, B. (1972) Notes on transference: universal phenomenon and hardest part of analysis. *Journal of the American Psychoanalytic Association*. 20: 267–302.

Blatt, S. and Blass, R. (1990). Attachment and separateness: a dialectical model of the products and processes of psychological development. *Psychoanalytic Study of the Child*. 44: 107–127.

Boesky, D. (1990). The psychoanalytic process and its components. *Psychoanalytic Quarterly*. 59: 550–584.

Bollas, C. (1987) *The Shadow of the Object*. New York: Columbia University Press.

Bollas, C. (1992) *Being a Character*. New York: Hill & Wang.

Boston Change Study Process Group (2002) Explicating the implicit: the local level and microprocess of change in the analytic situation. *International Journal of Psychoanalysis*. 83: 1051–1062.

Britton, R. (1998) Subjectivity, objectivity and potential space. In: *Belief and Imagination*. London: Routledge.

Britton, R. (2004) Subjectivity, objectivity, and triangular space. *Psychoanalytic Quarterly*. 73: 47–61.

Bucci, W. (2001) Pathways of emotional communication. *Psychoanalytic Inquiry*. 21(1): 40–70.

Cavell, M. (1988) Interpretation, psychoanalysis and the philosophy of mind. *Journal of the American Psychoanalytic Association*. 36(4): 859–880.

Cavell, M. (1998) Triangulation, one's own mind, and objectivity. *International Journal of Psychoanalysis*. 79: 449–467.

Chasseguet-Smirgel, J. (1974) Perversion, idealisation and sublimation. *International Journal of Psychoanalysis*. 55: 349–357.

Crastnopol, M. (1997) Incognito or not? The patient's subjective experience of the analyst's private life. *Psychoanalytic Dialogues*. 7(2): 257–278.

Crastnopol, M. (1999) The analyst's professional self as a "third" influence on the dyad: when the analyst writes about the treatment. *Psychoanalytic Dialogues.* 9: 445–470.

Cushman, P. (1995) *Constructing the Self, Constructing America.* Reading, MA: Addison-Wesley.

Davies, J. (1996) Linking the "pre-analytic" with the postclassical: integration, dissociation, and the multiplicity of unconscious process. *Contemporary Psychoanalysis.* 32: 553–576.

Ehrenberg, D. (1992) *The Intimate Edge: Extending the Reach of Psycho-Analytic Interaction.* New York: Norton.

Eliot, T.S. (1922) *The Complete Poems and Plays, 1909–1950.* New York: Harcourt, Brace & World.

Fishman, G. (1999) Knowing another from a dynamic systems point of view: the need for a multimodal concept of empathy. *Psychoanalytic Quarterly.* 68: 376–400.

Freud, S. (1912) Recommendations to physicians practising psychoanalysis. *The Standard Edition of the Complete Psychological Works of Sigmund Freud.* 12.

Freud, S. (1913) The disposition to obsessional neurosis. *The Standard Edition of the Complete Psychological Works of Sigmund Freud.* 12.

Freud, S. (1915) The unconscious. *The Standard Edition of the Complete Psychological Works of Sigmund Freud.* 14.

Frie, R. and Reis, B. (2001) Understanding intersubjectivity: psychoanalytic formulations and their philosophical underpinnings. *Contemporary Psychoanalysis.* 37(2): 297–327.

Friedman, R. and Natterson, J. (1999) Enactments: an intersubjective perspective. *Psychoanalytic Quarterly.* 68: 220–247.

Gerson, S. (1996) Neutrality, resistance, and self-disclosure in an intersubjective psychoanalysis. *Psychoanalytic Dialogues.* 6: 623–647.

Ginot, E. (2001) The holding environment and intersubjectivity. *Psychoanalytic Quarterly.* 70(2): 417–436.

Green, A. (1975) The analyst, symbolization and absence in the analytic setting. *International Journal of Psychoanalysis.* 56: 1–21.

Green, A. (2000) The intrapsychic and intersubjective in psychoanalysis. *Psychoanalytic Quarterly.* 69: 1–39.

Hoffman, I.Z. (1983) The patient as interpreter of the analyst's experience. *Contemporary Psychoanalysis.* 19: 389–422.

Hoffman, I.Z. (1998) *Ritual and Spontaneity in the Psychoanalytic Process.* Hillsdale, NJ: Analytic Press.

Jacobs, T. (1999) On the question of self-disclosure by the analyst: error or advance in technique? *Psychoanalytic Quarterly.* 68: 159–183.

Lacan, J. (1977) *Ecrits: A Selection* (translated by A. Sheridan). New York: Norton.

Lear, J. (1990) *Love and its Place in Nature.* New York: Farrar, Straus & Giroux.

Levine, H. and Friedman, R. (2000) Intersubjectivity and interaction in the analytic relationship: a mainstream view. *Psychoanalytic Quarterly.* 69: 63–92.

Lyons-Ruth, K. (1999) The two-person unconscious: intersubjective dialogue, enactive relational representation, and the emergence of new forms of relational organization. *Psychoanalytic Inquiry*, 19: 576–617.

Lyons-Ruth, K. and Boston Change Study Process Group (1998) Implicit relational knowing: its role in development and psychoanalytic treatment. *Infant Mental Health Journal*. 19: 282–289.

Maroda, K. (1991) *The Power of Countertransference*. New York: Wiley.

Mayer, E. (1996) Subjectivity and intersubjectivity of clinical facts. *International Journal of Psychoanalysis*. 77: 709–737.

Meissner, W. (2002) The problem of self-disclosure in psychoanalysis. *Journal of the American Psychoanalytic Association*. 50: 827–867.

Mitchell, S. (1997) *Influence and Autonomy in Psychoanalysis*. Hillsdale, NJ: Analytic Press.

Mitchell, S. (1998) The analyst's knowledge and authority. *Psychoanalytic Quarterly*. 67(1): 1–31.

Mitrani, J. (1995) Toward an understanding of unmentalized experience. *Psychoanalytic Quarterly*. 64: 68–112.

Momigliano, L. and Robutti, A. (1992) *Shared Experience: The Psychoanalytic Dialogue*. London: Karnac.

Ogden, T. (1994a) The analytical third: working with intersubjective clinical facts. *International Journal of Psychoanalysis*. 75(1): 3–20.

Ogden, T. (1994b) *Subjects of Analysis*. New York: Aronson.

Peirce, C. (1972) *Charles S. Peirce: The Essential Writings* (edited by E.C. Moore). New York: Harper & Row.

Renik, O. (1993) Analytic interaction: conceptualizing technique in light of the analyst's irreducible subjectivity. *Psychoanalytic Quarterly*. 62: 553–571.

Renik, O. (1995) The ideal of the anonymous analyst and the problem of self-disclosure. *Psychoanalytic Quarterly*. 64: 466–495.

Renik, O. (1996) The perils of neutrality. *Psychoanalytic Quarterly*, 65: 495–517.

Renik, O. (1997) Conscious and unconscious use of the self. *Psychoanalytic Inquiry*, 17: 5–12.

Renik, O. (1998) The analyst's subjectivity and the analyst's objectivity. *International Journal of Psychoanalysis*. 79: 487–97.

Renik, O. (1999). Playing one's cards face up in analysis: an approach to the problem of disclosure. Psychoanalytic Quarterly. 68: 521–540.

Rucker, N. and Lombardi, K. (1997) *Subject Relations: Unconscious Experience and Relational Psychoanalysis*. London: Routledge.

Spezzano, C. (1995) "Classical" vs. "contemporary" theory: the differences that matter clinically. *Contemporary Psychoanalysis*. 31(1): 20–45.

Spezzano, C. (1996) The three faces of two-person psychology: development, ontology, and epistemology. *Psychoanalytic Dialogues*. 6: 599–622.

Spezzano, C. (1998) The triangle of clinical judgment. *Journal of the American Psychoanalytic Association*. 46: 365–388.

Stern, D. (1989) The analyst's unformulated experience of the patient. *Contemporary Psychoanalysis*. 25: 1–33.

Stern, D. (1997) *Unformulated Experience*. Hillsdale, NJ: Analytic Press.

Stolorow, R. and Atwood, G. (1992) *Contexts of Being: The Intersubjective Foundations of Psychological Life*. Hillsdale, NJ: Analytic Press.

Stolorow, R., Atwood, G., and Brandchaft, B. (1994) *The Intersubjective Perspective*. Northvale, NJ: Aronson.

Vygotsky, L. (1978) Mind in society: the development of higher psychological processes (edited by M. Cole, S. Scribner, V. Johm-Steiner, and E. Sounder- man). Cambridge, MA: Harvard University Press.

Winnicott, D. (1953) *Playing and Reality*. New York: Routledge, 1989.

Zeddies, T. (2000) Within, outside, and in-between: the relational unconscious. *Psychoanalytic Psychology*. 17(3): 467–487.

Chapter 5

How to grow a psychoanalytic forest

A challenge going forward

Fred Busch

The eminent sociologist Robert Merton (1957) expressed the difficulty with the history of sociology in this way: "The conception of each (author) seldom built on the work of those who came before. They are often laid out as alternative and competing conceptions, rather than consolidated and extended into a cumulative product" (p. 5).

Based on what seemed like common sense and science at the time, it was thought that the best way to build a forest was to plant homogeneous saplings, where the underbrush was stripped away. Without *competitors*, it was thought, the newly planted trees would thrive. What happened instead was that, in comparison to old-growth forests, these new trees were more susceptible to disease and climatic distress. By analyzing the DNA in root tips and tracing the movement of molecules through underground conduits, scientists discovered that fungal threads link nearly every tree in a forest—*even trees of different species*. Carbon, water, nutrients, alarm signals, and hormones can pass from tree to tree through these subterranean circuits. Resources tend to flow from the oldest and biggest trees to the youngest and smallest. Chemical alarm signals generated by one tree prepare nearby trees for danger. Seedlings severed from the forest's underground lifelines are much more likely to die than their networked counterparts.[1]

It is my view that, for some time, psychoanalysts have been working like old-school foresters … cutting down older trees from which our psychoanalytic forest has grown and getting rid of the underbrush that sustained it. *What could have been additions* to what has often been labeled pejoratively as "classical analysis",[2] feeding and protecting others, and being fed and protected, becomes instead the new best replacement forest. Each new set of ideas becomes *the new* theory of psychoanalysis, with its own Journals, and authors only quoting like-minded analysts. Instead of feeding each other, new theories compete for the psychoanalytic equivalent of air, water, and nutrients necessary to grow a theory. Eagle (2021) noted that one might charitably think new theories emerging are attempts to correct inadequate explanatory concepts, "Rather they emerge as *self-sufficient theories* that claim to account for all aspects of human behavior" (p. 273).

DOI: 10.4324/9781003340744-7

To be clear, there are legitimate criticisms of Freudian theory, and I consider revisions an important part of psychoanalysis' growth. However, psychoanalysis' ability to flourish is stunted by splintering into separate groups. The history of science shows that the discoveries of core concepts are built upon and lead to new discoveries, but the core concepts are not dismissed as they still serve as explanatory reasons for some part of the eventual new discoveries. As the Nobel physicist Frank Wilczek (2021) explained, core concepts in physics are the first guiding principles that serve to understand how the world works. They are built upon and not dismissed. The remarkable achievement of speedily creating vaccines was the result of twenty years of work that built on certain core concepts.

A brief history

Rejecting Freud's basic ideas to build separate theories has been with us since the beginning of the psychoanalytic revolution.[3] I say "revolution" as sometimes we forget how radical, even post-modern, Freud's ideas were and still are. One of the earliest to discard Freud's basic assumptions was Adler, who in 1912 rejected the notion of sexual impulses as a basic factor in psychic life. Yet Freud's theories of sexuality were the foundation for the principle of intrapsychic causality, and thus crucial to the development of a psychoanalytic theory of mind. Jung also questioned sexuality as a fundamental part of Freud's theory on the motivation for psychic life. Instead, he proposed what Gyimesi (2009) described as "an obscure, scarcely rational life-force at the center of the human psyche" (p. 458).

The next wave of forest planters swore allegiance to Freud but rejected key parts of his views. I'm not sure if it was ever made clear that Klein's basic theory of technique remained connected to Freud's *first theory of the mind, while implicitly rejecting his second theory of the mind* (Freud, 1923; 1926). As an example, she continued to think of anxiety being reduced by bringing to the surface buried unconscious fantasies rather than following Freud's second view of anxiety as being due to a threat posed to the ego. Thus, early Kleinian analysts would interpret primitive unconscious fantasies in the first analytic session, while Freudian analysts would only consider working with preconscious derivatives of unconscious fantasies (Busch, 2006; Green, 1974). An important part of Freud's second theory of mind was the realization that resistances were unconscious, and therefore the analyst would need to work through resistances to transform the unconscious. Deeper interpretations were viewed as posing great danger to the ego and would lead to intense anxiety. Then Bion, who was basically a Kleinian (Ferro and Nocoli, 2017), developed a new language for psychoanalysis because of what he believed to be the plethora of meanings associated with each term. Bion, then, attempted to create his own view of psychoanalysis.

Greenson (1974) observed that discussions between Kleinians and Freudians at international meetings gave one the impression of people speaking two different languages at each other, with one ignorant of the other and both firmly prejudiced towards each other (Greenson, 1974). Yorke's (1971) comparison of Kleinian and Freudian approaches led him to state "The two approaches have little in common beyond one or two technical parameters and a language which serves only to blur the distinctions" (p. 153).

Lacan, despite his repeated claims that he is returning to pure Freud, largely ignores the structural, post-1923 Freud. He focused on Freud's work through the 1915 paper on the unconscious, as though Freud had never found reason to revise his theory.[4] Others have shown that Lacan rejected the value of analyzing unconscious defenses, a decisive break with what was at the heart of Freud's second theory of the mind.[5] After many attempts at international meetings to compare and contrast these different models, with little resolution, the International Psychoanalytic Association seems to have settled into a position where acceptance of all models is the norm.

Within the last half-century most attempts to promote a *new, better psychoanalysis* have come from the United States. Kohut's development of self-psychology included an attempt to *replace* Freud's instinct theory with a line of narcissistic development, culminating in his view of transference behavior (and pathology in general) in terms of narcissistic needs that are to be understood and partially met in the treatment. While many psychoanalysts saw Kohut's contributions on narcissism as important *additions* to our ways of understanding patients, he and his followers increasing believed that working with narcissistic pathology was *the* main factor in the curative process for *all* patients and led to increasing alienation from Freudian-based treatments. There were also Rapport's former students, Merton Gill, George Klein, and Robert Holt, who turned against Rapaport's Ego Psychology, proclaiming that Freud's theory did not fit with clinical data. Gill's belief in the early interpretation of transference was a break from an ego psychological position of the necessity of interpreting resistances before deeper interpretations and Freud's view of interpreting the transference only when it became a resistance. In fact, Gill's view was close to the Kleinian way of dealing with the transference. It is often not remembered that Gill (1984) later modified his views on the early emphasis on transference.

The relational and interpersonal schools highlighted the importance of the relationship as the curative factor in psychoanalysis, while believing that uncovering the role of the patient's unconscious played a secondary role. The forerunners of the relational and interpersonal views, Sullivan and Fromm abandoned free association for what Sullivan (1954) called the "directed inquiry," an active questioning of the patient in order to deconstruct his story. In reading of its current iteration (Levenson, 1988), it seems more like an inquisition to ferret out what the patient is hiding, an abandonment of the importance of working through resistances. Mitchell and Greenberg (1983) and Mitchell (1988) erroneously portray Freud's model of the mind as based upon drives alone, and then compare it to their relational model. Mitchel

(1988) "asks the reader to choose between the purely relational mode perspective and his version of the Freudian drive model. The message is clear—you cannot have both" (Bachant and Richards, 1993, p. 432). When Greenberg (1991) claimed there is hardly an author left who believes in the significance of the drives or the structural theory, he didn't consider the French whose thinking has influenced analysts in the world outside the United States, and the many American Freudians. Hatcher (1990) pointed out that Mitchell not only discarded drives, but also the importance of structures in Freud's theory, resulting in an impoverished, less vivid, less clinically useful theory. Protestations aside, he views Mitchell as making a radical shift from the intrapsychic to the interpersonal. As Hatcher (ibid) states, "He requires that his theory be dyadic rather than monadic, that it describe the mind at all times in interaction with others—this *is* the mind" (p. 133).[6]

The clinical psychoanalytic forest

For me, with some modifications, the goals of psychoanalytic treatment, have remained the same since its inception. Put broadly, and in current terms, we attempt to build complex, preconscious representations from simple unconscious representations and presentations.[7] It's difficult to think why a theory would be presented as "psychoanalytic" without including this basic premise. It is based on what Freud (1915) described, mixed with what we've learned since then, about the importance of representations (linking to Freud's *thing presentations* to *word presentations*), and the significance of the preconscious in making interventions in bringing what is unconsciously driving the person to seek help (Green, 1974). Further, as indicated earlier, I see most of what is portrayed as the "new great theory of psychoanalysis" as *additions* to the Freudian approach, not as replacement. Leo Rangell, known as a staunch defender of Freudian Ego Psychology, came to the conclusion that we need a composite theory.

> I favor one total, composite psychoanalytic theory, unified and cumulative: total because it contains all non-expendable elements, composite because it is a blend of the old and all valid new concepts and discoveries as fulfilling the criteria for what is psychoanalytic. Every viable contribution made by alternative theories finds a home in this composite theory. Under its embracing umbrella coexist drives and defense; id, ego, and superego self and object; the intrapsychic and interpersonal; the internal and external world.
>
> (Rangell, 2004, pp. 237–238)

For me, this is a blueprint for building what I would call a *psychoanalytic forest*, in that it relies on the principles of modern forest building where our theories need to be interconnected and feed each other. I would add the interpsychic (Diamond, 2014; Bolognini, 2004) and Kleinian approaches to this mix.

I consider myself a Freudian, who has tried to integrate many of the ideas developed over the last forty years in my clinical work. This is especially true of French psychoanalysis (Busch, 2013) while also considering the work of the post-Bionians (Busch, 2019), Kohut, relational psychoanalysis, and some Italian and Latin American psychoanalysts. As my earliest training was as a child psychologist, and my earliest research involved years of observing toddler and nursery groups, I have always maintained a developmental perspective. I agree with Abend's (2018) assessment when he describes how many of us were influenced by developments in psychoanalysis over the last thirty years:

> I attribute this expanded palette of sensibility on my part to the impact of relational thinkers, and to that of Kleinians, and self psychologists, and I might well add, to the impact of discussions with many of my other colleagues who have themselves been more or less influenced by, and have in turn exerted their influence upon, the changing psychoanalytic scene.
>
> (p. 441)

In summary, I use a variety of psychoanalytic theories to understand my patient, and my role in the analysis. However, when it comes to how and when I convey my understanding to a patient, I rely primarily on my understanding and elaboration of Freudian theory as expressed primarily in Freud's (1923; 1926; 1933) papers that elaborated the second topique or structural theory as defined in Hartmann's (1939) work.

An integrated Freudian approach

Over the last thirty years I've developed a way of working clinically that is closer to what the patient can understand without increasing unbearable anxiety. It is based on Freud's move to the structural model and a way of thinking about how analysts can analyze the terrifying fears the patient deals with when facing his unconscious. It was the basis of the development of Ego Psychology, which has been maligned based upon misunderstanding. Ego Psychology offers the best way to safely understand and approach the multi-layered unconscious. It involves working closer to what the patient can understand rather than what the analyst thinks he understands, which translates into speaking to the patient's preconscious (Busch, 2006; Green, 1974). Since Hartmann developed his adaptational point[8] of view, it has been possible (but not widely used) to help our analysands realize their difficulties are understandable and reasonable solutions to unconscious fantasies, and troubled early object relations that range from mismatches of temperaments, empty, cold, or distant relations, long separations, to chilling neglect, abuse, and the *unconscious fantasies that develop as a result* (Busch, 2005). This last element is indispensable in understanding our patients. Finally, I would add that the discovery of the *preconscious* as the place in the mind where we address our interventions has made the process of understanding more understandable to patients.

What I have felt important to incorporate into my psychoanalytic work are: greater attunement to and use of countertransference reactions; understanding the importance of analyst's empathic attunement; the role of the analyst as co-contributor to the analysis; the importance of understanding narcissistic development and problems along with borderline conditions, etc. Abend (2018) captured one element of a contemporary Freudian sensibility in the following:

> I am still just as convinced as I ever was that the analysand's past experience and the psychic structures to which they have contributed, go a long way toward shaping his or her transference attitudes. ... Furthermore ... I have come to recognize the validity of the subjectivist argument that undermines my former unquestioning faith in my ability to objectively discern these influences in my patients, [yet] I have not been persuaded that I therefore must abandon all confidence in my capacity to make usefully accurate judgments about what I observe in my patient's productions and behavior.
>
> (pp. 438–439)

The vignette I will present is, I believe, fairly typical of the way many contemporary Freudians work.

Clinical example

(My thoughts will be presented in italics.)
Harold, a 40-year-old full Professor at a prestigious university, came to treatment because of depression, often feeling he wasn't being appreciated, leading to his being distant from others and occasional outbursts of anger.

In the second year of analysis Harold started the session by telling a dream. As he began, he made a slip, and then there was a long silence. He then continued as if nothing had happened. *Previously, at times, he'd been able to view slips as a sign of an unconscious breakthrough and was open to analyze them. Not today though!*

I sensed Harold's irritation, and thought he was probably in a narcissistically deprived state and experienced his slip as stopping him from where he thought he was going. I had seen this before. At such times I thought I understood that Harold would experience any inquiry into the way he handled the slip as another interruption, a failure of mirroring, so I didn't say anything at that moment. Pre-Kohut I would have been inclined to interrupt Harold, and wonder about his non-reaction to the slip.

When he started talking again, he related how he hadn't heard from his brother. This was followed by a litany of complaints about people who hadn't responded to his emails and phone calls. *As he was talking, I could sense that my silence might have had another meaning for Harold ... i.e., he was irritated at not hearing from me. However, I still felt that if I had said something he would feel annoyed because I was not letting him find his own way. This was one dilemma in working with Harold, the conflict over wanting mirroring (i.e., appreciation of his wish to not deal with the slip at this moment) and feeling the longing to hear my voice, which aroused further conflict.*

Some theories might suggest the necessity of interpreting the transference meaning of Harold's complaints about not hearing from someone. However, I view the patient's readiness to hear and use transference interpretations as a central factor in whether such interpretations are enlightening. Often, I feel early interpretations of the transference lead to intellectualized understanding. To paraphrase Andre Green, the analyst cannot run like a hare while the patient moves like a tortoise.

Harold, as often happened, attributed not hearing back from others to some way he must have offended them. When he eventually heard back from those he believed he offended, the explanations for their not getting back to him right away were usually benign, but it had little effect on his view that he drove people away.

At this point I was struck with the force with which Harold was drawn to feel he'd offended someone in the face of their distance. He seemed drawn like a magnet to feel he had done something as the cause of the absence of the other. When I would occasionally point out something he told me which might lead to a more benign explanation for the person's absence,[9] it was vigorously rejected. That is, it seemed he needed to feel he was the one driving others away rather than being able to tolerate that it may have nothing to do with him. At this point I began thinking of how his mother was severely depressed after his birth. She became less depressed over time, but still depressed. That is, in Harold's early years she seemed to be physically there but emotionally absent. His father worked a lot and had little to do with Harold in his early years. It seemed likely that there was no one there for Harold as an emotional container in dealing with the stormy emotions of infancy, early childhood, and developmentally determined separations. Further into the analysis it became clear that he experienced frightening feelings of aloneness as a child. Ultimately, we learned more of the factors that played a role in Harold's self-criticism, but in the material just presented, this need to turn passive to active seemed closer to a workable surface (Paniagua, 1985), *and what I call working "in the neighborhood"* (Busch, 1993).

FB: It's my impression that when people don't return your calls or email, and you realize it wasn't because you offended them, it doesn't change your perception. It seems there's something very uncomfortable about feeling distant from someone, and not feeling you've done something to cause it.

This intervention begins with an analyst-centered intervention (Steiner, 1994), *followed by a clarification* (Bibring, 1954) *in the here and now* (Gray, 1994; Joseph, 1985) *to represent a preconscious* (Green, 1974) *defense in the manner of Anna* Freud (1936).

HAROLD: I just thought of a time when I accidently knocked over a glass of water, and my mother became furious with me. It didn't seem like the intensity of her anger was commensurate with the deed. However, at the time I felt I had done something very wrong. I think most people saw me as a pretty good kid. I did well at school, had a large group of friends, and was a good athlete. When I won awards for my academic and athletic prowess, I felt my mother was proud of me, but it didn't stop her from expressing what seemed like endless criticism. Only now I can see that she felt proud for narcissistic reasons like "Look what a great mother I am for having such a wonderful child." My mother outside the house was different than at home. Outside the house she seemed sweet, and pleasant. She was the favorite aunt amongst my cousins. At home she was distant, dour, and critical. Maybe now I can see how when she was so different at home, I felt it was me who caused her bad feelings.

FB: I think that's an important insight. Now maybe we can understand why you become so convinced when someone seems distant it's because of something you did. It seems your mother was most connected to you via criticism, and now it feels like an important way to keep connected to others when you feel their absence, which worries you.

Since Harold's associations went to his relationship with his mother, I felt it was important to both appreciate his insight and elaborate on it to reflect one aspect of what was happening in the transference and his interactions. While Freud and Hartmann were both criticized for ignoring object relations, this is a misunderstanding. Certainly, there is nothing about an object relations perspective that is inconsistent with a contemporary Freudian perspective.

HAROLD: Hmm! I don't remember ever not feeling that way. Last week you seemed tired, and I thought I was boring you. It was only when you cancelled on Friday because you weren't feeling well, I realized it wasn't because of me.

FB: Does something come to mind about this feeling I was bored?

HAROLD: Well sometimes it does seem like you're more involved in what I'm saying than others. Like when I tell you about departmental meetings once again, I think you get less involved.

FB: *As Harold's observation struck me as correct, I said,* I think you may be right. I'll try and watch for it.

HAROLD: Hmm! Well, that surprised me. In my previous analysis my analyst never confirmed a feeling I was having about him. Thank you. Silence. I was reluctant to say what I was thinking because it was the same old Harold. I was thinking of Julie (his wife) and how she was distant this morning and wondered what I had done.

FB: So, after feeling I gave you something that your previous analyst didn't, your thoughts go to someone being distant. It's like the closeness is uncomfortable.

HAROLD: It bugs me I keep on doing this.

After a pause, the session ended.

Discussion of the clinical vignette

In this section, to demonstrate why and how my responses are part of a Freudian approach that attempts to integrate insights from other perspectives, I will highlight certain moments from the vignette where I did or didn't respond.

- My decision to not respond to the patient's frustration and anger at his own slip represents a greater understanding of narcissistic problems over the last forty years. It is difficult to imagine being a psychoanalyst today without knowledge of Kohut's contributions to the understanding of narcissistic conditions. There are certain transferences (mirroring, twin, idealizing, etc.) that are best understood from a Kohutian perspective, and can lead to interventions or appreciative silence that, in general, can soften the impact on the patient's fragile narcissism. I have often observed that without this understanding the analyst, in the face of a narcissistic transference, feels irritated at the position he feels forced into, and then interprets the patient's angry feelings. This only further destabilizes the patient's narcissistic balance. In his countertransference the analyst misunderstands that the analysand is doing something to stabilize him-self, and not necessarily doing something to the analyst. Inherent in my approach is the necessity of being aware of the difference between thin-skinned and thick-skinned narcissists (Rosenfeld, 1987).
- My first intervention (i.e., "it's my impression") integrates my elaboration of Steiner's (1994) concept of analyst-centered interpretations, an important addition to working with self-critical patients.[10] Rather than telling the patient "you are" this way or that way, we soften the potential for self-criticism. "Experience suggests that ... containment is weakened if the analyst perseveres in interpreting or explaining to the patient what he (the patient) is thinking, feeling, or doing (ibid, p. 407, parenthesis added). My intent is to help the patient achieve some psychic space to reflect upon what I've suggested.
- In this and other interventions I am also using the under-utilized technique of clarification, introduced by Bibring (1954). "The reason for the need for clarification is simple: in the midst of conflict a patient's thinking is concrete. He can only think about what is immediately present. So, we need to bring together the strands of a patient's association in the immediacy of what he's been saying (i.e., in the here and now). For long periods of time, and even when the patient is freely associating, he is incapable of keeping track of the sequence of his thoughts while talking. It requires a great deal of time before we can make an interpretation that may be a word, or metaphor, capturing in a short form the essence of a reverie, and have some hope the patient will understand it in a non-intellectual fashion.

- In taking note of what I believed to be Harold's insight in my second intervention, I am using a form of Poland's (2000) concept of witnessing, which he describes as "the action of the analyst as a witness, one who recognizes and grasps the emotional import of the patient's self-exploration in the immediacy of the moment" (p. 17). It is my impression that we have sometimes focused exclusively on the tragic components of our patients' lives, while neglecting their attempts to analytically move forward. Appreciating a patient's reflections on his associations recognizes his growing partnership in the analytic process. I also clarify the genetic roots of his defense using Harold's preconscious associations (Busch, 2006).
- When I asked Harold about his view that I was bored, I didn't know if he had picked up something in my countertransference, and/or there was a fantasy affecting his perception. I believed it was important to corroborate his perception as I could recall feeling exactly what he described. To do otherwise can repeat the traumatic experience of many patients where what they saw and/or experienced was denied. This does not exclude considering perceptions as informed by fantasy.

Changing minds

The difficulty of getting analysts to open their minds to fresh perspectives is embedded within our training. We spend years immersed in one perspective or another, and there can be professional consequences for those who challenge the prevailing theoretical orientation of the Institute. For those Institutes who try to offer a variety of theoretical perspectives, there is often a prevailing perspective that is not openly acknowledged. Authors of one perspective most often quote their fellow teammates, and disregard critiques.[11]

In general, staying with what is familiar is typical of most of humanity. Many of us favor the comfort of conviction over the discomfort of doubt. We listen to opinions that make us feel good, instead of ideas that make us think hard. We see disagreement as a threat to our egos, rather than an opportunity to learn. We surround ourselves with people who agree with our conclusions, when we should be gravitating toward those who challenge our thought process. We think too much like preachers defending our sacred beliefs, and too little like scientists searching for truth. Intelligence is no cure, and it can even be a curse: being good at thinking can make us worse at rethinking. The brighter we are, the blinder to our own limitations we can become.

Notes

1 Based upon the *New York Times Magazine* article "The social life of forests", 6 December 2020.

2 It is fascinating how this term "classical," usually defined as representing an exemplary standard, traditional and long-established in form or style, has become used as a criticism.

3 A complete history of the those who openly or subtly rejected Freud's basic ideas, and tried to build their own psychoanalytic forest, is a longer story than warrants inclusion in this chapter. Therefore, I have chosen to present only a sketch of what has occurred.

4 While, in general, I don't think one can reduce theories based upon the theorist's personality, it is difficult to disregard Lacan's battles with Loewenstein (his analyst) as playing a role in Lacan's dismissal of what became known as Ego Psychology.

5 It is important to remember that Freud was ambivalent about the technical changes necessitated by his second theory (Busch, 1992; 1993; Paniagua, 2001; 2008).

6 See Tuckett, Chapter 3, for further ways Kohut and relational analysts have moved from what has been considered basic to a psychoanalytic approach.

7 Using Freud's (1915) term for what some now call unformulated representations.

8 Hartmann was harshly criticized based upon mischaracterizing what he meant. Critics saw this as the analyst attempting to have the patient to adapt to societal norms. What Hartmann actually proposed was that symptoms were an adaptation to a pathological environment, along with the demands off the unconscious. Thus, long before analysts recognized the importance of the outside world on the child's psyche, Hartmann proposed this idea.

9 A generally ineffective method we use when trying to stop the patient's brutal self-attacks.

10 Steiner's focus is on using analyst-centered interpretations to deal with the patient's projections, especially with borderline patients. As I've suggested previously (Busch, 2015), I think it can be usefully adapted with other patients.

11 In a remarkable book, Jon Mills (2020) presents a critique of relational psychoanalysis, and then invites relational analysts to critique his criticisms.

References

Abend, S. (2018) Contemporary Conflict Theory: The Journey of a Psychoanalyst. New York: International Psychoanalytical Books.

Bachant, J.L. and Richards, A.D. (1993) Relational concepts in psychoanalysis: an integration by Stephen A. Mitchell. Psychoanalytic Dialogues. 3(3): 431–460.

Bibring, E. (1954) Psychoanalysis and the dynamic psychotherapies. Journal of the American Psychoanalytic Association. 2: 745–770.

Bolognini, S. (2004) Intrapsychic-interpsychic. International Journal of Psychoanalysis. 85(2): 337–358.

Busch, F. (1992) Recurring thoughts on unconscious ego resistances. Journal of the American Psychoanalytic Association. 40: 1089–1115.

Busch, F. (1993) "In the neighborhood": aspects of a good interpretation and a "developmental lag" in ego psychology. Journal of the American Psychoanalytic Association. 41: 151–177.

Busch, F. (2005) Conflict theory/trauma theory. *Psychoanalytic Quarterly*. 74(1): 27–45.

Busch F (2006) A shadow concept. *International Journal of Psychoanalysis*. 87: 1471–1485.

Busch, F. (2013) *Creating a Psychoanalytic Mind*. London: Routledge.

Busch, F. (2015) Our vital profession. *International Journal of Psychoanalysis*. 96: 553–568.

Busch, F. (2019) *The Analyst's Reveries*. London: Routledge.

Diamond, M. (2014) Analytic mind use and interpsychic communication. *Psychoanalytic Quarterly*. 83: 525–64.

Eagle, M. (2021) *Toward a Unified Psychoanalytic Theory*. London: Routledge.

Ferro, A. and Nicoli, L. (2017) *The New Analyst's Guide to the Galaxy*. London: Karnac Books.

Freud, A. (1936) *The Ego and Mechanisms of Defense*. London: Karnac.

Freud, S. (1915) The unconscious. *The Standard Edition of the Complete Psychological Works of Sigmund Freud*. 14.

Freud, S. (1923) The ego and the id. *The Standard Edition of the Complete Psychological Works of Sigmund Freud*. 19.

Freud, S. (1926) Inhibitions, symptoms and anxiety. *The Standard Edition of the Complete Psychological Works of Sigmund Freud*. 20.

Freud, S. (1933) The dissolution of the psychical personality. New Introductory Lectures on Psychoanalysis. *The Standard Edition of the Complete Psychological Works of Sigmund Freud*. XXII.

Gill, M.M. (1984) Transference: a change in conception or only in emphasis? *Psychoanalytic Inquiry*. 4: 489–523.

Gray, P. (1994) *The Ego and Analysis of Defense*. Northridge, NJ: Jason Aronson.

Green, A. (1974) Surface analysis, deep analysis (the role of the preconscious in psychoanalytic technique). *International Review of Psycho-Analysis*. 1: 415–423.

Greenberg, J.R. (1991) Countertransference and reality. *Psychoanalytic Dialogues*. 1(1): 52–73.

Greenberg, J.R. and Mitchell, S.A. (1983) *Object Relations in Psychoanalytic Theory*. Cambridge, MA: Harvard University Press.

Greenson, R.R. (1974) Transference: Freud or Klein. *International Journal of Psychoanalysis*. 55: 37–48.

Gyimesi, J. (2009) The problem of demarcation: psychoanalysis and the occult. *American Imago*. (4): 457–470.

Hatcher, R.L. (1990) *Relational concepts in psychoanalysis: an integration by Stephen A. Mitchell*. PSA Books. 1(2): 127–142.

Joseph, B. (1985). Transference: the total situation. *International Journal of Psychoanalysis*. 66: 447–454.

Levenson, E.A. (1988) The pursuit of the particular – on the psychoanalytic inquiry. *Contemporary Psychoanalysis*. 24: 1–16.

Mills, J. (2020) *Debating Relational Psychoanalysis: Jon Mills and his Critics*. London: Routledge.

Merton, R. (1957) *Social Theory and Social Structure: Revised and Enlarged Edition*. Glencoe, IL: Free Press.

Mitchell, S. (1988) *Relational Concepts in Psychoanalysis: an Integration*. Cambridge, MA: Harvard University Press.

Paniagua, C. (2001) The attraction of topographical technique. *International Journal of Psychoanalysis*. 82(4): 671–684.

Paniagua, C. (2008) Id analysis and technical approaches. *Psychoanalytic Quarterly*. 77(1): 219–250.

Poland, W.S. (2000) The analyst's witnessing and otherness. *Journal of American Psychoanalytic Association*. 48(1): 17–34.

Rangell, L. (2004) *My Life in Theory*. New York: Other Press.

Rosenfeld, H. (1987) *Impasse and Interpretation*. London: Routledge.

Steiner, J. (1994) Patient-centered and analyst-centered interpretations: some implications of containment and countertransference. *Psychoanalytic Inquiry*. 14: 406–422.

Sullivan, H.S. (1954) *The Psychiatric Interview* (edited by S.W. Perry and M.L. Gawel). New York: Norton.

Wilczek, F. (2021) *Fundamentals*. New York: Penguin Press.

Yorke, C. (1971) Some suggestions for a critique of Kleinian psychology. *Psychoanalytic Study of the Child*. 26: 129–155.

Chapter 6

Affirming "that's not psycho-analysis!"

On the value of the politically incorrect act of attempting to define the limits of our field

Rachel Blass

> There should be some headquarters whose business it would be to declare:
> 'All this nonsense is nothing to do with analysis; this is not psycho-analysis.'
> (Freud, 1914, p. 43, on the establishment of the IPA)

Defining psychoanalysis is clearly a controversial issue.[1] There may be some consensus among analysts and analytic schools regarding broad definitions of the kind found in psychology textbooks or websites of analytic societies. It may, for example, be agreed that the field was founded by Sigmund Freud or that the practice involves a special relationship and intensive in-depth work aimed at fundamental psychic change. But when it comes to more specific and meaningful defining features, those that characterize the essence of psychoanalytic theory and practice, sharp differences are found. In part, this is merely a reflection of the sharp differences that exist between different analytic schools on issues of aims, method, epistemology, and what constitutes essential tenets of psychoanalytic thinking and practice (Blass, 2003a; Sandler and Dreher, 1996). As is well known, finding the common ground of psychoanalysis has always been a very difficult task for the psychoanalytic movement (Wallerstein, 1988). On various occasions Freud spoke of the Oedipus complex (Freud, 1905, p. 226), the unconscious (Freud, 1923, p. 13), and dream theory (Freud, 1914, p. 57) as "shibboleth[s] that distinguish ... the adherents of psychoanalysis from its opponents" (Freud, 1905, p. 226). But today even a concern with these broad concepts no longer defines the identity of many who regard themselves as psychoanalysts. Self-psychologists, for example, regard the conflicts of the Oedipus complex to be secondary, breakdown products of the self in a pathological state (Ornstein and Ornstein, 1980, p. 205) and many of those affiliated with American Relational psychoanalysis have adopted a postmodern perspective which puts in question the very existence of an internal reality such as the unconscious (see, for example, Philip Bromberg's comments in Dunn, 2003). Also, there is a growing tendency to expand the scope of the term unconscious, to refer primarily to all that is not immediately conscious (Freud's descriptive unconscious, rather than his

DOI: 10.4324/9781003340744-8

dynamic unconscious) so that apparent common ground is often only superficially shared (Dunn, 2003).

Alongside the absence of commonality in regard to central analytic concepts, almost from its inception there have been fundamental differences as to what defines psychoanalysis' essential aims and methods. For some, only a process based on verbal interpretation, allowing for lived insight into the latent truths of the mind, can be deemed analytic (see Caper, 1992, p. 289), whereas others hold much broader views, including as part of the analytic method the very act of fulfilment of various kinds of needs and forms of relatedness, absent in the patient's childhood. It has been suggested that Ferenczi, Balint, and Winnicott exemplify this broader perspective (Esman, 1990; Hoffer, 1991; Segal, 2006). The emphasis on empathy rather than truth that characterizes self psychology (Kohut, 1978, p. 676) and the view of "what is true *is* what works" that has been supported by a Relational approach (Renik, 1998, p. 492) may be seen to be additional contemporary alternative perspectives on what constitutes a specifically analytic method. There are differences also in regard to the essential nature of transference and the role of education and suggestion as part of the analytic enterprise. Whilst in 1988 Wallerstein speaks of psychoanalysis as united by a concern with transference, resistance, and "unconscious mental life expressed in unconscious fantasy and unconscious conflict" (p. 12), it would seem that this definition set forth originally by Freud would not encompass much of what is considered to be analytic practice today and was questionably applicable even 20 years ago. In 2002, Leo Rangell, tracing the development of psychoanalytic theory and practice, concludes that such a traditional analytic model "is today hardly recognizable" (2002, p. 1122).

In this chapter I am not concerned with the controversial issue of *how* to define psychoanalysis but rather with the controversy over the legitimacy of *the act* of defining psychoanalysis. For while indeed in the course of the history of psychoanalysis a variety of definitions of the field have been proposed, some of a more systematic nature (e.g. Rapaport and Gill, 1959), and some of less (e.g. Kernberg, 1999), and at times these definitions were disputed, even very openly and explicitly so (most notably in the "controversial discussions" [see King and Steiner, 1991]), in recent years it seems that the act of defining psychoanalysis has come to be considered an illegitimate one. We are now encouraged to describe what analysts *do*, but to refrain from judging what analysis *is* (Tuckett, 2008).[2]

Interestingly, the question of legitimacy of the act of defining does not arise when what is excluded from the definition are theories and practices whose promoters would not consider to be psychoanalytic per se (e.g. CBT or medication). It arises only when the exclusion meets opposition; when it is suggested that theories and practices regarded by some as analytic are not, in fact, so; that what they express is not psychoanalysis. Such a statement may be heard in private conversations but has come to be considered not only inappropriate in public psychoanalytic discourse, but futile and even hostile (Friedman, 2006, p. 689).

In my view, it is interesting that the issue of definition has come to be regarded in this way. To state that an idea, theory, or practice is not analytical is not to state that it is false, stupid, or non-therapeutic, but rather that its truth and/or value lies in another field. Why should such a statement be considered to be so disturbing? In most disciplines, being assigned to a different category of discipline would not be a source of great concern, much less a source of insult. Would a researcher trained as a psychologist be disturbed to hear that according to some his scientific contribution lies in the field of sociology rather than social psychology as he had thought? Would it make a difference if one's study, carried out in a chemistry laboratory, turns out to be in biology rather than chemistry, or *vice versa*, as long as the findings told us something true about reality? Would it even make a difference to a behaviourist to hear that he is a cognitivist, as long as it was agreed that the kind of treatment that he was offering worked well? I think not. Apparently, the very different reaction of the analyst to the matter of definition is tied to the fact the psychoanalyst is not merely concerned with contributing to the understanding of reality, with discovering true findings or with working therapeutically, but rather *the analyst is concerned with doing so psychoanalytically*. It is for this reason that to be told that one's work is interesting and helpful but non-analytic is to undermine the value of the work. A matter of identity is at stake.

In what follows I will first clarify the main arguments against defining the field of psychoanalysis and in support of the view that it is indeed inappropriate to posit that there are theories and practices which, while thought by their proponents to be analytic, in fact are not. I will then address the other side of the picture, explaining the reasons for defining psychoanalysis even if this entails the exclusion of theories and practices thought by some to be analytic. Finally, I will draw the broader implications of recognizing these considerations.

Arguments against defining psychoanalysis

We cannot define

This argument pertains to the *possibility* of defining psychoanalysis in a way that may exclude any existing perspective on what psychoanalysis is. One may take the position that it is not possible to do so because psychoanalysis is not a given, stable object that is open to objective scrutiny like a biological or physical entity. Rather, it is a certain kind of social construction. For this reason psychoanalysis can be defined only in terms of how in fact it is socially constructed or how it has been constructed over the course of history – not in terms of what it actually, in essence, is. In other words, all we can say of psychoanalysis is "this is how it tends to be or is usually regarded (or used to be regarded)", "this is a widely (or less widely) accepted definition of the field", not that "this *is* and this *is not* psychoanalysis". In contrast to essentialist definitions which would exclude certain views of psychoanalysis as simply wrong or unjustified, this social constructivist perspective leads to all-inclusive definitions, constantly changing to include the different ways in which psychoanalysis happens to be regarded.

In the light of this argument, exclusive definitions are simply personal opinions or preferences, the failure to regard them as such is error, and any attempt to justify or sharpen them is futile.

No person should define the field

This argument pertains to the authority to define psychoanalysis. It runs as follows: if indeed psychoanalysis is something that *is* definable in an exclusive way (counter to what was suggested above), if indeed there is a case to be made as to what is or what is not psychoanalysis, no individual person can assume or demonstrate that he is in a privileged position to put forth such a case. Therefore, if he does put forth such a case, he is granting himself an authority that is not his. Inherent to this argument is the relativistic notion that there is no objective way to arbitrate between opposing claims regarding the definition of psychoanalysis, and thus such claims must be treated as though they have equal validity and in turn no validity. That is, according to this view, no matter how well argued or reasonable one's position regarding the definition of psychoanalysis may be, it can never carry more weight than any other position on this matter, and hence there is no real reason to adopt a more restrictive definition. One would do so only if one ascribes authority to the analyst who puts forth the restrictive definition and to do so is both unfounded and dangerous. Unfounded because "who is to say" that the view of one person is better than that of another in this regard, and dangerous because unwarranted authority with the power to exclude threatens all innovation as well the very possibility of rational discourse.

In light of this argument, to define psychoanalysis in an exclusive way is to wrongly set oneself up above others – hence the presumptuousness and insult associated with this act. In contrast to the previous argument, however, the alternative here is not necessarily to define in an all-inclusive way. For if psychoanalysis is indeed something definable – and in this context it is claimed that it is – not all definitions would actually be equally true and valid. The alternative is to remain silent on the issue of definition or to adopt a kind of pluralism, whereby one affirms the validity of all definitions. Adoption of this pluralism contains what may be regarded as an inherent contradiction, involving the affirmation of the value of all definitions because of the difficulty in demonstrating the value of the definition that one actually holds to.

The negative consequences of definition

This argument is a pragmatic one. It affirms that definition is possible and that there are ways of evaluating the value and validity of different definitions. However, it is argued, putting forth such limiting definitions, albeit true and worthy, is not in the best interest of psychoanalysis. It creates feelings of dissent and tension within the analytic world and limits the numbers of analysts and in so doing it weakens psychoanalysis in its opposition to blatantly non-analytic approaches, most notably the cognitive-behaviourist camp. In other words, according to this view psychoanalysis benefits by being defined as broadly as possible, by including all those who define themselves as analysts, because as a broader body it has more influence both in the social and in the mental health contexts. Thus, finer distinctions that lead to the exclusion of this or that group should be put aside.

Another dimension of this pragmatic view refers not only to the potential damage of defining psychoanalysis in an exclusive way, but also to the fact that there is nothing to be gained by openly doing so. It is a futile and tension-arousing exercise leading nowhere.

The upshot of this argument is that on matters of definition one should, for pragmatic reasons, distinguish one's private from one's public stance. While privately one may rightly hold exclusive definitions, these should not be aired publicly. Instead, silence or broad definitions that focus on the common ground relative to blatantly non-analytic approaches are recommended.

Who cares? Psychoanalysis is and should be shaped by personal preference

This argument has some overlap with the previous ones, but here the claim is more specific. It is that (a) psychoanalysis cannot be defined because what is incorporated into the practice depends on personal preference, rather than on any considerations open to rational scrutiny, and (b) that this personal preference approach makes for a desirable state of flux, which would not be possible were one to try to define.

This argument appears, at times, in a more general version whereby it is simply stated that definition is unimportant because it is only a matter of semantics. In any of its versions the implication is that the question of the definition of psychoanalysis should simply be dropped – it is unnecessary and interferes with a natural process of personal selection in matters of clinical practice.

In sum, there are at least four main reasons why psychoanalysis should not be defined in a way that excludes ideas and practices that are considered by some to be analytic. It is not possible, justified, or beneficial for anyone to do so. At best it could lead to unnecessary tension and division; at worst it could bolster an authoritarian approach which would negatively determine the future of psychoanalysis. For these reasons it is necessary, or at least in the best interest of psychoanalysis, to refrain from definitions of this kind. This entails adopting very broad definitions, ones that would include all the new approaches as well as the old. Alternatively, it entails simply remaining silent on the issue of definition.

Thus, to speak on this topic is viewed as wrong and unhelpful. In turn it also comes to be regarded by many as inappropriate, a politically incorrect step, an act of divisiveness where unity and acceptance are most needed. I think that this latter view is not only predominant in contemporary analytic discourse, but also one which, because of the analytic political implications, is difficult to differ with. And yet I think that there is another side to which I now turn.

Arguments in favour of defining psychoanalysis

In presenting the arguments in favour of defining psychoanalysis, it is important first to establish the propositions that (a) psychoanalysis is a kind of entity that can be defined and (b) definitions may be supported and grounded and the quality of the support and grounding may be assessed.

It was noted earlier that there is the view that psychoanalysis is not a definable entity, i.e., it has no existence independently of the common perspectives regarding it, because it is a social construct, rather than a physical entity open to physical examination. Since a philosophical analysis of the problems with this view would take us too far afield, I will merely point to two intuitions that run counter to it.

Firstly, much of life deals with matters that are not physical entities, but which we do not, therefore, regard as defined by common opinion. Love, morality, and music, for example, are not physical entities, but rather are concepts that refer to certain occurrences or states of being. Indeed, the concepts are in a sense man-made, but we do not, therefore, tend to consider their definition to be determined by common opinion, or by summation of the different opinions that happen to prevail. Similarly in political matters, we do not tend to think that what defines a nationality or a country's borders is the kind of thing to be determined by an empirical survey of views on the matter. Rather, in such matters we consider these concepts to refer to non-physical entities, to some extent socially constructed, that have a substantive existence worthy of exploration and study.

The second intuition relevant in this context is that to recognize that one has a view about the definition of something (physical or non-physical) is to recognize that there is something to which one's definition refers. That is, we naturally make a distinction between views regarding the definition of things and the things themselves that are being defined (e.g., our own view of music and music itself, which our view hopes to capture). More specifically, in relation to psychoanalysis: to hold any view regarding *what* psychoanalysis is is also to hold *that* psychoanalysis is; in other words that it exists as an entity that has a nature or meaning that can be defined.

If psychoanalysis is a definable entity, then there can be better or worse definitions depending on how well these definitions grasp its nature or meaning. Can we ever know when one definition is better than another? As we have seen, coming from a relativistic stance, it may be argued that this is not really possible, that there is no way to arbitrate between opposing definitions (see point 2 above). All we have are personal opinions or declared allegiances. In contrast to this view, however, it may be claimed that definitions may be supported with evidence and arguments and the quality of these should determine our evaluation of the definitions. Various kinds of evidence and arguments may be relevant in this context and, while these would usually not lead to a conclusive definition with which all would agree, or that could be demonstrated to be true beyond objection, we may be able to justify maintaining one definition rather than another.

This is what happens when we come to define other non-physical entities, like the concepts mentioned above, of love, morality, music, nationality, and political borders. In determining these, it would seem reasonable to take into account historical factors (e.g. the history of a country's borders), rational arguments regarding what is unique to the concept (e.g. regarding the distinction between noise and music or between music and good music), appeals to common sense and reason (e.g. pointing to and defining instances which we would all agree constitute acts of love or of morality), as well as counterarguments which may reveal inconsistencies and incoherence of the proposed definitions, etc. All these are conceptual steps that would further our attempts to put forth meaningful definitions that would capture what is unique and essential to the entity in question and what distinguishes it from others. Of course, there may be several different viewpoints on these matters, but this would not mean that all viewpoints are of equal value and that none should be discarded, that they all can or need to be part of an all-inclusive definition, or that the attempt to define is futile. Where the history and evolution of a concept are not adequately addressed, where distinctions between different phenomena are blurred, where there is incoherence, or where arguments are rationally flawed, we may question the value or validity of a definition. And indeed, it is unlikely that there would be agreement even on what it means to take history into account in an adequate way, or what is considered a flawed argument, and yet this does not lead us to abandon our efforts to define. Rather, we continue to hold on to the truth of our views and hope that they will be corrected or refined through the debate with those of others.

The same considerations would hold true for determining the value and validity of the definition of psychoanalysis. Undoubtedly, defining psycho-analysis is a very complex task – there are no simple or clear-cut solutions to determining the boundaries of the field, its essence, or the range of possible developments that it can rightfully be said to encompass. For example, the multifaceted nature of Freud's writings invites different perspectives on what would be essential to psychoanalysis in order for it to be grounded in Freud's legacy. Indeed, Freud associates psychoanalysis with the concern with unconscious processes, but clearly having that concern would not in and of itself define analytic practice grounded in Freud. And, conversely, one may wonder which of the numerous additional concerns which Freud emphasizes (e.g. dream theory, sexuality, the Oedipus complex, developmental psychology, etc.) would have to be maintained for one's practice to be considered grounded in this way. If not all need to be accepted (and it is questionable whether they could be in a coherent way), then perhaps even his ideas regarding the unconscious could be discarded while still continuing the legacy. It would seem that there are no simple correct answers in this regard, and yet this does not mean that all attempts to answer are of equal value or of no value. Meaningful discourse regarding what is essential and unique is still possible (as in the other fields that I noted).

Beyond the issue of legacy, we may also see that the question of how to define what is essential to psychoanalysis may be impacted by different cultural influences and approaches to methodology that may determine clinical practice and in turn how this practice is to be understood. In this regard the differences between British, French, and North American views on what is essential to analytic technique and relationship are notable. And yet this does not mean that the different views are equally valid and are not open to debate. For example, one may question whether how psychoanalysis has come to be regarded in a specific culture allows it to be meaningfully distinguished from related fields of therapy or inquiry.

Moreover, it would seem that any definition of psychoanalysis would always be open to further questioning and debate as we are met with new findings and experiences that may pull towards change in theory and technique. All these considerations, however, do not deny the fact that there is some possibility of arbitrating between opposing definitions. The virtues and limitations of definitions can still be studied and one may legitimately think the position of another to be limited or mistaken.

This position on the possibility of defining psychoanalysis serves as part of the grounds for the following arguments in favour of doing so.

Scientific inquiry demands definition

By "scientific inquiry" I mean the inquiry into the nature of reality, into the truth regarding what actually exists, what things actually are. Putting aside for our purposes the complex question of how specifically to define such reality and truth in the context of psychoanalysis, consistent commitment to inquiry into its nature requires applying it to the study of what psychoanalysis is. Therefore, if the nature of psychoanalysis is something that could be investigated and defined (as we do other non-physical entities), then it is incumbent upon analysts concerned with the pursuit of truth to do so and in this way to discover or clarify what psychoanalysis truly encompasses. This means to define it as best one can, without imposing *a priori* limitations such as that the definition should not contradict or exclude any views held by other analysts.

Clearly, this argument will carry no weight for those who do not consider psychoanalysis to be an enterprise concerned with truth, and indeed with the expansion of the definition of psychoanalysis, one will find many who define themselves as analysts who do not have such a concern. But whether or not psychoanalysis can be considered dissociated from a concern with truth is ultimately a matter to be determined through discourse regarding the definition of the field.

Here, it is important to emphasize that any other form of scientific inquiry in the field of psychoanalysis (e.g. empirical, or clinical) rests on this more conceptual kind of inquiry into definition. This is because findings from other forms of inquiry could be considered relevant to psychoanalysis only if we first have a definition of what constitutes psychoanalysis. Accordingly, it may be seen that many of the disputes in psychoanalysis are not questions of what is empirically or clinically true (e.g. Does attachment or conflict play important roles in psychopathology?), but rather are questions of what truly belongs to our conceptualization of psychoanalysis (e.g. Is attachment relevant to psychoanalysis? Is psychoanalysis defined by its concern with conflict?). Once the definition is clarified, the scope of psychoanalysis narrows, as does the range of questions open to empirical or clinical investigation.

Training programmes require definition

To transmit psychoanalysis and to evaluate our success in doing so, we must have some definition of what psychoanalysis is.

The legitimate authority to define

To believe that one's own definition of psychoanalysis is true and that of others wrong is not necessarily to assume unwarranted authority. If there is some truth to the matter of the definition of psychoanalysis and if evidence and arguments can be and, in fact, are brought forth to support one's view, then, in upholding one's own definition, it is the authority of reason and rational considerations, not personal authority, that is coming into play.

"But who is to say that reason is on my side? That the reasoning of my opponent is not just as valid and that I am blind to his reasoning as he is blind to mine?" the analyst may ask. When such questions are pervasive and prevent adopting rationally grounded positions, they are, in my view, an expression of a kind of relativism of postmodern life, which invites us to abandon rational inquiry out of fear. The fear is of error – that not reason but the wish to impose one's own authority underlies one's stance, and hence the fear that voicing one's stance is a kind of attack rather than a form of dialogue. In light of this understanding, the question of the legitimate authority to define is ultimately one of whether one should trust one's reason with all the dangers that this involves, or whether awareness of these dangers should lead one to remain in perpetual doubt. According to at least some definitions of psychoanalysis, to opt consistently for doubt goes against the very grain of the analytic enterprise, which does indeed invite us to doubt our convictions and their underlying motives, but also holds that it is possible to come to truer convictions regarding the nature of reality, internal and external (Blass, 2003b). The idea that this is possible rests on the hope that through analysis the desire for truth will take precedence over the desire to think that we possess it (Blass, 2006).

In this context it is important to bear in mind that to put forth and uphold one's views on the matter of definition is not to have the final word on the matter. As in any rationally based inquiry, to present ideas on what is right and true is not to make claim to "The Ultimate Truth", but rather to take a step towards attaining a better grasp of reality as it is. Along similar lines, it should be recognized that defining psychoanalysis does not entail rejecting development or evolution of the field. Indeed, the definition of psychoanalysis sets limits and must take into account its roots and history (as in the process of forming an adequate definition of any concept), but this does not imply the imposition of static historical conceptions or bowing to the authority of the past. These distinctions and, more broadly, the tentativeness and uncertainty that are inherent to any serious claim to truth can be recognized as we better recognize the impact that fear of authority (either of being it or succumbing to it) may play in our attitude towards such claims.

The problem of all-inclusive definitions

By refraining from defining in an exclusive way, we either choose to remain silent regarding our exclusive definitions or in some form or other adopt an all-inclusive one. Not to define is not a possibility since we implicitly do so as part of meaningful discourse. In the very use of the term psychoanalysis, we imply that we think that it means something that distinguishes it from other things which are not psychoanalysis. The problem of all-inclusive definitions are as follows:

- *Contradiction*: If we reach all-inclusive definitions by summing the various specific definitions, there is the problem of psychoanalysis being defined with inherent contradictions. For example, psychoanalysis cannot be both a practice based *exclusively* on the verbal interpretation of unconscious conflict and a practice whose curative potential depends on the analyst fulfilling maternal needs which the patient consciously experiences to be absent.

- *Denial*: If contradiction is avoided by adopting the broadest definition possible, this entails denying the value and/or validity of the more restrictive views.
- *Loss of meaning*: By defining most broadly, psychoanalysis becomes associated with rather fuzzy ideas and practices. This fuzziness will impact the future development of psychoanalysis. Distinctions between psychoanalysis and psychotherapy or between psychoanalysis and any other form of talking treatment would be gradually lost.
- *Arbitrariness*: To determine the definition of psychoanalysis by including all views prevalent among those who call themselves analysts is a method that is not geared towards grasping that which is essential to psychoanalysis. It does not inquire into the nature of psychoanalysis, and rests on the views of a group whose credentials for defining psychoanalysis are unclear since their training is in a field that supposedly has no clear and limiting definition.
- *Authority*: To choose to define most broadly is still to choose to define. Thus, the question of authority that was raised in relation to exclusive definition could be raised here as well. On what authority can one decide that the most inclusive is the best or truest definition? While, as we have seen, an analyst offering an exclusive definition can respond to the question of authority through appeal to reason and the desire for truth, it would seem that because of underlying relativistic assumptions, such a response would not be possible when it comes to the all-inclusive definitions.

In this context it is important to reflect on the meaning and purpose of inclusive definitions. There are certain concepts that are inclusively defined to focus on the ground common to several groups that hold very different perspectives on the essential meaning of these concepts. This is most noted regarding political or religious definitions. For example, the basic tenets of Christianity are viewed very differently and in opposing ways in different Christian denominations. However, the concept of Christianity may be defined very broadly to refer to the ground shared by the different denominations – for example, some form of belief in Jesus Christ. This does not seem to entail the contradictions, denial, loss of meaning, or arbitrariness described above. Could we not regard the inclusive definition of psychoanalysis in this way? It is possible to suggest several reasons why not. First and foremost is the fact that in the present state of affairs it would be difficult to find any specific tenet that unifies all those who call themselves analysts. Secondly, by applying such an overarching definition it would still have to be agreed that this definition sets limits on who is and who is not a psychoanalyst. The arguments against exclusive definition discussed above would not allow for agreement on this point. Thirdly, regarding Christianity, it is clear to the various denominations unified by this overarching term that the term unites groups that are opposed on many basic issues. The opposition is openly expressed and is formalized in the different organizations in which each of the denominations develops. If, on the other hand, Christianity were viewed as a more specific term, one which should determine the schools one goes to and the teachings one learns, if it meant that the resources of all Christian denominations should be shared and that they should pray together in the same churches, disputes over the definition of the term would inevitably break out. This latter situation seems more applicable to the understanding of the term "psychoanalysis", which, while broad and clearly always referring to several different subgroups of theories and practices, is still regarded as a specific approach that demands of its proponents to learn and work together harmoniously.

In other words, unless some feature uniting all analysts is found and is taken as a shibboleth that separates analysts from those that are not, and unless the differences that exist between analysts beyond this unifying feature are given open and formal expression, then appeal to overarching definitions that are based on common ground is misguided.

On the importance of defining openly

This point comes to counter the idea that psychoanalysts should not openly air their differences in order to maintain unity in the face of the real opposition. Here, there are several considerations to take into account.

- *Who is the opposition?* In the absence of a clear definition of that which unifies psychoanalysis, the basis for standing together against another party seems unclear. Is Kleinian psychoanalysis truly guarding ground shared with self psychology in the opposition to cognitive-behavioural therapy? In the light of the profound differences between the former two both in theory and practice, one may in fact argue that the true opposition lies between them. Moreover, as the concept of analysis expands, the distinction between cognitive-behavioural therapy and some forms of psychoanalysis that acknowledge the use of suggestion and direction (e.g. Hoffman, 1996) or imply that what is most important is the verbalization of one's feelings (Westen and Gabbard, 2002) becomes unclear.
- *Honesty*: Given the fact that analytic approaches that are opposed in fundamental ways share some apparent formal similarities (e.g. use of the couch and the shared organizations), to fail to openly air differences regarding the very definition of psychoanalysis may be misleading. This is problematic from an ethical perspective. It may be argued that potential patients, students, and candidates should be allowed to know of differences that exist so that their choices could be better informed.

- *The dangers of stifling thought and the value of learning through debate*: By refraining from openly defining psychoanalysis in an exclusive way, the exclusive definitions do not disappear. Rather they remain unexamined and a latent source of animosity and consequently block dialogue and creative development of the field. Conversely, the open expression of views on the definition of psychoanalysis may allow for a meaningful exchange of ideas, and in turn lead to clearer thinking and understanding of the different views and of the nature of psychoanalysis itself. Indeed, openly presenting definitions that claim that certain theories and practices are simply not psychoanalysis may lead to divisiveness, tensions, and, ultimately, splits. But one may wonder whether living together in false and forced harmony is preferable.

Therapeutic definitions of psychoanalysis and psychoanalytic identity

One additional view on the issue of definition that should be taken into account is that we cannot define psychoanalysis because psychoanalysis evolves through the discovery of what is therapeutic. As the bodies of clinical experience and/or of empirical research expand, psychoanalysis too would change. Its procedure and understanding would be modified in order to incorporate what is learnt about what is helpful to our patients and in turn the definition of psychoanalysis would be in a constant state of flux. Thus, for example, if it is found that with certain kinds of patients deficits are more efficaciously treated through directive approaches than previously thought to be analytic, then the definition of psychoanalysis would have to be expanded to include the more directive approaches (Hurry, 1998, pp. 36–37).

This argument against definition differs from the previous arguments in a fundamental way (and for that reason was not included earlier). In a sense, in rejecting the idea of defining psychoanalysis it offers a single external criterion to determine the expanding definition of psychoanalysis and in this sense, paradoxically, is already based on a specific definition of the field. In other words, according to this view psychoanalysis is to be defined in such a way as to include all that is found to be curative to our patients.

It is important to recognize the striking flaw with this view and in so doing we may also see how rational considerations may be applied to demonstrate the limitations or failures of specific definitions of psychoanalysis. Undoubtedly, it is true that clinical experience provides us with a growing body of information regarding what is curative which psychoanalysts will incorporate into their work. Such learning from experience is reflected in all significant developments in psychoanalytic theory and practice. However, it is essential to distinguish here between curative in general and curative psychoanalytically. Were psychoanalysis to be defined by what is found to be curative in general, the absurd state of affairs would emerge whereby all forms of successful treatment, all methods with a positive outcome, would be called psychoanalysis (e.g. medication). We could then also never say that analytic treatment was combined with some other form of treatment, for once it is worthy of being combined it would become part and parcel of psychoanalysis. Nor could we say that there are successful treatments that are non-analytic. Our normal use of language, however, demands that such statements would be possible and that there would be a distinction between that which is therapeutic and that which is psychoanalytic.

It is in the context of this therapeutic view of the definition of psychoanalysis that we may see most clearly emotional or evaluative dimensions involved in the act of definition, which, I think, find expression to some extent in all attempts to avoid exclusive definitions. As noted at the beginning of this chapter, there is a question as to why the analyst who finds it so impossible to define the field still feels so strongly that its definition should exclude no one. Why the sense of insult at the suggestion that one is doing therapeutic work which falls outside the realms of psychoanalysis, so long as the work is thought to be helpful and based on valid findings? When we observe the attempt to refer to all things therapeutic as analytic, the issues underlying these feelings come closer to the surface. The analyst's desire to refer to his work as psychoanalytic, not merely therapeutic, even when (according to the analyst's own account) the only thing that makes it analytic is the fact that it is therapeutic, highlights what is to be gained by the use of the term psychoanalytic. It becomes apparent that it adds a positive connotation to certain therapeutic work, affiliates it with a kind of practice which, for therapists who developed in an analytically oriented milieu, points to the value, depth, and meaningfulness of one's work. As I mentioned earlier, there seems to be an issue of identity at stake here. In other words, when an analyst adopts a therapeutic kind of definition of psychoanalysis, what becomes more apparent is that he may be applying the term "psychoanalysis" to his work not because of its meaning, the fact that it refers to specific tenets or techniques which the analyst feels are central to his work – no such tenets or techniques are posited. Rather, it is applied because of the positive evaluation as well as the sense of identity that it offers. These could not be attained from an affiliation with the much broader context of therapy.

It may be suggested that at this point an additional evaluative factor comes into play. This is because if there is some recognition of the fact that one's affiliation is based on a desire for positive evaluation rather than on identification with some well-defined meaning or content, one may judge one's motives for affiliation negatively, recognizing that they are derived from narcissistic considerations, rather than realistic ones. One way of dealing with this would be by abandoning all attempts to define. That is, by "opening the doors" of psychoanalysis to all those who wish to enter, possible narcissistic motives for ascribing the term to oneself may be masked and counteracted. These emotional/evaluative factors contribute to the strange state of affairs in which the term "psychoanalysis" is held in high esteem and yet remains so undefined that all who wish to may refer to their work as psychoanalytic.

In this context one may again point to the value of defining what indeed is psychoanalytic, for it is through definition that affiliation with psychoanalysis may be grounded in true identification with what psychoanalysis is.

Conclusions

This examination of the arguments against putting forth exclusive definitions and the counterarguments in favour of so doing highlights that there is a price to be paid in attempting to define psychoanalysis in ways that include all those who call themselves analysts or, alternatively, to avoid defining altogether. To do so requires us to bracket a concern with gaining a better grasp of the nature of psychoanalysis in favour of harmonious existence among different analytic factions, whilst what is shared in this existence remains unspecified and unclear. In fact, as the concept of psychoanalysis becomes increasingly expanded and fuzzy, even the concern with gaining a better grasp on reality can no longer be deemed a shared analytic interest and so the price referred to here would not be meaningful to all contemporary analysts.

This examination, however, suggests that the dissipating concern with grasping reality, including the reality of psychoanalysis, is problematic. It leads to contradiction, meaninglessness, and denial of what is known and can be known. It also ultimately leads to authoritarianism and conformism, as inclusiveness comes to be demanded without rational grounding and dissenting exclusivist views are stifled out of considerations that may be popular, but irrelevant to the issue of truth, and hence are arbitrary.

There is no easy alternative. As discussed, there cannot exist any simple and agreed upon method for determining what is essential to a phenomenon such as psychoanalysis. Moreover, exclusivist definitions of psychoanalysis, which claim that certain practices that take place within the analytic world and under the rubric of psychoanalysis are simply not psychoanalytical, will undoubtedly arouse tension and dissent. It may lead to the necessity of recognizing that there are different camps that can no longer work together in harmony. As the definition of psychoanalysis is constricted so the number of analysts would be constricted as well, with possible implications for the political power of the psychoanalytic movement. There is also the real danger that greater freedom to exclude would result in the exclusion of valuable views in the absence of adequate grounds for this.

However, from a more hopeful perspective, it may be suggested that overt expression of differences is preferable to their remaining latent, and that the power of psychoanalysis is not measured only in numbers but in the strength and meaningfulness of its ideas. Moreover, it may be seen that the wrongful imposition of one's thinking, a danger inherent in any real attempt to develop rational discourse on the nature of reality, is not inevitable. If man's desire for truth is greater than his desire for power, then in the place of imposition one may envision the potential for productive dialogue between opposing views.

For this dialogue to take place and for psychoanalysis to evolve in a meaningful and enriching way, freedom of thought and expression on the definition of psychoanalysis is necessary. It must be permissible to voice one's views on what is and what is not psychoanalysis. As this chapter has stressed, these are not merely personal preferences and party affiliations, but rather issues that may be discussed and argued through rational considerations of historical and conceptual nature. It is through such freedom and the deeper understanding of the essence of psychoanalysis that it allows for that being excluded from the definition of psychoanalysis or being included within it can have any meaning at all.

Notes

1   Parts of this chapter were previously published and are here reprinted with kind permission: Rachel B. Blass (2010) Affirming "that's not psycho-analysis!" On the value of the politically incorrect act of attempting to define the limits of our field, The International Journal of Psychoanalysis, 91(1): 81–89, doi: 10.1111/ j.1745-8315.2009.00211.x, © Institute of Psychoanalysis, reprinted by permission of Taylor & Francis Ltd, www.tandfonline.com, on behalf of the Institute of Psychoanalysis.
2   A non-judgemental, descriptive approach of this kind may be of value in many ways but cannot determine our *definition* of what is essentially analytic. It tells us what is practised by analysts, but not what is essential to analytic practice. The latter requires a judgemental stance on what is and what is not analytic.

References

Blass, R.B. (2003a) On ethical issues at the foundation of the debate over the goals of psychoanalysis. *International Journal of Psychoanalysis*. 84: 929–943.

Blass, R.B. (2003b) The puzzle of Freud's puzzle analogy: reviving a struggle with doubt and conviction in Freud's *Moses and monotheism*. *International Journal of Psychoanalysis*. 84: 669–682.

Blass, R.B. (2006) A psychoanalytic understanding of the desire for knowledge as reflected in Freud's *Leonardo da Vinci and a memory of his childhood*. *International Journal of Psychoanalysis*. 87: 1259–1276.

Caper, R. (1992) Does psychoanalysis heal? A contribution to the theory of psychoanalytic technique. *International Journal of Psychoanalysis*. 73: 283–292.

Dunn, J. (2003) Have we changed our view of the unconscious in contemporary clinical work? *Journal of the American Psychoanalytic Association*. 51: 941–955.

Esman, A.H. (1990) Three books by and about Winnicott. *International Journal of Psychoanalysis*. 71: 695–699.

Freud, S. (1905) Three essays on the theory of sexuality. *The Standard Edition of the Complete Psychological Works of Sigmund Freud.* 7: 123–246.

Freud, S. (1914) On the history of the psycho-analytic movement. *The Standard Edition of the Complete Psychological Works of Sigmund Freud.* 14: 1–66.

Freud, S. (1923) The ego and the id. *The Standard Edition of the Complete Psychological Works of Sigmund Freud.* 19: 1–66.

Friedman, L. (2006) What is psychoanalysis? *Psychoanalytic Quarterly.* 75: 689–713.

Hoffer, A. (1991) The Freud–Ferenczi controversy: a living legacy. *International Journal of Psychoanalysis.* 18: 465–472.

Hoffman, I.Z. (1996) The intimate and ironic authority of the psychoanalyst's presence. *Psychoanalytic Quarterly.* 65: 102–136.

Hurry, A. (1998) Psychoanalysis and developmental therapy. In: A. Hurry (editor). *Psychoanalysis and Developmental Therapy,* 32–73. London: Karnac.

Kernberg, O. (1999) Psychoanalysis, psychoanalytic psychotherapy and supportive psychotherapy: contemporary controversies. *International Journal of Psychoanalysis.* 80: 1075–1091.

King, P. and Steiner, R. (editors) (1991) *The Freud–Klein controversies 1941–1945.* London: Routledge.

Kohut, H. (1978) *The Search for the Self,* P. Ornstein (editor). New York, NY: International UP.

Ornstein, P.H. and Ornstein, A. (1980) Formulating interpretations in clinical psychoanalysis. *International Journal of Psychoanalysis.* 61: 203–211.

Rangell, L. (2002) The theory of psychoanalysis: vicissitudes of its evolution. *Journal of the American Psychoanalytic Association.* 50: 1109–1137.

Rapaport, D. and Gill, M.M. (1959) The points of view and assumptions of metapsychology. In: M.M. Gill (editor). *The Collected Papers of David Rapaport,* 795–811. New York, NY: Basic Books.

Renik, O. (1998) The analyst's subjectivity and the analyst's objectivity. *International Journal of Psychoanalysis.* 79: 487–497.

Sandler, J. and Dreher, A.-U. (1996) *What Do Psychoanalysts Want? The Problem of Aims in Psychoanalytic Therapy.* New York, NY: Routledge.

Segal, H. (2006) Reflections on truth, tradition, and the psychoanalytic tradition of truth. *American Imago.* 63: 283–292.

Tuckett, D. (editor) (2008) *Psychoanalysis Comparable and Incomparable.* London: Routledge.

Wallerstein, RS. (1988) One psychoanalysis or many? *International Journal of Psychoanalysis.* 69: 5–21.

Westen, D. and Gabbard, G.O. (2002) Developments in cognitive neuroscience: I. Conflict, compromise, and connectionism. *Journal of the American Psychoanalytic Association.* 50: 53–98.

Chapter 7

Psychoanalysis and its future

Destiny at the crossroads

Arthur Leonoff

> Do you suppose that someday a marble tablet will be placed on the house, inscribed with these words: In this house, on July 24, 1895, The Secret of Dreams was revealed to Dr. Sigmund Freud.[1]
>
> (Sigmund Freud)

> To survive, to avert what we have termed future shock, the individual must become infinitely more adaptable and capable than ever before. We must search out totally new ways to anchor ourselves, for all the old roots – religion, nation, community, family, or profession – are now shaking under the hurricane impact of the accelerative thrust. [2]
>
> (Alvin Toffler)

Introduction

This is an essay on the future of psychoanalysis but not of the predictive kind or one that advocates for a specific choice or direction lest it suffers or, at worst, perishes. It is rather about how psychoanalysis has traditionally conceptualized its future and, specifically, the importance that Freud, a conquistador by self-reference, gave to destiny, which, I contend, remains an important driver of psychoanalytic politics today (Freud, 1900). Destiny in psychoanalysis not only charts a rightful goal, worthy of this founder's vision, it is also a deep, moral obligation to keep the field on track and make the right choice at every approaching crossroad. It is an enduring responsibility that inhabits the profession but, I believe, also works against important change, inhibiting the field, decreasing openness to other influences, fostering anxiety, and limiting the capacity of psychoanalytic organizations to adapt to an evolving future.

Pursuing this destiny has much to do with psychoanalysis' bold stand against conventional wisdom, its radical social critique, and pursuit of societal healing. It is an internalized ethos acquired through intimate intensive formation in psychoanalytic institutes and transmitted through the analytic generations, especially but not limited to the personal or training analysis.

DOI: 10.4324/9781003340744-9

Psychoanalysis evolves in sometimes surprising ways, but it is also impacted by this conviction of destiny that functions like a communal myth that is rarely articulated but informs its history.[3]

Myth and psychoanalysis

There is the history of psychoanalysis but then there is also the story. Myth belongs to the realm of story (Frye, 1990). It functions like an explanatory frame that underlies its history and reflects both individual and transgenerational transferences to the field. It concerns how psychoanalysis sees itself in respect to its history and what values and ideals it espouses.

Destiny thinking functions like a preconscious wish regarding the rightful but also lonely place of analysts in the world. Mostly, it remains out of awareness but, paradoxically, analysts are always aware of its pull. There is an implicit notion of a correct pathway that emanates from the momentum of Freud's powerful will and influence. We all know the short shrift he made of those whom he viewed as veering from the path. The myth of "splendid isolation" that he cultivated, corralled the recognition he clearly savored (Breger, 2009).

Myths, however, can be used to justify a surprising degree of authority and coercive control over what is deemed acceptable. Analysts easily tolerate those who are uninvolved in analytic life but there is a special enmity and fear reserved for those seen as betraying psychoanalytic destiny. Someone who is "dangerous to psychoanalysis" gets special attention and the troops are on guard.

In 1910, addressing the second Psychoanalytic Conference at Nuremberg, Freud's poetic rhetoric articulated this societal mandate that has guided psychoanalysis since, including its self-image as a stalwart defender of truth in the face of fierce resistance that requires unity and uniformity:

> Powerful though men's emotions and self-interest may be, yet intellect is a power too—a power which makes itself felt, not, it is true, immediately, but all the more certainly in the end. The harshest truths are heard and recognized at last, after the interests they have injured and the emotions they have roused have exhausted their fury. It has always been so, and the unwelcome truths which we psycho-analysts have to tell the world will have the same fate. Only it will not happen very quickly; we must be able to wait.
>
> (Freud, 1910, 147–148)

This is mythos endowing psychoanalysis with a social purpose and authority beyond the patient in treatment. It describes a clash of Titans: the anti-force of repression and resistance against the powerful logic of psychoanalysis. This is a Herculean task that has always demanded loyalty.

The notion of Freud's defense of ideas and, in parallel, his defense of psycho-analysis' rightful destiny for which he would need a "secret council" became blurred early in psychoanalysis' story (Freud, 1912). This duality seems to have characterized analysis as a clinical discipline but also a movement in pursuit of a lofty mission. Psychoanalysts as conquistadores, champions for a cause rivaling Galileo and Darwin, drove lofty idealism and ambition, first of Freud and then of the profession. As a result, Freud's insistence on infantile sexuality and the Oedipus complex generated powerful internal politics that saw some early adherents expelled and others severely criticized or marginalized. Destiny was always a greater goal than the fate of any individual within the movement.

Quo vadis?

Psychoanalysis' agenda was bold from the outset. Its members were one of the "impossible professions," which only added to the myth of the heroic, isolated analyst, facing truth about the mind, much of it unconscious and deeply in conflict with itself. It aimed to provide a window into the human condition that was imbued with intention. When Freud wrote: "*Where id was, there ego shall be*," he was outlining a destiny for psychoanalysis as a liberator of humanity and a freedom fighter for the mind (Freud, 1933, p. 80).

Yet, the field of psychoanalysis that seemed so clear when Freud penned this phrase is much more complicated today. It has many strands and exists in a neighborhood of therapies in which it strives to stand out as a unique and ambitious enterprise with very different goals than others. Its clients are as apt to suffer from unthoughts, non-represented states, and weak identity as from repressed ideas. There is still the old zeal and psychoanalysis is infectious wherever it takes hold in the world. Yet, it can also seem muddled, unsure, for instance, where psychoanalysis stops and psychotherapy begins. There is even disagreement about whether this distinction needs to exist at all.

If we understand destiny as opening a creative path to the future, something self-created and not fated, then psychoanalysis certainly warrants a destiny. On the other hand, destiny thinking, a conviction of one's specific place in the world, can mask omnipotent and even destructive currents that emerge whenever individuals, groups, or nations believe in destiny too much.

There are frustrations inherent to analytic practice in many parts of the world. Reality constraints unfavorable to working in the way one trained, and ongoing divisive political tensions within the field, can foster disillusionment. A profession that aspires to high ideals and standards bears a risk when reality fails to measure up to expectations. This could well be the case for psychoanalysis, which insists on its high standards above all else while, in contrast, much of the world expects far less in terms of standard mental health services. When analysts perceive a movement to lower psychoanalytic standards, tensions escalate sharply. This is existential and broadly linked to destiny in my view.

Bornstein (2004) noted this preoccupation with destiny in Freud's own response to independents such as Adler and Jung who were perceived as the first of the threats to psychoanalysis' existence:

> How vulnerable Freud must have viewed psychoanalysis is striking. He lacked confidence that it could withstand open and free inquiry. This belief is diametrically opposite the idea that scientific inquiry is intrinsic to psychoanalysis.
>
> (p. 77)

This vulnerability would not have been so evident when psychoanalysis was in an ascendant position in Europe and North America. There were many decades in the twentieth century when its flame was unrivaled before it suffered a precipitous fall in the public eye at a time that mental healthcare turned rather radically to imbalanced brain chemistry and behaviorism, both of which excluded mind. On the other hand, psychoanalysis never had an easy time even when it was at its pinnacle of esteem and popularity. Besides external threats and internal saboteurs and revisionists, internecine jealousies and rivalries riled the profession, leading to high-profile splits and transgenerational resentments.

In its ascendancy, analysts were in a privileged position in universities and communities. The field felt assured of its rightful destiny. The training analysts were the most revered. Everyone idealized Freud and every article was obliged to begin with his contributions. Psychoanalysis, thus, was venerated, along with its founder, for most of the twentieth century before it faced a reckoning with its own limits, excesses, and the availability of therapeutic alternatives. This rocked the profession in part because psychoanalysis had never had to justify its existence or efficacy. Indeed, there was a decidedly anti-research attitude within psychoanalysis and it was mainly unprepared to face external scrutiny.

The social atmosphere also changed, and it was not friendly to analysis. Freud was personally pilloried for supposed crimes such as an affair with his sister-in-law, Minna, and he was accused of turning his back on real sexual abuse to sell his theories (Mack and Kaufman, 2013). It was a time of nasty betrayals in which Freud and psychoanalysis were under regular attack. This was a long way from the Freud who hoped that a plaque would be placed in his honor at the very spot that he first deciphered the meaning of dreams. He was imagining a revered destiny for the profession. Psychoanalysis has always been a field prone to idealization and destiny thinking, which renders it vulnerable to attack from critics and adversaries. Fredrick Crews (2017) and his ilk are more successful than they should be because of this internal characteristic.

There is a consequence, though, to following in the footsteps of an intellectual giant. The late Janet Malcom's revelatory book, *The Impossible Profession* (Malcom, 1981) was limited to the New York Psychoanalytic Society's brand of analyst, but her chosen subject, Aaron Green, still seems identifiable through a contemporary lens. Malcom writes: "When a patient gets better, Green credits the psychoanalytic process; when he doesn't, he blames himself." Implicit is the notion that psychoanalysis is a graspable object, a thing unto itself that is to be treasured and protected. Analysts often feel responsible for the fate of psychoanalysis and to preserve its legacy. It goes well beyond the fealty that health professionals and therapists usually feel regarding their *métier*. Any analyst, especially a leader and training analyst, who acts discreditably is perceived to be attacking "psychoanalysis," not just their own reputational standing.

This is not an uncommon reaction among tight-knit groups with strong intra-group identification. When Bernie Madoff committed his heinous financial crimes, many Jews winced and felt it personally as a betrayal of his own people and the tenets of his faith in which integrity and philanthropy are so highly valued. In a *New York Times* article, a rabbi was quoted:

> "Jews have these familial ties," Rabbi Wolpe said. "It's not solely a shared belief; it's a sense of close communal bonds, and in the same way that your family can embarrass you as no one else can, when a Jew does this, Jews feel ashamed by proxy. I'd like to believe someone raised in our community, imbued with Jewish values, would be better than this."
>
> (Pogrebin, 2008)

Destiny was one reason that Freud (1911) chose a non-Jew as his successor. "*So let us go on toiling. We too have a destiny to fulfil,*" wrote Freud to Jung (pp. 472–474). In the end, of course, his theories mattered more to him than any narcissistic aggrandizement that Jung's Christian heritage would have won for psychoanalysis (Wittels, 1933). He was emboldened by destiny following his *stage* (internship) at the Salpêtrière Hospital with Charcot.

It is this same sense of destiny that colors psychoanalysis and continues to shape its politics. We are afraid to lose "it," no matter how this is conceptualized. It might be psychoanalysis itself or a key concept such as sexuality or the unconscious. Whatever its representation, it is understood that loss of this precious element would be tragic for psychoanalysis' destiny, if not for the world.

Freud believed that "it" was the Oedipus complex and infantile sexuality because without it there was no psychoanalysis to protect. There was also loyalty to a cause of which he was the representative and symbol. It was a narcissistic investment from the outset, deeply mythologized, and imbued with the equivalent of religious fervor. It took years to lessen this homage to the founder and to be freed from an insistence on fealty. Nonetheless, destiny thinking preoccupies psychoanalysis still and, in my view, remains an impediment.

In current times, what is perceived to be in danger is more likely identified with the frame and setting or whatever is deemed to make the process specifically psychoanalytic. The issue of session frequency is currently front and center. Death by dilution is seen as a very present danger by what is perceived as a reduction in training standards. It emerges as a fear that the imprimatur of Freud's analysis, 100 plus years in the making, will be lost to general psychotherapy by taking the wrong turn.

Today, psychoanalysis resides in a tough neighborhood. The field has been buffeted, even battered in the last decades. Healthcare culture has changed to accommodate fast-paced lives and technology. Taking time for personal development during the workday is no longer a cultural priority. Talk therapy is measured against psychoactive drugs for rapid symptom relief and no more. Symptoms are targeted and not the subject who experiences them.

Destiny thinking

In the face of these very real challenges for psychoanalysis, destiny thinking can be a salve that protects against disillusionment but makes it much harder to adapt. Freud (1925) described the myth of Oedipus as a "tragedy of destiny" in that our future is not a matter of fate but written in the unconscious and enacted with a form of intentionality and determinism (p. 63). Bollas (1989) referred to a "destiny drive," which he linked to the Winnicottian "true self." He wrote in this respect:

> I should be clear that I think that one of the tasks of an analysis is to enable the analysand to come into contact with his destiny, which means the progressive articulation of his true self through many objects.
>
> (p. 35)

The notion of "true self" is more aspirational than directional but it is embraced by many analysts. Could it apply to the field itself? In this regard, psychoanalysis as a field has no necessary final endpoint or destination although destiny thinking would imply that we either take the right path or risk seriously damaging the profession or, at worst, destroying it. As much as destiny thinking in psychoanalysis encourages idealization, the risks of disillusionment are then also greater.

In 1975, Heinz Kohut, himself a reformer, put it this way:

> It is my prediction, then, that psychoanalysis is not far from an important point in its development. At that point, it will be decided whether a critical developmental task will be avoided or whether it will be engaged. In the first case, analysis will enter a period in which it will restrict itself

to continuing its careful codification and systematization of the already
explored and will then die. In the second case, it will enter a more or less
prolonged period of questioning its past, of struggling against the temptation of rebelliously discarding its inheritance, followed by the examination of daring new paths into new territories. This will be a period
of great danger, of excited battles and debates—but analysis will have a
chance to emerge from it, to go on to live and to thrive.

(Kohut, 1975, p. 378)

Each generation of analysts bears responsibility for psychoanalysis' future. If
analytic standards are high, which they are uniformly within the International
Psychoanalytic Association, there are those that want them higher. There is
an experience of shame for not living up to the demands of this destiny. Some
also cast shame on those who are perceived as "selling out" by eradicating the
technical specificity of psychoanalysis, especially by merging it with psychotherapy or elevating psychotherapists to the ranks of analysts by lowering
standards. This is classed among cardinal sins and harsh judgment descends
on anyone accused of what is viewed as a betrayal of destiny.

Although the general societal view is that psychoanalysis is a form of psychotherapy, from inside the analytic profession, the distinction is imperative.
Here is where destiny intervenes in my view. Psychoanalysis as a theory of
mind could tolerate contiguity with psychotherapy but psychoanalysis as
a unique process cannot. This likely explains why the issue of session frequency in training becomes so controversial. Frequency is the most observable
delimiting feature of psychoanalysis when compared to psychotherapy, at least
when the practitioner is an analyst. It is not the only characteristic but others
are more intrinsic and subjective.

The loss of the unconscious is another worrying sign that has been noted.
Busch (2001), for example, wrote that "psychoanalysis is drifting into a state
of mindlessness." This is more than a technical argument in Busch's view but
entirely existential as he believes that it radically deviates from a core concept
that is elemental to Freud's legacy and psychoanalysis' destiny. Busch uses the
metaphor of "drift" to highlight deviation from destiny and its threat to the field.

In actuality, new developments in psychoanalysis are often measured
against an implicit standard that is linked to analytic destiny. Ego psychology, for example, through the eyes of André Green (2005), was a deviant
tradition that made far too much of adaptation, and he certainly railed about
supplanting the intrapsychic baby of psychoanalysis with the literal baby of
infant research. Green saw himself very much as a steward of this Freudian
destiny – preserving the originality and specificity of psychoanalytic thought.

He noted:

However interesting the information received from the field of related
disciplines may be, it seems to me that the essential aspect of research in

psychoanalysis should be situated in the area of psychoanalytic practice and clinical experience, reference to which is indispensable for keeping psychoanalytic thought pointing in the right direction.

(Green, 2002, p. 70)

As in this quote, destiny thinking always implies direction and what would take psychoanalysis away from its assigned future. In my view, though, it underestimates the organic fluidity of an analytic process, its self-creation and unpredictability. Once spun and unleashed, the analytic process marches to its own drummer and finds its own end. This is likely true of the field itself.

The problem with destiny thinking generally is that it promotes a sense of ideality and fealty to a cause, which can lead to a close mindedness, fear, as well as defensiveness. Rather than protect psychoanalysis, it renders it more fragile by creating precisely this idea of crossroads and choice points. This encourages a form of splitting of the field around the demands of destiny. Keeping one's bearings or losing them, a compass metaphor, is commonly heard in this context and describes this idea of straying so far from home that you can never get back. It identifies destiny with a specific pathway which can then be overdetermining and rigidifying.

This is burdening to psychoanalytic self-governance, which bears the responsibility to keep the field on its "true path" even if this remains vaguely defined.

Transmission of psychoanalysis: "how does your garden grow"

The pathway of destiny involves a process of transmission in which one generation of analysts instructs another, although always in an imperfect way. It is imperfect in the sense that it is never a mirror image of itself and this subtle misrecognition, on its own, changes the field. There is also a residue of what cannot easily be symbolized both in terms of clinical work and organizational life, which becomes the focus of work in the next generation. The new generation receives the information from the old but also creates something different with it than what existed previously. Analytic work then reacts to these subtle shifts.

Transmission is, thus, bi-personal and bi-directional even though the older generation is instructing the next. It is a co-creation. As such, knowledge is constantly being re-transcribed in both generations in real time. I have experienced on many occasions the novelty of how a patient hears what I say, and in the gap between intention and comprehension one finds truths and transference that become important markers of what works in psychoanalytic treatment. It changes what I understood about what I was saying as much as creating insightful and serendipitous experience for the patient. There is a mutuality to transmission.

This same process occurs in the educational context. Teaching is learning and a chance to deepen but also revise understanding and perspective. Transmission of psychoanalytic knowledge alters the very concepts that are being taught. Although this is happening independently in thousands of seminar rooms around the world, it is a collective rethink that finds its way into original journal articles that communally modify the field and, in the *après coup*, re-transcribe what had been understood previously.

Psychoanalysis, in my view, thus, follows no exact script, nor is there one sure and rightful destiny. Instead, reacting to the many environments and settings in which it functions, psychoanalysis is in constant revision while never destined to reach a final form. Its theory expands to encompass new thoughts, which in turn impact on and creatively modify what came before.

The problem of translation in a mindless world

Mind is in retreat in many cultures and societies not because of any specific antipathy but because the world does not make it easy to live a personal life. Besides neoliberal values that push people to work and consume, the private self is being coopted by the likes of Google and the contemplative self has been supplanted by a binging form of screen entertainment. There might be nostalgia for mind or, at least, for the time when contemplation could be its own purpose. Then again there is also nostalgia for print newspapers but this is not saving them. The search for meaning is still important but the search tends to be extra-psychic and, consequently, the familiarity with mind and mental phenomena is much less pronounced. Emotions like sentimentality easily triggered by social media gain favor over more profound affective responses. Cognitive behavior therapy is the treatment *de rigueur*. Mind has a very limited role to play. One sees a superficializing of culture to fit the medium of a hand-held device. If the medium is the message, then where does this leave mind? (McLuhan, 1967).

The challenge for psychoanalysis is one of translation for, whatever is its nature or variations, psychoanalysis is very much about mind. In an increasingly mindless world, the disconnect between psychoanalysis and society becomes that much greater because of the lack of a shared language. Nicoli and Tugnoli (2020) have written persuasively about this issue of translation in communicating psychoanalytic ideas. Although they speak about this activity in terms of community outreach and the IPA's "Freud's café" initiative, it would apply to all venues and contexts where intricate psychoanalytic ideas need to be communicated to others in plain language. Likewise, what is transmitted in psychoanalytic education should not be reduced to curriculum but instead fosters a way of thinking, being with the other's thoughts and ranging between "here and now" and "there and then."

The fundamental and at times radical shift of mental health treatment strategies away from mind underlines society's ambivalence regarding the murky depths of the psyche, which seem elusive and hard to pin down. It is this culture shift that has led to predictions of the demise of psychoanalysis, which has become a metaphor for mind. While late nineteenth and early twentieth century western culture repressed sexuality and was scandalized by Freud's insistence on infantile erotism, it is mind itself that is now in the crosshairs of repression.

Anti-mind trends infiltrate the body politic and can have something to do with the sense of crisis that pervades psychoanalysis (Aguillaume-Torres, 2016; Carlson, 2016; Azzone, 2018). Committed analysts with deep attachment to the field mourn its apparent decline and protest its causes. Writing prior to when the American Psychoanalytic Association aborted its controversial training structure, the Board of Professional Standards, Arnold Richards (2015) wrote movingly:

> Because our field is in crisis. Its prestige has plummeted along with its economic viability and even its population. It has lost much of its standing among the traditional academic disciplines, and almost all of its coverage as a psychotherapeutic technique. Even in departments of psychiatry its presence wanes. Analysts are getting older, and it is not clear who will replace us. Fewer candidates are seeking training, and there are fewer patients for them to analyze. A once-fascinated public distrusts psychoanalysis as unscientific, authoritarian, deluded, reactionary, trite, arrogant, sexist, and/or passé. We know its value and want to restore its health and reclaim for it the respect it once compelled, but to do that we have to be able to explain psychoanalysis in ways that make sense to other people and to ourselves. We cannot seem to do it. Why? What is it about psychoanalysis that makes us seem so powerless to halt its decline?
>
> (p. 390)

Although he was speaking from an American perspective at a point in time, the unsettling experience of crisis is still familiar. Disillusionment was in the air and too much disillusionment often leads to a sense of crisis (Leonoff, 2021). Within his text, however, is also a formula for recovery, a path to the future through translation; communicating psychoanalytic ideas in ways that it can be understood by others and ourselves. This seems essential.

Despite shifting cultural expectations and fears of catastrophe, psychoanalytic therapies have their place. The pool is certainly shallower if depth is measured in sessions per week in much of the analytic world, but the reach is greater than it has ever been. There is still a bigger need for psychoanalysis than there are analysts. Individuals with complex personality and mood disorders exacerbated by psychic trauma are drawn to the intensive work that analysts are trained and keen to do. Indeed, as far as I am aware, there is no drug or acronym therapy available that has the life-altering potential of psychoanalysis for such complex clinical problems.

There is general agreement that psychoanalysis needs to be protected although analysts differ on what this means. Should the field hold to its original structure – the basic encounter in an intensive treatment defined by frequency and couch in which psychoanalysis and psychotherapy are very different genres – or adapt to a cultural and mental health landscape that would redefine analysis as a way of thinking and being with the patient, cultivating a psychoanalytic mindset, but less bound to the original setup. Working through this complex issue can be hindered by destiny thinking because it creates fear as well as guilt for letting down Freud and those that follow, including ourselves.

As the divergence between training and practice has become wider in many parts of the analytic world, it has also been harder for practitioners to state when they are practicing psychoanalysis and when they are not. Binary thinking tends to pervade these debates. Analysts who spend most of their careers doing psychoanalytic psychotherapy bristle with the contention that they are not practicing analysis. Clearly, there are local conditions that determine how we practice. It is a complex mix of cultural, economic, regulatory, and third-party insurance availability. At the crossroads of its future, psychoanalysis needs to be defined on its own terms and in the context of its core values and history, but not so rigidly defined that it excludes many of its own practitioners and succumbs to endless nostalgia, losing essential flexibility and snapping when it most needs to bend.

This brings us back to the notion of destiny in psychoanalysis as the counterpoint to nostalgia. Destiny is mythical but myths are the drivers of human culture and politics. Psychoanalysis is no exception. Of course, the notion of destiny is, at its core, a defensive illusion against the impermanence of human enterprises. It becomes especially problematic in the face of significant and widespread stresses and disillusionments. At these moments, destiny thinking can intervene and impede the capacity to make necessary changes.

There is no doubt that psychoanalytic organizations have struggled with disillusionment: aging memberships, less market share, less candidates, isolation from universities, very public attacks and criticisms, and internecine struggles over training standards and training analysts, all of which have taken their toll. Destiny thinking, however, with its notion of the right path, does not help. It increases hand wringing and could well overlook that psychoanalysts have been increasingly adept at adjusting to changing conditions and sharpening their clinical skills to include new skills and novel modes of listening. What Freud experienced and expressed as destiny can be equated with this intimate process – to speak what has not been thought and to understand in a relationally fresh and meaningful way that is deeply life altering. As long as we continue to do this well, we do not need a destiny.

Conclusion

Psychoanalysis owes a lot to its past but this will not determine its future. At the same time, psychoanalysis does not need a destiny to evolve, nor is there really a crossroads. Change is inevitable as psychoanalysis evolves organically both clinically and organizationally. The challenge is to be ready and open for the future and to adopt practices and perspectives that will preserve core values while not resorting to destiny thinking and its penchant for crisis, disillusionment, and institutional conflict. There is something untranslatable about human subjectivity but this creates the opportunity for genuine novelty and surprise. This seems a worthwhile compromise: we forfeit the fixed idea of destiny but inherit a field that has room and capacity for infinite change and growth.

Notes

1   Freud, S. (1900). Letter from Sigmund Freud to Wilhelm Fliess, 12 June 1900. Letters of Sigmund Freud 1873–1939, 240–241.
2   Toffler, A. (1970). *Future Shock*. New York: Random House.
3   As of this writing, a PEP web search of the textual contiguity of the words "psychoanalysis" and "mission" yields 325 entries. These words have an inclination to appear in close proximity, which attests to the associative strength of the pairing.

References

Aguillaume-Torres, R. (2016) One psychoanalysis or two? *International Forum of Psychoanalysis*. 25(3): 150–156.

Azzone, P. (2018) Understanding the crisis: five core issues in contemporary psychoanalysis. *International Forum of Psychoanalysis*. 27(4): 255–265.

Bollas, C. (1989) *Forces of Destiny: Psychoanalysis and Human Idiom*. London: Free Association Books.

Bornstein, M. (2004) The problem of narcissism in psychoanalytic organizations. *Psychoanalytic Inquiry*. 24(1): 71–85.

Breger, L. (2009) *A Dream of Undying Fame: How Freud Betrayed His Mentor and Invented Psychoanalysis*. New York: Basic Books.

Busch, F. (2001) Are we losing our mind? *Journal of the American Psychoanalytic Association*. 49(3): 739–751.

Carlson, D.A. (2016) *Illusions of a future: psychoanalysis and the biopolitics of desire*. By Kate Schechter. Durham: Duke University Press. *Journal of the American Psychoanalytic Association*. 64(1): 245–249.

Crews, F. (2017) *Freud: The Making of an Illusion*. New York: Metropolitan Books.

Freud, S. (1900) Letter, February 1, 1900. *Letters of Sigmund Freud to Wilhelm Fliess, 1887–1904*. 397–398.

Freud, S. (1910) The future prospects of psycho-analytic therapy. *The Standard Edition of the Complete Psychological Works of Sigmund Freud.* XI: 139–152.

Freud, S. (1911) Letter from Sigmund Freud to C.G. Jung, December 17, 1911. In: W. McGuire (editor) (1975) *The Freud/Jung Letters: The Correspondence Between Sigmund Freud and C.G. Jung.* New York: Princeton University Press.

Freud, S. (1912) Letter from Sigmund Freud to Ernest Jones, August 1. In: *The Complete Correspondence of Sigmund Freud and Ernest Jones, 1908–1939* (edited by R.A. Paskauskas). Cambridge: Harvard University Press, 1993, pp. 147–148.

Freud, S. (1925) An autobiographical study. *The Standard Edition of the Complete Psychological Works of Sigmund Freud, Volume XX (1925–1926): An Autobiographical Study, Inhibitions, Symptoms and Anxiety, The Question of Lay Analysis and Other Works.* London: Hogarth.

Freud, S. (1933) New introductory lectures on psychoanalysis. *The Standard Edition of the Complete Psychological Works of Sigmund Freud, Volume XXII (1932–1936): New Introductory Lectures on Psychoanalysis and Other Works.* London: Hogarth.

Frye, N. (1990) *The Great Code: The Bible & Literature.* Markham, Ontario: Penguin Books.

Green, A. (2002) The crisis in psychoanalytic understanding. *Fort Da.* 8(1): 58–71.

Green, A. (2005) The illusion of *common ground* and mythical pluralism. *International Journal of Psychoanalysis.* 86(3): 627–632.

Kohut, H. (1975) The future of psychoanalysis. *Annual of Psychoanalysis,* 3: 325–340.

Leonoff, A. (2021) *When Divorces Fail: Disillusionment, Destructivity and High Conflict Divorce.* New York: Rowman & Littlefield.

Mack, K. and Kaufman, J. (2013) *Freud's Mistress.* New York: Putnam.

Malcom, J. (1981) *Psychoanalysis: The Impossible Profession.* New York: Alfred A. Knopf.

McLuhan, M. (1967) *The Medium Is the Message.* New York: Penguin Books.

Nicoli, L. and Tugnoli, S. (2020) "Bringing the plague:" groundwork for a transformative outreach of psychoanalysis. *International Journal of Psychoanalysis.* 101(3): 549–571.

Pogrebin, R. (2008) In Madoff scandal, Jews feel an acute betrayal. *New York Times,* 23 December 2008. www.nytimes.com/2008/12/24/us/24jews.html.

Richards, A. (2015) Psychoanalysis in crisis: the danger of ideology. *Psychoanalytic Review.* 102(3): 389–405.

Wittels, F. (1933) Revision of a biography. *Psychoanalytic Review.* 20(4): 361–374.

Chapter 8

Technique at the crossroads

Cecilio Paniagua

Crossroads in psychoanalytic practice have been categorized in different ways throughout the history of our profession: "orthodox" analysis *vs.* dynamic psychotherapy; Freudian *vs.* Kleinian and neo-Kleinian analysis; ego psychology *vs.* deep psychology with its ensuing content interpretations; drive analysis *vs.* Sullivanian interpersonal understanding; classical *vs.* Kohutian self-psychology *cum* corrective emotional experiences; topographical *vs.* structural technique, etc. At our present time I think that the most topical (or raging) crossroad in the analysis of the clinical material could be considered the, so-called, *one-person vs. two-person*, intersubjective or relational approaches.

Psychoanalytic techniques are aimed at attaining improvement of the analysand's symptoms and character pathology through the exploration of unconscious conflicts. We all would agree on stressing the crucial importance of comprehending and interpreting the patient's memories and fantasies stemming from his/her childhood experiences and manifested in transference phenomena. Now, which technical approaches are more effective in securing this goal? I don't think the thesis is defensible that all our criteria should be considered equal since there are no totally objective findings: what Freud (1933) berated as "the anarchist theory" (p. 175).

Some analysts extol the virtues of a strict abstinence and anonymity, discarding their own emotional reactions in the sessions. Others, on the contrary, maintain that these reactions constitute a reliable reflection of the analysand's inner fantasies conveyed through the mechanism of projective identification. Some analysts uphold a sharp separation of the concept "countertransference" from the apperception of the analysand's dynamics. Others adduce that this *one-person* stand spells the concealment behind a false self that perpetuates the myth of the aloof, expressionless analyst. It needs to be said that extreme characterization of these positions as *one-person vs. two-person* approaches seems somewhat of a misnomer. Psychoanalysis can never be a solipsistic exercise. As Stern stressed, intersubjectivity is an omnipresent matrix in analysis (*cf.* Levin, 2021). Of course, any exchange between two human beings is bi-personal. The point to discuss, though, is whether examination of

DOI: 10.4324/9781003340744-10

the themes in a session refer to the analyst's own occurrences and fantasying or rather to the analysand's reminiscences and present material. Here, I think we should take for granted that in our clinical practice two minds are at work for the analysis of one of them. As Abrams and Shengold (1978) stated distinctly, the purpose of the bi-directional analytic encounter should be the exploration of the intrapsychic processes of one of the participants: the patient.

For the exploration of the material, the most neutral analyst always displays in his/her interventions a personal style and prosody and, certainly, all of his/her reactions will contain some combination of personal transference, role responsiveness, and average expectable reactions. The evaluation of the elements in this spectrum with sufficient reliability is probably the main task of the analyst's personal analysis in what concerns his/her clinical competency. The analyst's praxis should contribute to his/her own introspection, but I would say that this undertaking is none of the analysand's business. The examination of the analyst's affective or visual pictograms belongs to his/her self-inquiry. In Heimann's (1950) words, "(The analyst) will find ample stimulus for taking himself to task again and again, and for continuing the analysis of his own problems" (p. 83, quoted in Busch, 2021). Additionally, this can be helpful as a diagnostic tool (*cf.* Stefana et al. 2021). However, the clinical use of the analyst's reactions would seem legitimate only as inspiration to connect observable material coming from the patient with inferences based on previous findings, assuming that such endeavor does not transgress reasonable criteria of projective attribution (*cf.* Busch, 2000; 2010; 2019).

Some authors in the *one-person* field claim that a so-called, *two-person* technique invariably entails crass acting out on the part of the analyst. Not so. One issue is to show empathy and genuine interest in the patient's psychology, and another thing is to exaggerate its expression in the session. One issue is to entertain daydreams stirred by the analysand's discourse, and another thing is to counteract them as belonging to the latter's mentation. An example of the latter is the use of the analyst's reveries as a trustworthy discharge of the analysand's unconscious contents onto the analyst's personal associations (*cf.* Busch, 2018). To my mind, interpretations based on this interpersonal phenomenon represent a form of enactment that hinders the analyzability of the patient's subsequent associations due to their hybrid nature. To *promote* insights in patients is not the same as *providing* insights forged in the analyst's associations, appealing as the latter may be both for the practitioner's secret claims of omniscience and the patient's dependency wishes (*cf.* Paniagua, 2003).

Bionian authors defend the idea that an essential part of the analytic endeavor ought to center on the transformation of the patient's "non-digested" preverbal expressions into verbal symbols. Their subsequent interpretations then mix the analyst's associations with the patient's, complicating the elucidation of what fantasies belong to whom in the dyad, making the analysand "less bold in tackling his problems" (Weiss and Sampson, 1986, p. 237). When the analyst opts for basing his/her technical approach on this type of *a prioris* or pre-conceived points, he/she will inevitably introduce distortion in his/her conclusions. In Freud's (1912) words, "if [the analyst] follows his inclinations he will certainly falsify what he may perceive" (p. 112).

Heimann (1950) is often considered the pioneer of a technique grounded on deeming the analyst's inner states reliably homologous to the patient's. She wrote, "The analyst's unconscious understands that of his patient ... Often the emotions roused in [him] are much nearer to the heart of the matter than his reasoning" (p. 82). This certainly can be true, but why this dichotomy between the "emotions" and the "reasoning" of the analyst? Heimann seemed to be replicating Reik's (1948) advice of following one's intuitions with "inner sincerity" (p. 57), since "the response of the analyst is the emotional answer to the communications of the patient" (p. 62). This eventually led to a conceptualization of countertransference not as manifestation of the analyst's own unconscious, but as an intersubjective creation of the analytic couple, which eventually became a different entity from both participants: an "analytic third" (Ogden, 1994), a "chimera" (De M'Uzan, 2008), i.e., an entelechy additional to the two subjects present in the treatment, "an entity outside of their personal contribution" (Ogden, 1997, p. 589).

In 1953, Racker commented on the "remarkable coincidence" between the mental processes of the analyst and those of the analysand, concluding that it was necessary for the practitioner to fuse "the present and the past, the continuous and intimate connection of reality and fantasy, of external and internal, conscious and unconscious" into an all-embracing notion of "total countertransference" (1957, p. 311). Other Argentinean authors, like the Barangers (2008), asserted that "The bi-personal field is ... something created *between* the two [participants] ... in the moment of the session, radically different from what each of them is separately" (p. 806), considering the approach that aims at analyzing the patients' individual representations a "reduced and impoverished scheme," and therefore, "a methodological error" (p. 813). Ferro (2005) is of the opinion that the analyst should use his/her own dreams as metaphors for interpretations. Ogden (2017) stated that "Dreaming the analyst's session is an experience created by patient and analyst ... These dreams are the dreams of the unconscious analytic third created by patient and analyst" (p. 19). This author ended encouraging the analyst to manifest his/her "spontaneous" reactions to the patient's dreams, verbalizing unplanned interpretations that "feel true" (2016, p. 423). To me, all this comes too close to the idea of telepathy.

From a Kohutian perspective, Geist reminded us recently how "a self-psychological approach dramatically changes the ambiance between the analytic partners – from frustration to emotional connection" (in Shane and Carr, 2021, pp. 221–222). This is not an unusual occurrence; however, I would add that such "dramatic" shifts should not be considered an end in themselves, but rather a springboard for further analytic elaboration. The communication of what the analyst may appraise as "the relational moments ... that connect deeply and authentically … patient and therapist … more as humans rather than as professional and patient" are often remembered by analysands as "peak moments" (Békés and Hoffman, 2020, pp. 1052–1053). This unsurprising finding should make us wonder what kind of defenses were mobilized impeding them to perceive us as human enough in the first place.

Nowadays, a good number of analysts defend the idea that the treatment is incomplete when the practitioner does not explore *intersubjectively* his/her inner dialogues, confusion, and enactments, sharing with the analysand his/her personal urgencies, idiosyncratic fantasies, somatizations, inhibitions, silences, compulsions, insecurities, and aggressiveness. Greenson (1967) wrote that the outpouring of the analyst's personal feelings could be seen as "a caricature of honesty" (p. 209). The two-person, dual-track practice tends to make an inadequate differentiation between average expectable responses, projective identifications, and countertransference *vera*. Neyraut (1974) emphasized the inseparableness of countertransference from transference, viewing their relationship as necessarily dialectical, a notion favored by many French authors. I think that the concept of transference and countertransference as an aligned phenomenon interferes with the analysis of the patient's own dynamics, while familiarizing him/her with the practitioner's personal preferences. In my experience, this outlook tends also to make the analyst counter-resist self-analysis while promoting an indulgence in all-knowing wishes.

Indeed, conceptualizing our field of study as a "total situation" (Joseph, 1985) does not seem an innocuous idea. Kernberg (2011) warned of the risk of fusion and confusion implicit in the hypertrophied mix of projective identification with the analyst's subjective experiences. Busch (2021) referred to the automatic attunement between the analyst's reactions and the patient's unconscious as a utopia, stressing that this conviction should be considered a matter of ethical responsibility. In his *Technique* book, Greenson (1967) wrote, "Some analysts practice analysis which suits their personality; some use their patients to discharge their repressed desires … Some use technique to project, others to protect their personality" (p. 221). In 1951, Reich already remarked that the analyst's *preference of technique* definitely could be determined by his/her countertransference. In the application of our analytic technique, keeping these underlying notions a blurred conglomerate may lead the analyst to (1) maintain unexplored his/her core countertransference; (2) enhance grandiose beliefs in mind-reading faculties; (3) protect his/her professional narcissism; (4) reinforce idealization of esteemed teachers and school. All this benefits the practitioners, not their patients (Paniagua, 2012).

Against the conceptualization of "countertransference" as "all the feelings which the analyst experiences towards his patient" (Heimann, 1950, p. 81), Sandler (1976; 1987) was one of the most eloquent authors, writing on "role responsiveness" to the patient's projections as different from the analyst's idiosyncratic reactions, and pointing to the dangers of "wild countertransference analysis" (1993, p. 1104). A clinical approach based on the totalistic concept of countertransference sidesteps the practitioner's relative ignorance about the intricate (dystonic and syntonic) compromise formations in the patient's unconscious, sparing the analyst the mortification produced by the acknowledgement of blind spots (what McLaughlin, 1981, called "dumb spots"), while vouchsafing the narcissistic belief in the trustworthiness of intuitions. At the same time, all this usually gratifies dependency wishes in the regressed patient who feels in the hands of a parental all-knowing mind-reader, while his/her complicity with the analyst's bi-personal interpretations help him/her dodge painful conflicts. In his 1937 *Constructions* paper, Freud stated, "It may be convenient for the [analysand's] resistance to make use of an assent … in order to prolong the concealment of a truth that has not been discovered" (p. 262).

I was trained in a U.S. institute considered "classical". Years after the return to my hometown I felt somewhat disconcerted about the proliferation of "two-person" theories of technique that seemed quite discrepant from the Contemporary Ego Psychology one I learned. I was exposed to different psychoanalytic currents prevalent in Southern Europe, trying to learn from them as much as I could with an open mind, but not so open that the brain fell out! I think I succeeded in incorporating some theoretical notions in my conceptualizations and my teaching, but after immersing myself in numerous clinical examples in which the new relational techniques were used, I felt that no significant *aggiornamento* of my analytic *modus operandi* was necessary. Despite the time past and the cultural differences, attainment of an understanding of the mind in unconscious conflict still seemed optimal when using the old methodology that permitted a detailed exploration of needs, wishes, categorical imperatives and the adaptation to external realities. In my opinion, inclusion of some of the recommended intersubjective strategies interfered with an effective analysis of life-long character pathologies (Paniagua, 1999). To this day, I share Loewenstein's (1951) idea that the more an analytic technique focuses on the articulation of characterological defenses, the less the patient's discoveries tend to be dependent on the analyst's personal associations.

Now I will set forth what I consider advantageous in the practice of the, so-called, *one-person* ego psychoanalytic approach I learned long ago, using for the purpose a brief clinical vignette without detailed anamnestic data or description of complex dynamics. Hopefully, its discussion will throw some light on alternative interpretive styles in our technical crossroads.

An analysand of mine of many years complained bitterly in a session about his feelings of humiliation for his dependence on me when the only defense he could think of for asserting his masculine self-esteem was to be provocative like his father. Then he added that he had been re-reading Shakespeare lately and he found him to be "a son-of-a-bitch". In his judgement, this author's grand theatrical dramas were devoid of realistic understanding for human tribulations. His expletive (which, I feel, sounds even rougher in Spanish) took me by surprise and I laughed mutely. The patient heard my nasal giggling and did not find it funny. He chastised me for "ridiculing" him about his opinion that the great Bard received "unfair praise all over the world for the hysterically exaggerated characters in his tragedies". I had taken for granted that he shared with me the idea that his derogatory expression was deliberately grotesque. It was not the first time that an exchange like this took place, and we had chuckled together appropriately. However, on other occasions, like this one, my attempt at serving the therapeutic relationship with a modest chuckling backfired. I seemed to have a blind spot about his humorlessness in certain situations – food for my self-analysis.

I believe that smiling and occasional laughter – of course, not when the patient is describing a dramatic episode or when he/she is angry – is part of "[sensing] that one's analyst is a real person out there" (Hall, 2021). I also realize that this manifestation of humanness on the part of the analyst can be seen as a *faux pas* depending on its intensity and the subcultural milieu. I remember that in my training in the U.S. one of my supervisors pointed out that the smiling, through which I tried to convey empathy and good will, could be seen as excessive by the patient. However, in my own society I consider it an average expectable response most of the time. On this occasion with my analysand, a different meaning of my chuckling dawned on me. I ended seeing in it an aspect of condescension which led me to reflect on a self-protective maneuver at a particular time in my life. Perhaps I tried to take partially as empathic reinforcement of the therapeutic alliance an unconscious stratagem aimed at hiding a countertransferential defense of mine.

Countertransference is an inevitable phenomenon that requires understanding and control by the analyst. To deny its existence is often fatal for the analysis, but to be swept by it is equally pernicious. Certainly, the fact that its intraclinical manifestation can be an obstacle to treatment does not mean that the concept can be dispensed with. As Spitz (1956) pointed out, problems arise not from the existence of countertransference, but from its acting out. The bi-personal relation with our patients prompts us to become aware of our countertransferential reactions, indeed. Racker (1957) stated, "[countertransference] may be the greatest danger and at the same time an important tool for understanding" (p. 303). For instance, this patient's utterance made me aware of some irreverent floating thoughts of mine comparing Othello, Lear, or Hamlet with characters from some Spanish classics. This idiosyncratic and prejudiced musing could have contributed to spark off my chuckling.

How should I have responded to this analysand's reproachful reaction? Was my mild chuckling really an appropriate response in my subcultural milieu? Was I repeating automatically some pattern learned in my own upbringing? Was the patient trying to shock me with his expression, and if so, how could this subject be broached, and to what extent was his reaction analyzable? I was well aware by then of his pent-up rage and his vengeful disdain for transference authority figures. This patient described the father of his childhood as demanding, punitive, and devoid of compassion, and he had a hard time seeing in me a stance or traits other than "new editions or facsimiles" (Freud, 1905, p. 116) of past experiences. He sensed I was driven by a wish to demean and ridicule him from my imaginary pedestal of masculine superiority. I thought he could be attempting to disconcert me through his reprimand, bringing me down to his level of past humiliations. I will discuss my reflections on this very brief vignette with further comments on the technical choice of paths in this clinical crossroad.

I could have remained silent, waiting for further associations that expanded his feelings about my chuckling and his response to it. I could have reminded him of similar past reactions in his interactions with me in order to identify additional transference displacements. I could have explored further his touchiness and the defensive nature of his annoyance on this occasion. Aware of how often he felt attacked or ridiculed, I could have tried to analyze what seemed an unusual opportunity for his reversing our roles. Possibly, I could have touched on his Oedipal rivalry with me. I could have asked him about further associations concerning Shakespearian characters. I could have alluded to his envy of accomplished men which became apparent in many previous occasions. I could have pointed out that he disqualified a gigantic author right after a painful mention of his perceived inferiority compared with his father and me. All of this with variable degrees of depth, perspicacity, empathy, close-process attention to the fluctuation of his defenses, and assessment of his receptivity, while I tried to call the register of my own peculiarities. I consider these possibilities consonant with a *one-person* technique.

Following what I understand to be a *two-person* approach, I could have told the patient also about (impromptu or deliberate) associations of mine at the moment, or about cognitive and emotional memories, either related to my childhood or my recent past. Also, I could have shared with him some fantasies, reveries, or "counter-dreams" (Bergstein, 2013) of mine, following Bion's (1962) dictum that the analyst should share with the patient the dreams that he/she cannot dream. Moreover, I could have voiced experiences about subcultural comparisons, as well as my knowledge of literature, manifesting myself as more "real". All this with the double purpose of showing my "humanness" *and* making purportedly a deeper connection with his unconscious. However, such an approach would have provided him with unnecessary extraneous material for associations, true, not devoid of "genuine qualities" (Tauber, 1954). The problem here was that he would have mixed then this knowledge about my ideas and inclinations with his own associations as justification for defensive intellectualizations. Without any doubt, this participation on the part of the analyst would have colored significantly the subsequent material related to his anger, envy, and persecutory feelings related to his own biographical experiences, thus hampering the analysis of transferential phenomena.

I think that interpretations based on this type of self-disclosures, often rationalized as empathy (or "concordant identification" in Racker's [1957] typification), represent an anti-analytic concession that inevitably weakens the exploration of the patient's original fantasies. Nevertheless, they seem attractive due to their implicit gratifications for both, analyst and analysand. As Shane and Carr (2021) stated, "This kind of bi-directional, relational experience provides the patient a sense of feeling understood that is strengthening to the patient's sense of self. And it helps the therapist bear confusion, uncertainty, and anxiety that could be overwhelming" (p. 222). Indeed, the analyst can discharge parts of his/her countertransference load, feeling at the same time influential and helpful. Simultaneously, the patient, under the magnetic spell of suggestion in a setting that fosters regression, is induced to an immersion into the atmosphere of the omnipotent parental figure whose ascendancy he/she yearned – all this despite the occasional irritation for the analyst's intrusiveness. No wonder that some applications of a *two-person* method turn out to be an appealing resource, making us forget that said gratifications are made at the expense of the patient's achievement of deeper insights. The following comment – or confession – from Winnicott (1969) comes to mind: "It appalls me to think how much change I have prevented or delayed in patients ... by my personal need to interpret" (p. 86).

To me, many of the clinical examples described in our literature about using *two-person* approaches sound like a return to square one, i.e., obliviousness of the powerful and omnipresent role of suggestion typical of the pre-analytic talking cures and the topographical technique (Paniagua, 2001). Grünbaum's (1980) contention that the suggestive factor can never be completely eliminated is so true, but why not try our best? The main issue I am attempting to raise here is that for the minimization of the irrational influence of suggestion, not all technical methods were born equal, since not all facilitate optimally a veracious approximation to our field of study: the analysand's complex unconscious realities.

I think that *abstinence, neutrality,* and *anonymity* (not to be mistaken with detachment, remoteness, indifference, or haughtiness) still should play a fundamental role in our profession. In our web-times anonymity has become more difficult, indeed, and it is utopian anyway to think that analysands will not notice realistically personal traits of ours, especially in long treatments. But why shouldn't these perceptions plus the ensuing associations and allusions suffice? Why complicate matters further with inappropriate disclosures? And, granted, a strict application of the above triad would be inappropriate in cases that are *not* psychoanalytic. We need to bear in mind that the *raison d'être* for said technical rules is to bring about an exploration as pristine as possible of the patient's transference, and this aim is not always a priority in many psychotherapies where supportive measures and interpersonal influence ought to be employed significantly.

I favor interventions based on Freud's structural theory that seem more ego-syntonic and digestible to the analysand. With the years, I have become more convinced of the remarkable efficacy of those "low level" interpretations that Bibring (1954) labeled *clarifications*, which facilitate the patient's expansion of his/her own production. The result of their use often surprises the analyst for the depth, newness, and completeness of the patient's responses (Paniagua, 2006). In the case I described, instead of addressing my interventions to his fear of "unmasculine" dependency, his homosexual longings, or his unbearable feelings of humiliation, I preferred to address his attention to his difficulty in the working through the reasons for his irritation. Patients' timely discovery of their own multidetermined truths seems more reliable and therapeutically more effective. Resistance analysis still seems to me the best way to explore the compromise formations between forces and defensive counterforces that eventually became the character traits the patient had to arrive to during the formative years of his/her psychic life. I think that this endeavor still constitutes the essence of clinical psychoanalysis.

References

Abrams, S. and Shengold, L. (1978) Some reflections on affects and the psychoanalytic situation. *International Journal of Psychoanalysis*. 59: 395–407.

Baranger, M. and Baranger, W. (1969) *Problemas del Campo Analítico*. Buenos Aires: Kargieman.

Baranger, M. and Baranger, W. (2008) The analytic situation as a dynamic field. *International Journal of Psychoanalysis*. 89: 795–826.

Békés, V. and Hoffman, L. (2020) The "something more" than working alliance: authentic relational moments. *Journal of the American Psychoanalytic Association*. 68: 1051–1064.

Bergstein, A. (2013) Transcending the caesura: reverie, dreaming and counterdreaming. *International Journal of Psychoanalysis*. 94: 621–644.

Bibring, E. (1954) Psychoanalysis and the dynamic psychotherapies. *Journal of the American Psychoanalytic Association*. 2: 745–770.

Bion, W.R. (1962) *Learning from Experience*. London: Heinemann.

Busch, F. (2000) What is a deep interpretation? *Journal of the American Psychoanalytic Association*. 48: 237–254.

Busch, F. (2010) Distinguishing psychoanalysis from psychotherapy. *International Journal of Psychoanalysis*. 91: 23–34.

Busch, F. (2018) Searching for the analyst's reveries. *International Journal of Psychoanalysis*. 99: 569–589.

Busch, F. (2019) *The Analyst's Reveries: Exploration's in Bion's Enigmatic Concept*. New York: Routledge.

Busch. F. (2021) Responsible countertransference (unpublished manuscript).

De M'Uzan, M. (2008) *La Chimère des Inconscients*. Paris: Presse Universitaires de France.

Ferro, A. (2005) Four sessions with Lisa. *International Journal of Psychoanalysis*. 86: 1247–1256.

Freud, S. (1905) Fragment of an analysis of a case of hysteria. *The Standard Edition of the Complete Psychological Works of Sigmund Freud*. 7: 7–122.

Freud, S. (1912) Recommendations to physicians practicing psycho-analysis. *The Standard Edition of the Complete Psychological Works of Sigmund Freud*. 12: 109–120.

Freud, S. (1933) New introductory lectures on psycho-analysis. *The Standard Edition of the Complete Psychological Works of Sigmund Freud*. 22: 5–182.

Freud, S. (1937) Constructions in analysis. *The Standard Edition of the Complete Psychological Works of Sigmund Freud*. 23: 255–269.

Greenson, R.R. (1967) *The Technique and Practice of Psychoanalysis*. New York: International Universities Press.

Grünbaum, A. (1980) Epistemological liabilities of the clinical appraisal of psycho-analytic theory. *Noûs*: 14(3): 307–385.

Hall, J. (2021) ApsA MEM, 5 March.

Heimann, P. (1950) On countertransference. *International Journal of Psychoanalysis*. 31: 81–84.

Joseph, B. (1985) Transference: the total situation. *International Journal of Psychoanalysis*. 66: 447–454.

Kernberg, O.F. (2011) Divergent contemporary trends in psychoanalytic theory. *Psychoanalytic Review*. 98: 633–664.

Levin, C. (2021) Addendum. ApsaA MEM, 26 March.

Loewenstein, R.M. (1951) The problem of interpretation. *Psychoanalytic Quarterly*. 20: 1–14.

McLaughlin, J.T. (1981) Transference, psychic reality, and countertransference. *Psychoanalytic Quarterly*. 50: 639–664.

Neyraut, M. (1974) *Le Transfert*. Paris: Presse Universitaires de France.

Ogden, T.H. (1994) The analytic third: working with intersubjective clinical facts. *International Journal of Psychoanalysis*. 75: 3–19.

Ogden, T.H. (1997) Reverie and interpretation. *Psychoanalytic Quarterly*. 66: 567–595.

Ogden, T.H. (2016) On language and truth in psychoanalysis. *Psychoanalytic Quarterly*. 85: 411–426.

Ogden, T.H. (2017) Dreaming the analytic session: a clinical essay. *Psychoanalysis Quarterly*. 86: 1–20.

Paniagua, C. (1999) Das konzept der intersubjetivität –einige kritische Bemerkungen. *Psyche*. 53: 958–971.

Paniagua, C. (2001) The attraction of the topographical model. *International Journal of Psychoanalysis*. 82: 671–684.

Paniagua, C. (2003) Problems with the concept "interpretation". *International Journal of Psychoanalysis*. 84: 1105–1123.

Paniagua, C. (2006) Técnica interpretativa y la sorpresa del analista. *Revista de Psicoanálisis*. LXIII(1): 163–178.

Paniagua, C. (2012) Countertransference: a confusing concept. *Oedipus*. 8: 391–406.

Racker, H. (1953) A contribution to the problem of countertransference. *International Journal of Psychoanalysis*. 34: 313–324.

Racker, H. (1957) The meanings and uses of countertransference. *Psychoanalytic Quarterly*. 26: 303–356.

Reich, A. (1951) On countertransference. *International Journal of Psychoanalysis*. 32: 25–31.

Reik, T. (1948) The surprised analyst. In: B. Wolstein (editor). *Essential Papers On Countertransference*. New York: New York University Press, 1988, pp. 51–63.

Sandler, J. (1976) Countertransference and role responsiveness. *International Review of Psychoanalysis*. 3: 43–47.

Sandler, J. (editor) (1987) *Projection, Identification, Projective Identification*. Madison, CT: International Universities Press.

Sandler, J. (1993) On communication from patient to analyst: not everything is projective identification. *International Journal of Psychoanalysis*. 74: 1097–1107.

Shane, E. and Carr, E.M. (2021) Afterward – the many faces of self psychology: two reflective essays. *Psychoanalytic Inquiry*. 41: 213–226.

Spitz, R.A. (1956) Countertransference comments on its varying role in the analytic situation. *Journal of the American Psychoanalytic Association*. 4: 256–265.

Stefana, A., Hinshelwood, R.D., and Borensztejn, C.L. (2021) Racker and Heimann on countertransference: similarities and differences. *Psychoanalytic Quarterly*. 90: 105–137.

Tauber, E.S. (1954) Exploring the therapeutic use of countertransference data. *Psychiatry*. 17: 331–336.

Weiss, J. and Sampson, H. (1986) *The Psychoanalytic Process*. New York: Guilford.

Winnicott, D.W. (1969) The use of an object and relating through identifications. In: *Playing and Reality*. New York: Basic Books, 1971, pp. 86–94.

Chapter 9

Those who listen

Harvey Schwartz

During the period after World War II there was an influx of clinicians seeking psychoanalytic training. This was said to be the result of many having observed and worked with senior analysts in their wartime caring for soldiers and veterans. The younger generation felt that there was something different about how the analysts engaged with and thought about their patients. The oft quoted refrain was "The psychoanalysts knew things that the others didn't." This comports with what many of us have rediscovered over the years. In our addressing our field's future we need to revisit these questions. What is it that we know? What is it that we bring that's unique to those who seek our healing? Are we in fact healers and if so of what particular sort? We know that our clinical task is one of healing. We also know that the likelihood of that occurring is diminished if we assume the mantle of being the healer. More about this later.

I'd like to begin by approaching this from a wide-angle perspective. It isn't at all obvious to the general population, those who might seek treatment, that we psychoanalysts have something to offer, much less something unique. For as long as that remains the case our future is precarious. Many other practitioners fill the airwaves with their new treatments that promise to relieve suffering. Further, new biological discoveries are revealing hidden aspects of our bodies that are as revolutionary today as the discovery of the hidden aspects of our minds were a century ago. The exciting findings emerging from this project, the research on the mind/body connection, are leading many to approach the mind primarily through the body. These newly recognized physical forces within our soma are being demonstrated to impact our mood, our health, and our longevity (Cryan et al., 2019).

There is currently a revolution in medicine that is emerging from the awareness that there are vastly more cells in our body that are not human than are and they belong to the microbiome. The presence of these microbes – bacteria, viruses, and fungi – and their biologically active metabolites impact every facet of our life including the likelihood of our becoming depressed (Chinna Meyyappan et al., 2020), getting cancer (Suraya et al., 2020), and

DOI: 10.4324/9781003340744-11

succumbing to Alzheimer's disease (Sun et al., 2020). We are just at the beginning of understanding these forces and of then being able to engage them therapeutically. Interventional studies using fecal microbiota transplants (Antushevich, 2020), as well as pre- and pro-biotic supplements (Amirani, 2020), are beginning to show results in preventing and treating a remarkably wide variety of illnesses. Dietary changes have also demonstrated an ability to impact our microbiome and from that to prevent and ameliorate illness (Wang et al., 2021).

I don't intend these few words on the vast area of the microbiome to be a diversion from our topic of the crossroads and future of psychoanalysis. We do though exist in the twenty-first century and we must recognize the state of research in the caretaking professions within which we function. The microbiome is perhaps the most fundamental change we live in but certainly not the only one. Psychedelic medicines have been demonstrated to offer important relief to those suffering from depression (Bouso et al., 2020), addiction (Nutt et al., 2020), post traumatic states (Krediet et al., 2020), and in those who are dying (Bernstein, 2020). In addition, mindfulness training (Querstret et al., 2020), reduction in inflammation (Gialluisi, 2020), and breathing practices that increase parasympathetic functioning (Brown et al., 2013) are all promising interventions that are being turned to by individuals seeking relief of their distress.

Our future as analysts is to live among these and other unforeseen new developments. We must demonstrate that we have something unique to offer beyond the comfort of providing attentive listening. We can fill our office hours with those who simply wish to be heard manifestly. However, there are many practitioners who can offer this service, and do, who are not trained in psychoanalysis. Are we different?

Back to our foundation. It must start with the relationship. Ours is one that is uniquely and peculiarly both literal and metaphoric, predictable and illusory. This is our calling card; this is what we do that no one else does. This is what makes analytic work different from cognitive treatment and pre-biotic supplements – as useful as they may be. We offer a relationship that is healing through our capacity to remain ambiguous. Not ambiguous about our interest in the well-being of our analysand. Just ambiguous about what it is that we are attuned to – the music, not the notes. This present though elusive quality of our encounter, shorthanded as "neutrality," is famously seductive and is best brought forth with those who can play in such a symbolizing arena. Like all potentially life-changing treatments, there are side effects if applied without care. Especially for those who were raised with lacunae in their experience of dependable trust, a mostly metaphoric analytic presence can awaken more terror than reflection. As such, it needs careful titration and inevitably entails misjudgments in both directions. Indeed, the ongoing recalibration of our illusory presence can yield vital insights into analysands' histories.

If our peculiarly analytic presence is a vehicle for our healing efforts, how does that come about? What is it about serving as a container, one albeit with flexible walls, that we claim offers so much to our analysands? To approach this, we must begin with our own minds. I mentioned earlier a caution about assuming the role of the healer least we compromise our freedom to be received as idiosyncratically as our patient's imaginings will allow. This studied caution and the self-consciousness it reflects is our instrument of attentiveness to the latent experiences of the other. This self-awareness is different from those therapies that limit their attention to manifest level-thinking processes. It is also different from the ruminative self-consciousness that characterizes our inhibited patients. Their sense of self-awareness is defined by a view of themselves as seen in the projected eyes of an accusatory other. In contrast, ours is a self-consciousness oriented towards our engagement with the "other". It operates through maintaining our interest in our own reactions to patients' various enticements rather than either ignoring them or seeking to gratify them for our own needs. We listen to ourselves in order to better hear our patients. Any fixed self-representation we would maintain, healer or otherwise, would be in service of personal satisfaction and would obstruct our fluid attunement to the necessarily ever-changing inner imaginings that emerge from within our analysands. This capacity for even hovering availability currently goes by the term *reverie* – an apt characterization of our uniquely multi-faceted intimacy.

Still the question remains, what is it about this poetic state of mind that facilitates new freedoms in those in our care? For that, we must now turn to how they react to our inviting presence. Of course, patients can only engage us as they characteristically do. That is, with their own unknowing seduction to draw us into their familiar schemas organized by their version of their past. It is at such moments that a particular analytic encounter occurs. It is precisely when they live out with us in a manner based on their assumption that we are a familiar internal object that our availability as a novel metaphoric presence proves invaluable. We are a familiar object and we are not. We are warmly interested in their discomfort at our unavailability to serve that familiar role. Our commitment is to provide words for this new and creative opportunity.

New experience is such a laden notion that we should spend a moment on it. This encounter where we are expected quite naturally to be in the patient's familiar scenario catches them short. After all, their life as all of ours is built upon such assumptions. They came to us for change – but not *that* kind of change. They didn't know they had such assumptions, syntonic as they are – like "water to a fish" – and they certainly had no sense that they were modifiable. We are in this moment with the patient where they are certain, even without knowing it, that we evaluate them, feel retaliatory towards them, find them repugnant, etc. When we bring this projected latent conviction to their attention, we discover that it is quite adhesive. It turns out that despite it being a source of distress they are quite attached to it. So much so that in the face of our generally not having demonstrated such negativity towards them, they will still choose it over the *uncertainty* associated with our being an external benevolent object with an interest in knowing them. Our relating to them autonomously from their assumptions creates a space for new experiencing. This is where we get to know their history of assumed dangers that they have associated with attachment, dependency, and affections towards those registered as separate from them. Through trial and error in these realms they slowly come to recognize that tolerating the uncertain possibilities in our relationship opens up their own world of possibilities. Freeing us from any assigned roles does the same for them. This is what we have to offer.

In the face of our presence as a related someone with new possibilities for how they experience themselves and others, we encounter what are called *resistances*. It is such an unfortunate term. Unfortunate because it is so easy to confuse our term *resistance* with the colloquial term resistance. This latter word is defined as "the refusal to accept or comply with something: the attempt to prevent something by action or argument" (Google, 2022). If we confuse *resistance* with resistance, we would be reinforcing the patient's self-critical inclination to focus on manifest opposition rather than on layered and latent meaning.

Simply put, our meaning of *resistance* is that it is the best way a patient has available to them to represent their affects, fantasies, and reality considerations at a particular moment in time. It is a compromise for these intrapsychic elements in as adaptable form as they are capable. It is our charge to demonstrate how they contain yet-to-be-realized possibilities for their more authentic future. It is, though, their best effort *at this time* to be present and object-related. This is wholly distinct from the everyday meaning of resistance. That refers to a binary oppositional mindset that is limited to distracting provocation.

An analyst functions by being able to simultaneously tolerate patients' seductions to represent themselves in the unidimensional manner of resistance while also keeping present a curious sense of them as struggling with multifaceted *resistance*. Analysands themselves more or less live in the world of experiencing themselves as resisting. In contrast, the analyst endeavors to be cognitively and emotionally in tune with the underlying elements of *resistance* that are always in operation. This is our way of keeping in our minds a sense of their potentials. By our piecemeal analysis of the components of their *resistance*, especially as it emerges in relation to the transference, we facilitate their discovery of their inner complexity and nuance. This is the case, for example, with acting out and acting in. They are *resistances* that are containers of meaning, compromise, and communication. Both patients and non-analysts view them as resistances – badnesses that need to stop. Our perspective on this is the gift of psychoanalysis – initially, for analysands to learn that they have a defensive structure and then to come to recognize its particulars including its history. This is our unique healing ability.

It gets more personal than that. The act of maintaining in our reverie those elements that belong to the analysand's manifest self-representations while also experiencing their latent *resistances* requires an investment of more than just intellectual fortitude. Our capacity to do so floats on an emotional investment in their well-being. This is where Glover's felicitous phrase "the true unconscious attitude" (1937) of the analyst proves pivotal. To tolerate the often difficult tension between the analysand's manifest insistences and their latent conflicts requires a good deal of caring, of a particular sort. Further, as treatment progresses, patients will find themselves in the midst of what is a confusing though therapeutic shift of self-awareness. This entails a progression in their sense of self and time whereby timeless repetition slowly gives way to vulnerable temporality. They come to experience that their biological lives are in fact moving through time and it is not endless. This creative awakening will more likely deepen if they have a sense that they are not alone in the process. The dangers that they presume lurk in leaving their syntonic waters behind will be lessened if they feel a link to an understanding and available partner, however layered that may be. This too requires the analyst's affective availability. Those analysands who can register to at least some degree their analyst's accessible benevolence have a better chance of building on and with it. Those who register even this background attentiveness as danger-filled face a more precarious future.

There's more than this particular version of caring that distinguishes us from other practitioners in the future mental health marketplace. As mentioned, we work clinically in the distinction between patients' manifest self-awareness and their latent conflictual life through our knowledge of their mind and our internal registration of their potential future. We interpretively invite the patient to share in our curiosity about their defensive style. This enables us to recognize that they have a defensive structure, its nature, and with that its history. We discover with them that their protective constructs, their *resistances*, carry their early life history in holographic form – each particular aspect links to a constellation of childhood perceived difficulties.

Our attitude of curiosity about these compromised formations orients the analysand towards our accepting mindset. This includes our receptivity towards those hidden aspects of their minds, that which they withhold from themselves, that are deeply shameful to them. Our interest in these presumptively humiliating and forbidden imaginings is no more or less pressing than our interest in their obscuring mechanisms. For example, when we are faced with the varieties of sado-masochism that present to us, in both its pre- and post-triangulation iterations, our attention is on the obscuring forces as well as on the hidden overstimulations and desires that are being obscured. This balanced curiosity, an essence of neutrality, introduces such a capacity for the analysand to discover within themselves.

It is through the here and now recognition of patients' transference-organized inhibitions, their past-living-in-their-present, that we engage their capacity to observe the static nature of time within which they have been existing.[1] Unbeknownst to them and through our careful and caring analysis of their historically driven defensive organization, we awaken them to the needless limitations in their constricted current functioning. In this manner, we together free time, more or less, from its childhood adhesiveness. With the repeated trial of new capacities and freedoms of thought in the transference, creative potentials can be actualized. This too marks a unique aspect of the healing of depth treatment.

However, when we endeavor to clinically engage those who seek our care but are without histories of safe attachments that would enable them to receive it, we are faced with an encounter of a different sort. Our attentive interest along with our insightful observations lack the traction with which to awaken their curiosity. Now *resistances* are indeed resistances – all or nothing demands to meet their presumed needs in the here and now.

Words are essentially actions mostly lacking in metaphoric capacity. The analytic playing field has moved from the co-created "third" to our guts. The analysand's internal life is now lived inside us in the projected traumas and part objects of their forgotten past. They unknowingly have assigned us their historical victim role and vengeance is now theirs. When, in the face of this, we are able to, albeit imperfectly, hold on to our good internal objects in order to survive the at times painful nuanced assault on our benevolence, we can continue to offer the possibility of healing. Our capacity at such times to maintain our object relatedness offers these individuals a novel counterweight to their otherwise self and other alienation. It maintains the possibility of their (re)connecting with their own positive self-representations.

Off the couch – in the community

The capacity to observe and tolerate these projected distortions of our core intentions is a fundamental, though difficult, analytic competency. It is vital when endeavoring to make contact with ego-limited and traumatized individuals. It is also an essential tool when applying our analytic mindset in venues "off the couch." The challenge for us in these alternative settings is to appreciate the presence and impact of current-day destructive forces *in their own right* as influencers on intrapsychic processes. The temptation has been to consider them significant only to the extent that they reverberate with childhood perceptions and events. This may prove to be mostly the case. However, in weighing the question, we need to be aware of the comfort we collect in sparing ourselves something of the vulnerability of sharing adult-onset danger and violence. We've all learned from the pandemic how powerful our simultaneous immersion in current danger is on the analytic process. We also have learned of its association with childhood fears.

This work outside the office can also represent an aspect of our profession's future. It raises the question, though, what is it exactly that we analysts can bring to these "off the couch" settings that facilitates healing? The obstacles are obvious and many. These encounters take place in the outside world, which is endowed with literalness, i.e., refugee centers, hospitals, prisons, community clinics, etc. It is where the pressing external forces, often overwhelming, are at least initially without representation and sit ripe for externalizations. Time is only *now*. It is often challenging for anyone so afflicted to come to consider how these elements of reality also function as *resistances*. To repeat, this is the case as well for ego-limited analysands in the office. There, in our familiar setting, the likelihood of the healing hinges on our maintaining a connection with our good internal objects despite pressures to the contrary. Such holding introduces a similar potential for these struggling patients. They too, through repetitive trial, have the opportunity to discover their own version of good internal object in the face of projected danger. For some, after long periods of shared literalness, pockets of metaphoric imagery become recognizable, allowing for more nuanced self-awareness and relatedness. These nascent capacities facilitate the transformation, in the transference, of literal imitation to more autonomous identification.

It may be that we can learn from this manner of work with "on the couch" ego-limited individuals who *endow* their environments with destructiveness and apply it "off the couch" with those who live in environments that are *actually* destructive. Our analytic capacity to maintain internal attachments of a benevolent sort is for both the first step in helping someone outside of us to locate *hope*. It's important that this internal function of ours exists in some sort of sharable form. The co-participated positive transference in the form of *hope* is an essential discovery for those who struggle to survive in war, with cancer, and in pandemics. It introduces a background of affection and gratitude that are the building blocks for the capacity to symbolize. Symbolization in place of often covert dissociation is vital for those with untrustworthy backgrounds as well as for those overwhelmed by current-day trauma. Such efforts of ours link us with those of the benevolent clergy who have been a source of comfort to vast numbers of people throughout the millennia.[2] Such interdisciplinary considerations could lead us as well to be interested in the substantial neurophysiologic changes that have been demonstrated to underlie the effectiveness of placebo interventions (Frisaldi et al., 2020). This data may elucidate the biologic basis for the healing impact of our foundational "other" orientation.

In essence, our core and differentiating healing ability is built upon our capacity to be affectively interested in the latent conflicts, imaginings, and potentials of those who present for our care. For those patients lacking a history of dependable trust our attentiveness may elicit suspiciousness. Our metabolizing of this self-protective paranoia into its elements that contain object hunger offers the individual the possibility of discovering safe attachments. Alternatively, for the neurotically struggling individual, the more playful third space allows for a less tumultuous analytic arena within which we can both engage in productive reverie.

Only clinicians who have struggled to co-discover these regressive states of mind within themselves are in a position to make them available to those in their care. Our ability to experience, observe, and reflect on these countertransferences is what allows us to put them in service of the "other". This "in service to the other" relatedness offers a background context of healing in all treatments. It is the ground upon which our analytic figure takes shape. For some patients who can make use of additional interventions, the particular information that we are able to glean through our self-awareness allows us also to relate to them interpretively. Nevertheless, this "other" orientation, elaborated upon by Levinas (1961), is the crucible of our clinical focus. The rest, as it is said, is commentary.

I would like to add two caveats to this capacity. I note a tendency in our profession to at times "turn a symptom into a virtue." I'm referring to the occasions when we valorize the act of becoming distracted by theoretical constructs when faced with an awkward clinical exchange. These are the situations when after making an interpretive intervention one experiences a sudden onset of self-conscious concern such as "Is this analytic?" or "Is this properly Freudian, Kleinian, etc?" These questions are often taken seriously on their face. What would ordinarily be easily recognized as a countertransference restriction is otherwise bypassed if theory is in the content. At such moments, analytic listening is being attenuated – anxiety about one's group allegiance emerges and is not recognized as the countertransference distraction that it is. The skill of testing the usefulness of one's interventions by following patients' associations to it is in fact what defines our engagement as psychoanalytic. It is that attentiveness that we strive to offer – the relinquishment of our self-focused gratification of "being analytic" and instead maintaining, to the best of our capacity at any moment, a persistent analytic interest in the experience of the "other."

My emphasis on the "other"-oriented benevolence as an essential aspect of our clinical care draws us to recognize those areas where other forces imbalance us. That is true in the consulting room certainly but more obvious outside of it. I'm referring to the well-known and peculiar characteristic of psychoanalytic organizations where the attunement with which we engage analysands stands in sharp contrast to our attitude towards colleagues with whom we disagree. Multiple and conflicting perspectives are, of course, vital within any living profession. I'm referring not to differing points of view but to the disregard for decency which often characterizes such psychoanalytic disagreements. Ad homonem abuse may usefully remind us of the universality of splitting but nevertheless burdens our discourse with a suffocating cloud of malevolence. It may be that this predilection of ours is especially inviting in the absence of theory-specific outcome data that would otherwise ground us in greater modesty.

To conclude with a return to my opening historical recounting of when military psychoanalysts were recognized as "knowing something that the others didn't." I'd like to enrich this perhaps screen memory through an associative personal recollection.

I was sitting in a case conference with an analyst presenter with both analysts and non-analysts as observers. The patient being described was especially awkward. Those around the conference table were invited to comment on the clinical process that was being presented. As usual in such settings the reflections varied in their degree of thoughtfulness. I noted the content of the differing comments and it certainly occurred to me that the analysts in the group "knew something that the others didn't." That observation, however, was short lived. What caught my attention was something else. I noticed that some clinicians in the room were laughing at the oddities of the patient. They were laughing *at* the patient. *They were snickering.* As I looked around the table it was clear to me that there was something different about the attitude of the analysts. It wasn't simply that they knew something that the others didn't. It was that their attitude towards the struggling patient was different.

I suggest that this is the quality that drew the young military clinicians to wish to identify with their analyst teachers. I suggest that this is the quality that analysts have to offer those who seek our care that indeed makes us different from other clinicians. I see this quality as defining our crossroad and assuring our future. There will always be a place for healers. There will always be those who will seek out those who are different. They don't snicker. *They listen.*

Acknowledgments

I would like to express my appreciation to my colleagues who carefully read and generously commented on earlier drafts of this chapter. I'm grateful for their thoughtfulness.

Notes

1 Odors can stimulate tracts in the brain that elicit with uncanny immediacy and literalness specific memories and images from one's past. However, the brain pathways for non-olfactory stimulated remembering are not as direct (Guangyu, 2021). Perhaps then, the analyst's presence along with her interpretive focus are necessary to facilitate for the patient the linkage between present-day transference rhythms with the past memories that they encode.

2 While our approach shares elements of support with the clergy, unlike them, our goal is to return to the individual the full array of affects that are otherwise externalized on to their priests and deities. Ultimately, our intent is to help facilitate their ownership of their empowering creativity freed as much as possible from the denial of our human helplessness.

References

Amirani, E., Milajerdi, A., Mirzaei, H., Jamilian, H., Ali Mansournia, M., Hallajzadeh, J., and Ghaderi, A. (2020) The effects of probiotic supplementation on mental health, biomarkers of inflammation and oxidative stress in patients with psychiatric disorders: A systematic review and meta-analysis of randomized controlled trials. *Complementary Therapies in Medicine.* 49: 102361. doi: 10.1016/j.ctim.2020.102361. PMID: 32147043.

Antushevich, H. (2020) Fecal microbiota transplantation in disease therapy. *Clinica Chimica Acta.* 503: 90–98.

Bernstein, I. (2020) At the intersection of palliative care, psychedelic medicine, and healthcare reform: a call for a new hospice and palliative care movement. *Journal of Palliative Care.* 37(2): 93–96. doi: 10.1177/0825859720946898. PMID: 32752931.

Bouso, J.C., Ona, G., Dos Santos, R.G., Hallak, J.E.C. (2021) Psychedelic medicines in major depression: progress and future challenges. In: Kim, YK. (editor) *Major Depressive Disorder. Advances in Experimental Medicine and Biology.* 1305: 515–533. Springer: Singapore. doi: 10.1007/978-981-33-6044-0_26. PMID: 33834416.

Brown, R.P., Gerbarg, P.L., and Muench, F. (2013) Breathing practices for treatment of psychiatric and stress-related medical conditions. *Psychiatric Clinic of North America.* 36(1): 121–140.

Chinna Meyyappan, A., Forth, E., Wallace, C.J.K., et al. (2020) Effect of fecal microbiota transplant on symptoms of psychiatric disorders: a systematic review. *BMC Psychiatry.* 20: 299.

Cryan, J.F., O'Riordan, K.J., Cowan, C.S.M., Sandhu, K.V., et al. (2019) Review: the microbiota-gut-brain axis. 1. *Physiological Reviews.* 99(4): 28.

Frisaldi, E., Shaibani, A., and Benedetti, F. (2020) Understanding the mechanisms of placebo and nocebo effects. *Swiss Medical Weekly.* 1: 150.

Gialluisi, A. Bonaccio, M., Di Castelnuovo, A., Costanzo, S., De Curtis, A., Sarchiapone, M., Cerletti, C., Donati, M.B., de Gaetano, G., and Iacoviello, L. (2020) Lifestyle and biological factors influence the relationship between mental health and low-grade inflammation. *Brain, Behavior, and Immunity.* 85: 4–13.

Glover, E. (1937) Symposium in the theory of the therapeutic results of psychoanalysis. *International Journal of Pharmaceutics.* 18: 125–189.

Google (2022) Dictionary. www.google.com/search?q=resistance+definition&rlz=1C1CHBF_enUS842US842&oq=resistance&aqs=chrome.2.69i57j46i39i275j35i39j0i67j0i67i433j0i67l2j69i60.6347j1j4&sourceid=chrome&ie=UTF-8

Guangyu, Z., Olofsson, J.K., Koubeissi, M.Z., Menelaou, G., Rosenow, J., Schuele, S.U., Xu, P., Voss, J.L., Lane, G., Zelano, C. (2021) Human hippocampal connectivity is stronger in olfaction than other sensory systems. *Progress in Neurobiology.* 201: 102027. doi: 10.1016/j.pneurobio.2021.102027. PMID: 33640412. PMCID: PMC8096712.

Krediet, E., Bostoen, T., Breeksema, J., van Schagen, A., Passie, T., and Vermetten, E. (2020) The potential of psychedelics for the treatment of PTSD. *International Journal of Neuropsychopharmacology.* 23(6): 385–400.

Levinas, E. (1961) *Totality and Infinity: An Essay on Exteriority.* Livonia, Michigan: XanEdu.

Nutt, D., Erritzoe, D., and Carhart-Harris, R. (2020) Psychedelic psychiatry's brave new world cell. 181(1): 24–28.

Querstret, D., Morison, L., Dickinson, S., Cropley, M., and John, M. (2020) Mindfulness-based stress reduction and mindfulness-based cognitive therapy for psychological health and well-being in nonclinical samples: a systematic review and meta-analysis. *International Journal of Stress Management,* 27(4): 394–411.

Sun, M. et al. (2020) A review of the brain-gut-microbiome axis and the potential role of microbiota in Alzheimer's disease. *Journal of Alzheimers Disease.* 73(3): 849–865. doi: 10.3233/JAD-190872. PMID: 31884474.

Suraya, R., Nagano, T., Kobayashi, K., and Nishimura, Y. (2020) Microbiome as a target for cancer therapy. *Integrative Cancer Therapies.* 19: 1534735420920721. doi: 10.1177/1534735420920721. PMID: 32564632. PMCID: PMC7307392.

Wang, D.D., Nguyen, L.H., Li, Y., et al. (2021) The gut microbiome modulates the protective association between a Mediterranean diet and cardiometabolic disease risk. *Nature Medicine.* 27: 333–343.

Chapter 10

Crossroads, cloverleaf overpass, or skein

The relationship between some neurocognitive research and the development of the unconscious mind

Allannah Furlong

The concept of *crossroads* is very ancient. From the literal sense of where two roads intersect, it was long associated with liminality, a place neither here nor there, betwixt and between. Outside of the settlement, it symbolized a locality where two realms touch, such that at the center of the crossroads, communication with spirits could take place. Thus, before the more modern sense of the confluence of wayfarers in the exchange of goods and ideas, with its metaphorical extension as turning point or opportunity to change course, the crossroad was lieu of fear and uncanniness where criminals and suicides were buried. In the *fundamental anthropological situation* described by Laplanche (1999; 2011c), two realms touch, that of the child's mind and body and that of the adult, but the intersection is deeply asymmetrical at first. At this cross-road, the quality of the adult's communication not only summons the child's *spirit* but either facilitates or hampers its coming into existence. Of outmost interest to psychoanalysts, what occurred at this meeting place is constructed in every analytic dyad's work and theorized in one way or another by every major psychoanalytic thinker.

As new technologies have permitted ever more precise study of the brain's functioning, there is ongoing excitement among colleagues about what insight neuroscience research into the mother–baby encounter can bring to psycho-analytic thinking about it. It is my impression that this research in relation to psychoanalytic thinking is one of the major interdisciplinary crossroads psychoanalysis faces and will continue to face in the future. As we will see, the purported overlap between the two fields needs to be rigorously examined both in order to respect the possibly unbridgeable epistemological separate-ness of the two domains and in order to examine carefully in *what manner they touch*, hence my title of *"crossroads, cloverleaf overpass, or skein?"* How to concep-tualize the *articulation* between the brain realm of neurophysiological activity and the psychic realm of intersubjective symbol-exchange remains, for the moment, far out of reach.

DOI: 10.4324/9781003340744-12

For the moment, let us look at some subfields of neurocognitive research which might enlighten our psychoanalytic reflection about what is, or was, happening betwixt and between the minds of the former babies our patients were and that of the adults who were ministering to them. With limited expertise and limited space together preventing a global overview of the relevant literature, what will be shared here is a personal selection. Although I emerge amazed by the stupendous discoveries occurring in many laboratories across the world, *it will become clear that my impression is not as enthusiastic as those of some colleagues about what this new research can offer psychoanalysis.*

A good place to begin is with the work of Michael Meaney who is credited with launching the fusion of **epigenetics and neuroscience**. Stahl (2010) gives a nice precis of what epigenetics is about:

> Genetics is the DNA code for what a cell can transcribe into specific types of RNA or translate into specific proteins. Epigenetics is a parallel system that determines whether any given gene is actually made into its specific RNA and protein, or if it is instead ignored. If the genome is a lexicon of all protein "words," then the epigenome is a "story" resulting from arranging the "words" into a coherent tale.
>
> (p. 221)

Meaney's highly original and innovative research started with the study of maternal care in rats. He zeroed in on the relationship between maternal care and stress response in offspring by looking at the changes in the transcription of specific genes that regulate adult stress responses and synaptic plasticity in these animals. He has not only shown that good rat mothers (high liking and grooming) produce offspring who are able to withstand stress better than those whose mothers licked and groomed them less as pups. This result in itself is not surprising. Spitz's studies in the 1940s of children in a foundling hospital (paralleled twenty years later by Harlow's experiments with rhesus monkeys) proved beyond a doubt that adequate nutrition, hygiene, and housing are not enough to ensure normal development. The secret ingredient is the devoted attention of a loving adult, usually the mother. What was new was Meaney's (2001a) demonstration that qualitative changes in the hypothalamic – pituitary – adrenal (HPA) axis underlay the differences in stress tolerance. One commentator (Schramek, 2005) has called Meaney's research an "ode to a mother's touch." When a rat mother licks her pups, she somehow turns on the gene involved in reducing the quantity of glucocorticoids that will be released in the face of stress.

Fascinating though this research may be, I will introduce a first reservation: in what way might these newly discovered physical correlates of maternal care alter an analyst's listening? In fact, Alan Schore (2001; 2009; 2021) has devoted his career to answering this question, though his research has mainly looked at other levels of brain functioning, namely that of hemispheric differentiation. He too has reached the conclusion that *loss of ability to regulate the intensity of feelings (mediated by the same glucocorticoid pathways studied by Meaney and associates) is a far-reaching effect of early trauma and neglect.* Early "affect-transacting" interactions specifically shape the maturation of specific structural connections within the brain that underlie, he argues, both the interpersonal and intrapsychic aspects of all future socioemotional functions. Schore explicitly integrates attachment theory into his understanding of brain development.

However, I find myself occasionally skeptical reading Schore since he tends to churn out a disconcerting mélange of neuroscientific findings and clinical observations as if each "proved" the other, *whereas one often has the impression that psychoanalysis has provided the language with which to think about the biology.* Already familiar psychodynamic formulations operate as attributions of meaning for the neuroscientific findings. There is a risk of circular reasoning. Does inadequate right-brain activity "cause" some mothers to be depressed and speak depleted babytalk or do these traits of some mothers *cause* the underdeveloped right-brain functioning that appears in brain imaging? Or are we observing matters on entirely different material planes, speculating about parallel processes or of cloverleaf-like over- and under-passes whose articulation remains deeply mysterious?

As a working clinician, Schore's goal has always been to comb the research for clues in the construction of an ideal model of psychotherapy, and many of his conclusions about the importance of identifying affect and of the emotional implication of the psychotherapist are both reasonable and reasonably familiar, I warrant, to any experienced psychotherapist. Moreover, he has read and been inspired by much of the psychoanalytic literature. Yet he turns his findings of right-brain to right-brain synchronicity in affectively attuned human pairings into a concrete goal of psychotherapy.

> In line with current developmental and relational models I have argued that right-brain to right-brain communications represent interactions of the patient's unconscious primary-process system and the therapist's primary-process system ... and that primary process cognition is the major communicative mechanism of the relational unconscious.
>
> (2009, p. 128)

A recognizable – and controversial among psychoanalysts – idea of unconscious-to-unconscious transmission has now been attributed to "right-brain to right-brain communications." I was tempted to dismiss Schore's formulation, at first, as merely dressing an old observation in new biological apparel. But Peter Goldberg's recent study of an article of Winnicott's reminded me that similar conceptualizations have appeared often enough in the psychoanalytic literature. In the presentation Winnicott made in San Francisco in 1962, we are invited to think about a *direct* communication in early life which "does not look like communication at all, because it is carried out implicitly, silently, or at least without the need for articulation" (Goldberg, 2021, p. 456). This form of communication does not pass through words and in joining "us together unconsciously and thoughtlessly" (p. 456) sounds a lot like Schore's notion of right-hemisphere to right-hemisphere transmission. The arena of human experience Winnicott had in mind takes place in a world of objects not yet differentiated from me as not me. As Goldberg comments, "It is meant to be *lived*, not prematurely known or dismantled" (p. 457). Goldberg goes on say "[t]hus Winnicott introduces a theory of symbolization, slipping it in without announcing its significance or momentousness: using words and symbols ... must not displace or replace this ongoing way of being-with that does not need language, the dimension of inseparable unison with others" (p. 461). Not possible in this article, it certainly would be interesting to make a more detailed comparison between Schore and Winnicott's ideas on "unconscious communication."

There exists an ideological bias, or a kind of exhortatory appeal, in Schore's work (and one might say the same of some of Winnicott's writings), in a disproportionate fascination with trauma, dissociation, safety, and the therapeutic value of empathy. As explanation for laboratory results, we have a romantic and simplified evocation of evolutionary theory, as though thousands of years of collective culture has not made a dent in our postulated neolithic fright-flight adaptation to a dangerous day-to-day world on the steppe or the savannah. "A general principle of this work is that the sensitive empathic therapist allows the patient to reexperience dysregulating affects in *affectively tolerable doses in the context of a safe environment, so that overwhelming traumatic feelings can be regulated and integrated into the patient's emotional life*" (Schore, 2009, p. 130). It is the empathic clinician's *psychobiologically attuned interactive affect regulation* that helps effect change.

Even if we can sympathize with Schore's criticism, shared by Winnicott, of overly "cognitive" therapeutic approaches, is there not a risk in swinging too far in the opposite direction in this notion of a "psychobiologically attuned interactive affect regulation"? Albeit my knowledge of the brain imaging field of baby–adult interaction is very limited, but so far, I have not come across much regard for the symbolic nature, conscious or unconscious, of adult–infant exchanges. One can criticize both Schore and Winnicott for writing as though "affective" exchanges were not inevitably imbued with symbolic, culturally shared, meaning, and as though the patient's *interpretation* of the situation does not mediate his or her emotional reaction. Nonverbal does not mean nonlinguistic. Though Schore shares the psychoanalytic "fascination with the mysterious and marvelous transmutative power of conversation within a human dyad" (2003), he nevertheless also claims that for him, "intersubjectivity," as well as countertransference, are *essentially* "psycho-physiological" events.

The way Schore expresses himself, it is as though the co-construction *mediated through the analyst's interpretive work* were an aftermath of a psycho-physiological synchronicity rather than, just as plausibly, the other way around. There is a huge literature in psychoanalysis about psychosomatic functioning where somatic events in either the patient or the analyst have presumed psychic, symbolic, meaning. Schore's conclusions may sound similar, but they are fundamentally different. He refers to transference as a triggering of concrete deposits of prior experience in the right brain, memory networks echoing with one another. For him "a conversation between limbic systems" is synonymous with a "spontaneous emotion-laden conversation." In Schore's universe of "bottom-up interactive regulation," *the idea of words, and the representations they express, as causes, indeed as causes of affective states, is not apparent*. What makes Schore frustrating to read is that what he synthesizes are indeed breathtaking insights into the development of the baby's brain but at the same time he blithely squishes together findings from separate ontological levels to an extent which, on occasion, verges on psychobabble. Nevertheless, one needs to avoid the risk of throwing the baby out with the bathwater, since the supposed existence of unconscious transmission has a pedigree in the psychoanalytic literature going back to Freud.

On the other hand, Schore's therapeutic fervor is also characteristic of other neuroscientific researchers who openly aspire to "personalize" therapeutic interventions. The stated goal of eventual *individualized* treatment plans for most mental health problems is ironical: patients are explicitly objectified as suffering from pathological ideations or emotions, with the hope of finding biological measures and manualized treatments which can deliver efficient and predictable results. An uncritical reference to a presumed human normality is part and parcel of this aim. Two publications by Stahl (2010; 2012) are marred in this way. While he is persuaded that the strictly verbal exchanges of psychotherapy *can cause* epigenetic changes, at the same time, he attributes the source of psychiatric illness to malfunctioning brain circuitry. Thus, the kind of psychotherapy he favors is a form of cognitive behavioral therapy that succeeds by "improving the efficiency of information processing in these circuits, just like effective drug therapy is thought to do" (p. 252). To address *malfunctioning brain circuits in* psychiatry, Stahl (2012) endorses psychotherapy as an *epigenetic drug* because it "can hypothetically induce epigenetic changes in brain circuits that can enhance the efficiency of information processing in malfunctioning neurons" (p. 259). Somehow, the goal of biological efficiency of information processing has leapfrogged over the goal of integrating unconscious aspects of oneself.

In contrast to other health-related disciplines, psychoanalytic publications never provide *guidelines* that supersede former practices, which is why the old literature can be just as inspiring to the contemporary analyst as the more recent. In its account of the unconscious *presentations and representations* analysts and their analysands have uncovered, the analytic literature adds to the treasure chest of signifiers at our disposal to apprehend and put into words the unique experience of other patients and other analysts. It is an instigator to thought: nothing more, and nothing less. The internal framework of the analyst is more parsimoniously described as an evolving mindset than as a particular set of neurological patterns.

Despite its astounding new methodologies, neuroscience is still very much in its infancy. Raz (2010) is cognizant of the immense epistemological divide still at our feet. As he puts it: "Everything is biological, certainly, but everything is also social. We should probably pay as much attention to a new social phenomenon as we do to a new molecule" (p. 58). In an important article, Meaney (2001b) expressed a related cautionary note: "Simply put, it is biologically impossible for gene and environment to operate independently of one another ... Neurotransmitter and hormonal activity is profoundly influenced, for example, by social interactions, which lead to effects on gene activity, or expression. At no point in life is the operation of the genome independent of the *context* in which it functions" (emphasis added, p. 52). As psychoanalysts, I am assuming that we expect the symbolic universe of our conscious and unconscious identifications and drives (not instincts) to act as significant "context" for our individual genomes. *Biological context is not just physical; it is equally intersubjective and symbolic.*

In this connection, I would point out that, in general, no baby operates outside the context of a culture, and of a system of signs and words. In espousing a semiotic concept of culture, the anthropologist Clifford Geertz (1973) would certainly have agreed. "Believing ... that man is an animal suspended in webs of significance he himself has spun, I take culture to be those webs and the analysis of it to be therefore not an experimental science in search of law but an interpretive one in search of meaning" (p. 311). In this sense, we have another way of expressing Winnicott's famous dictum that *there is no such thing as a baby* because there is always some adult about, and *the first thing most adults want to do around a baby is talk to it*. This association brings me to one more field of developmental and neurocognitive research which crosses over with psychoanalytic curiosity about the fundamental anthropological situation as *communication*. When addressing infants, most adults adopt a particular type of speech, known as infant-directed speech (ID or IDS) to developmental researchers and as *baby talk* or *motherease* to the rest of us.

Baby talk can be observed in many languages and is not restricted to mothers. It is characterized by exaggerated intonation, as well as reduced speech rate, shorter utterance duration, lots of positive affect, and grammatical simplification. Many studies have examined the impact on the child's learning of the *quality of adult infant-directed speech*. It has been found that depressed mothers show substantially different speech patterns with their babies. Compared with non-depressed mothers, depressed mothers have a lower mean pitch and pitch range, speak less frequently, respond more slowly verbally to their babies, and are rated as expressing less positive valence in their voices (Lam-Cassettari and Kohlhoff, 2020; Spinelli and Mesman, 2018; Kaplan et al., 2015; Herrera et al., 2004; Thiessen et al., 2010; Saint-Georges et al., 2013). *The human mother's touch is evidently more than physical, it seems.*

These studies are fleshing out the intricacies of the period we psychoanalysts call prehistoric, that is, the period in human psychic life that can only be the subject of retrospective conjecture in adulthood. None of these laboratory findings, however, appears to undermine or call for a realignment of what psychoanalysts already know about this period either from direct observation, work with children, or through joint constructions with adult patients (the work of Freiberg, Furman, and Anna Freud are only some examples).

The same can be said about the position of Gabbard (2000; Westen and Gabbard, 2002a and 2002b), who has been one of the psychoanalytic forerunners of the belief in the relevance of "developments in cognitive neuroscience" for psychoanalytic theory. In his collaboration with Westen, Gabbard also stresses the notion of affect regulation focused upon by Meaney and Schore, though without noting a long line of psychoanalytic thinking going back as far as Hartmann (1950),[1] followed by Winnicott, Green, Loewald, and others, in which the child's affect regulation has been understood as an outgrowth of an evolving *articulation* between primary processes and secondary thought. The parents' role is seen as *facilitating environment*, that is, as aiding the child to acquire secondary process thinking without cutting itself off from the hallucinatory vitality of primary-process thought.

When Westen and Gabbard further elaborate on the *connectionist model* in neuroscience, which means that "temperament and experience have laid down strong neural 'tracks' that predispose [everyone] to take on particular roles … under certain circumstances" (p. 118), I start to feel queasy. Are they serious when they propose that "A node in a network is like an hypothesis. It can be 'on' or 'off,' signaling whether some part of a representation appears to match current sensory input, if it fits with other details of a memory of an encounter, or appears useful as a potential solution to a problem" (p. 104)? Yet did Freud (1899) not caution against such one-on-one equations between sensory input and childhood memories in declaring "a number of motives, with no concern for historical accuracy, had a part in forming them"? (p. 322).

While Gabbard's work *is always thoughtful* and the articles I am citing are full of astute insights, I personally feel that by pointing out ways of conceptualizing psychoanalytic findings as biological brain activities, these articles are trying to convince us to *believe in psychanalysis by seeing*. Westen and Gabbard's argument is not convincing that the new *biological empirical* data coming out of neurocognitive research has led them to a more sophisticated view of transference. On the contrary, it is far more likely that their understanding of transference has changed over time with clinical experience and theoretical debate with colleagues. Why are the imagined neurological parallels more useful than our own accumulated knowledge?

From the psychoanalytic perspective, infant-directed speech and singing are much more than qualities of prosody, pitch, and verbalization. They are usually the epitome of adult-acquired transitional thinking, offering a there-and-not-there playfulness in interaction which is associated with a subjective *quality of thinking*. At the same time, the normal baby is never exposed to the elements directly; his or her mental (and physical) environment is always mediated, filtered, through the caretaker's own mind which offers an optimal violence of interpretation,[2] an optimal parental seduction, and an already-there of secondarized "reality." The mother's reverie precedes – as well as accompanies – her baby's beta productions. Before there are ever *beta elements*, there are optimally already a lot of environmental *alpha elements*. In the case of human development, the *ode to a mother's touch* in its impact on neuronal differentiation will eventually want to account for qualitative aspects of her psychic functioning and the libidinal and aggressive messages it contains.

In the beginning is a psyche/soma which forms part of a caretaking adult–infant unit. The famous Maslow hierarchy of needs is fundamentally misleading. Needs for nourishment, for hydration, for warmth, for cleanliness, even for primary mammalian body-to-body bonding are not more "basic" than the child's need to be named, to be spoken to, to be desired, to be "addressed" as an individual, and to be "recognized" as a wished-for addition to the human species (Furlong, 2013). The baby is from the beginning more than a helpless body "calling" out to the adult; adults precede the baby's cries with their own wishes for recognition, with their own projected meanings, which cleave to the baby's body as snugly as any infant bodysuit. As Lacan puts it, the baby swallows the signifier along with mother's milk. Long before the "I think, therefore I am" there must be "I think because I am thought about and spoken to by a (loving) adult."

What the baby optimally encounters is not a series of benevolent physical gestures followed on a virtual level by communicational symbols, but rather *a word-and-caretaking-gesture amalgam*. It would be hard to imagine a loving caretaker ministering to a child without at the same time speaking to it. It would be equally difficult to imagine a loving caretaker speaking to a child without some urge to touch it. The adults' earliest words to the child are always incarnated: the musicality and tonalities of the voice welded into the mumbo jumbo of baby talk as well as into the tenderness and efficacy of each caretaking gesture. *From the psychoanalytic point of view, the deeply corporeal nature of infant-directed speech is also part of a "mother's touch."* The development of the child's psyche/soma will be as stunted by not being regularly spoken to as by not receiving an adequate caloric intake. When the depressed mother has trouble feeding and cleaning her child, she has at the same time trouble talking to it.

It may be too early for neuroscientists to look at the depressed or inadequate mother as part of the same continuum as the happier mother, though IDS researchers are aware of the *hostile* side of depressive mothering and are trying to measure its impact on babies. But no parenthood can escape ambivalence, much of it unconscious. How in the world might a researcher measure the transmission of adult *enigmatic messages to the child and the child's unconscious translations of them*? How would he or she measure unconscious erotic excitement or hostility in the relationship with the child? Is not our specialized method of listening to the semiotic content arising in our own minds and bodies and in those of our patients the only serious way of measuring this level of immaterial reality? And a more parsimonious and less expensive technique at that?

But being able to point to an image can make concepts *appear truer*. Aristotle wrote that "All men by nature desire to know ... we prefer seeing to everything else. The reason is that this, most of all senses, makes us know and brings to light many differences between things."[3] Aristotle may be right that we prefer seeing to everything else, but this sensorial mode is not well equipped to detect the immaterial intersubjective reality of the messages we send to one another, and which form a major part of the reality we study as psychoanalysts in our offices. Not being able to "see" a transferential "message" does not mean it does not exist.

"Neuropsychoanalysts must exercise prudence and desist from attempts to rehabilitate the psychoanalytic doctrine by exaggerating its compatibility with the findings of cognitive neuroscience" (Raz, 2010, p. 61). This may be more *à propos* than Raz realizes. I am not the first to conclude that research's ever-expanding reach into the incredible biological complexity of the brain *does not necessarily bring us closer to the psychic reality studied by psychoanalysts*. There are substantial epistemological differences between the two realms, though most would agree that they must touch each other, cross, somewhere ... but how? Is the how of this "touching" a direct translation? Transmutation? Tangent? Parallel process? Crossroad? Cloverleaf overpass? Tangled skein? Emergent property? In the meantime, certain distinctions are essential.

Quite a few readers will recall the muscular decade-long debate hosted by the *International Journal of Psychoanalysis* between Blass and Carmeli on one side and a selection of neuroscientists and neuropsychoanalysts on the other (see Blass and Carmeli, 2007; 2015; 2016, and Carmeli and Blass, 2013; Canestri, 2015; Yovell, Solms, and Fotopoulou, 2015). Neither side managed to win over the other. Yet, from where I sit, Blass and Carmeli's reasoning was far more persuasive. Not only did they demonstrate with detailed illustrations that the so-called "contribution" of neuroscientific findings to the psychoanalytic process is illusory, but they also show how this "contribution" can actually harm the *as-if* quality of the analyst's listening. On their side, the neuroscientists accuse Blass and Carmeli of ivory tower purity, a contention which may be linked to the equation made by the former between psychotherapeutic and psychoanalytic. Defining psychoanalytic work as the *analysis, or deconstruction, of discourse* (verbal and nonverbal) in pursuit of unconscious derivatives, Laplanche (2011a) has stated that not all of what goes on in psychoanalytic sessions is psychoanalytic *per se*. Much of it is psychothera-peutic, defined by Laplanche as interventions that construct an integrating narrative.

But *this new narrative can sometimes curtail or shortcut analytic work*, as Blass and Carmeli reiterate. The illusion of a concrete physiological brain cor-relate as "explanation" can halt the slide of signifiers by obviating the dyad's fantasy-freeing reverie. In Schore's theoretical progression, the patient's ego can be bypassed by the neuropsychoanalyst's cognizance of a deeper, unknown biological part of the patient's mind. When the analyst divines the uncon-scious ("absent content") content behind the patient's utterances, "we give him no help about his inability to know that for himself, and leave him to some extent dependent on the analyst for all such knowledge" (Searl, 1936, p. 478[4]). *In other words, attempts to use neuroscientific knowledge in clinical situ-ations could become a new form of authoritarian technique instead of helping the patient understand himself on the level of his psychic reality.* Though Busch (1995) was at the time referring to Searl, his words might apply equally to attempts to sub-stitute brain scans for free association: "deep interpretations of absent content enforce a type of passivity on the patient. They also encourage a belief in the analyst's omniscience" (p. 337).

In his inimitable, limpid, fashion, Laplanche (2011b) sets out very useful clarifications as to the separate "contributions" to human knowledge of attachment/developmental/neuroscientific theory and psychoanalysis. On the one side, there is affection, adaptation, reciprocity, self-preservation, mutuality, synchronicity, emotional regulation, and intersubjectivity (in the conscious, phenomenological sense). On the other there is infantile sexu-ality, part-object non-adaptation, asymmetry, inter-generational difference, lack of emotional regulation, and a conflicted/cloven subjectivity. Moreover, Laplanche reminds us that the "absent content" and lack of ego integration of interest to psychoanalysts is a register of the human mind which neces-sarily precedes the development of the developmental processes studied by neuroscientists, because the adult's mind ineluctably precedes that of the baby at the crossroad of their initial encounters.

*There is **empirical evidence in the discourse** of our patients; there is a science (and an art) to our decortication of the **messages** (manifest, latent, or ambiguously expressed) we send to each other,* and which have been discerned in (or hypothesized from) the associations of our patients. At the same time, there are ethical reservations to intervening in more concrete, and unsymbolic, ways directly into the brain of patients. In any case, as Blass and Carmelli have stated many times: dreams of direct neurological correction may be attractive to some and are surely valuable in many cases, but it *is not the therapeutic pathway which makes psychoanalysis what it is.* In the register of immaterial intersubjective reality which characterizes psychoanalytic work: "The slide of signifiers will always dissipate a bound meaning and subvert any act of solidarity" (Bollas, 1992, p. 202).

The very possibility of subjectivity, of intersubjectivity, of a sense of self, of a sense of a mind of one's own, or of mentalization is inconceivable outside of language, nor can any of these aspects of self-consciousness emerge except in and through the language addressed to us as babies. There is an asymmetry in the fundamental anthropological situation, which is obviously mediated by brain processes, but which does not reside in them *per se*. The depressed mother's *baby talk* is stunted because she is deeply confused and conflicted about her desire for the existence of a new mind and about her capacity to take care of it. Our minds only develop as places we live in because our early caretakers projected an interlocuter into us, addressed us and spoke for us until we could speak for ourselves. We are "called forth" as minds. The happy *mother's touch* is more than a caress; it is the beginning of a *sacred conversation*[5] which must indeed be transmuted into intracranial physiological activity. The latter follows. If dysfunctional, the brain can inhibit the intracranial substrate of this sacred conversation, but it does not initiate, induce, or cause it.

More and more, I think we are faced with independent ("unsyncronized") ways of thinking among ourselves about the necessity of "scientifically proving" psychoanalytic hypotheses by recourse to biological parallels. The arguments advanced on one side do not seem to alter the other's mind. Could there be something personal about the stance we take, something of the order of divergent *convictions* which do not seem to yield easily to argument? Lavie (1999) questioned the illusion that we are the free authors of rationally held beliefs that owe nothing to our personal pasts. He argued – and most psychoanalysts would agree with him on principle – that our ideas hold us rather than the other way around. Contrary to the tendency of Schore and others interested in the neuroscience of affect regulation, Lavie contends that we are not all like-minded; we will *not* be attuned to one another because we have had different personal trajectories.

An extensive overview of contemporary neurocognitive research has led Mark Solms (2021) to propose "deep revisions" of Freud's drive theory. A full critique of this monumental effort is beyond my expertise. Yet, it is astonishing that such a huge synthesis of contemporary experimental and theoretical research is grounded solely on an adaptive, homeostatic model where no conceptualization of precocious intersubjectivity, no serious engagement with the destructive forces in human life, no reference to mediation/alienation in language, and no theory of infantile sexuality or unconscious fantasy make an appearance.

Cassirer (1944) argued that we cannot discover the nature of man in the same way that we can detect the nature of physical things. Whereas physical things may be described in terms of their objective properties, man may only be described and defined in terms of his consciousness. This fact poses an entirely new challenge not solvable by our usual modes of investigation. "For it is only in our immediate intercourse with human beings that we have insight into the character of man" (p. 5). For this most passionate student of symbolic systems of all kinds, contradiction is part and parcel of human existence. I imagine that Cassirer would also have had reserves about some neuropsychoanalytic claims. At least, this is how I read his assertion that "Man has no 'nature' – no simple or homogeneous being. He is a strange mixture of being and nonbeing" (p. 11).

Notes

1   My thanks to Fred Busch for pointing out Hartmann's priority in this theorization.
2   I am borrowing Aulagnier's (2001) observation that the baby's cognitive and physical incapacity requires the mother to *attribute meaning* to the baby's behavior long before the latter can formulate its own needs.
3   Aristotle, *Metaphysics*, as quoted by E. Cassirer, p. 2 in *An Essay on Man*.
4   I thank Fred Busch for bringing this article to my attention.
5   In art, *a sacra conversazione*, meaning holy (or sacred) conversation, is a genre developed in Italian Renaissance painting, with a depiction of the Virgin and Child amidst a group of saints in a grouping in which there is implied spiritual and conversational exchange.

References

Aulagnier, P. (2001) *The Violence of Interpretation: From Pictogram to Statement*. Translated by A. Sheridan. Hove, East Sussex: Brunner-Routledge.

Blass, R.B. and Carmeli, Z. (2007) The case against neuropsychoanalysis. On fallacies underlying psychoanalysis' latest scientific trend and its negative impact on psychoanalytic discourse. *International Journal of Psychoanalysis*, 88(1): 19–40.

Blass, R.B. and Carmeli, Z. (2015) Further evidence for the case against neuropsychoanalysis: how Yovell, Solms, and Fotopoulou's response to our critique confirms the irrelevance and harmfulness to psychoanalysis of the contemporary neuroscientific trend. *International Journal of Psychoanalysis*, 96(6): 1555–1573.

Blass, R. and Carmeli, Z. (2016) Response to Kessler, Sandberg, and Busch: the case for and against neuropsychoanalysis. *International Journal of Psychoanalysis*, 97(4): 1155–1158.

Bollas, C. (1992) *Being a Character: Psychoanalysis and Self Experience*. New York: Hill and Wang.

Busch, F. (1995) Neglected classics: M.N. Searl's "some queries on principles of technique". *Psychoanalytic Quarterly*. 64: 326–344.

Canestri, J. (2015) The case for neuropsychoanalysis. *International Journal of Psychoanalysis*. 96(6): 1575–1584.

Carmeli, Z. and Blass, R. (2013) The case against neuroplastic analysis: a further illustration of the irrelevance of neuroscience to psychoanalysis through a critique of Doidge's *The Brain that Changes Itself*. *International Journal of Psychoanalysis*. 94(2): 391–410.

Cassirer, E. (1944) *An Essay on Man: An Introduction to a Philosophy of Human Culture.* New Haven and London: Yale University Press.

Freud, S. (1899) Screen memories. *The Standard Edition of the Complete Psychological Works of Sigmund Freud.* III: 299–322.

Furlong, A. (2013) An example of dehumanization as a shield against our helpless openness to the other. *Journal of the American Psychoanalytic Association.* 61: 471–490.

Gabbard, G.O. (2000) What can neuroscience teach us about transference? *Canadian Journal of Psychoanalysis.* 9: 1–18.

Geertz, C. (1973) Thick description: Toward an interpretive theory of culture. In *The Interpretation of Cultures: Selected Essays.* New York: Basic Books.

Hartmann, H. (1950) The *Ego and the Problem of Adaptation.* New York: International University Press. Originally published in German in 1939.

Herrera, E., Reissland, N., and Shepherd, J. (2004) Maternal touch and maternal child-directed speech: effects of depressed mood in the postnatal period. *Journal of Affective Disorders.* 81(1): 29–39. doi: 10.1016/j.jad.2003.07.001. PMID: 15183597.

Kaplan, P., Danko, C., Cejka, A., and Everhart, K. (2015) Maternal depression and the learning-promoting effects of infant-directed speech: roles of maternal sensitivity, depression diagnosis, and speech acoustic cues. *Infant Behaviour and Development.* 41: 52–63. doi:10.1016/j.infbeh.2015.06.011.

Lam-Cassettari, C. and Kohlhoff, J (2020) Effect of maternal depression on infant-directed speech to prelinguistic infants: implications for language development. *PLOS One.* 15(7): e0236787. https://doi.org/10.1371/journal. pone.0236787

Laplanche, J. (1999) *Essays on Otherness*, Translated by L. Thurston. London and New York: Routledge.

Laplanche, J. (2011a) Psychoanalysis and psychotherapy. In: *Freud and the Sexual*, J. Fletcher, J. House, and N. Ray (translators). New York: Unconscious in Translation, pp. 279–284.

Laplanche, J. (2011b) Sexuality and attachment in metapsychology. In: *Freud and the Sexual*, J. Fletcher, J. House, and N. Ray (translators). New York: Unconscious in Translation, pp. 27–51.

Laplanche, J. (2011c) Starting from the fundamental anthropological situation. In: *Freud and the Sexual*, J. Fletcher, J. House, and N. Ray (translators). New York: Unconscious in Translation, pp. 99–113.

Lavie, J.-C. (1999) Lettre sauvage à Umberto Eco. *Trans.* 10: 29–39.

Meaney M.J. (2001a) Maternal care, gene expression, and the transmission of individual differences in stress reactivity across generations. *Annual Review of Neuroscience.* 24: 1161–1192.

Meaney, M.J. (2001b) Nature, nurture, and the disunity of knowledge. *Annals of the New York Academy of Sciences.* 935: 50–61. doi: 10.1111/j.1749-6632.2001. tb03470.x.PMID: 11411175.

Raz, A. (2010) From dynamic lesions to brain imaging of behavioral lesions: response to commentaries. *Neuropsychoanalysis.* 12(1): 46–65.

Saint-Georges, C., Chetouani, M., Cassel, R., Apicella, F., Mahdhaoui, A., Muratori, F., Laznik, M.C., and Cohen, D. (2013) Motherese in interaction: at the cross-road of emotion and cognition? (A systematic review). *PLOS One*. 8(10): e78103. doi: 10.1371/journal.pone.0078103. PMID: 24205112; PMCID: PMC3800080.

Schramek, T. (2005) *Michael Meaney: Ode to the Mother's Touch*. Montreal: Douglas Mental Health University Institute.

Schore, A.N. (2001) The effects of early relational trauma on right brain development, affect regulation, and infant mental health. *Infant Mental Health Journal*. 22: 201–269.

Schore, A.N. (2003) *Affect Regulation and the Repair of the Self*. New York: WW Norton.

Schore, A.N. (2009) Right-brain affect regulation. An essential mechanism of development, trauma, dissociation, and psychotherapy. In: *The Healing Power Of Emotion: Affective Neuroscience, Development, and Clinical Practice*, edited by D. Fosha, D. Siegal, and M. Solomon. New York: W W Norton, p. 112–144.

Schore, A.N. (2021) The interpersonal neurobiology of intersubjectivity. *Frontiers in Psychology*. 12: 648616. doi: 10.3389/fpsyg.2021.648616.

Searl, M.N. (1936) Some queries on principles of technique. *International Journal of Psychoanalysis*. 17: 471–493.

Spinelli, M. and Mesman, J. (2018) The regulation of infant negative emotions: the role of maternal sensitivity and infant-directed speech prosody. *Infancy*. 23: 502–518. https://doi.org/10.1111/infa.12237

Stahl, S. (2010) Methylated spirits: epigenetic hypotheses of psychiatric disorders. *CNS Spectrums*. 15: 220–30. doi:10.1017/S1092852900000055.

Stahl, S. (2012) Psychotherapy as an epigenetic "drug": psychiatric therapeutics target symptoms linked to malfunctioning brain circuits with psychotherapy as well as with drugs. *Journal of Clinical Pharmacy and Therapeutics*. 37: 249–253.

Thiessen, E., Hill, E., and Saffran, J. (2010) Infant-directed speech facilitates word segmentation. *Infancy*. 7: 53–71. https://doi.org/10.1207/s15327078in0701

Westen, D. and Gabbard, G.O. (2002a) Developments in cognitive neuroscience: I. Conflict, compromise, and connectionism. *Journal of the American Psychoanalytic Association*. 50: 53–98. doi:10.1177/00030651020500011501.

Westen, D. and Gabbard, G.O. (2002b) Developments in cognitive neuroscience: II. Implications for theories of transference. *Journal of the American Psychoanalytic Association*. 50: 99–134.

Yovell, Y., Solms, M., and Fotopoulou, A. (2015) The case for neuropsychoanalysis: why a dialogue with neuroscience is necessary but not sufficient for psychoanalysis. *The International Journal of Psychoanalysis*. 96: 1515–1553.

Part II

Psychoanalysis and social issues

Chapter 11

Difference

Our legacy and our future

Harriet Wolfe

Introduction

The invitation to think about psychoanalysis in the twenty-first century, both as a contributor to this volume and as an elected officer of the International Psychoanalytical Association (IPA), was a welcome one, but it has kept me awake at night. I ran for president of the IPA with the idea that the Association is a huge reservoir of expertise that could help our troubled world. I first dreamt this addition to the IPA's mission in Warsaw in 2018. The European Psychoanalytic Federation (EPF) had its annual meeting there shortly after a Polish law was passed that made it illegal to speak about Poland's having had an involvement in the Holocaust ("Full text," 2018). I had not read the law, nor had most other participants. But it was experienced as frightening. For me it was an alarming example of how false facts can become law.

One of the psychoanalytic interventions that occurred at the Warsaw meeting was a two-part large group meeting conducted in Group Relations style to discuss the theme "Life after atrocities in Europe" (Erlich and Erlich-Ginor, 2018). Analysts shared their individual experiences from as early as 5 years of age to as recent as the past week. The general feeling was one of threat: feared revival of fascist governments, electoral gains by populist leaders, growing evidence of inhumane policies, increased public violence. The ghosts of genocide and war were alive in the room.

As analysts in the group meeting wondered what psychoanalysts could do, I thought that the expertise of the people in the room and throughout the IPA represented a unique resource for the understanding of societal as well as individual conflict. I thought there might be a way that plain-language psychoanalytic educational interventions could move members of the general public to take action in the face of threats to the planet and to psychologically, socially, and economically endangered populations.

In the interim I have been asked in relation to my ambitions: "Do you wish to change the profession?" It is a surprising question that I think reflects an inordinate, intense focus on psychoanalysis as a clinical profession. I cannot imagine a public psychoanalytic intervention having a notable effect unless it

DOI: 10.4324/9781003340744-14

grows out of a deep clinical psychoanalytic understanding. It must come from an "in-your-bones" type of understanding that occurs only with a foundation of rigorous training and clinical experience. It may seem to be an additional skill to say what we understand in non-technical, plain language. But we do that in the confines of our consulting rooms all the time: we use plain, relevant, emotionally connected speech.

During my two years as president-elect and now six months as president, I have witnessed dramatic differences of opinion arise between individual analysts and between regional groups. The IPA's greatest strength – a highly educated and committed membership – could become its nemesis if professional differences remain irresolvable and continue to be an organizational preoccupation.

When one's personal, local, or regional psychoanalytic identity is challenged, potential shifts in emphasis within the IPA may be felt as an existential threat. This is particularly prominent today in relation to training standards and guidelines for clinical practice. The Janus face of the IPA reflects the fact that we always look inward but we also look outward, personally and in our work; at the same time continually encounter linguistic, cultural, and scientific differences among ourselves. When the dual experience of inward and outward awareness represents two aspects of an integrated self or organizational process, it is possible to make prudent choices about which direction is more important at which time. The optimal outcome is neither compromise nor consensus; it is the ability to make the best choices possible given lessons of the past and knowledge of current and future circumstances, to the extent they are predictable.

Psychoanalysis is under threat at a time in history when it has never been more needed. There is widespread opinion that it is too expensive, too time consuming, too focused on the individual mind, and disconnected from reality. These allegations are not new, but they have intensified in the context of the pandemic. The emergent crossroad is, in my mind, a matter of how psychoanalysis positions itself in relation to the external world and how psychoanalysts manage the pressure to grow and change in the sense of being "modern" in a way that preserves the integrity of the clinical method and also contributes to social justice.

To explore psychoanalytic engagement with social justice, I will revisit historical events and then shift to the tension between inner and outer realities, between subjectivity and objectivity, and how psychoanalysts are inclined, or not, to recognize when their thinking is impacted by the societal surround. Finally, how do most psychoanalysts conceive of reality? Is it in the consulting room, the streets, the past, the future, interpersonal exchange, social media exchange, or all of these and other fields simultaneously? How does our interest in the unconscious and its timelessness prepare us to play a constructive role in our troubled world? How will we manage our professional differences in ways that allow for respectful, productive, collegial problem-solving and, at the same time, establish us as an international collective that benefits the world?

A historical perspective: theoretical and clinical psychoanalysis in the 1920s

Psychoanalysis first developed as a recognized clinical and socially relevant profession in Vienna and Berlin in the 1920s and early 1930s during a time of great social need. Psychoanalysts were deeply identified with the social democratic spirit of that era. In the twenty-first century a similar progressive involvement has become controversial within psychoanalysis. A political stance is anathema to many in the profession and, to those colleagues, socially relevant commentary can seem inappropriate. But this is not where and how the profession stood after World War I.

As we are aware, World War I resulted in massive loss of life, dramatic levels of traumatic "war neuroses," and severe social needs throughout the former German Empire. The Versailles Treaty negotiations that followed World War I, which did not include Germany, imposed conditions on Germany that resulted in political chaos at first and ensured severe economic decline through the demand for Germany's reparation of war costs to the Allied Parties. The German public suffered widespread humiliation, socioeconomic stress, and personal losses: husbands, fathers, sons, neighbors, and entire families lost to combat or bombings close to home.

The German Weimar Republic (1919–1933) developed a new and fragile democracy that reduced political chaos and aimed to address social problems. It was gradually undermined by right-wing populist forces. Similar to false fact becoming law in Poland in 2018, the decline of democracy in Germany and the rise of a charismatic fascist leader in the 1930s resonates with the current presence of international political leaders who polarize and distort social truths. They disenfranchise citizens who have needs that do not align with their own or those of their constituencies. One might wonder whether even a relatively sturdy, historically based democracy such as that of the United States is secure in the face of organized political assaults on such values as social equity and the freedom to vote.

The sociopolitical environment after the Great War demanded accountability and public involvement on the part of professionals, including psychoanalysts. Cultural receptivity to the ideas Freud had introduced, including the ubiquity and importance of sexual drive, was alive and well in Red Vienna and Weimar Berlin. But resistance was fierce on the part of medical doctors to competition from the new Freudian profession. They were dismayed by its focus on sexual forces and emotionality as relevant to behavior and physical health.

Freud charted a social mission as joined to the clinical one when he gave an inspiring speech in Budapest in 1918 at the fifth IPA Congress. He urged the development of "institutions or out-patient clinics ... where treatment shall be free. The poor man should have just as much right to assistance for his mind as he now has to the life-saving help offered by surgery" (Freud, 1918, as cited in Danto, 2005, p. 17). He set the care of the individual into the broad context of civic responsibility. In his mind it was the social responsibility of the entire psychoanalytic community to be therapeutic regardless of economic class.

The first free clinic was opened in Berlin in 1920 under the guidance of and with the financial support of Max Eitingon. It was known as the Berlin Poliklinik. The Ambulatorium in Vienna opened in 1922.[1] The public quickly took advantage of the help offered. Ambulatorium records show that patients were predominantly male, and their most frequent presenting complaint was impotence, a common symptom of war neurosis. The notion that female hysterics dominated the clinical psychoanalytic landscape is erroneous (Danto, 2005). But there was an emphasis on maternal infant care and home visits were common. This was an early form of psychoanalysis in the community, not only free of classism but showing the recognition and hope that childism, prejudice against children (Young-Bruehl, 2009), could and should be overcome by psychoanalysts.[2] Psychoanalysts of the 1920s recognized that developmental forces could be thwarted by social forces.

Similar to today, patients were assessed in terms of their early childhood stressors, their genetically determined aspects of personality, and their social environment. In the social democratic post-World War I context, there was also an acute awareness of classism. There was severe social inequity and the inability of people in need of care to pay for it. This inequity fueled an intense altruistic psychoanalytic commitment to public access to care. It was supported not only by community outreach through maternal–infant support programs and public lectures about child development and family well-being. Programs for prevention and treatment of juvenile delinquency began. School reforms were led by psychoanalysts. Foster children were treated, and observation of their strengths as well as their vulnerabilities became foundational to child development theory.

As the free clinics in Vienna and Berlin developed, the analysts delivering care met regularly and engaged in lively discussions of parameters of treatment from a scientific point of view. They explored their experience with frequency of sessions, length of sessions, and whether interruptions of treatment were useful. The clinical response to the social surround was flexible. The frequency and length of session were debated but ultimately reflected a balance between the pragmatics of urgent clinical demand and the insistence on intensity of treatment. Treatment was to be delivered with attention to personal privacy and a high level of expertise.

A search began for pragmatic solutions to the high levels of clinical need and the relatively limited professional resources. More analysts were trained. But treating patients several times per week became difficult. Waiting lists grew. Experiments with "fractionated" treatment, which included interruptions, and less frequent sessions occurred in the face of patients' need to manage family and work obligations. Although care occurred as often as five times per week, a frequency of three sessions per week became the standard in Berlin by 1926 (Danto, 2005, p. 180). The ideal length of a session was thought to be 60 minutes, but again this proved impractical. At first, sessions were reduced to 30 minutes, but the experiment was considered unsuccessful. The response to crowded schedules became session lengths of 45–60 minutes based on level of individual need and motivation.

Before and after Hitler became Chancellor in 1933 there was ample evidence of a striking theme: the vulnerability of psychoanalysis to internal and external political conflicts. There were internal skirmishes over local clinic or society leadership. There was competition for Freud's approval as well as objections to his leadership. In the 1920s external politics involved the medical profession's wish to limit competition for patients and right-wing disparagement of attention to psychological health as a sign of weakness. As the 1930s approached, economic conditions worsened considerably, both in Europe and in the United States. A good deal of financial support for psychoanalytic programs had come from American foundations. Sadly, it came to an end.

The characteristic focus of the profession on internal organizational matters may have contributed to the slow recognition by some psychoanalysts in the early 1930s of extreme and life-threatening external political threat. Hitler's swift rise to power over just three months, January to March of 1933, and the goal of aryanization had a dramatic effect on all psychoanalytic endeavors. It was a mortal threat to the many psychoanalysts who were Jewish. Most left Germany and Austria but a few stayed and became active in the resistance movement. The IPA remained very distant from fascist politics. It seemed to turn a blind eye to analysts who were apprehended by the Nazis. It supported the continuation of the Deutsche Psychoanalytische Gesellschaft (DPG) in Berlin despite evidence that psychoanalysis was being perversely redefined by Hermann Goering's cousin, who was a psychotherapist, and others. Psychoanalysis became a psychotherapy that aimed to enhance national character.

Fast-forward 100 years: theoretical and clinical psychoanalysis in the 2020s

Just over a hundred years since Freud's Budapest speech, the world is in the midst of a perfect storm of environmental, political, economic, and social stressors, compounded by the challenges and uncertainty of a global pandemic.

The psychological pressures of such severe stressors point to the vital importance of psychoanalysis as a method of treatment and a way of thinking deeply
about human reactions to uncertainty, loss, and trauma. Nevertheless, psychoanalysis as a profession has been slow to engage fully in the complexity of
societal suffering.

There are many psychoanalysts working in such settings as jails, hospitals,
courtrooms, schools, and low-cost clinics. But the IPA as the organizational structure for the profession continues to focus primarily on standards
of treatment and training. While maintaining professional excellence and
rigorous, standard-based training is essential, the absence of an explicit
organizational commitment to social issues is a regrettable deficiency. Some
institutes consider community psychoanalysis to be a legitimate aspect of psychoanalytic training (González and Peltz, 2021). But many programs consider
work in the community to be "applied psychoanalysis" and to have no place
in psychoanalytic training. For such programs, community psychoanalysis is
perceived as a threat to the essence, the "pure gold," of psychoanalysis.

The choice of terms like "pure gold" and "applied" rather than "psychoanalytic" captures a current divide within the profession. It is not entirely new
to have hotly contested divides while the world around us is being destroyed.
In the early 1940s Melanie Klein and Anna Freud exemplified one form of
difference: Melanie was focused on the interpretation of the infantile unconscious and Anna on psychoanalytic interventions that recognized children's
social adaptation and allowed them to resume their development. Winnicott's
famous communication to colleagues during the Freud–Klein debates that
bombs were falling outside did not serve as an effective wake-up call. Melanie
Klein's rejoinder that he seemed to have forgotten that psychoanalysis concerns
itself with the internal world is close to the mindset of large segments of
today's professional collective. We often fail to actively explore how we too are
subjects of powerful external societal events and structured attitudes.

Prominent clinical and theoretical contributors like Hanna Segal took
psychoanalytic thinking to the problems of the world in the late twentieth
and early twenty-first centuries. Similar to Edith Jacobson who actively
participated in the Nazi Resistance during the 1930s, Segal participated
in sociopolitical debates, particularly in the movement against nuclear
armaments. Her psychoanalytic paper "Silence is the real crime" (Segal,
1987) was an important contribution to the nuclear debate. After the Gulf
War and 9/11 she wrote:

> What does the future hold? It is pretty grim, because global oppression,
> which includes mass murder as well as total economic exploitation, leaves
> desperate terrorism as almost the only weapon for the oppressed ... This
> expanding global empire, like all such things, has to be sustained through
> control of the media – and this is of necessity based on a series of lies.
> From the humane (and psychoanalytic) point of view we are led as citizens

to struggle with the unending task of exposing lies for the preservation of sane humane values – this is our only hope.

(Bell and Steiner, 2011)

In today's IPA, in the absence of an explicit organizational commitment to social issues, there is no fusion of insight therapy and community responsibility as was the case in the 1920s. There is no implicit political mission recognized in psychoanalysis. The frequently misused ethos of "neutrality" contributes to analysts' reluctance to be active in the external world for fear of corrupting or weakening an analysand's transference. However, this perception of "neutrality" has become controversial.

Analysts line up on opposing sides of the neutrality issue much as politicians line up on progressive and conservative sides of policy discussions. It is a small example of how the profession of psychoanalysis is a microcosm of the external world and remains unprotected from large group dynamics and sociopolitical tensions. Perhaps because of its isolation, psychoanalysis forgets what Freud and later Segal knew: neutrality is a clinical attitude in the consulting room; it is not to be confused with the attitude of an engaged, concerned, and expert member of society.

Isolation from other scientific and humanistic disciplines feeds into additional dramatic divides. There has been a proliferation of psychoanalytic research in the last decade (Leuzinger-Bohleber and Kaechele, 2015; Leuzinger-Bohleber et al., 2020; Wallerstein, 2009). But many psychoanalysts continue to dismiss neuroscientific thinking and psychoanalytic research that includes biological markers (González-Torres, 2013). This was true also in the last century when the profession's physical models were Newtonian and linear. The brilliant outline of neurophysiologic research Freud articulated in his 1895 *Project for a Scientific Psychology* (Freud, 1950) was abandoned as unlikely to be fruitful. However, psychoanalysis has been shown to prolong life (Jeffery, 2001) and has been shown to raise the I.Q.s of children (Kliman, 2018). Trauma, untreated, has been shown to shorten life (O'Donovon et al., 2011) and lower the I.Q.s of children (LeWinn et al., 2009; van Os et al., 2017). Although a focus on the interior of the unconscious individual mind can of course be clinically useful, the refusal to consider other realms of data that enlighten us about human behavior and humans as social animals seriously constricts the profession's theoretical paradigms and their value inside and outside the profession.

The relationship between inner and outer reality

I struggle with the question of why organized psychoanalysis seems blind to the impact of the social surround. Its theory about the impact of trauma on the collective is meager compared to its theory about its impact on the individual or its transgenerational transmission in families (Faimberg, 1988;

Volkan, et al., 2002). Despite the advances of Group Relations Theory and its recognition of a social unconscious (Hopper, 2003), some psychoanalysts seem disinterested, even dismissive, of the constitutive impact of the social surround, of culture and of structured systems of prejudice on the development and thinking of the individual and the group. There are notable exceptions (Dajani, 2017; González, 2020; Kaës, 2007: Moss and Zeavin, 2022; Tubert-Oklander, 2014). But mainstream psychoanalytic debate today often focuses on whether the suspension of distance training rules during the pandemic will have a deleterious effect on the profession going forward.

Thoughtful colleagues see a cautionary tale in the maintenance by the IPA of the DPG in the 1930s. The mindset that psychoanalysis in Germany needed to be – and could be – saved had grave consequences. The goal of professional organizational "survival" in a time of immense societal disruption overshadowed the question of whether it was possible in the particular Nazi environment to rescue psychoanalytic practice and its values of truth, insight, fairness, and freedom of thought. The influential psychoanalytic leaders at the time, Ernest Jones and Anna Freud, were unable to pay enough attention to the urgent sociopolitical surround and the impact of a fascist regime. They seemed to feel that psychoanalysis could somehow remain protected in spite of what was going on around it. Are we vulnerable to a predominance of similar thinking today?

I encounter evidence of a present-day professional concern that psychoanalysis will be corrupted if too much attention is paid to the circumstances of the pandemic and other pervasive social issues. A central concern relates to the suspension of distance training rules at the beginning of the pandemic. Most analysts around the world, including analysts-in-training, have worked at a distance since March 2020 with all of their patients, and they continue to do so in the many areas where Covid variants have made in-person meetings unsafe. The worry is that an emergency measure will get translated into permanent change and the profession will lose its experiential core. Analysts have found that distance analysis through use of the telephone or an internet platform is possible. That of course does not mean that all analysts favor it or feel the absence of two people in the room is desirable. There is widespread agreement that in-person experience is vital to a full understanding of the intimate and challenging task of a deep psychoanalytic treatment.

The current professional debate centers on whether distance analysis permits the successful training of future analysts, i.e., whether the embodied presence of two persons in the consulting room is essential for successful psychoanalytic training. A more meaningful question may be whether distance analysis permits the training of competent analysts – who are greatly needed in a world struggling to cope with unprecedented challenges – when social circumstances interrupt or render in-person analytic training impractical, extravagant, or impossible.

We do not have enough data to help us answer the question of whether an ongoing adaptation that supports greater flexibility in training threatens the formation of competent analysts. The Research Committee of the IPA will pursue the question, but rigorous research is not done quickly.

I have spent more hours on the effort to articulate this professional dilemma than I wish to count. It strikes me as an enactment. During a perfect storm of environmental, political, economic, and social stressors, compounded by the challenges and uncertainty of a global pandemic, there is a prevailing focus on psychoanalytic training. Clearly, we need truly competent analysts if the profession is to make a positive difference in the world, in whatever arena we enter psychoanalytically. But the profession's ability to divorce itself from the considerable pressures of today's external world is alarming to me.

I think my difficulty in capturing the dilemma that the profession is focused on with clarity and efficiency has important personal and professional roots. It reflects my own confusion regarding what is subjective and how I know if I am being objective. Given the violence with which systemic classism, racism, childism, anti-Semitism, and other intersecting social inequities have come to the surface in the past few years, it is both confusing and essential to explore how the social unconscious and my individual unconscious constitute my subjectivity. I will continue to think (rather than conclude) and pursue a prudent path despite the pressure to act and to appear certain.

Tolerating uncertainty in the service of authentic discovery is at the heart of what we do. As analysts we are always piecing things together (Moss, 2022). Uncertainty is a constant. We have progressed insofar as we know we cannot know the truth of another, or the content of their unconscious fantasy. But we can assist in the search and remain open to surprise.

Herein lies the essence of my enactment. Organizationally, I am devoted to helping a group work well together. I am not as interested in the outcome or the decisions made as I am in the principle of respectful, thorough inquiry. As a clinical analyst, I am interested in helping others with authentic discovery of personal meaning.

A relevant screen memory of mine relates to a period rather late in adolescence, and was no doubt presaged by similar less consciously retained experiences. I was at a family gathering. We were celebrating my sister's graduation from college. I was in from New York where I was studying for a Master of Arts degree in Germanic Languages and Literature, and I was enthusiastically describing the progressive, liberal thinking of my friends and colleagues at Columbia and Union Theological Seminary. My frequently compassionate father looked me in the eye and said: "Never speak that way again!" Short and sweet and violent. He was a Republican and averse to current efforts going on to unionize his business in which he felt he had been quite generous to his employees.

This vignette could be thought of as capturing patriarchy, misogyny, hatred, love, terror, and/or empathy. Somatically, I felt someone (my father) had put a knife to my throat. It was a true gag order. As much as I hated him for his attack on my thinking, I could see he was suffering despair over his business and could not tolerate progressive thinking that challenged his norm. Was I being weak because I understood his pain and did not yell at him or become a true activist going forward? That is the sort of question I continue to struggle with as a remnant of my internalized patriarchy. Happily, I had a wealth of close, supportive mentors in my mother, grandmother, and family doctor, all strong women. I learned through those models that integrity and group cohesion require persistent loving, listening, and openness to discord.

The painful reality for my father, myself, and the current psychoanalytic profession was/is the experience of helplessness. The enactment I spoke of in regard to writing a section of this essay reflected helplessness, personal and professional, individual and collective. As a profession we aspire to do good, yet we fight doggedly over frequency and whether analysis must occur in person. Are we in danger of missing the fact that we are part of a greater scientific and social world? If we insist on dyadic isolation and yet aim to have wide social influence, we perpetuate illusions that are unhelpful. I think our irresolvable professional conflicts reflect an unconscious determination to be more than we can be and to achieve certainty when the lack of it is too painful to bear.

Early in this essay I asked an ingenuous question: How do most psychoanalysts conceive of reality? Is it in the consulting room, the streets, the past, the future, interpersonal exchange, social media exchange, or all of these and other fields simultaneously? The obvious answer is "all of the above." Yet the answer is not obvious when we consider the tension we know to exist between internal and external experience and the dynamic influence of unconscious fantasy. From our point of view reality is both internal and external. How each person manages the tension between desire and restraint, love and hatred, caring and violence results in a complex reality. We are helpless to define anything as certain; our work embodies the uncertainty principle.

Psychoanalytic thinking as a guide through human experience

Psychoanalysts are more aware than most professionals of the reality and pervasive influence of helplessness and how frightening it can be. Sometimes our special training can cloud our awareness of our vulnerability, however, and the fact that we engage in defensive reactions as all humans do. Each of us is a product of a particular culture as well as of biology and developmental experience.

Disciplines such as philosophy, sociology, history, literature, and the arts often depict or describe human experience in profoundly complementary and instructive ways. A German sociologist, Hartmut Rosa, is interested in resonance as vital to lively human experience. He has written a short book entitled *The Uncontrollability of the World* in English (Rosa, 2020); the German title is *Unverfuegbarkeit* (2018). His introduction to the English translation describes how difficult it was to translate the German word/concept. The difficulty resonates with so many of our experiences in international psychoanalysis, where we seek to share something we know that the other will want to think about too and will find familiar in some way, yet words fail us to give the true sense of what we wish to convey.

As a sociologist, Rosa (2020) casts light on the nature of modern society, on its intense anxieties as underlying the common desire to make the world controllable. But an aggressive effort to render modern life controllable results in frustration, anger, and despair. He captures the importance of an openness to the uncontrollable with the concept of resonance and posits experience is deadened in the absence of resonance. When I think of resonant, some nourishing experiences I imagine to be universal come to mind: a gorgeous sunset, a light falling snow, a smiling baby. Each of them and countless others are completely out of my control. That which is uncontrollable is also a source of joy.

From a sociological point of view, modern society risks killing the world, literally and figuratively, by trying to control rather than understand it. An area of life where psychoanalysis offers hope is in its deep recognition of the timelessness of the unconscious. That recognition informs our commitment to listening, taking time, respecting the complexity of human experience, and our tolerance for disturbing affects and difficult realities. The challenge becomes: How do we use that important awareness? Might we stay silent or listen too long when suffering becomes intolerable or when our patients define their political allegiance very differently from our own? Janine Puget (2008) introduced the notion of sharing an opinion as a clinical intervention that supports recognition within the analytic dyad of "a difficult coexistence between what is known and what is alien/foreign" (translated by González, 2020). With such an intervention, how the two analytic parties' subjectivities are influenced differently by external reality can become evident rather than being inadvertently buried or set aside.

Alterity is a challenging experience that is often denied as opposed to accepted, celebrated, explored, or respected. When politicians or psychoanalysts remain entrenched on opposing sides of an issue and contribute to polarization, "otherness" becomes toxic as opposed to informative and growth-promoting. When we remain silent about what endangers the planet, our local community, or the greater world, we are, in my view, hiding from reality. The question becomes how to fully engage in the complex social realities that confront us in the consulting room as well as in the outside world.

Psychoanalytic thinking offers hope in its devotion to an ethical stance. Viviane Chetrit-Vatine (2012/2014) references Levinas when she articulates a matricial ethic that keeps the clinician centered in the context of the psychoanalytic seduction of another person into an intimate encounter in which the analyst must manage desire, despair, disgust, and intense pressure to act in a very careful and ethical manner.

This ethical core informs our clinical work. I think it must also inform our engagement with questions of how to understand and how to engage actively with society at large. If we enter the public sphere with the specific goal of enhancing our private psychoanalytic practices, I doubt we'll have much success. Our motives must be more than self-serving, although whatever we can do to bring our insights and the power of our method and theory into the public sphere will enhance our standing in the public eye and encourage potential trainees and patients to seek us out.

The activity of speaking out from a psychoanalytic point of view about societal issues is not appealing to every analyst. For example, I myself shy away from forensic settings where attorneys appear to be intent on diminishing my thinking, yet another remnant of my experience with my father. Other analysts are more comfortable with both the attorneys' and their own aggression and, given that foundation, can enlighten a jury regarding the humanity (or lack of it) in a legal situation and the nature and impact of the trauma in question. Once it is stated in simple language, the human side of an argument about responsibility for damage can become crystal clear, and the path to justice opens up.

As a profession we have a legacy of differences. We also have a legacy of generativity and growth based on our acknowledging and exploring our differences. Divisiveness may too often be the proximal experience in our organizational discussions, but our differences remain a significant source of richness and creativity.

My plan for the IPA is to ensure we find ways to use our knowledge and our ethics to develop and support the efforts of our members, their societies, and their communities to face the social stressors, historical forces, and political and environmental threats that have risen to alarming levels in the world. These external factors have subtle, demanding, inevitable presence in the subjectivities present in the consulting room. The psychoanalytic leap going forward will be a theoretical advance regarding the impact of the social surround on individual and group development. Essential to that advance in theory is the private work of analysts to investigate the ways in which their subjectivity is molded by their culture and by current social dynamics.

Notes

1   Additional free clinics opened subsequently in Budapest, Buenos Aires, London, Los Angeles, New York, and Rio de Janiero (Danto, 2005).
2   "Young-Bruehl sees childism as occurring when 'people as individuals and in societies mistreat children in order to fulfill certain needs through them, to project internal conflicts and self-hatreds outward, or to assert themselves when they feel their authority has been questioned' (p.1)" (Ablon, 2012, p. 1340).

References

Ablon, S.L. (2012) Review of the book *Childism: Confronting Prejudice against Children*, by E. Young-Bruehl. *Journal of the American Psychoanalytic Association*. 60(6): 1339–1347.

Bell, D. and Steiner, J. (2011) Hanna Segal obituary. *The Guardian*. www.theguard ian.com/science/2011/jul/14/hanna-segal-obituary

Chetrit-Vatine, V. (2014) *The Ethical Seduction of the Analytic Situation: The Feminine-Maternal Origins of Responsibility for the Other*. London: Karnac. (Original work published 2012).

Dajani, K.G. (2017) The ego's habitus: an examination of the role culture plays in structuring the ego. *International Journal of Applied Psychoanalytic Studies*. 14(4): 273–281. https://doi.org/10.1002/aps.1553

Danto, E.A. (2005) *Freud's Free Clinics: Psychoanalysis and Social Justice, 1918–1938*. New York: Columbia University Press.

Erlich, S. and Erlich-Ginor, M. (2018) Life after atrocities in Europe. The 31st Annual Conference of the European Psychoanalytical Federation, Warsaw, Poland. www.spi web.it/wp-content/uploads/2017/06/epf-2018-en.pdf

Faimberg, H. (1988) The telescoping of generations. *Contemporary Psychoanalysis*. 24(1): 99–118. https://doi.org/10.1080/00107530.1988.10746222

Freud, S. (1950) Project for a scientific psychology (1950 [1895]). *The Standard Edition of the Complete Psychological Works of Sigmund Freud*. 1(1): 281–391.

Full Text of Poland's Controversial Holocaust legislation (2018). Times of Israel. www.timesofisrael.com/full-text-of-polands-controversial-holocaust-legislation/

González, F.J. (2020) First world problems and gated communities of the mind: an ethics of place in psychoanalysis. *Psychoanalytic Quarterly*. 89(4): 741–770. doi: 10.1080/00332828.2020.1805271.

González, F.J. and Peltz, R. (2021) Community psychoanalysis: collaborative practice as intervention. *Psychoanalytic Dialogues*. 31(4): 409–427. doi: 10.1080/10481885.2021.1926788.

González-Torres, M.A. (2013) Psychoanalysis and neuroscience: friends or enemies? *International Forum of Psychoanalysis*. 22(1): 35–42. https://doi.org/10.1080/08037 06x.2011.602359

Hopper, E. (2003) *The Social Unconscious: Selected Papers*. London: J. Kingsley Publishers.

Jeffery, E.H. (2001) The mortality of psychoanalysts. *Journal of the American Psychoanalytic Association*. 49(1): 103–111. https://doi.org/10.1177/000306510 10490011001

Kaës, R. (2007) *Linking, Alliances, and Shared Space: Groups and the Psychoanalyst*. London: The International Psychoanalytic Association.

Kliman, G. (2018) Reflective network therapy for childhood autism and childhood PTSD. *Neuropsychoanalysis: An Interdisciplinary Journal for Psychoanalysis and the Neurosciences*. 20(2): 73–86.

Leuzinger-Bohleber, M. and Kächele, H. (editors) (2015) *An Open Door Review of Clinical, Conceptual, Process and Outcome Studies in Psychoanalysis* (3rd edition). London: International Psychoanalytic Association.

Leuzinger-Bohleber, M., Solms, M., and Arnold, S.E. (2020) *Outcome Research and the Future of Psychoanalysis, Clinicians and Researchers in Dialogue.* London: Routledge.

LeWinn, K.Z., Stroud, L.R., Molnar, B.E., Ware, J.H., Koenen, K.C., and Buka, S.L. (2009) Elevated maternal cortisol levels during pregnancy are associated with reduced childhood IQ. *International Journal of Epidemiology.* 38(6): 1700–1710. https://doi.org/10.1093/ije/dyp200

Moss, D. (2022) On hating in the first person plural: thinking psychoanalytically about racism, homophobia, and misogyny. In: Moss, D. and Zeavin, L. (editors). *Hating, Abhorring and Wishing to Destroy: Psychoanalytic Essays on the Contemporary Moment (The New Library of Psychoanalysis "Beyond the Couch" Series)*, pp 13–31. London: Routledge.

Moss, D. and Zeavin, L. (2022) *Hating, Abhorring and Wishing to Destroy: Psychoanalytic Essays on the Contemporary Moment (The New Library of Psychoanalysis "Beyond the Couch"* Series). London: Routledge.

O'Donovan, A., Epel, E., Lin, J., Wolkowitz, O., Cohen, B., Maguen, S., Metzler, T., Lenoci, M., Blackburn, E., and Neylan, T.C. (2011) Childhood trauma associated with short leukocyte telomere length in post-traumatic stress disorder. *Biological Psychiatry.* 70(5): 465–471. https://doi.org/10.1016/j.biopsych.2011.01.035

Puget, J. (2008) Coartada social y psicoanálisis [Social alibi and psychoanalysis]. *Psicoanálisis.* 30(2–3): 321–322.

Rosa, H. (2018) *Unverfugbarkeit.* Vienna: Residenz Verlag.

Rosa, H. (2020) *The Uncontrollability of the World.* Cambridge: Polity Press.

Segal, H. (1987) Silence is the real crime. *International Review of Psychoanalysis.* 14(1): 3–12.

Tubert-Oklander, J. (2014) *The One and the Many: Relational Analysis and Group Analysis.* London: Karnac.

van Os, J., Marsman, A., van Dam, D., and Simons, C.J.P. (2017) Evidence that the impact of childhood trauma on IQ is substantial in controls, moderate in siblings, and absent in patients with psychotic disorder. *Schizophrenia Bulletin.* 43(2): 316–324. https://doi.org/10.1093/schbul/sbw177

Volkan, V.D., Ast, G., and Greer, W.F. (2002) *The Third Reich in the Unconscious: Transgenerational Transmission and its Consequences.* New York: Brunner-Routledge.

Wallerstein, R.S. (2009) What kind of research in psychoanalytic science? *International Journal of Psychoanalysis.* 90(1): 109–133. https://doi.org/10.1111/j.1745-8315.2008.00107.x

Young-Bruehl, E. (2009). Childism—prejudice against children. *Contemporary Psychoanalysis.* 45(2): 251–265. https://doi.org/10.1080/00107530.2009.10745998

Chapter 12

Conviction, lies, and denialism

Psychoanalytic reflections

Roosevelt Cassorla

Psychoanalysis, in showing us the existence of a psychic reality beyond material reality, has deepened the controversial philosophical discussion in relation to what exists and is true.

Considering the first Freudian topography, we observe that elements of the psychic reality are represented in the conscious and unconscious systems. However, there are experiences – which are unrepresented – that do not belong to either of the two systems. These are potential realities that only become present when stimulated by the relationship with another person. Freud (1937) referred to these aspects in his text "Constructions in Analysis", broadening the field into what we would today call unsymbolized areas or areas with symbolization deficit.[1] We are confronted with situations in which the primitive mind was unable to carry out this task or had, traumatically, been attacked. The analyst seeks to draw them out through imaginary narratives or constructions on what might have happened during the initial stages of development. The validation of the constructions derives from the *conviction* manifested by the patient. This feeling would indicate contact with fragments of the "historic reality", which, in turn, is constantly being transformed by new emotional experiences.

An important factor for the feeling of conviction derives from the emotional impact that occurs within the analytic field. The patient has the experience of engaging with their analyst, who in turn – using their emotions and reveries – is looking for symbols to give a name to what is happening, symbols that the patient is lacking. The emotional truth of the moment is experienced, and this truth is the only one to which both members of the dyad have access. When the analyst suggests, for example, that the patient, in their early life, felt devastated by the sensation of abandonment due to their mother's illness – something they will never remember – the analyst is attempting to connect fantasies which are occurring in the "here and now" of the analytic field.

The patient's conviction derives as much from the fictional hypothetical account as from the impact of the emotional truth present in

DOI: 10.4324/9781003340744-15

the relationship. It matters little if this abandonment on the part of the mother really happened – what matters is that a *new* experience is being lived which attracts associations linked to unconscious factors. The analyst's constructions are the fruit of the accumulation of emotional experiences that emerged seeking dreamers who could dream them. The unsymbolized elements – non-dreams – are transformed into dreams-for-two thanks to the intersubjective relationship.

As we have seen, there is only access to the reality or truth of the moment when the patient and the analyst are connected, at-one-ment (Bion, 1970). This truth is an isolated instance and as soon as it manifests it is already being transformed. The participating observer is transformed by the facts that they observe just as the facts are transformed by the observer. Attacks on the truth are ever present (Cassorla, 2013).

The characters and narratives that are placed in the analytic field (or their absence) show us the development as well as the attacks on the capacity to give meaning to emotional experiences, and manifest at various points on the dream ⟷ non-dream spectrum (Cassorla, 2018b).

Myths, if we consider them to be humanity's dreams, also use narratives. Both have their roots in primitive experiences which have been transformed over the life of the individual and/or the history of human groups. As the dreams-for-two expand the capacity for dreaming and thinking, the patient knows more about himself and is convinced of this fact. The same thing occurs with myths.

At the end of his text Freud (1937) speculates:

> The delusions of patients appear to me to be the equivalents of the constructions which we build up in the course of an analytic treatment – attempts at explanation and cure, though it is true that these, under the conditions of a psychosis, can do no more than replace the fragment of reality that is being disavowed in the present by another fragment that had already been disavowed in the remote past. ... so the delusion owes its convincing power to the element of historical truth which it inserts in the place of the rejected reality.
>
> (p. 267)

Freud is telling us that "wrong" constructions do not do the patient any harm because the latter is unaware of them. However, practice shows us that they can be detrimental in situations where a vulnerable patient latches on to an idealized analyst who is unprepared or unscrupulous, or when there is a chronic enactment (Cassorla, 2018b). The patient has the *conviction* that their analyst is helping them, but this is a false conviction.

Similar situations may arise in families and groups, and in wider society when the latter is subject to manipulative or malevolent leaders and when the capacity for thinking becomes obscured. Freud (1937) warns us:

If we consider mankind as a whole and substitute it for the single human individual, we discover that it too has developed delusions which are inaccessible to logical criticism and which contradict reality. If, in spite of this, they are able to exert an extraordinary power over men, investigation leads us to the same explanation as in the case of the single individual. They owe their power to the element of *historical truth* which they have brought up from the repression of the forgotten and primaeval past.

(p. 268)

The study of attacks on the capacity to think constitutes a crossroads in psychoanalytic knowledge which has proved fruitful. Could this knowledge help us to understand similar occurrences that manifest in social groups?

Our investigation will draw on a short story by Jorge Luis Borges, published in 1935 (Borges, 1975). The reader will not be presented with the "true" story. The initial distortions appear with translations. My summary will falsify it even further.

The short story

In April 1854 a ship called the *Mermaid* which was sailing from Rio de Janeiro to Liverpool sank in the waters of the Atlantic. Among the dead there was a young man called Roger Tichborne, an English army officer who grew up in France and who came from one of the prominent families in England.

His mother, Lady Tichborne, refused to believe that her son was dead and placed heart-rending advertisements in all the newspapers with the largest readership.

One of these advertisements fell into the hands of Bogle, a heavy-set black man who lived in Sidney, who was getting on in years and in authority. There was a second condition: the sudden stroke of genius. He was a well-mannered and decent man, described by Borges as having had his old African ways curbed by the uses and misuses of Calvinism. He could be considered normal apart from the fact that he harboured a great fear of being run over by a vehicle.

Bogle had a very good friend called Arthur Orton, the third and principal character in the story.

Orton was born in Wapping, a poor suburb of London, and like many living in the English slums, he felt the call of the sea and became a sailor. Borges describes him as a man who is at once quiet and dull. He didn't starve to death due to his dim-witted good humour, his fixed smile, and his unremitting meekness. Orton deserted in Chile and these characteristics led him to be loved and adopted by a certain Castro family, from whom he took the surname, thus becoming Tom Castro.

Castro reappears in Sidney where, while crossing a street, he notices the terror of a huge black man, the aforementioned Bogle. Extending his arm to shield him, a protectorate emerges: that of the solid and unsure black man over the obese dimwit from Wapping.

In September 1865 they both read Lady Tichborne's advert in a newspaper looking for her missing son. Bogle's great idea was as follows: Orton should take the first ship back to Europe and satisfy Lady Tichborne's hopes by claiming to be her son. The plan, says Borges, was outrageously ingenious. This was because Tichborne was a gentleman, slight in build, with a precise way of speaking and lively eyes. Orton was a man of low intelligence, with heavy-lidded eyes, and his speech was dim or non-existent.

Bogle knew that an exact likeness of Roger Tichborne would be impossible to achieve and that all the similarities attained would only highlight certain inevitable differences. He therefore steered clear of all likeness. His intuition told him that this fact would serve as convincing proof that no fraud was afoot. But Bogle was counting on one thing, the most important thing, for his plan to work: Lady Tichborne's certainty that her beloved Roger was not dead. Plus the fourteen years that had passed since the shipwreck.

Tom Castro/Orton wrote a letter to Lady Tichborne on Bogle's orders and to confirm his identity, he cited the unimpeachable proof of two moles located on the left side of his chest and the memory of the childhood episode of his having been attacked by a swarm of bees.

The fake story told by the two friends compelled Lady Tichborne – through her tears – to come up with the memories of these things that did not happen.

When Orton arrived, with his manservant Bogle, the tearful mother instantly recognized him and welcomed him with an emotional embrace. Now that she had her son back, Lady Tichborne relinquished the diary and letters that Roger had sent her from Brazil, which had sustained her in her grief through fourteen years of absence.

Bogle smiled to himself: now he had a way to flesh out Roger's ghost.

The story would have ended here, with three happy people: the mother, her fake son, and the successful conspirator.

But Lady Tichborne died in 1870, and her relatives brought suit against Arthur Orton for false impersonation, since they did not believe that this nearly illiterate man was her real son. However, Orton had the support of his numerous creditors who wanted to be paid what was owed to them by Tichborne.

Bogle had a new idea. He arranged for a stream of fake letters to be sent, claiming that Tichborne was an impostor. These letters were signed by priests from the Society of Jesus. Decent people everywhere soon noticed that Tichborne was the target of a Jesuit plot.

During the ensuing trial, one hundred witnesses swore that the defendant was Tichborne, including four officers from his dragoon regiment. He couldn't be an imposter, because if he was then he would have made some effort to imitate portraits from his youth. And besides, his mother couldn't have been wrong.

Bogle ends up being killed in a vehicle accident, as he had foreseen. Orton loses his guru and self-destructs. He continued to lie, but with waning enthusiasm and obvious discrepancies. In February 1874 he was sentenced to fourteen years of forced labour. In prison he got himself liked – this was his calling. His good behaviour secured him an early release. He toured the United Kingdom giving lectures in which he alternately pleaded his innocence or his guilt, whichever the audience wanted to hear at that moment in time.

"Dreaming" the characters

The psychoanalyst does not have the tools to consider a work of art or a social factor like a "patient". However, there is nothing to prevent him from "dreaming" the emotional experiences that result from contact with the work, in other words, from using his imagination to seek out moments of emotional truth. He should remain aware of the reductionism involved.

Let's start with Lady Tichborne. Faced with the pain of the possibility of having lost her son, Lady Tichborne looks for any sign to confirm that he is alive. It doesn't matter if these signs are false or untruthful. As a result, Orton's task becomes easy. Here is a receptive container for his lies. Lady Tichborne came to recall episodes from her son's childhood that did not actually happen. Other "constructions" (in the sense used in Freud's text) were based on letters she had given to her fake son. Possibly to give him more elements to enable him to confirm the desired fraud.

Now let's dream about Orton. This helpless character has one characteristic that facilitates his life – his great capacity for adaptation, his ability to become what others want him to be, like a chameleon. He does not think – he is thought up by Bogle and by all those he takes possession of, transforming them into protective shells which, in reality, are empty. Orton reminds us of the title of the book by Italo Calvino, *The Nonexistent Knight*. The shell that is merged with Bogle disintegrates when the latter dies, and it becomes impossible to regain the defences.

Curiously, both Orton and Lady Tichborne share a false adaptation whose objective is to escape from situations that are experienced as traumatic. Orton needs to build a false self, at all times, to substitute the sensation of non-existence. Lady Tichborne seeks to supplement the loss of a part of herself. These substitutive structures are overlaid with the delusions indicated in Freud's text.

Let us focus for a moment on Bogle, the man with the great idea. Borges leads us to dream about the wild parts of the mind contained by a Calvinist superego. This configuration is complicated by the terrifying contact of threatening aspects, projected in the fantasy of being struck down by a vehicle. Bogle feels attracted to Orton's adhesive side (which protects him from his helplessness in crossing the street). At the same time, he employs obsessive control, recruiting Orton and – through him – Lady Tichborne.

Our dreams have shown us some rather similar aspects among the characters in the short story. Traumatized individuals, experiencing fears of annihilation, combating their helplessness and despair through the fantasy of omnipotent control over reality. Bogle creates lies, Orton disseminates them, Lady Tichborne believes them. Executioners and victims complement each other.

Lies and denialism

The Borges story will serve as a model to allow us to discuss certain aspects relating to conscious lies, without overlooking the fact that they are based on unconscious factors. The liar's capacity for symbolization is sophisticated, since they must know the truth in order to conceal it with lies (Bion, 1970; Meltzer, 1983). For them to be convincing, they must have a certain coherence with the truth.

We can draw a distinction between the lie and the falsehood. The latter refers to an error of perception or judgment. For example, the sun setting over the horizon leads to the false idea that it turns around the Earth. The Inquisitor, who knows that the Earth turns around the sun, *lies* when they condemn Galileo. The patient, whose unconscious defences attack the perception of reality, is not lying, because they do not have access to their defences. Although we may be able to undo them and, in this way, get closer to the truth, it always escapes us. This is part of its unknowable nature. Those who are delusional, the mystics and fanatics, are certain that they have found it.

At one end of the scale there are protective lies and at the other end there are malevolent lies. We can classify lies according to their relationship with the other. We can use as a model the narcissism ⟷ socialism continuum (Bion, 1992). In the area of socialism, where there is respect for the object, we identify lies that are *heroic* and *altruistic* (when someone lies to save someone else's life, for example), *compassionate* (to avoid suffering) and *protective* (to protect someone or a group).

Moving towards narcissism we encounter the *self-protective lie* and the *narcissistic lie*. This attacks otherness, consciously. It is followed by the *malevolent lie* which involves malice. Lemma (2005) proposes the *sadistic lie*, which humiliates the object, and the *self-preservation lie*, which aims to attract the object or avoid its intrusion.

Another perspective reveals a gradient that ranges from a white lie, bordering on astuteness and intelligence, offered gladly and elegantly, to a negative polarity of usage that is obligatory, widespread, growing and, above all, hostile, destructive and self-destructive (Stella and Ferro, 2019).

All the types described above can merge into one another and coexist, sometimes in a way that is confused and split off from the rest of the personality. New lies attempt to justify others, creating a complex web of lies.

Malevolent lies can be used to dominate people and human groups. Sophisticated systems of propaganda convince people of "truths" that are in the interest of the dominant group. The victims remain insecure and confused about what is true. The destruction of knowledge facilitates the conquest of a certain kind of power, one that will "save" people from their insecurity. These lies go beyond *political lies* – supposedly for the good of the people – defended by Plato and Machiavelli (Arendt, 1967).[2]

Lies and falsehoods are articulated within the study of denialism, a social phenomenon that has been becoming more evident in recent times. Initially used to deny historical facts, it has spread in other directions. The denialist scorns evidence, which he considers to be false or deceitful. He commonly creates another reality, opposed to the one that he denies. Denialism may be accompanied by fanaticism. The denialist is convinced of his truth, like Lady Tichborne. Bogle is a false denialist since his only objective is to benefit himself. In between the two we have Orton, the dim-witted follower who is unconcerned with truth or lies: all he needs is a leader who can make him feel like he exists. It wouldn't surprise us if a large part of the current denialist fanatics resembled Orton.

The new reality created by the denialist has its own characteristics: it appeals to a mythical imagination involving ancestral aspects of the individual, the group, or humanity as a whole, transformed into idealized constructions. This hypothesis takes the Freudian idea that there would be a fragment of historical truth – in this case one that is idealized – connected to the history or pre-history of the group, which would contribute to the feeling of conviction.

There is a close relationship between helplessness and the need for idealization. We recall that the universal fantasy of death, as an ending, does not make emotional sense. After death an idealized world awaits us. This other life is merged with ideas of Paradise, a return to the maternal uterus, going back to Mother Earth. This fantasy seems to have been important for our survival as a species. A perfect world is omnipotently created, which is split off from a threatening world. The Islamic suicide bomber, along with the Christian from the Crusades, will be taken to Paradise after killing the infidels. The fanatical groups surrounding Jim Jones and Heaven's Gate killed themselves in the certainty that they would have a special life after death. Followers of the Jehovah's Witnesses prefer to die rather than receive a blood transfusion. Lady Tichborne prefers to imagine an indissoluble mother–child relationship, in life.

The fantasy of omnipotence is projected in myths, ideologies and religions, yet it also persists within the primitive mind. Human groups feel, like the mythical baby, like "creators of the world", fanatics who are in possession of the truth. In order to feel superior, it is crucial that inferior groups exist. The permanent danger is that the truth will be attacked by envious rivals. This is why they must be controlled, dominated or, ultimately, eliminated.

Fanaticism and denialism become more evident during phases of intense changes that are experienced as traumatic, in individuals – for example, during childhood and adolescence – as well as in social groups. People feel confused and helpless, and they become easy targets for leaders to whom they submit themselves blindly. Studying the origins of Nazism in Germany reveals its relationship with the circumstances of helplessness, hatred and resentment among the population as a result of the defeat and the reparations imposed after the First World War.

Freud (1925) has shown us that denial simultaneously conceals and reveals the hidden reality. Other times there is a splitting of the ego: one part disavows the perception of something whilst another accepts it. The thing that is disavowed is substituted for a fetish that represents a perception that occurred shortly before or after the traumatic event – originally castration (Freud, 1927a). We can use these models for the phenomena studied.

Let us suppose that the newborn was expelled from Paradise (intrauterine life) suffering the terrible trauma of falling into Hell. Paradise will be found again in the first breastfeed and Hell will return at some point. Between moments of Paradise and Hell the experience with the other means that we can live in an Earth where infernal hauntings are administered in conflict with idealized gods. What is important to us, in this model, is the fetish that the baby (or humanity) creates to replace the trauma of expulsion from Paradise: total completeness, the oceanic feeling (Freud, 1927b) which will be found in fanatical groups who promote Paradise on Earth and/or in heaven.

It is possible that the plethora of current cases of fanaticism and denialism is being influenced by the difficulty human beings have with coexisting within democratic systems. Power and its transformations must be negotiated all the time and in a transparent way. Conflicts are permanent and lead to different degrees of instability. There are those who prefer to sacrifice freedom in the name of "order". Commonly this "order", which gives rise to repressive regimes, seeks to reinstate privileges that were suspended by the democratic system.

We are aware of the complexity of the phenomena studied, which require interdisciplinary exploration in greater depth. We run the risks inherent to reductionism, wild speculation and ethnocentric bias (Abella, 2018). We appreciate the contributions of social scientists who have demonstrated the relationship between situations of helplessness and the capitalist system, neo-liberalism, the hypertrophy of reason, the idealization of the market, liquid modernity, the narcissistic society, the decline of the paternal function, necropolitics – resulting in dehumanization – themes that we are unable to discuss here.[3] This text proposes that fanatical and denialist behaviour is simultaneously a product of and reaction against these social instabilities linked to individual factors.

The hypotheses outlined help us to shed some light on denialist choices which, as we have seen, seek a return to an idealized past. This past may be recent (for example, the nostalgia for the dictatorship in Brazil) and commonly turns to anti-enlightenment ideas.

When a religion feels threatened this strengthens fundamentalist groups, that is, those who evoke the Scriptures, which are evidently interpreted in a way that is in the interest of the fanatic. The denial of science involves a higher Being who determines everything and protects us if we follow its orders and teachings. Darwinism is experienced as an enemy – its error being to suppose that we, Men created by God in his image and likeness, are only a link in the evolutionary chain. Racists and white supremacists are nostalgic for the times when they were the superior race, dominating all "inferior" races. The Nazis revived myths of their origins such as being descendants of the Aryans, a superior race. Mussolini's model was the power of ancient Rome. Evangelical groups have appropriated Jewish symbols in the expectation of the coming of the Messiah, who will supposedly convert Jews to Christianity. The denialism of the power of vaccines is also based on a fantasy that everything that is "natural", meaning, that which is God-given, will save us. We don't have to worry about climate change, as though we could return to the dawn of time when God kept nature intact and mankind simply enjoyed it. Women and homosexuals are threatening because they stimulate desires and needs in beings considered to be superior.

Curiously, the risk of nuclear war (Segal, 1990) is no longer discussed. Le Goff (1994) shows us how the medieval imagination continues to be present in our culture. This was an age in which there was order, chivalry and loyalty. The idealization of the dominant class (the nobles and landowners) conveniently overlooks the impoverished, submissive and oppressed population.

Fanaticism may also manifest itself among those in the opposing camp. The fanatic who evokes the Scriptures may be set against the fanatic who wants to destroy any vestige of tradition. Sometimes, different fanaticisms clash within the same religious and ideological groups, each of which considers itself to be "purer" than the other.

Fanaticism and denialism attack the individual or group who employs reason, who allows for and seeks out debate, controversy, who respects the evidence and opinions of others. The greatest threat to the fanatic is freedom of thought. That is why, behind all denialism, there always exists in latent form the hatred of freedom, of creativity, of the fertile coexistence with the other, of the capacity to think, feel and transform the world by learning through experience.

The fanatical denialist cannot bear otherness. There are strong indications that the initial flaws in his development have led him to cling symbiotically or parasitically to idealized objects, reactive formations against terror and helplessness. To these emotional configurations we can add the inculcation of fanatical ideas, primarily among babies, children, adolescents and/or in situations of severe helplessness. These constitute destructive and malevolent narcissistic organizations that feel threatened by everything that is non-self. The enemy must be seduced, conquered, threatened or eliminated. Potentially, the very apparatus of perception may be attacked and the fanatical behaviour may become confused with the psychotic (Cassorla, 2019).

We are currently observing the expansion of so-called destructive populism, whose objective is to destroy democratic institutions, particularly those that seek to mitigate social suffering (Bollas, 2020). The omnipotently destructive affects are idealized and the container function of democratic society is distorted or destroyed. This implies the permanent escalation of destructive-exciting acts that seek to maintain the symbiotic relationship of destructive narcissism (Zienert-Eilts, 2020).

Bogle and Orton influenced dozens of people because these people wanted to believe them. Vulnerable populations seeking magical solutions allow themselves to be convinced. The leader employs emotional influence. They use prosody, mellifluous and/or threatening intonation that accompanies speech. Variations in vocal intensity, timbre and pauses induce emotions through acts of speech (Austin, 1962). Marching music reflects the heartbeat of the mother, heard by the baby. Klemperer (2013) has shown how Nazism deceptively transformed the meaning of words. In 1948 Orwell (2009) described "new-speak" in his book *Nineteen Eighty-Four*. Political propaganda uses the same mechanisms in democracies, too. All these resources are amplified by social media, using sophisticated artifices to attack the thinking capacity of victims who in turn are also in search of certainties. In recent times we have seen terms emerge such as "post-truth" to describe the lie induced emotionally and "truth decay" for the distortion of the truth.

We cannot conclude without addressing the psychoanalytic movement. Psychoanalysts are human beings. It is arrogant to attribute superiority to having "undergone analysis". We know about the support of psychoanalysts for Nazism, for dictatorial governments, for situations of social violence. Psychoanalytic training itself carries risks: there are Institutes where certain authors and ideas are denigrated – which is itself a form of denialism. There exist certainties surrounding "what is psychoanalysis" and "what is not psychoanalysis" based on beliefs and ideologies. There exist courses in which only a single author is studied. This can be a result of thinking becoming obstructed because certain authors are treated as though they were gospel. There are real sects in which the disciples follow a certain master. Disputes over political power can make creative investigation difficult. Racist and homophobic psychoanalysts exist. Ultimately, nothing different to what takes place among other human groups.

Curiously, the prestige of psychoanalysis has led it to mix with beliefs and religions. In my country there has been a trend for mental health professionals to call themselves psychoanalysts, even if they do not know about or use psychoanalytic knowledge. More dangerous has been the use of the title by groups of evangelical pastors, who have trained over three thousand "psychoanalysts" in courses lasting two semesters. These groups are pressuring the government to regulate the profession using criteria such as … two semesters of training.

The Brazilian Societies linked to the IPA have fought against this legislation, but everything seems to indicate that it will end up happening.

Does psychoanalysis have something to offer in the treatment of liars, fanatics and denialists? The majority of people with these characteristics do not seek psychoanalysis and are usually against it. However, we can identify these defences in some patients who seek us out for other reasons and help them get to know themselves better. Without the presumption – which is also arrogant – that we are turning them into a "better" person.

Our greatest challenge is to find ways in which the discoveries of psychoanalysis can benefit society. We are at a crossroads. Many studies – which we are unable to address in this text – have brought forth valuable reflections on the relationship between psychoanalytic knowledge and the violence that manifests between human groups. On the other hand, there are colleagues who argue that psychoanalysis should not dedicate itself to these areas. I take a divergent view.

This text has focused on a small section of Evil. Green (2010) illustrates dehumanisation at its highest level when he describes aspects of the de-objectalizing function:

> You do not exist. ... I don't even need to hold my nose any longer to protect myself from the nauseous smell you give off, for I can no longer feel anything that comes from you. To feel or sense what you exude, what you show or give me to understand, would be to accept implicitly your existence. But you don't have any existence. You are not even a piece of shit. You are a pile of ashes. Dust. And your death is retroactive. You have only ever existed, in fact, by virtue of an accident, which has to be resolved. The mourning that takes place for you will confer a retroactive existence on you. Thus it must not happen. You are a non-lieu.
>
> (pp. 109–110)

Our understanding of the inhuman falls short. Facing it, we feel perplexed, terrified and powerless. We can ignore it, or conform ourselves. We also run a formidable risk of naïvely imagining that we can fight inhumanity with more inhumanity. We must "question evil with its own logic, so that, beginning with the denunciation of its false premises, it can become undone or ... be highlighted when it tries to camouflage itself" (Chuster, Soares, and Trachtenberg, 2014, p. 119; our translation).

Notes

1 Freud (1923) had already anticipated this: "the *Ucs.* does not coincide with the repressed; it is still true that all that is repressed is *Ucs.*, but not all that is *Ucs.* is repressed" (p. 17).
2 Cassorla (2018) addresses the lie that manifests in the analytic field.

3   A review of the social aspects can be found here: https://plato.stanford.edu/entries/
postmodernism/

References

Abella, A. (2018) Can psychoanalysis contribute to the understanding of fundamentalism? An introduction to a vast question. *International Journal of Psychoanalysis*. 99(3): 642–664.

Arendt, H. (1967) Truth and politics. *The New Yorker*.

Austin, J.L. (1962) *How to Do Things by Words*. Cambridge: Harvard University Press.

Bion, W.R. (1970) *Attention and Interpretation*. London: Maresfield.

Bion, W.R. (1992) *Cogitations*. London: Karnac.

Bollas, C. (2020) Civilization and the Discontented. YouTube.

Borges, J.L. (1975) Tom Castro, the implausible impostor. In: *A Universal History of Infamy*. New York: Penguin, pp. 30–39. (In Portuguese: O impostor inverosímil Tom Castro. In: *História Universal da Infâmia*. Lisboa: Assiria e Alvim, pp. 27–36.)

Cassorla, R.M.S. (2013) When the analyst becomes stupid. An attempt to understand enactment using Bion's theory of thinking. *Psychoanalytic Quarterly*. 82: 323–360.

Cassorla, R.M.S. (2017) The dreaming field. In: Katz, S.M., Cassorla, R.M.S., and Civitarese, G. (editors). *Advances in Contemporary Psychoanalytic Field Theory*. New York: Routledge pp. 91–112.

Cassorla, R.M.S. (2018a) Breve ensaio sobre a mentira (A brief essay on lying). *Revista Brasileira de Psicanálise*. 52: 81–96.

Cassorla, R.M.S. (2018b) *The Psychoanalyst, the Theater of Dreams and the Clinic of Enactment*. London: Routledge.

Cassorla, R.M.S. (2019) Fanaticism: reflections based on phenomena in the analytic field. *International Journal of Psychoanalysis*. 100: 1338–1357.

Chuster, A, Soares, G., and Trachtenberg, R. (2014) *W.R. Bion: A Obra Complexa*. Porto Alegre: Sulina.

Freud, S. (1923) The ego and the id. *The Standard Edition of the Complete Psychological Works of Sigmund Freud*. 14.

Freud, S. (1925) Negation. *The Standard Edition of the Complete Psychological Works of Sigmund Freud*. 19.

Freud, S. (1927a) The future of an illusion. *The Standard Edition of the Complete Psychological Works of Sigmund Freud*. 2.

Freud, S. (1927b) Fetichism. *The Standard Edition of the Complete Psychological Works of Sigmund Freud*. 21.

Freud, S. (1937) Constructions in analysis. *The Standard Edition of the Complete Psychological Works of Sigmund Freud*. 23.

Green A. (2010) *El pensamiento clinico*. Buenos Aires: Amorrortu (*La pensée clinique*. Paris: Odile Jacob, 2002).

Klemperer, V. (2013) *The Language of the Third Reich*. London: Bloomsbury.

Le Goff, J. (1994) *The Medieval Imagination*. Chicago: Chicago University Press.

Lemma, A. (2005) The many faces of lying. *International Journal of Psychoanalysis*. 86: 737–753.

Meltzer, D. (1983) *Dream-Life*. Reading: Clunie Press.

Orwell, G. (2009) *Nineteen Eighty-Four*. New York: Albatross.

Segal, H. (1990) *Dream, Phantasy and Art*. London: Routledge.

Stella, G. and Ferro, A. (2019) *True lies. Un'apologia della menzogna*. Milano: Mimesis.

Zienert-Eilts, K.J. (2020) Destructive populism as "perverted containing": a psychoanalytical look at the attraction of Donald Trump. *International Journal of Psychoanalysis*. 101: 971–991.

Chapter 13

First do no harm

David Bell

What I have to say will be divided into three sections.[1] In the first, I will elaborate on what I have learnt about the healthcare of transgender children, and the serious clinical and ethical concerns that I, like many others who have become involved in this field of work, have come to recognise. I will then note some sudden developments that we have been witnessing in this field, and I will go on to discuss some of the socio-cultural factors that may be relevant to understanding them. Lastly, I will examine some of the characteristics of a peculiar form of thinking, or more precisely, non-thinking, that seems to have come to dominate the discourse in this area.

The understanding/knowledge that I have been developing comes from a number of sources, including my engagement with colleagues in the United Kingdom, in other European countries (particularly Sweden), Australia and the USA. But the main source was in my engagement with staff from the Gender Identity and Development Service (GIDS) at the Tavistock and Portman NHS Foundation Trust.

Firstly, I need to state an important rider – and the fact that I have to do so is symptomatic of the highly charged atmosphere in which discussions of this area take place, resulting in important and often highly motivated misunderstandings. What I wish to make clear at the outset is that questions about the appropriateness of medical and surgical intervention, most particularly in children, need to be kept entirely distinct from questions of discrimination. I say this as there is pressure for these two matters to be elided, and I will return to this later. We are all appalled by any violent hatred that many trans people have to suffer and indeed we may have some psychoanalytic thoughts as to its sources. I also need to make it clear that I can see that for *some* individuals, medical transition is the only reasonable option.

Background

The last ten years witnessed a massive increase in referrals of children and adolescents to GIDS, as shown in Figure 13.1. This increase has continued and the latest figure I have is 2700 (in 2019/2020).

DOI: 10.4324/9781003340744-16

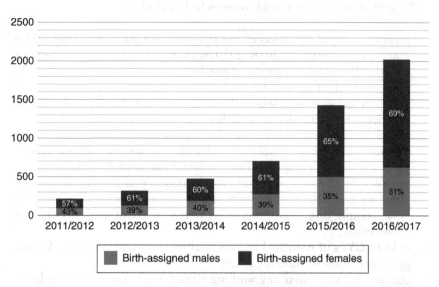

Figure 13.1 Referrals to the Gender Identity Development Service by birth-registered gender, April 2011–April 2017

I have shown in Figure 13.1 the clear geometric increase in referrals, but I would like also to draw your attention to the rising proportion of natal females – a relatively new phenomenon.

In 2019 I was in the last year of my term as a member of the Council of Governors of the Tavistock and Portman NHS Trust (from now on referred to as the Tavistock) – I was employed by the Tavistock for nearly 25 years. The Council is a structure made up of stakeholders (representatives from communities near to the Tavistock (the boroughs of Camden and Islington), from the rest of London and the rest of England, universities, general practice and staff. I was a staff governor representing academic and clinical staff. Around January 2019 some staff working on GIDS approached me as they had profound ethical and clinical concerns as to the way the children and young people (CYP) were being managed. Over the next nine months or so ten staff in all sought me out (that is roughly 1/3 of all the staff working in the service. They came from different disciplines and were mixed in seniority. All except one felt unable to see me in my room at the Tavistock for fear of being seen and instead were interviewed at my private consulting room – this alerted me to the level of threat and intimidation they were exposed to and this was a constant throughout the period I was involved. They had attempted to raise these concerns with their managers, with the medical director and with the Trust 'speak up' guardian – all without success.

The staff all raised very similar issues which included:

- pressure of rapid expansion of the service over a short time from 90 (in 2009) to 2700 referrals 2018–2019, without pause to enquire into what underlay this massive increase in numbers;
- huge caseloads of up to 140;[2]
- very inexperienced staff seeing the cases (that is, with very little clinical experience and certainly no specialist experience);
- serious levels of staff distress; rapid staff turnover;
- absence of appropriate (scientific) attitude of enquiry and uncertainty given the sudden changes and experimental nature of the treatment;
- serious ethical issues as regards the inadequacy of consent in minors, often with very little discussion of the potential brain, cognitive and bone complications, nor the infertility and sexual dysfunction that would ensue;
- risks to CYPs of hormonal and surgical interventions without adequate assessment time or thinking space;
- absence of discussion of any working clinical models or knowledge base;
- atmosphere of threat and intimidation/fear of being 'found out' for whistle-blowing – endemic fear of being accused of being 'transphobic';
- 'politically correct' culture privileging a kind of proceduralism in a complex situation where time for thought and reflection is needed;
- inappropriate involvement in GIDS of highly ideologically motivated 'trans' lobbies such as Mermaids;[3]
- very little capacity to resist pressures from family and social media; inability to stand up to pressure from trans lobbies for fear of being seen as transphobic;
- Perhaps as a result of GIDS being a nationally funded service, there was unclear governance and accountability of lead staff, a tendency for the service to see itself as accountable not to the Tavistock but instead directly to NHS England (NHSE)- this may have contributed to the sense of the service as existing completely detached from the traditions and culture of the Tavistock;
- an oversimplified view of cases with certain ones being viewed as 'straightforward' – how a child with gender dysphoria seeking medical and surgical intervention could be thought of as 'straightforward' was of course very concerning[4] – the clinicians who spoke to me regarded these CYP as among the most difficult and complex cases they had seen – often with multiple problems and highly disturbed families;
- poor levels of engagement with the children, pressure to push them through on to the medical pathway – partly attributable to the highly politicised pressures and long waiting lists;
- some children only seen once or twice before being referred for the prescription of puberty-blocking drugs;

- no real clinical model that could form a basis for understanding these CYPs; and
- the service at that time had a trans affirmative position (that is, an unquestioning acceptance of the declared gender identity of their child patients), and this stance was extremely difficult to question.

The service model was made at a time when there were 50 referrals a year and the very large majority came off puberty-blocking hormones after a lengthy period of engagement; now there were 2500 referrals per year (that is, a year-on-year increase of about 100%) but no attempt of the service to reconsider the model in the face of these massive changes in the characteristics of the population under their care – further, nearly 100% now remained on puberty blockers and went on to opposite sex hormones; so commencing them on puberty blockers was in effect starting them on a road to opposite sex hormones and probably towards surgery, that is, the decision to commence puberty blockers was heavily freighted with that knowledge – but instead it was taken lightly and assurances were given of 'reversibility'.[5]

Little interest had been expressed into understanding what may have led to the geometric increase in referrals in such a short time, nor in understanding of the reason for the change over from the majority being biological males seeking transition to female, to the majority being females seeking transition to male – it is, of course, reasonable to assume that poorly understood social and cultural factors are involved.

The low level of engagement was complicated by the fact that the CYPs often arrived with a rehearsed script. Some had gone online, or been scripted by parents, learning what were the 'right answers' to the questions – that is, the answers that would be likely to secure starting on the medical pathway to transition. Obviously, it would take considerable care, sensitivity and maturity for the clinician to be able to get past this defensive system – but more than anything it would take time, and time was what they did not have.

Parents who raised doubts and were concerned about the advisability of affirming the child's new gender identity were often alienated from the service or pressured to accept the child's position.

Many discussed systemic homophobia and intimidation of gay and lesbian staff. When they raised the difficult problem of homophobia in the families of children they were seeing, they were themselves intimidated or taken off the case (I discuss this further below).

I was impressed by the fact that the same issues came up again and again in the interviews, and deeply shocked to hear that CYPs were being neglected and placed on treatments for which there is *no* evidence (there having been no follow-up studies) and subjected to serious risk. I became convinced that that GIDS and thus the Tavistock had abandoned its duty of care and safeguarding to these CYPs.[6]

The service seemed to these staff to be completely cut off from what they viewed as Tavistock core values.[7] For example, senior staff were largely hostile to notions of the unconscious and psychoanalytic thinking in general.

Most of the staff I interviewed had left or were leaving the service for ethical reasons. Others stayed on to try and fight the battle and do their best to try and get proper treatment for their cases. There were some sites of good practice which individual clinicians struggled to maintain, often at considerable cost to themselves.

As a result of hearing these very serious concerns, I wrote a report which was submitted to the Board of the Tavistock. Management attempted to block my circulating the report to the Council of Governors and threatened me. However, I took my own legal advice and submitted the report. This marked the beginning of a very difficult relationship between myself and the management of the Tavistock, which continued until I retired in January 2021. However, I received support from analytic colleagues within the Trust and thus was able to continue to work securely in the adult department.

Management carried out a 'review' of the service led by the medical director that unsurprisingly functioned to reassure the service and the organisation that there were no serious problems.

Around this time a group of parents of adolescents contacted the Tavistock, concerned that young people were being fast-tracked on to a medical pathway.[8] Their letter raised many of the issues that had been brought to me – and, of course, made me more confident in my conclusions.

My report and its subsequent publicity (it was leaked to the press) formed part of a chain of circumstances which has led to increasing critical understanding of the inappropriate treatment of gender dysphoria in children and young people.

Legal action was taken by ex-patient Keira Bell (no relation) and an anonymous parent which took the form of judicial review seeking guidance from the Court as to whether or not children were legally in position to give consent to medical interventions whose consequences were unknown, but for which there was very reasonable concern as to the long-term consequences and potential serious damage.[9] Central to these proceedings was consideration of how the child's level of maturity and the presence of very significant psychological disturbance might interfere with the capacity of that child to make a reasoned consenting decision. The judgment, delivered in December 2020,[10] found that children were *not* in a position to give consent. The judges also expressed very serious concerns about the very poor governance of GIDS. In particular, they mentioned the lack of data on comorbidity, the lack of any proper follow-up and the lack of knowledge as to what percentage of the children seen in the clinic went on to opposite sex hormones or to surgery.

The Court of Appeal overturned this judgment in September 2021.

This latter finding has been very widely misunderstood – the Court did *not* give an opinion on whether children/young people can or cannot consent. Instead, it took the view that the Divisional Court (which had heard the judicial review) lacked the authority to reach such a judgment. By analogy, if a court finds that an official who had issued a traffic fine had no authority to do so, this would overturn that decision but would have no bearing on whether or not the offence had been committed. The appeal judges did state that it was assumed very great care would be taken by clinicians over issues of consent – but, of course, there was considerable mounting evidence that this was not the case.

Further, this appeal necessarily and properly addresses the finding of the judicial review *only in relation to consent* – the other serious issues raised concerning the poor governance of GIDS remain unchallenged.

The next major event in this sad story was the Sonia Appleby case. Sonia Appleby is the child safeguarding lead for the entire Tavistock. GIDS had undermined her position, sought to prevent staff from raising child safeguarding concerns with her and subjected her to intimidation (for raising concerns about the adequacy of child safeguarding on GIDS), and this led her, eventually, to take legal action against the Tavistock. The Employment Tribunal that heard the case found in her favour, that is they agreed that she had suffered reputational damage and had been prevented from doing her work on safeguarding as a result of raising legitimate concerns. They ordered the Trust to pay damages.[11] Over and above the immediate impact of this finding, its implications were very grave as it supported the claims made by GIDS staff that there was an atmosphere of threat and intimidation directed towards any staff who raised concerns about GIDS.

Lastly, the Care Quality Commission (responsible for ensuring appropriate levels of clinical care) visited the service in 2020. Their report, again, raised very serious concerns about the level of clinical care and governance of the service and also commented on staff's fear of retribution for raising concerns. In June 2021 NHS England took action by going in to the Tavistock in order to have oversight of the management and governance of the organisation.

The Tavistock initiated disciplinary proceedings against me. I provided a detailed written response to all the allegations they made. Following receipt of this response, they failed to convene a disciplinary hearing and I left on my planned retirement date.

In response to the now widespread concern about the provision of a potentially harmful treatment without any proper evidence base, NHS England have set up a wide-ranging review of clinical guidelines (known as the 'Cass Review') which released its interim report earlier this year (https://cass.inde pendent-review.uk/publications/interim-report/). The report echoed many of the concerns I and others have raised – for example about the inappropriateness of the 'affirmative model', the lack of appropriate care of the patient group, the lack of evidence for puberty blockers. NHS England, in view of the report, has since announced the closure of the service In the meantime, Sweden's Karolinska Institute has ended the use of puberty-blocking drugs or cross-sex hormones for minors (outside of ethically approved clinical studies)[12] and Finnish authorities have issued guidelines[13] that state that psychotherapy, rather than puberty blockers and cross-sex hormones, should be the first-line treatment for gender-dysphoric youths.

I now move away from this local story to consider more general issues.

Concerns regarding the understanding and treatment of trans children

It is vital to differentiate gender dysphoria (GD) from transgender – the former refers to deep feelings of discomfort with the sexual body which have multiple sources and multiple appropriate therapeutic approaches. 'Transgender' refers to those individuals who have completed or are embarking upon medical and surgical interventions aimed at altering their gender identity. However, services pressured by trans lobbies and by an increasingly hegemonic *zeitgeist* fail to discriminate between the two, with disastrous consequences.

There are multiple routes to GD – the list is long but would include the presence of various psychological disorders including depression and autistic spectrum disorder,[14] and children who, for multiple and complex reasons, live a lonely and isolated life, feeling that they just have no place in the world, and are psychically lost and homeless. Serious family disturbance is common, often with intergenerational transmission of major trauma such as child abuse in the mother/maternal line (sometimes a source of the mothers not being able to cope with a daughter now showing signs of entering puberty). Some families have suffered other major traumas; for example, the death of, say, a female child brings her brother to seek transition to support the identification with the dead sibling – returning the loved deceased daughter to the bereft parents.

A very important causal route, well described in the literature, is related to homosexuality. It is not uncommon for a gay boy, for example, to think that because he is attracted to the same sex he must 'really' be a girl. Some children who show characteristics of being gay/lesbian find this is not tolerated by the family (often very overtly, but equally often in a more subtle, even unconscious way); the children internalise this intolerance of their sexual orientation which becomes manifest as hatred of their own sexual bodies.

There is considerable evidence that a large number of these children, if helped in a proper manner, desist from transition and develop into gay or lesbian adults.

This also illustrates a further very important issue in the Tavistock service and which is reflected around the world – the peculiar absence of consideration of sexuality, which had become completely blotted out by the category of gender – of course, from a psychoanalytic perspective, considerations of sexuality and gender are completely intertwined within the psychology of a person.

We can suggest, then, that in any population of CYP who present with gender dysphoria there are two groups of children: Group A who will persist with medical/surgical intervention, and Group B who, with sufficient appropriate neutral support, will desist (that is, accept their natal sex and, in many cases, develop into non-conforming gay and lesbian adults). But, given the complete lack of evidence, we have no way of determining which group any particular child belongs to – although it is very clear that Group A is highly likely to be very small indeed.

How is it conceivable that we can go ahead and risk doing irreparable damage to children's bodies on this basis?

Thus, while it is clear that we are dealing with a highly complex problem with many causal pathways, and in any particular case no single aetiological factor, GIDS and other similar services around the world tend towards a damaging simplification. There are various reasons that underlie this, not least the huge increase in case loads and long waiting lists, leading to pressures to process the children rapidly rather than providing a service aimed at understanding the individual cases in any depth. Of course, alignment with affirmative lobbies (that is, lobbies that seek to 'affirm' the wish to change gender, tending to see it only as a positive choice to be encouraged) acts as an ideological support for this simplification.

Many services lack any understanding of, and are overtly hostile to, any thought about the unconscious issues. Even thinking about cause is very often regarded as an act of hostility – for the only acceptable explanation is that the child is *literally* in the wrong body and all suffering is secondary to this 'fact'. It needs to be borne in mind that there is absolutely no evidence for this assertion. Although the lobby group Mermaids asserted this until recently, they have now deleted it from their website.[15]

Sudden increase in incidence of gender dysphoria and the factors underlying it

It must, I think, be clear that such a rapid escalation of cases, the increase in natal females, the sudden appearance of 'rapid onset gender dysphoria', where the onset takes place over short period of times measured often in weeks or months, cannot be explained by individual factors alone, nor is it likely to be caused by a large number of individuals feeling free to 'come out' in this new 'liberal' atmosphere. It must be derived from socio-cultural forces that are as yet poorly understood or even investigated. It is therefore regrettable that treatment for children and adolescents has been increasing exponentially, without any enquiry into this broader determining socio-cultural context and also no real knowledge of the consequences as there is no adequate follow-up data. In the USA gender transitioning has become a huge growth industry.

Perhaps it is worth stating here that *all* psychological disorders arise from the interaction between the individual and the culture around her. That is, no psychiatric disorder can be understood as purely to do with the individual. There is considerable evidence (see, for example, Marchiano, 2019) that the recognition of a new condition, and the creation of specialist clinics to diagnose and treat it, result in a massive increase in the apparent incidence of the condition (this was true for hysteria and false memory syndrome). For example, certain core conflicts regarding sexuality in girls will express themselves in different ways,: hysteria, eating dirorders, various personality disturbances, gender dysphoria.- depending on the cultural context

What I offer here is only a preliminary sketch of some of the factors that may be relevant to this sudden change (see also Figure 13.2).

1. The ever-increasing penetration of the market form into all aspects of life reaches deep into the psychology of the person, reformulating identity so that identity comes to manifest features of the commodity form; identity moves from being something that one lives with, and struggles with over time, to a more transient structure which, somewhat like a commodity, is exchangeable. Commodity exchange, because of its extra-ordinary rapidity, supports the illusion of instantaneous transformation. It should be clear that I do *not* mean that a trans person just chooses a new identity, without any painful struggle, but only that this underlying socio-cultural change acts as a tendential force influencing the way we all think.

    This development is increasingly expressed in the relation between doctors and patients, which degenerates into its perverse form, a celebration of customer-hood (misunderstood as democratisation). Here, the distinction between need and wish evaporates – that is, we have been used to a world where a patient requests X treatment, but the professional can disagree, introducing a triangulation that may be welcomed or resisted. However, powerful social forces misrepresent this triangulation as only representing a kind of patriarchal power play, and where this is successful, externality collapses.

2. Overburdened child mental health services which cannot cope with the combination of increasing demand and cutting of resources are stretched to breaking point (for the UK situation, see the Association of Child Psychotherapy report 'A Silent Catastrophe'[16]). Faced with children suffering complex, serious disorders, it is understandable that any mention of gender problems can result in referral to specialist gender services, and in the process, complex disorders (now filtered through the prism of gender) can be left completely unaddressed (as has been most

recently stated in the Cass review (op cit). This can also lead to a damaging foreclosure of the ordinary turbulence and confusion of adolescence.

3. Another major change is to be found in the transformation of political life so that identity politics (race, gender) moves into a dominant position. This movement started off life as liberal and progressive but then (and this has been brilliantly discussed by feminist and black theorists[17]) it twists and turns, coming to manifest the very characteristics it sought to challenge; it becomes fixed, narrow and all-determining; critical engagement now recast as the enemy to be silenced.

4. The increasing recourse to medical and surgical intervention enacts a breakdown in the boundary between the bodily self and technology. As Rosine Perelberg (2018) has put it:

> the scale to which technology has penetrated the human body (is) worldwide. If Foucault's writings were ground-breaking indicating the control that society has exercised over the body, it seems that now there is a step further taken in that the new technologies and new form of capitalism takes over the production of the body itself.[18]

5. I think that in our current conjuncture we are witnessing a growing misogyny. What I have in mind here is this: since the Second World War up until the late 70s, a strong femininity, expressed by the increasing theorisation and respect for maternal caring, and in the British Context the creation of the Welfare State, maintained a certain social dominance. However, that version of strong caring has come to be represented in its perverse form, 'nanny state', a contemptuous attack on femininity.[19] This is both expressed and reinforced by ideological forms that promote the delusion of the autonomous man seeking to service only his own needs, enacting a hatred of all forms of dependence. It is further evidenced by the growing acceptance of the degradation of women through the normalisation of porn. In the UK female students who prostitute themselves to manage their difficult financial situation have been 'affirmed', even celebrated as choosing 'sex work' as a free choice – this has been the object of considerable critique from feminist groups. In my view, the increasing stereotyping of female gender identity (I discuss this further below) is a manifestation of this misogynistic turn. These various degradations of femininity may be having profound effects on girls and, in conjunction with more individual factors, support the internalisation of this hatred of femininity, transformed into a hatred of their female sexed bodies.

Affirmation thus colludes with a girl's disgust/hatred of her sexual body. Most of these children/young people to do *not* present with the belief 'I am a boy not a girl' but with a feeling of deep hatred and disgust of their sexual body experienced as a trapping claustrophobic prison from which they desperately need to escape. The sexual body, thus, in ways that are, psychoanalytically, utterly unsurprising, becomes the location for all sorts of other unbearable conflicts. This situation gives rise to the belief (supported culturally) that 'there is a place (another body) I can get into/occupy ... this will cure me ... I will be at last at peace'. Social transition is not a benign act as it too colludes with the hatred of the sexed body and also makes it increasingly difficult for the child to accept normal puberty. This type of understanding makes the prescription of puberty blockers even more concerning: 'puberty blockers as well as blocking the physical changes that puberty brings also block the developmental process whereby dysphoria often resolves' (Joyce, 2021).

6.   The internet/social media is a major determining force and occupies a position that is both causal *and* a vehicle for other causes. Through a kind of viral social contagion,[20] children who feel lost in the world become radicalised online, and join trans groups that provide them at last with an identity and social belonging, and also an explanation for all their suffering. Further, because of its overwhelming ubiquity and power, it is the medium through which the other factors listed above are transmitted at speed and with no obstruction.

   This factor is of considerable importance in the very marked increase in the occurrence of rapid onset gender dysphoria – there is considerable evidence of social contagion in schools.

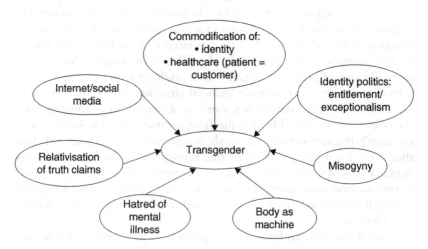

Figure 13.2 Some factors contributing to the sudden growth of gender dysphoria in children and adolescents

A peculiar mode of thinking

I will here elaborate on some aspects of the peculiar form of thinking, or rather non-thinking, that has come to dominate the discourse in this area.

As I think I have made clear, thoughtful engagement is treated as a kind of enemy and this is certainly the experience of many clinicians working in gender services. The wish to think over time and understand why a particular child has developed gender dysphoria comes to be seen as an expression of 'transphobia', creating a world where "You are either with me or against me", that is, a paranoid universe where there is no room for a mind that just wants to think about things. The intolerance of doubt and thought that characterises certain kinds of mental states here leaks out and becomes a force in the social realm.

The term 'transphobia' has, for our psychoanalytic community, a particular unfortunate resonance, namely, the homophobia that is a part of our history. I have in mind that dark history of conversion therapies for homosexuals (particularly, though not only, in the USA); I believe the fear of repeating this has interfered with our capacity to think through these issues and has led us to turn a blind eye to the damage being caused to young people. But it is vital to distinguish between conversion therapy and a wish to think. As I see it, the rapid decisions as regards the provision of medical and surgical intervention *is itself* a form of conversion therapy – like the past 'treatments' for homosexuality, it seeks to refashion the body as the only permissible solution to painful conflicts about gender. That is, it brings about transformations in the body, converting it in order to satisfy insufficiently examined individual, family and social agendas. The Lesbian, Gay and Bisexual Alliance supports this position (see https://lgballiance.org.uk/end-conversion-therapy/).

Lastly, the possession of a particular identity is taken as supplying one with a peculiar kind of higher authority. Let me explain: if, for example, a person says 'as a gay man, or Jewish man, or disabled man, or black woman, or whatever', it would be reasonable to accept that such a person, because of their specific experiences, will enrich any discussion of the world with which they identify. But this does *not* bring entitlement to an unquestioned higher authority. That is, by belonging to X or Y group, my views as to what is true of the world, particularly about the group to which I belong, remain as open to question as the views of any other person. However, in these discussions membership of the relevant group is assumed to grant a 'higher authority', exhibiting a kind of entitlement (that can in part derive from the link between a particular identity and the traumatising experience of victimhood), an entitlement that must not be questioned. This is, in other words, a demand to be exempt from the ordinary canons as to what counts as good judgement -there can be no personal or group sovereignty as to what counts as true. There is here, I believe, a link to the attack on truth value that is also a characteristic of our 'postmodern' age. I have discussed this elsewhere (Bell, 2009).

If we take it as a fact that gender identity is largely socially constructed, then there is a paradox at the heart of the trans phenomenon. The apparent freedom/liberation it expresses is totally undermined by locating all possibility of change only concretely, in material alteration of the body, rather than in the mind.

There has been a peculiar regression in thinking. In our contemporary world we are (at least in urban liberal environments) generally tolerant, even celebrate, a certain fluidity in expression of gender and sexuality. We are less interested in who a person goes to bed with, less bothered by a man being somewhat feminine or a woman being, so to speak, unfeminine. This exists alongside a toleration of certain limitations arising from the body. In the ideology of the militant trans lobbies, there is a peculiar rigidity of gender identity coupled with a belief in the total fluidity of the body, a most peculiar reversal. This is coupled with an essentialist mode of thought; that is, gender identity is confused with anatomical sex and so is seen as biological and fixed rather than psychological, social and fluid.

Bea Campbell (2016) has said:

> The sexual revolution wrought by feminist and gay activism has, of course, changed the political landscape in which trans lives can be lived. It co-exists with the commodification of gender archetypes and the reinstatement of seemingly polarised and parodic masculinities and femininities.

This resorting to stereotypical views of femininity undoes the work of generations of feminist women. Helen Joyce (2021), in her brilliant book *Trans*, describes this as putting women 'back in the box'.

One wonders if the peculiar intransigence of these beliefs is at times a result of the awareness of doubt, a doubt that is disowned and projected into the other, who then must be silenced.[21] Thinking, here, becomes the enemy to be destroyed – nothing should stand in the way of an unobstructed pathway to irreversible medical and surgical procedures that will result in a lifetime of medication whose long-term consequences remain unknown.[22]

I will end with a story.

As a medical student, I attended a lecture by Eysenck on his electric shock treatment to decondition gay men. In the discussion, a young gay philosopher asked if there were not ethical matters that needed consideration. Eysenck responded that these men were suffering as a result of being homosexual and sought help. We have, he said, the technology to relieve them – there is no further ethical consideration. The questioner suggested a thought experiment. Let us imagine, he suggested to Professor Eysenck, that you are an orthopaedic surgeon and that one day a man approaches you complaining 'I cannot bear my arm, it is ugly, I never know what to do with it – my wife also hates it – look, it's covered in bruises as I always knock it – could you please remove it?'. 'Well,' said the questioner, 'I think you might send him to a psychiatrist to find out what is wrong in the relation between the man and his arm; I don't think you would just say, we have the technology to relieve him of his suffering and so proceed to amputation.' There was a deafening silence in the room. The point here, of course, is that the homosexual man who seeks treatment of this type is *not* sovereign over decisions as to what afflicts him – for there are individual, family, social determinations (including living in a world where hatred of homosexuality would be a daily experience) that affect him and may be beyond awareness.

However, the last time I told that story I was disturbed to learn that in the USA there *are* surgeons who *will* amputate under these conditions;[23] here patient-hood has collapsed completely into customer-ship, and so wish transcends any conception of need – externality is annihilated.

It is indeed strange to be living in a world where, on my Unit at the Tavistock, I received a referral from a plastic surgeon of a woman who has asked for surgery on her nose, the surgeon having informed the patient that there was nothing wrong with her nose, but with her relationship to it. After a year's psychotherapy, she gave up her wish for surgery, having understood the complex identifications that underlay her belief. Meanwhile, a person with acute gender dysphoria, within only a few consultations, may well find agreement to change her name, commence medication and thus be heading for surgical removal of her breasts and genitals, any questioning peremptorily foreclosed.

Many years ago, if your television seemed not be functioning you would use various controls to reset it. But sometimes a message from the broadcaster appeared: 'Do not adjust your set; there is a problem with the signal'. A version of this made its way into a political slogan of the time which is also fitting to ours: 'Do not adjust your set; reality is disturbed'.

However, the current predicament is much darker than this. Serious questions have been raised concerning the ethics and safety of many of the medical and surgical treatments that are being commonly applied; treatments which may be offering medical solutions to psychological problems.

It is hoped that this discussion may be contribute to the growing critical engagement in this area. There is now much broader debate in the media than would have been possible only a few years ago, so the pendulum may be starting to swing the other way,[24] but there are many beleaguered colleagues who are struggling to maintain thought and ethical responsibility in a highly toxic climate, who would greatly value our support.

Notes

1   This chapter contains material that was previously published, which is here reprinted with kind permission of Catherine Humble, Executive Editor, *The International Journal of Psychoanalysis*. Following the NHS England external review of gender services led by Dame Hilary Cass, the GIDS service at the Tavistock will be closed down. This review upheld the criticism raised in this chapter.

2 One member of staff explained that in her prior job, if she thought about a family she had seen, one aspect (for example, a family in which there had been a significant loss) would bring all the features of the case back to mind. But at GIDS, given the pressure to push the children through, the huge case loads and the fact that many of the children said exactly the same thing as they had rehearsed a script, they all just faded into each other and no child could be remembered. She took this as a manifestation of the lack of any real clinical engagement with the children in their own individuality and specificity.

3 One of the directors had, concurrently, an important role in a trans lobby organisation, Gendered Intelligence.

4 The director Polly Carmichael, who I interviewed, told me that some cases were 'straightforward' and also that the service was 'not a clinical service'. By this she meant they were an assessment service (but how assessment could be seen as not constituting a clinical engagement was not explained).

5 Workers in the field often refer to 'reversibility' of puberty blockers – by which they mean that when they are stopped, puberty commences. However, this is a serious misrepresentation. The body/mind of a child is not like a video recorder where you can press the 'pause' button and then recommence by pressing 'play'. At the age of puberty, the brain, the hormonal system, the child's psychology and also the psychosocial world in which they function are all 'ready' for puberty. Pausing puberty and recommencing some years later means the child is embarking on puberty when in a different bio-psychosocial state. In any case, serious concerns have been raised as to the effect upon brain function, cognitive development and bone growth (see below). In any case, the fact that nearly 100% of CYPs do not desist but go on to to opposite sex hormones makes even these false claims of reversibility irrelevant.

6 I later learnt that in 2015 an external consultant had regarded the service as dysfunctional and recommended an immediate cap on the service (advice that was ignored), and that Dr David Taylor in 2005, in his role as medical director, had conducted an internal review raising many of these same concerns – see: www.bbc.co.uk/news/uk-54374165; again no action was taken.

7 Given that the service is directly funded by NHSE, there seemed to be a real possibility that lines of accountability may have become very unclear, leading to the service functioning as if independent from the rest of the Trust.

8 See: www.theguardian.com/society/2018/nov/03/tavistock-centre-gender-identity-clinic-accused-fast-tracking-young-adults

9 Serious concerns have been raised as to long-term effects on bone and brain developments, as well as on psychological development – see, for example, https://blogs.bmj.com/bmjebmspotlight/2019/02/25/gender-affirming-hormone-in-children-and-adolescents-evidence-review/

10 See: www.judiciary.uk/wp-content/uploads/2020/12/Bell-v-Tavistock-Judgment.pdf

11 See: https://assets.publishing.service.gov.uk/media/6149eb48d3bf7f05ac396f79/ Ms_S_Appleby__vs___Tavistock_and_Portman_NHS_Foundation_Trust.pdf

12 See: https://segm.org/Finland_deviates_from_WPATH_prioritizing_psychoth erapy_no_surgery_for_minors

13 See: https://segm.org/Finland_deviates_from_WPATH_prioritizing_psychoth erapy_no_surgery_for_minors

14 Rates of a diagnosis of autism spectrum disorder vary from about 15% to over 30%. It tends to be higher in girls.

15 See: https://mermaidsuk.org.uk/news/do-you-still-use-the-phrase-born-in-the-wrong-body/

16 See: https://childpsychotherapy.org.uk/acp-report-silent-catastrophe

17 See, for example, Haider Assad (2018).

18 Perelberg discussed this (2020).

19 I wrote on this in a paper at the time of the entry of the market form into the NHS, which marked the beginning of the destruction of the welfare consensus, see Bell (1997).

20 See https://journals.plos.org/plosone/article?id=10.1371/journal.pone.0202330
    The most explosive of Littman's findings may be that among the young people reported on – 83% of whom were designated female at birth – more than one-third had friendship groups in which 50% or more of the youths began to identify as transgender in a similar time frame.

21 Here I am drawing on Theodor Adornos' brilliant discussion of Freud's understanding of group psychology in his paper 'Group psychology and the understanding of fascist propaganda'.

22 It is high time that the manufacturers of drugs used for preventing puberty were barred from providing support for conferences given their direct interests in maintaining what has become a very lucrative market.

23 See 'A new way to be mad', *The Atlantic*, 2020. www.theatlantic.com/magazine/archive/2000/12/a-new-way-to-be-mad/304671/

24 The UK government's full-scale review of gender services mentioned above; Mermaids, a very powerful trans lobby that had managed to achieve influence at government level, tweeted last year that 'no child is born in the wrong body' – a sudden complete reversal of its position it had previously promoted. Government advice to schools, which read as if written by trans lobbyists and which emphasised affirmation and alienation of parents who wish to hold off intervention, has been rewritten in a manner which is very welcome (www.gov.uk/guidance/plan-your-relationships-sex-and-health-curriculum). They state: 'We are aware that topics involving gender and biological sex can be complex and sensitive matters to navi-gate. You should not reinforce harmful stereotypes, for instance by suggesting that children might be a different gender based on their personality and interests or the clothes they prefer to wear. Resources used in teaching about this topic must always be age-appropriate and evidence based. Materials which suggest that

non-conformity to gender stereotypes should be seen as synonymous with having a different gender identity should not be used and you should not work with external agencies or organisations that produce such material. While teachers should not suggest to a child that their non-compliance with gender stereotypes means that either their personality or their body is wrong and in need of changing.'

References

Bell, D. (1997) Primitive mind of state. *Psychoanalytic Psychotherapy.* 10(1): 45–57.

Bell, D. (2009) Is truth an illusion? Psychoanalysis and postmodernism. *International Journal of Psychoanalysis.* 90: 331–345.

Campbell, B. (2016) Letter to *London Review of Books.* 38(1): 1–2.

Haider, A. (2018) *Mistaken Identity, Race and Class in the Age of Trump.* London: Verso.

Joyce, H. (2021) *Trans: Where Ideology Meets Reality.* London: Oneworld Publications, p. 73.

Marchiano, L. (2019) Transgender: The new hysteria, in H. Brunskell Evans and M. Moore (eds), *Inventing the Transgender Child and Adolescent.* Newcastle: Cambridge Scholars.

Perelberg, R.J. (2018) *A Psychoanalytic Understanding of Bisexuality in Psychic Bisexuality: A British French Dialogue.* London: Routledge, pp. 1–57.

Perelberg, R.J. (2020) *Sexuality, Excess and Representation: A Psychoanalytic Clinical and Theoretical Perspective.* London: Routledge and New Library of Psychoanalysis, p. 33.

Chapter 14

On whiteness, racial rhetoric, identity politics, and critical race theory

A crucial moment in American psychoanalysis

Jon Mills

There is a scandal that has recently developed in the world of psychoanalysis, and I want to tell you about it.[1] Some would prefer to have it simply go away quietly, hush it up, or sweep it under the rug, but organizational politics aside, I think it is best to confront such matters head on rather than bury our heads in the sand, remain silent, deny it, blame the accusers, or worse, try to pulp it from the record through a spin doctor. Psychoanalysis already has an image problem, which now has become worse.

After reading the Abstract of Donald Moss' (2021a) recent provocative and controversial paper, "On having whiteness," published in the *Journal of the American Psychoanalytic Association*, at first glance I thought this might be a joke, satire, or a hoax, like the Sokal affair,[2] using some postmodern nonsense as argument; but when I saw that Moss is the Chair of the Program Committee of the American Psychoanalytic Association, I realized it was not. And this inflammatory text has garnered international attention in the news and social media outlets largely condemning it as racist hate speech (Bandyopadhyay, 2021; Brown, 2021; Chasmar, 2021; Jackson, 2021; Leeman, 2021; Mulraney, 2021; Schrader, 2021; Wilford, 2021). As esteemed evolutionary biologist Jerry Coyne (2021) puts it,

> it's a horrid, racist *gemisch* of obscurantist chest-beating in the guise of antiracism … a steaming pile of psychoanalytic scat … Second, the Journal of the American Psychoanalytic Association has no credibility and, apparently, no standards … Imagine if this paper used any ethnicity other than "whiteness." It would not have been publishable, and the author would have been damned and demonized forever for racism.

A very damning indictment indeed, if not damaging to the profession, especially when the American Psychoanalytic Association is accused of promoting anti-white racism (Huff, 2021). Not only is Moss' essay viewed as a racist embarrassment, *JAPA* may have also suffered a serious if not irreparable blow to its credibility as a premier psychoanalytic journal. To make matters worse, the editor of *JAPA*, Mitchell Wilson, has attempted to wash the scandal by

DOI: 10.4324/9781003340744-17

not allowing responses to Moss' article that do not promote his version of the narrative he wants to control. Before I critique Moss, I want to tell you about the backdoor shenanigans that go on behind the scenes, as it is most concerning to the integrity of psychoanalytic publishing and the greater issue of academic liberty.

I wrote a response to Moss' article as a Letter to the Editor, which Wilson wanted to chop in an attempt to downplay the disgrace he has contributed to for publishing a non-peer reviewed article that has brought shame and castigation to the profession. Wilson essentially wanted me to say what he wanted said, to omit my own arguments, water down the controversy, and mention nothing of the journal, the American Psychoanalytic Association, or how psychoanalysis is being publicly perceived and denounced in international news and social media forums in the United States, Canada, the UK, Australia, and New Zealand, just to name a few. Since when does an editor edit a Letter to the Editor, especially when the established protocol of the journal is to publish letters in response to an article and then allow the author to reply? I have not encountered this level of censorship before, as I find it an affront on free thought, and hence this is why I am offering this criticism. I cannot in good conscience allow someone else to tell me how to think or what I should say in print, as this violates the very premise, veracity, and honor of academic freedom. Not only do I believe Wilson is abusing his power as editor by hegemonically wanting to silence a particular voice he finds irritating, as it does not support his view of reality, but this type of cronyism of publishing a colleague who serves as a program chair with the same organization I find most egregious,[3] especially as he tries to protect his own ass over publishing a non-peer reviewed paper that created a scandal. He has not done us a favor by doing so. But the greater issue at stake here is allowing a free exchange of ideas, which Wilson is deliberately blocking. This exploitation of authority should not go unnoticed, as it affects us all.

Now back to Moss, where I offer this rejoinder in the hope that any tarnished misperceptions of the profession are remediated, as Moss does not represent the views of all psychoanalysts. I will let you be the judge of whether this critique lacks scholarship or deserves to be pulped.

Moss' central thesis is that being white or having the properties of whiteness is a parasitic affliction that is inherently pathological, "a way of being" (p. 356) with "no cure," where hatred, epistemological entitlement, superiority, and the need to dominate all other non-white peoples based on difference and otherness is present "at birth" (p. 358), as it "infiltrates our drives early on" (p. 356) in "infancy" (p.357). Although Moss offers a nebulous disclaimer that Whiteness is not the same as being phenotypically white, since Whiteness is an inherent property of being white, his distinction is unconvincing at best if not indefensible—as phenomenal properties cannot be independent from their ontological source, only the way in which they appear. For Moss they appear "as a condition one first acquires and then *has*—a malignant, parasitic-like condition to which 'white' people have a particular susceptibility" (pp. 355–356). He further states this condition is "foundational," hence essential and deterministic to a *baby's* sense of being, which is acquired after coming out of the womb instantiated as the pulsional desire to dominate, enslave, and exploit others without scruple. On face value, the claim is absurd.

Contrasting Whiteness with whiteness is an ontic distinction without ontological difference (as an ordinal property of a property) and is itself incitive. Whiteness is a synecdoche for racism, something Moss confusingly asserts is at once socially acquired, presumably through the attachment system, and inherent to white people as part of their embodied thrownness.[4] Instead of using a parasitic *metaphor*, he concretizes it as if it were an infectious medical disease that is uniquely susceptible to whites when psychoanalysis has long identified prejudice to be a universal human proclivity.

It is important to note that Moss' claim is quite different from the claim that racism is institutional, structural, or societally systemic, hence based on (largely discredited) implicit bias research (Church, 2020; Pluckrose and Church, 2020), which assumes implicit (unconscious and conscious) biases in individuals scale up in aggregate forms to systemic discrimination. Since drives are innate to our embodiment, Moss makes racism an a priori, *inborn* capacity inherent to infantile development and personality formation, which is pathological from the very beginning of life by attributing causality to simply being born white. In other words, all white people are biologically condemned to be racist by virtue of being thrown into a white-skinned body with certain morphological features. Whether or not Moss considered the political implications of such generalizations is moot, for this is a tacit assumption most readers would reasonably conclude from his essay, as it has already spurred international outrage on social media platforms and in the news, hence calling it a "racist and pseudo-scientific claim" (Lendrum, 2021).

Let us apply Moss' (2021a) assertion, passed off as if it is a scientific fact, that "Whiteness ... [is] a malignant, parasitic-like condition" (pp. 355–356) to other racialized groups:

> Blackness is a malignant, parasitic-like condition that is foundational, generating characteristic ways of being in one's body, in one's mind, and in one's world. Parasitic Blackness renders its hosts' appetites voracious, insatiable, and perverse. These deformed appetites particularly target non-black peoples.
>
> (Quote adapted)

How does that make you feel? Are you offended? Sounds like racist cant, does it not? The language is inflammatory, abusive, hostile, and incites outrage. To continue on a gratuitous point, let us compare Moss' proposition to a Nazi anti-Semitic propaganda book, *The Pestilential Miasma of the World*, published by Robert Ley (1944), head of the German Labor Front, where he says: "*Who is the Jew?* ... We call destructive elements in nature parasites ... They devour their hosts. They fall like locusts on them, suck their life away, destroy them ... *The Jew is such a parasite!*" (Bytwerk, 2004, translation, italics in original). What lovely sentiment from a hating humanity.

Here are just some of the troubling quotes from Moss' paper:

> Any infant is vulnerable to the parasite of Whiteness.
>
> (p. 357)

> Whiteness originates not in innocence but in entitlement ... We [whites] are *licensed at birth*, and therefore entitled, to find, capture, dissect, and overpower our targeted objects. As such, we will finally come to know and take dominion over them.
>
> (p. 358, italics added)

> The voice of Whiteness's entitled dominion, inside or out, is firm and final: You [non-whites] are not a people; you are labor. You are not a person; you are a deviant. This is not desire; this is sickness. You are not in need; you are a failure. You are not your own; you are ours.
>
> (p. 361)

And this one:

> Color provides a universe of suitable objects, placed there like gifts, to be captured and crushed, all at a whim, like, for so many Gullivered children, ants are there to be crushed underfoot, butterflies to be locked in a jar. These crushed ants and suffocated butterflies—victims of a nearly cellular narcissism—offer Whiteness a platform on which to begin.
>
> (p. 361)

One might wonder why a white man would write such sensational things, if only to garner attention based on identity politics under the guise of appeasing diversity optics, yet it reads as subversive ideology at the expense of truth and rigorous scholarship. Whether Moss is indulging in identity politics is subject to debate, so I will leave that for others to decide, but it is an increasing phenomenon gathering popularity as psychoanalysis continues to adopt the postmodern turn (Gherovici, 2017; Layton, 2020; Mills, 2017; 2020) including *woke* sensibilities and critical race studies (Andrews, 2020; Frosh, 2013; George and Hook, 2021; Thakur, 2020; Tuhkanen, 2009) where Whiteness Theory has become an offshoot.

As an academically trained philosopher and psychoanalyst, my reading of Moss' essay is that *it is illogical at best, uses racist rhetoric and emotional hyperbole that implicitly casts all white people into a homogenous pathological category, and makes universal statements that are not tenable, supported by empirical evidence, or true.* He (a) essentializes all people based on race, (b) makes drives (*Triebe*) in infancy the locus of hate toward all non-white others based on differences in skin color alone (as if race could even be conceptualized as a social-political category by the infantile mind), (c) fails to take into account cognitive and moral development and familial/socialization/cultural practices that undermine such broad-sweeping propositions, and (d) ignores racial, ethnic, and cultural contexts that inform our being in the world. For example, if a so-called white person were born and raised in India, Japan, or Brazil, let's say, the tables would be turned around, as per Moss' logic, whites would innately be bad objects for others to loathe and sadistically defile. How then can the universal proclamation of whiteness apply without taking into account historicity, context, and social identity that informs a collective cultural ethos? Even the founder of postcolonial theory, Edward Said (1993), rejects such racial and cultural binaries when, reflecting on the hybridized nature of contemporary life, he writes:

> Partly because of empire, all cultures are involved in one another; none is single and pure, all are hybrid, heterogenous, extraordinarily differentiated, and unmonolithic. … Far from being unitary or monolithic or autonomous things, cultures actually assume more "foreign" elements, alterities, differences, than they consciously exclude. Who in India or Algeria today can confidently separate out the British or French component of the past from present actualities, and who in Britain or France can draw a clear circle around British London or French Paris that would exclude the impact of India and Algeria upon those two imperial cities?
>
> (pp. xv and 15)

Moss' provocative essay appears to be based on ideological deference to far-left politics (postmodernism, critical race theory, whiteness studies) informing the need to address diversity imbalances and power differentials, but it has gone too far afield and is conceptually unsophisticated, if not dangerous incendiary incitement. Moreover, it is destructive to race relations that are currently tempestuous in our multicultural societies. This type of identity politics actually reinstalls and reinforces racist thinking and racialized categories into our social discourse and schemes of conceiving distributive justice that polarizes groups even further rather than facilitating dialogue and reconciliation. Every deplorable sin in culture is now because of whiteness or white privilege/entitlement/supremacy, a rather pathetic reaction formation where "whitey" (see Horowitz, 1999) must pay for the sins of their forefathers. More ridiculous is the premise that STEM subjects such as mathematics should be taught in school that they are historically based in white supremacy (Klainerman, 2021) despite the fact that major advances in the field have come from Egyptians, Babylonians, Greeks, Chinese, Indians, and Arabs—and whatever ethnicity a mathematician is, they seem to get similar results.

Another recent deplorable event by a psychoanalyst was a lecture given by Aruna Khilanani at Yale University School of Medicine who said: "There are no good apples out there. White people make my blood boil," further claiming that all "White people are out of their minds," are "psychopathic," and that she publicly confessed to having murderous "fantasies of unloading a revolver into the head of any white person that got in my way, burying their body, and wiping my bloody hands as I walked away relatively guiltless with a bounce in my step. Like I did the world a fucking favor (Time stamp: 7:17)"[5] (Herzog, 2021; Shetty, 2021), a lecture that was widely denounced as hate speech and an incitement to violence (Gustavo, 2021; Malekoff, 2021). This kind of race-based vitriol is a symptomatic expression of extremist ideology that has gained wide currency both in the academy and broader society. This trend in our culture is the complete opposite of Martin Luther King's exhortation to judge people not on the color of their skin but on the content of their character (see Taibbi, 2020 contra DiAngelo, 2018). Now skin color is primary and "whiteness" is an index of debasement and pathology. Although I have no need to be a defender of being white and perpetuate the current polarization in race relations, it is a further embarrassment to the profession when psychoanalysts now look like "racist psychobabble" buffoons who get on *Fox News* (Halon, 2021; Kudlow, 2021; Sky News Australia, 2021) bequeathed with the titles "Dr. KhilaWhiteMan" (Mercer, 2021) and "Dr. Woke" (Human Events, 2021).

The undisciplined use of racist tirades by professionals only foments more abhorrence, disgust, and hurt, especially when they are perceived by others as undermining the legitimacy of what we write in professional journals, which further sullies our image to the public, one already plagued by crisis and ideology (Mills, 2021; Richards, 2015). Furthermore, I find value judgements making universal statements based on skin color to be inane, if not immoral, socially divisive, and gravely irresponsible as they simply stoke more division and animus that already exist in our troubled racist times. How could the claim that the inherent or innate pathological disposition of "whiteness," itself a social construction, applies to all people who are identified or labelled as white, let alone advance any constructive discussions about social justice, systemic power imbalances, cultural/ethnic differences, race matters, and their possible amelioration, where this is where the work lies?

There is current debate surrounding antiracist theory among the black intelligentsia, i.e., Adolph Reed (New York Times, 2020), Thomas Chatterton Williams (2015), Glenn Loury and John McWhorter (Loury and McWhorter, 2021; Perry, 2021; Weiss, 2021), and others (see Hughes, 2020; 2021; Riley and McWhorter, 2020), and we should be mindful that these ideas do not represent black people across the board, but I point to them as evidence of a diversity of views contested by black professionals themselves (Weinstein, 2020). Among these are critiques of Ibram X. Kendi's (2019) *How to Be an Antiracist*, what Coleman Hughes (2019) calls "anti-intellectual" based on its empirical inaccuracies and ideological drift over rigorous data-based analysis, as well as against diversity consultants like Robin DiAngelo's (2018) *White Fragility*, what John McWhorter (2020) refers to as a "racist tract," which Jonathan Church (2018; 2020) further denounces as flawed science based on epistemologically dubious implicit bias research generalized to society as a whole. These critics point out how a dehumanizing, supercilious condescension occurs when antiracist sentiment is used as an argument to dignify BIPOC (Black, Indigenous, People of Color) when it in fact diminishes them as people, like the racism Moss attributes to all whites. All this does is, predictably, lead to provoked defensiveness, outrage, and white backlash, hence making social rifts, indignation, resentment, and animosity more pronounced.

Despite the fact that critical race theory (CRT) originated in legal studies examining how race and racism is correlated with institutional, structural, and systemic practices as well as other social justice inequities, these historical antecedents have been interpreted and subsumed within contemporary critiques in the phenomenology of culture that are predicated on "race" itself, or it would not have attracted such fervor from common citizens and US legislators who have introduced proposed bills and have already passed laws that ban teaching CRT in elementary and secondary school (Ali, 2021; Friedersdorf, 2021; Gerstmann, 2021; Greenfield, 2021; Iati, 2021; Wallace-Wells, 2021). Despite misinterpretations or distortions of CRT, not to mention the silly notion of making it illegal to teach or even talk about race in schools and society, which violates free speech amendments and academic freedom alike, the culture wars on the very concept of race have stoked deep resentments and social-political divisions surrounding identity. When identity is reduced to the color of one's skin, we have devolved into a very ignoble economy of signifying difference based on splitting. Here we will never be able to reconcile opposites when we remain oppositional to one another.

The problem with treating white people *en masse* as a homogenous category is that it succumbs to a *reductio ad absurdum* argument that fails to take into account pluralities and a whole array of mutable differences in people mediated by other complex social factors, as if whites as a social collective are responsible for the suffering of all non-whites. Given the historical fact that human civilization was largely built on slavery orchestrated by numerous races, nations, and ethnicities before white imperialism, the focus on parasitic colonial white supremacy as determinate ontological oppression in contemporary society neglects the most egregious problems with universalizing race in the most totalizing ways. This pseudo-reasoning is not only a category mistake, it is a prejudicial ideology based on the bankrupt circular premise that claims (implicitly or explicitly) that all whites oppress alterity by virtue of being white, hence an obtuse causally reductive proposition, itself a racist belief—nothing short of bigotry. If "race" is used as a dog whistle to condemn one group while condoning another based on skin color alone, then we have an inherent contradiction or antinomy based on the paralogism of pitting one identity against another in the service of identity politics that will meet with no resolve. This will only produce vehement resistance, reproach, and retaliatory rebuke by the targeted group under assault.

People speaking on behalf of a whole category of peoples, such as race, ethnicity, or skin color, fail to recognize the infantilization, if not frank racism, in such attempts to universalize representations of a whole class of social collectives, as if every individual could be represented by a generic generalization. How can you represent them? To assume that you can is to already reduce them to being an object or thing that devolves into classification alone. How could such totalizing claims/universal representations be empirically valid? By making such sweeping generalizations about whites, Moss is also inviting people to adopt and attribute his views of whites by non-whites, which is not accurate nor fair-minded for him to impose on any group of peoples.

In my book *The Ontology of Prejudice* (Mills and Polanowski, 1997; also see Mills, 1998), I was one of the first contemporary psychologists to address the notion of universal racism based on unconscious predisposition, but provide ethical arguments for why we (as humanity) must transcend this primitive form of thinking based on a simple economy of identity and difference. It pains me to witness the growing split and social rupture I anticipated 25 years ago when I wrote that book. People should be called out when they violate a humanistic collective ethos, especially when it potentially justifies and leads to retaliatory racism, such as we are currently witnessing with the rise of anti-Semitism and anti-Asian hate crimes, as it perpetuates more disdain and a perverse, distorted logic directed toward alterity as the evil Other (Mills, 2019a; b), when this type of mentality is under the sway of unconscious ideology looking for an emotional whipping boy to pillory regardless of what skin color, ethnicity, or (trans)gendered subject is pointing the finger.

It is my understanding that Moss has received threats as well as the organizations he is affiliated with,[6] which is most unfortunate, but not surprising. Given that *JAPA* published a racist piece under the guise of antiracist sensibility, no wonder people would get worked up and there would be counterattacks on social media. When racist sentiments are disseminated in professional public space, liberally minded people on the left as well as the conservative right get pissed off, especially those who take offense at being labelled white racists.

Not only Moss, but the reputation of the journal, the Association, and the greater image of psychoanalysis is now under scrutiny. Given this scandal has gone viral, there is no use trying to cover it up or dress it up in new garb intended to dismiss or placate dissent. The worse possible thing to do is to try to deny the racist overtones of the paper through a pompous justification, patronizing excuse, or redirecting shift to focus blame on aggressive critics or threats from others as if the journal did nothing wrong. Nor should they try to conceal the deed by manipulating the APsaA's presence on the web, and act like other "crazies" out there are attacking them—like the Tucker Carlsons and David Dukes of the world. This will only look like a public relations ploy in order to save face and redirect culpability. The editor made a *faux pas* and should not have allowed such an incendiary text to be published without undergoing a blind review process, as such gaffes and racist remarks would have been prevented from appearing in their current form. Because the paper cannot be retracted, *JAPA* should issue a public apology and allow open criticism, scholarly critique, debate on the Moss paper, and the greater social issues that are at stake, rather than trying to whitewash it, pun intended.

Acknowledgements

I wish to thank my friends and colleagues who I consulted with on this paper and who expressed their wishes to remain anonymous.

Notes

1 This chapter is in response to an article written by psychoanalyst Donald Moss (2021a) in a recent volume of the *Journal of the American Psychoanalytic Association*. Moss' essay is nebulously presented as a paper reviewed by the *JAPA* editorial board, when it was not. Thomas Newman, Executive Director of the American Psychoanalytic Association, posted a letter to the APsaA Membership Listserv on behalf of Kerry Sulkowicz and Bill Glover on 29 June 2021 stating the following: "Don's piece is a highly personalized essay—not a peer-reviewed scientific article."

2 In a publishing hoax exposing the lack of "intellectual rigor" in postmodern studies, physics professor Alan D. Sokal (1996) published an article called "Transgressing the boundaries: towards a transformative hermeneutics of quantum gravity", where he deceived the journal's editorial reviewers and readers in arguing that quantum gravity is a social and linguistic construct. In "Transgressing the boundaries: an afterword," published in *Dissent* and, in slightly different form, in *Philosophy and Literature*, Sokal tells us: "anyone who believes that the laws of physics are mere social conventions is invited to try transgressing those conventions from the windows of my apartment. I live on the twenty-first floor" (see fn. 3; www.physics.nyu.edu/sokal/afterword_v1a/afterword_v1a_singlefile.html).

3 To be sure, it is no coincidence that Moss (2021b) recently published a glowing review of Wilson's latest book called *So What – Reflections on Mitchell Wilson's The Analysts Desire: The Ethical Foundations of Clinical Practice*. This is a fine example of political partisanship endorsing the "buddy system" of mutual self-promotion.

4 This is Heidegger's technical word to explain our facticity and historicity of being thrown into a world, a body, a time and place, culture and language, and all exogenic conditions where we have no control over or say in the matter whatsoever, as they are merely the situations we find ourselves in as causally *given*.

5 The time stamp refers to the transcript of the recorded lecture at Yale.

6 Sulkowicz and Glover (2021) tell us that "Don and the three institutions that he
   was identified as having an affiliation with—APsaA, the New York Psychoanalytic
   Institute and Society, and the San Francisco Center for Psychoanalysis—received
   threatening emails and phone messages that resulted in having to close offices and
   engage security guards."

References

Ali, S.S. (2021) Amid growing critical race theory legislation, education experts say
   textbook content could be next. Education experts say the restrictions on teaching
   critical race theory may spill over to textbooks as book review commissions worry
   about violating bans. *NBC News*, 10 July. www.nbcnews.com/news/us-news/
   amid-growing-critical-race-theory-legislation-education-experts-say-textbook-
   n1272682

Andrews, L.M. (2020) Just like Freud's psychoanalysis, critical race theory will ultimately collapse. *The Federalist*, 23 September. https://thefederalist.com/2020/09/23/
   just-like-freuds-psychoanalysis-critical-race-theory-will-ultimately-collapse/

Bandyopadhyay, A. (2021) Donald Moss compared to Aruna Khilanani, called "Nazi"
   for saying "whiteness is malignant". Many on Twitter wondered if Donald Moss'
   research was a satire, while asked him to join hands with Aruna Khilanani. *MEA
   WorldWide*, 10 June. https://meaww.com/donald-moss-whiteness-malignant-paras
   ite-research-slammed-join-aruna-khilanani-racist-reactions

Brown, L. (2021) NYC psychoanalyst calls whiteness incurable "parasitic like condition". *New York Post*, 10 June. https://nypost.com/2021/06/10/psychoanalyst-calls-
   whiteness-incurable-parasitic-like-condition/

Chasmar, J. (2021) NYC psychoanalyst diagnoses "Whiteness" as a "malignant,
   parasitic-like condition". *The Washington Times*, 10 June. www.washingtontimes.
   com/news/2021/jun/10/donald-moss-nyc-psychoanalyst-says-whiteness-a-mal/

Church, J. (2018) The epistemological problem of white fragility theory. *Areo
   Magazine*, 21 December. https://areomagazine.com/2018/12/21/the-epistemologi
   cal-problem-of-white-fragility-theory/

Church, J. (2020) *Reinventing Racism: Why "White Fragility" Is the Wrong Way to Think
   about Racial Inequality*. Lantham, MD: Rowman & Littlefield.

Coyne, J. (2021) A new paper by a psychoanalyst looks like a hoax, but isn't. *Why
   Evolution Is True*, 11 June. https://whyevolutionistrue.com/2021/06/11/a-new-
   paper-by-a-psychoanalyst-looks-like-a-hoax-but-isnt/

DiAngelo, R. (2018) *White Fragility: Why It's so Hard for White People to Talk About
   Racism*. Boston: Beacon Press.

Friedersdorf, C. (2021) Critical race theory is making both parties flip-flop. The
   battle over teaching race in North Carolina schools prompts an ideological role
   reversal on both antidiscrimination and speech. *The Atlantic*, 8 July. www.theatlan
   tic.com/ideas/archive/2021/07/north-carolina-critical-race-theory-ban-free-speech/
   619381/

Frosh, S. (2013). Psychoanalysis, colonialism, racism. *Journal of Theoretical and Philosophical Psychology*. 33(3): 141–154.

George, S. & Hook, D. (editors) (2021) *Lacan and Race: Racism, Identity, and Psychoanalytic Theory*. London: Routledge.

Gerstmann, E. (2021). Should the states ban critical race theory in schools? *Forbes*, 6 July. www.forbes.com/sites/evangerstmann/2021/07/06/should-the-states-ban-critical-theory-in-schools/?sh=60c4751e111a

Gherovici, P. (2017) *Transgender Psychoanalysis*. London: Routledge.

Greenfield, N.M. (2021) Why are states lining up to ban critical race theory? *University World News*, 12 June. www.universityworldnews.com/post.php?story=20210612085115831

Gustavo, D. (2021) Yale University hosted speaker who shared fantasies about murdering white people. *World Socialist Web Site*, 13 June. www.wsws.org/en/artic les/2021/06/14/yale-j14.html

Halon, Y. (2021) "Whiteness" a "parasitic-like condition" with no cure, medical journal article claims: the author, with ties to organizations in New York City and San Francisco, was accused of promoting "racist psychobabble at its worst". *Fox News*, 9 June. www.foxnews.com/media/whiteness-a-parasitic-like-condition-with-no-cure-medical-journal-article-claims

Herzog, K. (2021) "The psychopathic problem of the white mind": a psychiatrist lecturing at Yale's Child Study Center spoke about "unloading a revolver into the head of any white person that got in my way". Podcast. *Common Sense with Bari Weiss*, 4 June. https://bariweiss.substack.com/p/the-psychopathic-problem-of-the-white

Horowitz, D. (1999) *Hating Whitey: And Other Progressive Causes*. Dallas, TX: Spence Publishing.

Huff, E. (2021) American Psychoanalytic Association promotes anti-white racism, calls "whiteness" a "parasitic-like condition". *Natural News*, 13 June. www.natu ralnews.com/2021-06-13-american-psychoanalytic-association-promotes-anti-white-racism.html

Hughes, C. (2019) How to be an anti-intellectual: a lauded book about antiracism is wrong on its facts and in its assumptions. *City Journal*, 27 October. https://www.city-journal.org/how-to-be-an-antiracist?fbclid=IwAR3nY0IupA4kNsG8Z2Xxm h9gT6KX2fLxkq9vV6_9Vkhyo4L0-OroJlBkz1M

Hughes, C. (2020) Stories and data: reflections on race, riots, and police. *City Journal*, 14 June. www.city-journal.org/reflections-on-race-riots-and-police

Hughes, C. (2021) Coleman Hughes on the case for color-blindness. Podcast. *Conversations with Coleman, Season 2*, 18 March. www.youtube.com/watch?v=Zq6x J2vFlaA

Human Events (2021) Psychoanalyst calls Whiteness a "parasitic-like condition". *Human Events*, 11 June. https://humanevents.com/2021/06/11/psychoanalyst-calls-whiteness-a-parasitic-like-condition/

Iati, M. (2021) What is critical race theory, and why do Republicans want to ban it in schools? *The Washington Post*, 29 May. www.washingtonpost.com/education/2021/05/29/critical-race-theory-bans-schools/

Jackson, J. (2021) Research article in medical journal describes Whiteness as "malignant, parasitic-like condition". *Newsweek*, 21 June. www.newsweek.com/research-arti cle-medical-journal-describes-whiteness-malignant-parasitic-like-condition-1599129

Kendi, I.X. (2019) *How to Be an Antiracist*. New York: One World.

Klainerman, S. (2021) There is no such thing as "white" math. Podcast. *Common Sense with Bari Weiss*, 1 March. https://bariweiss.substack.com/p/there-is-no-such-thing-as-white-math

Kudlow, L. (2021) Yale alum "ashamed" by school's handling of "crazy" speaker. *Fox Business*, 8 June. www.youtube.com/watch?v=a9FR_ESzeq0

Layton, L. (2020) *Toward a Social Psychoanalysis: Culture, Character, and Normative Unconscious Processes*. M. Leavy-Sperounis (editor). London: Routledge.

Leeman, Z. (2021) "Whiteness" is a "parasitic" condition with no "permanent cure," according to a psychoanalyst desperate to boost his woke points. *RT*, 16 June. www.rt.com/op-ed/526765-whiteness-parasitic-condition-woke/

Lendrum, E. (2021) Medical journal article calls "Whiteness" a "parasitic-like condition". *The Tennessee Star*, 13 June. https://tennesseestar.com/2021/06/13/medical-journal-article-calls-whiteness-a-parasitic-like-condition/

Ley, R. (1944) *Pesthauch der Welt*. Dresden: Franz Müller Verlag. Bytwerk, R. (translator), The Pestilential Miasma of the World (2004). https://research.calvin.edu/ger man-propaganda-archive/pesthauch.htm

Loury, G. and McWhorter, J. (2021) Critical race theory in U.S. schools. *The Glenn Show Podcast*, 4 May. www.youtube.com/watch?v=82HA4raBiOw

Malekoff, A. (2021) The back road: the strange case of Dr. Aruna Khilanani. *The Island Now*, 6 June. https://theislandnow.com/opinions-100/the-back-road-the-stra nge-case-of-dr-aruna-khilanani/

McWhorter, J. (2020) The dehumanizing condescension of *white fragility*: the popular book aims to combat racism but talks down to Black people. *The Atlantic*, 15 July. www.theatlantic.com/ideas/archive/2020/07/dehumanizing-condescension-white-fragility/614146/?fbclid=IwAR2P2eKlSLVDKfoRBG2bmKH0UCXml-7ldoxZ6nYFY2lov1ITeHL8H5iBFbA

Mercer, I. (2021) NY shrink Aruna KhilaWhiteMan: a made-in-America monster. *CNC News*, 11 June. www.cnsnews.com/commentary/ilana-mercer/ny-shrink-aruna-khilawhiteman-made-america-monster

Mills, J. (1998) Prejudice and its vicissitudes. *Human Studies*. 21(1): 187–196.

Mills, J. (2017) Challenging relational psychoanalysis: a critique of postmodernism and analyst self-disclosure. *Psychoanalytic Perspectives*. 14: 313–335.

Mills, J. (2019a) Recognition and *pathos*. *International Journal of Jungian Studies*. 11(1): 1–22.

Mills, J. (2019b) Dysrecognition and social pathology: new directions in critical theory. *Psychoanalysis, Culture & Society*. 1: 15–30.

Mills, J. (2020) *Debating Relational Psychoanalysis: Jon Mills and his Critics*. London: Routledge.

Mills, J. (2021) Crisis and ideology in psychoanalysis. *International Journal of Controversial Discussions*. 4: 111–127.

Mills, J. and Polanowski, J.A. (1997) *The Ontology of Prejudice.* Amsterdam/ New York: Rodopi.

Moss, D. (2021a) On having whiteness. *JAPA.* 69(2): 355–371.

Moss, D. (2021b) So what – reflections on Mitchell Wilson's The Analysts Desire: The Ethical Foundations of Clinical Practice. *Division/Review.* 25: 8–10.

Mulraney, F. (2021) "INCURABLE" WHITENESS: outrage as psychoanalyst claims being white is "a malignant, parasitic like condition with no cure". *The U.S. Sun,* 10 June. www.the-sun.com/news/3055102/donald-moss-whiteness-parasite-no-cure/

New York Times (2020). A black Marxist scholar wanted to talk about race. It ignited a fury. *New York Times,* 18 August. www.nytimes.com/2020/08/14/us/adolph-reed-controversy.html

Perry, M.J. (2021) Glenn Loury on the irony of "systemic racism". *American Enterprise Institute,* 29 April. www.aei.org/carpe-diem/glenn-loury-on-the-irony-of-systemic-racism/

Pluckrose, H. and Church, J. (2020) The flaws in white fragility theory: a primer. *New Discourses,* 8 June. https://newdiscourses.com/2020/06/flaws-white-fragility-theory-primer/

Richards, A. (2015) Psychoanalysis in crisis: the danger of ideology. *The Psychoanalytic Review.* 102(3): 389–406.

Riley, J. and McWhorter, J. (2020) Critical race theory: on the new ideology of race. *Manhattan Institute,* 16 December. www.youtube.com/watch?v=ZuvhrXM3v7Uht tps://www.youtube.com/watch?v=ZuvhrXM3v7U

Said, E.W. (1993) *Culture and Imperialism.* New York: Vintage.

Schrader, A. (2021) "Whiteness is a malignant, parasitic like condition": journal of the American Psychoanalytic Association publishes paper by white psychoanalyst that claims whiteness is "voracious, insatiable, and perverse – with no permanent cure". *The Daily Mail,* 9 June. www.dailymail.co.uk/news/article-9670579/Psycho analyst-condemned-paper-branding-whiteness-malignant-parasitic-like-condit ion.html

Shetty, M. (2021) Who is Aruna Khilanaani? *Biography Daily,* 5 June. https://biograp hydaily.com/2021/06/05/who-is-aruna-khilanani/

Sky News Australia (2021) Psychiatrist condemned after discussing fantasies of shooting white people in lecture. *Sky News Australia,* 7 June. www.youtube.com/ watch?v=KYCLW_f-qkY

Sokal, A.D. (1996) Transgressing the boundaries: an afterword. *Dissent,* 43(4): 93–99.

Sokal, A.D. (1996) Transgressing the boundaries: an afterword. *Philosophy and Literature.* 20(2): 338–346.

Sokal, A.D. (1996) Transgressing the boundaries: towards a transformative hermen-eutics of quantum gravity. *Social Text.* 46/47: 217–252.

Sulkowicz, K. and Glover, B. (2021) APsaA comments on JAPA controversy. Email communication to APsaA Membership Listserv, 29 June.

Taibbi, M. (2020) On "white fragility": a few thoughts on America's smash-hit #1 guide to egghead racialism. *TK News,* 28 June. https://taibbi.substack.com/p/on-white-fragility

Thakur, G.B. (2020) *Postcolonial Lack: Identity, Culture, Surplus*. Albany, NY: State University of New York Press.

Tuhkanen, M. (2009) *The American Optic: Psychoanalysis, Critical Race Theory, and Richard Wright*. Albany: State University of New York Press.

Wallace-Wells, B. (2021) How a conservative activist invented the conflict over criticalrace theory. *The New Yorker*, 18 June. www.newyorker.com/news/annals-of-inquiry/how-a-conservative-activist-invented-the-conflict-over-critical-race-theory

Weinstein, B. (2020) Black intellectual roundtable. *Bret Weinstein's DarkHorse Podcast*, 13 July. www.youtube.com/watch?v=pHGt733yw3g

Weiss, B. (2021) What is systemic racism? John McWhorter, Lara Bazelon, Glenn Loury, Kmele Foster, Chloé Valdary and Kenny Xu weigh in. *Common Sense with Bari Weiss*, 28 April. https://bariweiss.substack.com/p/what-is-systemic-racism

Wilford, D. (2021) WHITE NOISE: white man calls his skin colour a "parasitic-like condition". *Toronto Sun*, 10 June. https://torontosun.com/news/weird/white-noise-white-man-calls-his-skin-colour-a-parasitic-like-condition

Williams, T.C. (2015) Loaded dice. *London Review of Books*. 37(23): 3.

Part III

The role of psychoanalytic institutes

Chapter 15

The training and supervising analyst system in the United States

Current issues

Eric R. Marcus

Introduction

The future of psychoanalysis is clouded by two fights within the profession. It is also threatened by external forces. The first fight within the profession has to do with a splintering of theory and the fights, infiltrated with narcissistic grandiosity, about theory. For a review of this see Marcus (2018). The second battle within the profession, infiltrated with narcissistic rage, is about the training analyst system: its certification and appointment standards. The external threat is economic. This chapter will discuss the training and supervising analyst battle and the underlying economics. (For a complete review see Zagermann, 2021.)

The training and supervising analyst fight

We are at a crossroad. The crossroad is to keep the training and supervising analyst system or abolish it. It is actually a bit past the crossroads already and that's probably good and holds the opportunity for moving forward. There seems to be a rough majority consensus to keep it in some form. But if the war is over, the peace is far from signed.

The system is seen as an existential issue with its problems in ethics, power differential, and economics. Is the cure to reform it or to ditch it? It is this training and supervising analyst battle which this chapter will focus on. I will discuss each of these issues.

This chapter will make two claims. The first is about psychoanalysis as a profession, and a healthcare profession, and therefore with its own expertise requirements. The second is the relationship of the fight about the training analyst system to the economics of training and practice at this time. The chapter will explore each of these issues and try to move past the politics to the underlying formative forces at play. It will then propose some solutions.

DOI: 10.4324/9781003340744-19

The existential issue

The existential argument says that the category of training and supervising analyst is destroying organized psychoanalysis: it is not needed, is exclusionary, is falsely constructed, and produces a bogus, detrimental two-class system of practitioners. The problem with this argument is that social groups tend towards hierarchical segmentation as a universal, especially so when the social group is a collection of complex task professionals where there is a ladder of experience. Does this equate to a ladder of expertise? If so, are other criteria for expertise also relevant? Regardless, does intra-group segmentation strengthen or cripple such groups, or both?

In all complex endeavor groups, those seen as having expertise tend to be categorized and labeled. This can be organized and standardized or it can be natural and ad hoc. But from planting corn, to herding cattle, to building a table, to doing surgery, people seek to attain expertise as both the purveyor and the consumer.

Without internal professional criteria, self-identification through external criteria of marketing and advertising wins because in the purchase of complex goods and services, the purchaser may be woefully ignorant until after the purchase. This is why all professions and crafts have standards for belonging, excellence standards for purveyor and product quality, ethical standards for marketing and advertising, and standards and traditions for education and training. In professions and crafts, the goal is to do it right, according to what is seen as right at that time. Will it be our our craft or the marketplace that decides?

The power issue

The ostensible fight about power is about power within organizations: positions of power, the politics of power, the abuse of power. The power is seen as the power to control organizations: their structure, their political functions, their education systems, and their distribution of economic and honorific resources. The abuse of power is seen also as a psychological abuse, with a two-class system, one supposedly looking down on the other but also, the feeling of being looked down upon.

But the training and supervising analysts' political power, their organizational power, as a monopolistic phenomenon within institutes, is long gone. Non-training analysts serve on all committees and within the governance and educational system of most institutes. And as candidates get fewer and fewer, the monopolistic advantage shrinks.

But even with little power, even with more equal distribution of esteem, all those in a system of shrinking resources tend to feel insecure. This professional and institutional insecurity easily becomes an insecurity about the professional self that easily becomes about self and others. Because external independent causal variables can be hard to control, the focus rapidly becomes the internal, dependent variables. The idea of the limited good, the limited esteem, becomes dominant in all such groups. "I know why I have less – it is because someone else has undeservedly more." This is often true. But in organized psychoanalysis and its institutes, this truth is long gone. This is because nobody has much anymore!

There are fewer candidates, fewer patients, lower fees, fewer faculty vying for positions.

Of training and supervising analysts in the United States, according to the American Psychoanalytic Association surveys, half average between one and two formal psychoanalytic cases a year. The other half has zero. Now, the argument may debase itself into accusation and counter-accusation about who destroyed the system and poisoned the well. Was it the training analyst system through exclusion that destroyed it or was it the attack on the training system that destroyed it? These attacks are on the dependent, internal variables rather than the independent, external variables; they are attacks on us and our system rather than the external forces to which we poorly adapt.

That training and supervising analysts in the bad old days had narcissistic features and used their power sadistically is a common experience everyone my age and older has had. But it wasn't universal. And those of us with a modicum of self-confidence took what was useful and stood up to the bullying. Standing up to bullying and hierarchies is necessary in any hierarchy but also in every market. You don't get away from it even in social organizations ostensibly without formal hierarchy. In all systems and non-systems, there are bullies.

This issue of the free market and bullying is no better illustrated than in the free market of opinions in the open line of our own American Psychoanalytic Association. There you can see the opponents of the training analyst system bullying in exactly the same way they accuse the old training analyst of being. Without rules, bullying emerges. And with or without titles can come bullying in favor or against any particular issue. Bullying is an attitude. It is neither a title nor a system. But bullying in open systems is why rules developed. The law, said Sir Thomas Moore, are trees to hide behind when the cold wind blows. And a bully is a cold wind, indeed.

It does not take rage to stand up to a bully in any system. Rage is often counterproductive because it only brings about more bullying and counter-bullying. It takes self-confidence. You don't have to punch a bully to get him to back down. You just have to deny him access. The access required is to your own self-esteem in a psychological war that is ultimately within your power because it depends on your being intimidated. A bully indicates their vulnerability by being a bully.

The freedom of choice issue

The freedom issue is described as the freedom to practice unrestrained and the freedom of choice the candidate should have in choosing anyone to be their analyst. This argument says that it is wrong to restrain them and, perhaps more importantly, it deprives us of potential candidates. What we don't know is the incidence and prevalence. Does our system deprive us of candidates? Which candidates and how often? We don't know. Presumably, it is those prospective candidates who are already in treatment with a non-training analyst. We also don't know whether such potential candidates not accepting this stricture would ever accept other strictures that education requires. Candidates go to institutes for education and all education systems articulate themselves through some system of curating: courses, readings, faculty, graduates, and analysts who treat candidates. If they don't like the curating of one institute they have free choice in applying to another.

The democracy issue

The democracy issue is stated as access by all. But democracy doesn't mean access for all. That is libertarianism. Democracy means access of opportunity for all. Education is ideally opportunity equal in the sense of the opportunity to be able to work to achieve the requirements of education according to one's ability and work effort. Democracy also means equal opportunity to participate in governance. This we should all aspire to and some institutions are better than others, although all are better at it than they were. But there are always sub-groups and cliques fighting for power, disguised by idealized and righteous ideals, under any system of political organization. When there is equal access to decisions in power, there is equal access to the democracy fights, fair and foul, as different interest groups try to cut the limited resource pie, including the narcissistic resources. This we see in growing technicolor now that the fight for certification and accreditation has moved from our national organization to our local institutes.

The ethics issue

The ethics issue is posited as the ethical right of the candidate to choose their analyst free of interference.

This ethical approach rightly claims that if it isn't free choice, it isn't an analytic relationship and this would cripple any attempt at an analytic treatment. But, of course, candidates choose to do training, to do their analysis within that educational system, and also the institute to which they go. These choices are theirs to freely make.

That they must adhere to certain educational criteria is the ethics required of educational systems, of professions, of teachers, and also of students. To avoid these organizational ethics is unethical. We also can't overlook the bad ethics of providing candidates with analysts for their training who don't do analysis or who have never done enough to develop consistent expertise.

Thus, is the ethical issue more complicated than usually argued. What is sauce for the goose is sauce for the gander. If ethical treatment must be rendered the individual, ethical treatment must also be rendered the professional education mission and its articulating educational organizations.

There are always ethical issues involved in the relationship between individuals and groups, between justice for the group and justice for the individual. This dilemma has been the topic of philosophy, of politics, of governance, of religion, and of economics in the learned tomes of Western civilization for centuries. The analytic manifestation is relatively simple since from the point of view of available free choice, to join or not join the educational organization, there may be practical conflicts but it is no longer an ethical conflict.

What are we? A profession? A healthcare profession?

One of the major issues about organizational psychoanalysis is a basic question. Are we a profession? If so, are those of us who practice it practicing within a healthcare profession? What are the definitions by which we might understand how to answer? If we answer in the affirmative, what does that require of us?

A profession is a circumscribed area of knowledge and its practitioners who apply that knowledge. A profession is an area of endeavor that requires expertise. It therefore has methods and quality ideals. It therefore usually requires training and qualifications.

There are always the occasional autodidacts but they rise to acceptance by the profession through their meeting of qualifications in their product and their ability.

In order to grow and develop as an entity of applied knowledge, the profession circumscribes a boundary of expertise. Professions define their areas of expertise. They then try to do the job right and well, according to what the profession views as right and well at a particular time and a particular place.

Once there is the concept of doing it well and doing it badly and doing it right and doing it wrong, the idea of criteria and competencies is inevitable. A profession almost by definition must have levels of expertise acknowledging those with education and training of a particular type, and those without and, more importantly, within the profession, the beginners from the more experienced.

That levels of expertise be recognized is primarily about quality within the profession. Any power differential should be only the power of knowledge but the whole point of a profession is that professional knowledge does give one power, the power of the ability to apply knowledge to the professional task. Any organizational or economic power may be hoped for but is not inevitable.

In organized psychoanalysis, power was marked in the old days and insignificant nowadays. Whether one views this as fortunate or unfortunate, it is a fact. Except in the eye of the beholder. And there is the narcissistic injury. But it is a narcissistic injury of yesteryear and therefore of an aging group within our profession.

The issue with criteria for expertise is not just an education and training idea, it is an experience immersion idea. Those who do it may learn it. Those who do more of it may do it better. They may not but they may. But those who never do it probably never learn to do it. Those who used to do it but don't anymore fall out of practice in doing it. These are elementary and time-honored educational concepts that have logic and observations on their side.

If we are a profession, the next question is, are we a healthcare profession? That question means are we trying to help people and if we are, are we trying to help them in some way deal with illness effects or with health improvement? If we answer affirmatively to these questions, then we probably consider ourselves a healthcare profession. Certainly, the regulatory bodies of healthcare around the world consider that healthcare is a profession and is to be done by healthcare professionals. Regulatory bodies of healthcare require evidence of proficiency.

If we are not a healthcare profession, are we an education profession teaching people to know their minds and to live in a better-adapted way? Are we enlightenment practitioners showing others the true enlightened way? But both education and enlightenment tasks also have organizations and experienced or less experienced practitioners. This does not avoid gradients. Gradients tend to labeling. Master teacher. Ultimate guru.

This does not avoid competitive and crowded marketplaces. Both the education and enlightenment markets are quite crowded. Selling for education or enlightenment rather than healthcare is a very crowded market indeed. There, advertising and marketing are crucial. Some would say they are more crucial than expertise because mass markets tend towards the lowest common denominator of consumer because they are much more common than the sophisticated. "No one ever went broke underestimating the intelligence of the American public," supposedly said P.T. Barnum, who made his fortune in circuses.

The whole history of the healthcare profession has been the emergence in the nineteenth century of professionalism with proficiencies and certification, coincident with the scientific advances at that time. When you have expertise, sell expertise. When you have expertise, define your area of expertise and certify your members. Thus, it has been for 100 years. Do we have expertise? The passivity and ignorance of we ourselves about our research that justifies intensive long-term treatment is remarkable. We actually have better data about such efficacy then the short-term treatments (Shedler, 2010).

All healthcare professions tend to be licensed by the states and professional organizations by the United States Department of Education. The requirements are to specify your area of expertise and certify the expertise of your members. The certification must be done by independent boards and not by membership organizations. This is so that political issues do not dominate education and practice expertise issues.

These policies apply to all professions, not just healthcare. They apply not just to the professions but to the skilled crafts that intersect with human welfare. They therefore apply to plumbers, electricians, barbers, and educators themselves.

The standards issue

The standards fight is fighting a battle 50 years old with information and opinions that are 50 years old.

"Standards" is no longer an educational term. The ABP and AAPE do not use the term. They use the term "competencies." And the specifics of evaluation are called criteria. And the developmental progression is called from novice to expert (Benner, 2001). All crafts, all professions, all colleges, all professional training schools and universities, use these terms for their developmental ladder.

Competencies are what all medical board specialties do. That's what medical education does, and has done for the last 20 years. Competencies – what are they? How do we measure them? What is the minimum immersion for progression to the next stage of development?

Now the objections. It is said that measurement of qualifications has no validity. This is an error in two ways. First, it is a misuse of the word validity. What they mean is it has no applicability, presumably to the kind of psychoanalysis they do or want. Validity has to do with the integrity of the test itself. Does it measure what it says it measures? All tests measure only a piece of a complex phenomenon. And even test validity is a complex issue. There are different types of validity. Construct, content, criteria, and face are all different types of validity. What type is meant when validity is criticized?

Reliability has to do with the consistency of the measurement result when tested repeatedly or in different settings. Again, it is about the test, not so much about the phenomena the test measures. This is true of all tests. Test measure an aliquot or derivative of the phenomena. Temperature will tell you something about the weather but by itself not necessarily how cold you will feel. That depends also on other variables like humidity, wind direction and speed, and on terrain.

The second objection is the implication that because qualifications often have to do with qualities, they can't be fairly measured because they can't be objectively and reliably measured. Kernberg (2014) endorses that it can and clarifies this with his usual eloquence in a paper often mis-cited as the opposite.

The argument that there can't be validity, even assuming the term is used correctly, about quality measures is an argument that refutes all of social science research. In fact, our competency criteria tests have solid validity and reliability when social science procedures are properly used.

Markets and equal access

The free market is useful and may be crucial for the emergence of new ideas and their pruning and scaling. They may reward originality and new ideas. They also reward efficiency of delivery. But it is far from clear that this works with highly skilled services and their delivery. Furthermore, unregulated markets can be exploitative, from which emerge the very very rich and the very very poor; the very powerful and the very powerless. Do not expect democracy in free markets. Totally free markets, markets without any regulation, start to organize themselves in very unfree ways. This is what the market regulation laws are about.

In education services, it is precisely because of the vagaries of the free market and the need for regulation that criteria in medical education emerged with the Flexner report in 1910, which resulted in the closing of most proprietary medical schools in this country, about two thirds of the medical schools at that time, which had little or no criteria for medical education and were referred to as diploma mills. You paid your money and you got your diploma.

Hobbes said that man in nature is a war of all against all where life is nasty, mean, brutish, and short. Even Rousseau, with the opposite philosophy of gentle man in gentle nature, changed his mind as he got older.

The idea that eliminating the training and supervising analyst system will open up the marketplace, and democratically and fairly, with free, i.e., equal, access to all, is a myth about the free market. The myth is based on the unstated assumption that equality of access to markers of achievement is what the marketplace needs to have if it is to equally function as a purveyor, consumer, and adjudicator of quality, and therefore, there's the rub, of success in the market. Look at the American market for goods and services and you will see the falsity of that assumption. Cheap inferior goods flood the marketplace, hence the term *caveat emptor*. If you want to capture the mass market, forget expertise. If you want to capture a specialty niche market, treasure and identify expertise. Know your market is a basic professional standard of marketing.

Our psychoanalytic market is a niche market of educated and sophisticated consumers. Without a training and supervising analyst category, those of us who have a presence in lecturing, writing, opinionating, gesticulating, and now especially those of us who understand and have presence in social media will emerge more successful in the market.

Those complaining about the present system of access beware. There is worse. Worse is called a totally free market. And especially because there is never equal access. Hard work, intelligence, knowledge, persistence, talent, cleverness, and unscrupulousness all may help gain an advantage. So does financial access like inheritance.

So how is the average good practitioner, the person you might actually want to treat you or your family, because they are focused on treating people not advertising, how will they be able to identify themselves? The tried-and-true way is identification between colleagues who know your work. But that is a networking issue, at which some of us are better than others. For those who are not good at marketing or don't want to take the time to do so, credentialing is the most available access route to the market.

Conclusion – in life, one never has total equality. We are born with unequal assets and challenges; we have unequally traumatic formative events. One wishes therefore for equality of opportunity. For equality of opportunity, it helps to have a clearly demarcated path. It helps to have appropriate professional criteria to which all can aspire and work towards, equally. For many years, one ladder of success has been the training and supervising analyst system. We could change it for another system but no system at all is probably worse. We can and should make it more equal in opportunity.

The training and supervising analyst economic issue

Sometimes, an economic issue is claimed whereby the training and supervising analysts supposedly have an economic advantage in patient recruitment via monopolistic access to the candidate pool of patients via a marketable imprimatur of the training and supervising analyst title. The real issue is not whether any of these issues are good or bad, on which grounds the fight usually occurs, but whether any of this is any longer factually true.

The economic issue is that the training and supervising analyst has economic power because the designated class carries monopolistic access to candidates and a quality imprimatur to other patients. But no non-candidate patient has ever asked me whether I'm a training and supervising analyst. I assume this is because only someone in the profession would know the title.

But as fees for candidates and other patients have gotten lower and lower, because of the cost of the frequency of sessions for analytic treatment, a cost in both time and money, and as overhead of practice and family life has gotten higher and higher, the training analyst position is an economic disadvantage and has been for quite a while. Training and supervising analysts make enormous economic sacrifices to treat candidates at lower fees, to provide supervision free or at lower fees, to teach classes for free, and to lecture for minimal or no compensation. My teaching, supervising, and low-fee analytic training cases amount to a donation to my university and institute of about $100,000 a year at my private practice rate. So the idea of two classes, one economically powerful and one powerless, is a group fantasy perhaps generated by the progressive loss of power all of us have had in the marketplace of ideas and in the economic survival of psychoanalytic practice. It is a fantasy of the plentiful other as a wishful albeit envious fantasy of survival. The idea is that it really is out there and I can get it except that it's being hogged by somebody else. But when some find out the economic sacrifice of the modern training and supervising analyst, they no longer want it. At most institutes, the prospective training and supervising analyst has to be recruited. There isn't a long line! Understandably.

The real economic issues

As the old saw says about psychoanalysis, those who have the money don't have the time and those who have the time don't have the money. This means that there is a paucity of patients in analytic treatments.

This affects all of us: training analysts, non-training analysts, candidates. This issue for younger and mid-career analysts is the real economic issue.

The economic situation in the United States has changed dramatically over the last 40 years with dramatic income shifts. The middle and upper-middle classes have had to work harder and longer to stay where they are. 60-hour weeks and dual-income families are common. The struggling are struggling even harder.

These economic forces are depriving our profession of immersion in our work. That is the issue that is draining our morale and sabotaging our educational institutes. There is the pressure to decrease or eliminate immersion criteria for graduation and promotion. This economic issue is the main energizer of our political training and supervising analyst battle.

This puts stress on education and professional criteria for immersion. It has been the primary driver of the movement for change to teaching psychotherapy and for changing the immersion standards for graduation and promotion. About a third of our institutions have no candidates, one third are struggling for candidates, and a third are doing reasonably OK. The bottom wants to sell availability and the top wants to sell exclusivity. Both of them want national organizations to back their position. Either one will admit anyone with a palpable pulse and so it's really a question of advertising and marketing. But it is seen as a life or death existential struggle at the institute level, and it may be.

This is not a narcissistic issue. This is a fundamental economic issue. It is a fundamental issue of the marketplace, not just of ideas but of practice. Economic rage trumps narcissistic rage even as it evokes it. It is natural for those in need to attempt to get into the shrunken marketplace by trying to expand our work and profession into a more available albeit diluted marketplace. But then we lose our specialness and compete with a larger pool. Maybe we want to. Maybe we don't. Maybe we want some of both. Let's skip the raging because we need to be calm in order to think very carefully. Our survival depends on it.

What to do?

Darwin's message was adapt or die. But for high-quality professional services, the problem is complex.

We don't want to not adapt and therefore die but we also don't want to adapt and therefore die. How much do you give up by trying to adapt? Where is the sweet spot? How do we not throw out the baby with the outdated bath water? How do we keep the baby alive without some warm bath water? We are trying to adapt to economic changes in society.

Proposed solutions

What is needed to help ourselves? What might be the necessary adaptations to the economic vicissitudes of our times? We need to look at our educational system for candidates. We need to look at our training analyst system for graduates.

How can we keep our profession regenerating itself?

Do we lower immersion criteria? Do we eliminate immersion criteria? For candidate graduation as well as for prospective training and supervising analysts? How can we change to meet the economic times? The main issue now is access to immersion. The main issues are the economics of practice and education that prevent immersion.

Marketing

We must harness the dystopian economic forces that batter us. We can't change them. Some aspects of this harnessing are called marketing. Marketing need not be a dirty word. At its best, marketing is about letting people who need your services know about you and what you can do.

Institutes need to reach out to appropriate arenas. Talks at health services in schools, colleges, hospitals, and corporations may all help connect with pools of patients in need and services that screen them. Talks to other professional groups can help. Providing services to human resource divisions of corporations and law firms can also help. Teaching at all levels of education can really help. Institutes can also reach out with lectures and education offerings to the voluntary organizations where those with means gather.

In crisis there is opportunity. The intensity and time drain of work is also generating a need: for more self-reflective treatments. Video treatments, mandatory during the pandemic, inferior to in person, nonetheless may be adaptive for the time-challenged patient. It eliminates transit time and can be done at their work place. Transit time is potential money.

The vultures of cost management firms are now moving in to feed off the carcass of broken and unguarded healthcare. In doing so, they kill off the remains. They are turning healthcare into profit points and services into money. But in crisis is opportunity. What emerges is a group of people in the consumer market with money to buy healthcare who are faced with a deteriorated quality of mass market care. University healthcare systems, once the home of individualized and available expertise, are now mass market, middle-class clinic systems. Because insurance coverage is less and less, they attempt to make up income by increasing volume. The only way to do that is to industrialize the system, which means the patient is the organization's and not the doctor's. Healthcare tends to shift to diagnosis and treatment by algorithm not individualized, which takes more time. And algorithms fit better into computerized systems for specific and automatic billing. Time with the doctor is rationed, both accessibility and duration of appointment.

Thus emerges the new private practice market for quality care. It's sad because it preserves the old two-class, really three-class, healthcare system but for those of us who wish to practice at the highest level of quality and who also have a public health concern, we may divide our careers in two, each informing the other. I'm not the only one who has done so. But we must reach out to the new class who need our treatments and can pay for them. Our institutes must get involved in savvy professional marketing.

If we want to politically fight, our true fight is with the economic forces of managed-cost companies (Lazar, 2010). They must not be allowed to constrain private practice for those who can afford it and want it. In order to try to capture that market, they will try and are trying to destroy us, ideologically and financially, with limits and carve-outs of out-of-network care. Here is where the free market helps us. We don't really need them. They need us because the availability of professional resources in mental health is quite limited. There is our true fight. It isn't with each other.

Institutes can also organize markets within themselves by keeping track of graduates' practice interests and availability and providing referral services. This is crucial as an aspect of helping our young devote themselves to and survive in psychoanalytic practice.

Forming our own markets will free all of us and our institutes.

We should not fear the research issue. We have good research. We have research on the increased efficacy of frequency and duration (Huber et al., 2012). We have RCT research that CBT say only they have (Lilliengren, 2017).

Psychotherapy

Perhaps, it is said, part of the answer is psychotherapy. Do analysts do better psychotherapy? Many feel we do. This is perhaps obvious for dynamic psychotherapy and for TFP, but also true for CBT (Beck was an analyst), IPT, and supportive.

I believe this is especially so when applied to the expanded scope of sicker patients. Sicker patients, the psychotic and near psychotic, are often avoided by analysts because of the severity of illness issue and the medication issue.

But there can be split treatments and there are also those of us experienced with medication and conjoint treatments. All need the supportive and interpretive help of the analyst. Some patients will need and benefit from intensive psychoanalysis, either beginning when very ill or when better and their personality issues come more to the fore (Marcus, 2017).

Is psychoanalysis continuous with or a separate category from psychotherapy? Much ink has been spent on that issue! They are on a continuum, overlapping in the middle, and are also, at the extremes, categorical (Sripada, 2015). So what? The fact is, most of us do both. Most patients I analyze began with psychotherapy; some began with medication. Analytic training helps me with using medication both because it helps me understand the person to be able to better strengthen the doctor–patient relationship and therefore medication cooperation and also it helps me understand mind to clarify the diagnosis and therefore the type and dosing of medication targets. Severe psychiatric illness leaves its characteristic signature on the patient's ego functions and symbol formation processes and contents (Marcus, 2017). Personality leaves its characteristic signature on attitudes in the transference.

The totally separate question is how to teach this and whether it is best taught through teaching psychoanalysis proper as a base for then teaching its application in dynamic psychotherapy. It is easier to teach the application of something you know than something you don't know. It's easier then to see the application and apply it. How to teach and what and when to teach it, how to apportion limited curriculum, are educational issues that all educators wrestle with for any curriculum.

Will teaching psychotherapy help recruit candidates? I think it will help us as residency training programs and psychology PhD programs and social work programs no longer teach dynamic psychotherapy. It has been slowly removed from medical student training over many years (Asch and Marcus, 1988).

Regardless of its overlap with psychoanalysis, psychotherapy also needs to be taught as special techniques. Special aspects of technique and of theory are needed when one applies an area of knowledge to a specific task. Techniques of therapy, especially with medication, require attention to ego function. Less frequent sessions may at times require special techniques to maintain the unfolding, deepening process. These, done effectively, often motivate a full psychoanalysis or obviate the need for a full psychoanalysis. For some patients, psychotherapy does the job better than a full psychoanalysis. Most of us in practice for a while have come to this conclusion. So the fight over it is increasingly irrelevant.

Teaching psychotherapy at the institutes now takes different forms. Some do it as part of the first two years. Some do it as separate tracks. Some do it as courses spread throughout the curriculum. Some do it only as electives to senior candidates. Some do it with careful consideration to the differences from psychoanalysis. Some do it with careful consideration to the similarities.

Some want to change the immersion criteria for graduation and appointment to TSA so that psychotherapy counts. Whatever the merits of this drop in immersion, it will not end the fight over how much and what type and who gets to decide. This crucial issue has no quick or easy answer and requires careful thought and study about educational best practices as well as practicalities.

Psychoanalytic education adaptations

We must make psychoanalytic education less economically burdensome. Tuition should be free. Supervision should be free. Institutes should very actively help with patient recruitment. We can extend the years of education, making half time and quarter time available despite the risk of too little. This would be making the present economic drain less. Some classes can be online, making travel time available for practice.

Or do we lower our immersion criteria? That depends on how far you lower. Immersion is key to what we do both with each patient and in our own training. Immersion causes saturation which informs treatment. Immersion teaches transference and counter-transference tolerance, the crucial basis of our work.

From this immersion experience comes our ability to interpret accurately, have a real therapeutic relationship, to grow and develop within ourselves, and to catalyze growth and development in our patients. Immersion is the intense condensation of emotional experience about another person, which is what we wish to de-condense over time in the analytic process. It is a definition of psychoanalytic treatment. The main thing we sell is intensive emotional experience. It is our method. Immersion. Do we really want to give that up? That is the necessary bath water. Some say it's the baby.

My own observation over many many years as a director of medical education programs in academic medical education is that if you lower the quality of education or training, you lose your special market niche. You lose candidates. In an attempt to fit into the broader marketplace you lose your entrée and leverage if you lower your quality because you lose your marketing edge of specialness. We need to enter the broader marketplace from a position of higher expertise in quality. We sell quality, expertise, and availability. It is what our increasingly industrialized medical system no longer sells.

Training and supervising analyst criteria

The issue is twofold. First is why we need criteria. Shouldn't graduation be enough because we are supposed to graduate competent analysts? The problem is graduates most often don't do much analysis after graduation. This isn't bad because they are applying their analytic knowledge to psychotherapy and to other psychiatric and psychological tasks. But they don't do psychoanalysis.

So then comes the issue of training analyst. Do we really want training analysts who don't do analysis?

If we don't, then there must be some gating criteria. This brings up the issue of whether competencies for training can be both described and evaluated. Notice I use the word evaluate, not tested. All complicated professions and crafts have levels of expertise and criteria of competence for those levels, with ways of evaluating them. The problem has to do with defining and evaluating qualities, not just quantities. This is social science and qualitative research.

For specifics of competence criteria for certification and evaluation for training analyst appointment, see the websites of the American Board of Psychoanalysis criteria in the American Academy for Psychoanalytic Education. This will give an idea of how the competencies are described and how they are evaluated. Make up your own mind about its reasonableness. Certainly, institutes can have their own. But it might be helpful to see what some experienced educators come up with. Those competencies, as in all of education, are continuously being discussed and evolved. They look at what is actually happening in the analysis, not at the theory used. Cases are presented and discussed with the evaluators. The evaluators use certain competency criteria guidelines for their evaluation. These guidelines have developed within study and learning groups of the certifying organization. That is what certifying organizations do. Universities have done it for PhD candidate theses and for faculty hiring and tenure over many generations. Teaching, learning, evaluation, levels of competence and experience, and evaluation are basic to the university concept.

The real problem isn't whetehr we can describe and evaluate training analyst competency but rather that fewer and fewer will have any immersion. This is where a developmental pathway may be useful.

Developmental pathways take recent graduates who wish to proceed to the training analyst level and help them. The goal of such programs is not only educational, not only evaluation, but developmental. They help the graduate grow in experience and knowledge. The assumption of the developmental programs is that every analytic graduate has the ability to gain the knowledge and experience necessary to meet the training analyst competencies.

The programs should help with the different types of learning, with relevant readings, with discussions, with supervision both individual and peer group, with practice building, with professional networking. Those institutes that do this either spontaneously or naturally or through programs build back better! In those programs, there is a ladder of opportunity presented to the recent graduate. The developmental ladder leads naturally and almost inevitably to the final goal.

It also should be a developmental ladder for private practice. It must involve teaching about building and managing a practice. It must teach the recruitment and maintenance of a referral network. It ideally would have a referral source. Supervision for private practice is priceless for practice building and maintenance. And, of course, it comes from the experienced and is given to the inexperienced.

It will take time depending on the graduates' immersion and ability. So what? Some of our most highly respected and universally acclaimed as gifted training analysts took their time getting there! They are proud of that generative time and often recommend it.

Summary and conclusion

Let the bitter arguments stop. Move past the narcissistic insults of the past. Put the rage to work in building our future. End the complaining and start the building. Adaptation leads us in a certain direction. Let us get on with it. We need to catalyze and help the next generation. We know how much the broad range of psychoanalytic treatments helps patients. Do not give in to what seems to be overwhelming economic and political forces. Let us devote ourselves to the mission and carry it forth. Best wishes to us all.

References

Asch, S. and Marcus, E.R. (1988) Current status of psychoanalysis in medical student education in the United States: A preliminary overview. *JAPA*. 36(4): 1033–1057.

Benner, P. (2001) From novice to expert. *Clinical Psychology and Psychotherapy*. 22: 469–487.

Huber, D., Zimmermann, J., Henrich, G. and King, G. (2012) Comparison of cognitive-behaviour therapy with psychoanalytic and psychodynamic therapy for depressed patients: A three-year follow-up study. *Psychosom Med Psychotherapy*. 58(3): 299–316.

Kernberg, O. (2014) The twilight of the training analysis system. *Psychoanalytic Review*. 101(2): 151–174.

Lazar, S.G. (editor) (2010) *Psychotherapy Is Worth It: A Comprehensive View of its Cost Effectiveness*. American Psychiatric Publishing.

Lilliengren, P. (2017) Comprehensive compilation of randomized controlled trials (RCTs) involving psychodynamic treatments and intervention. www.researchgate.net/publication/

Marcus, E.R. (2017) *Psychosis and Near Psychosis: Ego Function, Symbol Structure, Treatment* (3rd edition). Routledge.

Marcus, E.R. (2018) Does psychoanalysis have a meta-theory? *Psychodynamic Psychiatry*. 46(2): 220–239.

Shedler, J. (2010) The efficacy of psychodynamic psychotherapy. *American Psychologist*. 98–109.

Sripada, B. (2015) Essential psychoanalysis: toward a re-appraisal of the relationship between psychoanalysis and dynamic psychotherapy. *Psychodynamic Psychiatry*. 43: 396–422.

Zagermann, P. (2021) *The Future of Psychoanalysis. The Debate about the Training Analyst System*. Routledge.

Chapter 16

Why does psychoanalytic education cause such dissension?

Alan Sugarman

The history of psychoanalytic education is fraught with controversy. Its difficulties have been described for so many years (Auchincloss and Michels, 2003; Balint, 1948; Bernfeld, 1962; Goodman, 1977; Kernberg, 1986; 1996; 2000; Kachele and Thoma, 2000; Kirsner, 2000; Knight, 1953; Lewin and Ross, 1960; Reeder, 2004; Zagermann, 2017) that one might wonder how our field has survived. These controversies seem to outnumber our theory wars, even. That is, "the most pressing issue and the one charged with the greatest emotion has always been that of training" (Knight, 1953, p. 210). As early as 1953, Knight was lamenting:

> The spectacle of a national association of physicians and scientists feuding with each other over training standards and practices and calling each other orthodox and conservative or deviant or dissident, is not an attractive one, to say the least. Such terms belong to religions, or to fanatical political movements and not to science and medicine. Psychoanalysis should be neither a 'doctrine' nor a 'party line'.
>
> (p. 210)

To paraphrase Janet Malcolm (1980), are those of us who identify as psychoanalytic educators trying to practice an impossible profession?

Almost seventy years later, our disagreements continue and reverberate in both APsaA and the IPA. Four years ago, the American Psychoanalytic Association completely revised its organizational structure and bylaws in an effort to bring a ceasefire to the decade's long strife about its educational practices. "In all three IPA regions most of the conflicts have centered on training standards" (Perdigao, 2020, p. 1). Compounding, perhaps even exacerbating, educational conflicts is the external reality situation that psychoanalytic institutes are having greater difficulty in attracting candidates, maintaining adequate numbers of qualified faculty to teach them, and remaining visible enough in their broader local communities to promote a

DOI: 10.4324/9781003340744-20

vision of psychoanalysis as a worthy enough treatment to attract patients for their faculty and candidates.

Remarkably for a profession that advocates a multi-deterministic understanding of causality, the usual sole explanation for the multitude of problems besetting psychoanalytic education is to blame the training analyst (TA) system. A host of literature describes the many problems of this aspect of the Eitingon tripartite educational model (Kirsner, 2000; Zagermann, 2017). Many analysts, including some luminaries in our field, have complained of both blatant and more insidious problems caused by the training analyst system. Two broad categories have been elaborated: (1) the creation of an organizational in and out group leading to schisms, and (2) a hierarchical and authoritarian system stifling creativity and the open-mindedness that should be the hallmark of an analytic mind and identity.

The underlying problem

But blaming the TA system focuses on a symptom, not the underlying causes of our regular and ongoing battles about how to educate fledgling psychoanalysts. I accept that most of the criticisms of the TA system are valid and that recent changes within most APsaA psychoanalytic institutes do not solve the many problems caused by such a designation. But I suggest that we lose the opportunity to think more deeply about the problems underlying psychoanalytic education when we lay them at the feet of the TA designation. Just as with clinical psychoanalysis, failing to understand the deeper underlying contributors will make it impossible to ameliorate the problems besetting psychoanalytic education.

It is true that our educational enterprise can be overly hierarchical, authoritarian, and rigid. But I do not think the TA system is the cause of this authoritarian hierarchy and rigidity. Rather, I postulate that the creation of the TA system reflected preexisting tendencies of psychoanalytic educators. The originators of formal psychoanalytic education already preferred authoritarian rigidity, and so built into the educational structure this element to promote it. And it did that quite well (Zagermann, 2017; Kirsner, 2000; Reeder, 2004). But it is important to keep in mind that an authoritarian mindset contributed to the creation of the TA system: not the other way around. Kirsner (2017) describes how the analysis of the aspiring analyst played a subsidiary role in training until Eitingon formed the Berlin Institute in 1920. Eitingon then created the International Training Commission to set, that is, mandate, psychoanalytic training standards for the entire world. Thus, the TA system originated in Eitingon's preexisting preference for rigid, hierarchical authority. "To judge from remarks of Jones about Eitingon, the latter often tried to formalize good practice into rules, as Euclid turned 'common notions' into axioms" (Lewin and Ross, 1960, pp. 28–29). Similarly, Pyles (2017) reports,

It seems that the training analyst system did not arise out of any unique educational or analytic necessity to do it in that particular way, but was, in fact, a natural consequence of the German educational system and methods of child-rearing, which were particularly regimented and hier- archical, or, to use Sigfried Bernfeld's term, 'Prussian'.

(p. 225)

History is clear that rigid, authoritarian hierarchical tendencies preceded the TA system.

But it has been 100 years since the formation of the Berlin Institute; psy- choanalytic education is now practiced in most areas of Europe, in North America, in South America, and in Asia, far from this Prussian culture. Yet it often remains rigid, hierarchical, and stimulates emotionally intense peda- gogical conflicts despite geographical distance and cultural differences. One must assume that there are multiple and complex underlying reasons for this situation given the psychoanalytic principle of multiple function (Waelder, 2007). Describing two of them will occupy the rest of this chapter. These reasons are not meant to be exhaustive. Rather, my hope is to be heuristic to promote greater consideration and discussion. Essentially, I believe that con- tinuing, often unspoken and unreconciled ambiguities in our field cause many to insist on "self-evident" and prematurely consolidated "truths" about the nature of psychoanalysis and the sort of education and preparation it requires.

That is, our educational battles highlight the lack of consensus on what defines psychoanalysis and how to prepare future analysts despite all of us agreeing that quality education is important. Such ambiguity breeds anxiety manifested in rigid, authoritarian polemics to contain it. Consequently, it should be helpful to explicitly articulate two of these ambiguous areas. Doing so can help all to keep in mind the dialectical tensions embedded within psy- choanalytic education in order not to defensively avoid uncertainty through a retreat into rigid orthodoxy, binary views, and premature closure of study and debate.

Scholarly discipline v. guild

One source of ambiguity is aptly captured in one's choice of terminology about the psychoanalytic educational enterprise. Is there psychoanalytic training or is there psychoanalytic education? The American Psychoanalytic Association opted for the latter in 2018 because it wanted to move beyond defining itself solely as a guild that only trains. That goal is reflected in the original vision statement of its new Department of Psychoanalytic Education:

Psychoanalytic education can be informed by and inform other discip- lines, particularly those from which we draw candidates. That is, the evo- lution of our discipline includes both advances from within, based on new clinical experience, research, and ideas, and from without, via challenges to adapt its theory and practice to findings from these other disciplines. This integration helps our candidates adapt to changing social realities and helps all of us make psychoanalysis a respectable academic discipline.

The subcommittee members rewriting APsaA's educational standards in 2018 were explicit among themselves about wanting psychoanalysis to be grounded in a scholarly approach. The term "training" as it is used in training analysis, on the other hand, derives from an emphasis on learning clinical practice, not scholarly, academic deliberation. Kernberg (1986) describes four possible and currently interacting models for psychoanalytic institutes: (1) the seminary model, (2) the university model, (3) the trade school model, and (4) the art school model. Similar distinctions were made even earlier. Lewin and Ross (1960), for example, suggested that there are three models often conflated in psychoanalytic institutes: "(1) that the institute is a professional school, a medical school of sorts; (2) that it is a graduate school, like a university graduate department; and (3) that it is (perhaps also) a research organization" (pp. 37–38).

Many of the problems blamed on the training analyst system really have to do with the overemphasis on teaching psychoanalysis as primarily a clinical technique. To the degree that this becomes the definition of psychoanalysis, candidates are essentially apprentices spending years perfecting their skills with master artisans – their training and supervising analysts. The paradigm becomes a master–disciple relationship (Arlow, 1972). Historians of psychoanalytic education report that the implementation of the training analyst system was part of a larger attempt to formalize psychoanalytic training to create such skilled practitioners.

> Before the 1920's, formal psychoanalytic training did not exist. Psychoanalytic societies were scientific clubs with no accredited schools or curricula. In Europe, for the first twenty years of psychoanalysis, there were no training institutes and no mandatory training analysis. … The 1925 Bad Homburg IPA Congress unanimously established the International Training Board, chaired by Max Eitingon, to set uniform standards for psychoanalytic training around the world.
>
> (Kirsner, 2017, p. 164)

That is, the training analyst system originated in a broader attempt to formalize psychoanalytic training to establish psychoanalysis as a profession, not as an academic discipline. Unfortunately, this prioritizing of the guild or profession dimension of psychoanalysis contributes to psychoanalytic education too often being reduced to rigid, concrete attempts to carry on the legacy of Freud instead of developing a scientific discipline (Bergmann, 2004). Wallerstein (1977) noted:

To maintain and perpetuate that practice we have developed our institutes to be basically independent of other organized entities in function and structure and have developed them in their familiar 'tripartite' educational form. We have come with justification to regard them as adequate vehicles through which to give *training for our profession and to protect its standards from erosion and its central truths from dilution*.

(p. 309, my italics)

Prioritizing this professional or guild dimension of our field leads inevitably to an emphasis on "protecting" standards. Too easily, evolution in thinking and new developments in technique coming from within psychoanalytic experience or from external, related disciplines are labeled threats to the true essence of psychoanalysis. And this guild emphasis has directly contributed to some of the tensions in organized psychoanalysis. Perdigao (2020) reports: "In the 1950's many in the French psychoanalytic community began to object to the Eitingon model believing it was akin to vocational training" (p. 5).

Analysts who wish our field was a scholarly discipline, with clinical psychoanalysis being just one of its practical applications, feel stifled and devalued. They admonish,

If we are to produce research and researchers, if we are to continue to advance our scientific frontiers in concert and imbricated with other related bodies of knowledge, with all the hoped for consequences for psychoanalysis in its therapeutic application, as a growing science, and as an integral part of the fabric of the wider intellectual-scientific-academic world, then we are declared, in our present organization to be grossly deficient.

(Wallerstein, 1977, p. 310)

Having psychoanalytic education overseen by practitioners (skilled craftsmen) has consequences.

The purpose of a professional organization is the strengthening of professional identity by the reinforcement of standards *in adherence to tradition*. Deviations from accepted patterns of thought are viewed with suspicion and frequently discouraged. Academic institutions have the opposite function: they need perpetually to question assumptions and established beliefs and must encourage the search for new truths by the pursuit of research. They welcome new information and must be willing to modify theories in the light of new findings.

(Rogawski, 1989, p. 175, my italics)

For these reasons, some advocate that psychoanalytic institutes need to ally themselves with universities (Kernberg and Michels, 2017).

This guild or profession definition impacts typical institute functioning. A common lament among analytic candidates and pedagogues is that the didactic classwork is the weakest or most disappointing part of the educational process. As Aaron Green, Janet Malcolm's (1980) pseudonym for the New York psychoanalyst she interviewed, says,

> The courses turned out to be disappointing. There were a few exceptions, taught by good teachers, but mostly they were boring discussion classes, in which I had to sit and listen to my fellow students – who knew even less than I did. The classes were at night, from eight-thirty to ten, three times a week. Analytic institutes are night schools.
>
> (pp. 54–55)

Though some institutes emphasize the need for course syllabi to use up-to-date readings, many continue to rely on outdated "classic" readings. The Standard Edition continues to be a staple in many institutes. Some have complained about this tendency (Arlow, 2010; Kernberg, 1996; Sugarman, 2012). "We are, in fact, the only science that uses textbooks that are almost 100 years old. As a result, our candidates are indoctrinated with what psychoanalysis was and not with what psychoanalysis is" (Arlow, 2010, p. 9). Such tendencies carry an implicit message that the psychoanalytic body of knowledge stopped expanding decades ago. In addition, there is minimal vetting of pedagogical ability in teaching faculty in many institutes. Candidates are often taught by faculty having an impoverished understanding of the material they are teaching, are unable to link analytic concepts to clinical material, or stimulate class discussion or critical thinking. Contrast this situation with the amount of deliberation that goes into selecting training or supervising analysts. Clearly, proficiency in the trade is prioritized over pedagogical ability.

This overvaluing of the trade or professional dimension of psychoanalysis even affects the selection of supervising analysts. Most institutes automatically make all TAs supervisors despite the educational standards of both APsaA and the IPA allowing that function to be separated from the training analyst designation. "As we have seen, it has almost always been taken for granted that anyone commissioned to be a training analyst is also suited to be a supervisor, which, to say the least, is a loose assumption" (Reeder, 2004, p. 233). The fact that different skills are needed to be a competent supervisor is ignored. Many excellent TAs work in a primarily intuitive manner. They can be excellent craftsmen but are unable to explain what they are doing or why. Hence, they cannot teach candidates how to think about their patients or the clinical process, too often just suggesting specific interventions for the candidate to apply in a rote manner.

Is psychoanalysis a natural science or a hermeneutic discipline?

Within the academic, scholarly dimension of psychoanalysis, we run into the other ambiguity causing anxiety. What sort of scholarly discipline are we? Too often we fail to acknowledge the competing epistemologies in psychoanalysis. "Is analysis a science or an interpretive discipline? Are we interested in causes or reasons? Are our theories to be understood as mechanisms or metaphors?" (Rees, 2007, p. 896). From the beginning, Freud (1895) sought to place psychoanalysis squarely within the natural scientific realm in his Project for a Scientific Psychology, a goal continued by the prominent early ego psychologists (Hartmann, 1964; Hartmann, Kris, and Loewenstein, 1964; Rapaport, 1951; 1960) with their view of psychoanalysis as a general psychology (Loewenstein, Newman, Schur, and Solnit, 1966; Rosenblatt and Thickstun, 1977). Neuropsychoanalysis (Solms, 2014; 2000) is one current iteration of this definition of psychoanalysis. Many believe that a natural science approach both demonstrates the validity of psychoanalysis and helps it to regain prestige and a place in academia (Sugarman, 2022).

A significant challenge for these aspirations is that Freud, and many after him, saw the clinical psychoanalytic process as the research tool for this science (Saks, 1999). The data that his science studied could only come from the analytic hour. But most question whether the clinical process qualifies as a scientific methodology and research tool. After all, it involves a specific kind of data-feelings, longings, fears, fantasies, memories, wishes, and so on that cannot be directly seen by a neutral observer (Rosenblatt and Thickstun, 1977). Instead, the data are communicated to this observer by the words of the subject/patient, causing it to be often criticized for its lack of objectivity and vulnerability to transference/countertransference distortion. Regardless, the real scientific issue rests on how reliable data are (Rosenblatt and Thickstun, 1977). Can different observers agree consistently on the pattern or relationship of this data? Some critics argue that data must also be quantitative to be scientific. But most philosophers of science insist that quantification is not an inherent aspect of science (Sherwood, 1969). "The goal of scientific investigation is to discover order in phenomena that can be expressed in lawlike form. Quantification is necessary only if such laws are to be expressed numerically" (Rosenblatt and Thickstun, 1977, pp. 12–13). Most important is whether the observed patterns have the potential to disprove the hypothesis using "observation in situations where some commitment of knowledge is made, in which hypotheses or beliefs are in some way placed in jeopardy, made relevant to and potentially falsifiable by the outcome of that situation" (Sherwood, 1969, p. 51). The difference between science and faith ultimately rests on whether the belief can be shown to be false. If that is not possible, psychoanalysis is in the realm of faith.

Because of concerns about clinical data being scientific, several prominent analysts influenced by Ricoeur (1977) suggested that it is better classified as a hermeneutic discipline. Schafer (1976), for example, noted that the natural science approach "excludes meaning from the center of psychoanalytic theory. … But meaning (and intention) is the same as 'psychic reality' – that which is at the center of psychoanalytic work" (p. 199). He also argues that "the biological language of functions cannot be concerned with meaning. … the primary psychoanalytic language is a language of and for meanings and the changes they undergo during development and during the psychoanalytic process" (p. 89). Schafer, like many of Rapaport's students, concluded that much of the metapsychology used by Rapaport and the other ego psychological theorists to claim a scientific status for psychoanalysis is inappropriate and inadequate for explaining the essential data of psychoanalysis. Sugarman (2022) has said similar things about neuropsychoanalysis. One problem with seeing psychoanalysis as scientific lies with the economic model according to Schafer (1976), Gill and Holzman (1976), George Klein (1976), and Mayman (1976). In one way or another, they and others see the economic model as providing an illusion of being scientific by thinking that reframing psychological phenomena in terms of psychic energy and its transformation explains causality.

> This … model is superimposed upon analytic experience, ignoring its derivation from the work of reconstructing an individual history on the basis of scattered fragments. Most seriously, this model is in many ways antecedent to analytic experience, as we see in the Project, and it imposes its reference system on this experience: quantifiable energy, stimulation, tension, discharge, inhibitions, cathexis, etc.
>
> (Ricoeur, 1977, p. 851)

One way to reconcile this important ambiguity about the nature of the psychoanalytic discipline might be to consider it both a scientific and a hermeneutic discipline, rather than insist on a black and white dichotomy. Psychoanalysis involves a variety of models that explain different aspects of human functioning: (1) a model of mind, (2) a developmental model, (3) a model of pathogenesis, and (4) a model of mutative or therapeutic action. Perhaps some of these models, or parts of them, are best studied and thought about through the lens of a natural science approach while others are best understood from the perspective of hermeneutics. For example, Pulver (2003) thinks that neuroscience is irrelevant for clinical psychoanalysis while being quite important for our model of mind. Ours is a complex discipline as is not unusual for academic disciplines.

> As Thomas Kuhn describes in his analysis of the history of science, different paradigms often exist side by side within a scientific discipline.

… It seems to me that the above-mentioned understanding of psycho-analysis as a critical hermeneutics of the 1970's and 1980's is still currently represented in French psychoanalysis and partly in the Latin-American IPA societies (see e.g., Ahumada & Doria-Medina, 2010; Bernardi, 2003; De Mijolla, 2003; Duarte Guimaraes Filho, 2009; Green, 2003; Perron, 2003, 2006; Vinocur de Fischbein, 2009; Widlocher, 2003), while in the Anglo-Saxon and German-speaking psychoanalysis, the discussion, or perhaps even the adjustment to an empirical-quantitative research para-digm, has been pushed to the fore.

(Leuzinger-Bohleber, 2015, pp. 6–7)

The psychoanalytic model of the mind

Solms (2020) situates his model of the emotional mind squarely in the camp of natural science, postulating three basic premises for a psychoanalytic model of the emotional mind that can be studied scientifically and proven true or false: (1) the human infant is born with a set of innate needs and is not a blank slate; (2) mental development involves creating the capacities to meet these needs in the world; and (3) most ways humans learn to meet their needs are implemented unconsciously. A corollary is that pathogenesis involves failure to find successful ways to meet these needs. In essence, he uses developmental psychology to place the psychoanalytic model of mind clearly in the natural science domain in line with Emde (2020).

Everything we do in psychoanalysis is predicated upon these three claims. If they are disproved, the core scientific presuppositions upon which psy-choanalysis (as we know it) will have been rejected. But as things stand currently, in 2018, they are eminently defensible, strongly—indeed increasingly—supported by accumulating and converging lines of evi-dence in neighbouring fields.

(Solms, 2020, p. 27)

Let us examine his claim.

As a discipline, psychoanalysis began at the interface of mind and brain and always been about … loving, hating, what brings us together as lovers, parents, and friend and what pulls us apart in conflict and hatred. These are the enduring mysteries of life and especially of early devel-opment – how young children learn the language of the social world with its intertwined biological, genetic, and experiential roots and how infants translate thousands of intimate moments with their parents into a genuine, intuitive, emotional connection to other persons.

(Mayes, Fonagy, and Target, 2007, pp. 2–3)

Research provides overwhelming evidence that the human infant is not simply a blank slate upon which the environment inscribes a mind. The importance of maturation in mental development, originally conceptualized as autonomous ego functions, or the ego's conflict-free sphere, is supported by academic cognitive and developmental psychology, and remains an essential part of contemporary psychoanalytic developmental thinking. "There is an expected sequence of emerging functions in the psychic apparatus leading to progressively differentiated structures of hierarchical organization. The sequences, the functions, and the structures are rooted in biological sources" (Gilmore and Meersand, 2014, p. 11). Infant research (Beebe and Lachmann, 1988; 1997; De Litvan, 2007; Emde, 1994; Fonagy, Gergely, Jurist, and Target, 2002; Gergely and Watson, 1996; Jurist, Slade, and Bergner, 2008; Sander, 1988; Tronick, 2007) and attachment research (Ainsworth, 1985; Ainsworth, Blehar, Waters, and Wall, 1978; Main and Solomon, 1990; Sroufe, 1996) support this psychoanalytic premise that the human infant comes into the world with innate needs and capacities for getting those needs met. Trevarthen (1979), for example, found that infants are wired to coordinate their actions with others. Such research demonstrates that the psychoanalytic model of development can be studied from a natural science perspective (Mayes, Fonagy, and Target, 2007).

Solms's second premise is that the task of development is to find ways to meet one's emotional needs in the world. Adaptation involves the infant, then child, and finally adolescent learning strategies to achieve satisfaction and minimize frustration. Both psychoanalytic theory and developmental research demonstrate that this learning involves the interaction between inborn potentialities/capacities and the environment (Gilmore and Meersand, 2014; Mayes, Fonagy, and Target, 2007) mediated primarily through mentalization, a mental function that emerges from adequate parenting and affects subsequent object relating (Fonagy et al., 2002; Mayes and Cohen, 1996). It promotes affect-regulation, crucial for the broader self-regulation necessary for relating to others in ways that ensure need satisfaction (Jurist, 2018; Sugarman, 2018). Hence, there is ample evidence that the developmental model of psychoanalysis fits well within a natural science paradigm. To the degree that the overarching psychoanalytic model of the mind is a developmental model, it seems reasonable to regard these studies as offering partial confirmation of its scientific validity as well.

Another important premise of the overarching psychoanalytic model of the mind is the importance of unconscious mental processes. Freud's original definition of psychoanalysis as the science of the unconscious has been updated (Leuzinger-Bohleber, 2015; Leuzinger-Bohleber, Arnold, and Solms, 2017). As Solms (2020) puts it, "Most of our methods of meeting our emotional needs are executed unconsciously" (p. 26). Evidence to support this premise has been provided by Bargh and Chartrand (1999) who report that only 5% of goal-directed actions occur consciously (Solms, 2020). Equally important is the expansion of the psychoanalytic theory of the unconscious beyond the traditional "dynamic unconscious" of drive–defense conflicts (Emde, 2020; Leuzinger-Bohleber, Arnold, and Solms, 2017). Based on neuroscientific research, "unconscious mental functioning is now appreciated to involve adaptive domains of skill-based procedural and implicit knowledge and these domains are importantly included in neuropsychological assessments, including those of executive functioning and their emotional connections" (Emde, 2020, p. 39).

Furthermore, a host of psychoanalytically oriented research supports Britton's (2015) conclusion that there is a system in the system Ucs. Britton (2015) reverses Lacan's idea that the unconscious is structured like a language and suggests that "language is structured like the unconscious" (p. 20). Regardless of which is like the other, research supports a central scientific premise of psychoanalysis that the unconscious has structure (Schore, 2019; Weinberger and Stoycheva, 2019). Robert Holt (1978) has done and chaired extensive research using projective tests to measure the primary process, a key component of the unconscious's structure. Similarly, the elements of procedural or implicit relational paradigms, now considered to be essential parts of unconscious mental functioning, have been supported by a host of projective test research stimulated by the thinking of Mayman (1963; 1967; 1968), Blatt (1975; 1990), Blatt and Lerner (1983), Blatt and Sugarman (1980), and Blatt, Brenneis, Schimek, and Glick (1976). Students and collaborators of theirs have published exhaustively on the relationship between these internal relational paradigms and a host of clinical and developmental issues and disorders (Harder, 1979; Hatcher and Krohn, 1980; Krohn and Mayman, 1974; Kwawer, 1980; Ryan, 1970; Segal, Westen, Lohr, and Silk, 1993; Spear, 1980; Spear and Sugarman, 1984; Urist, 1977; Westen, 1991; Westen, Lohr, Silk, Gold, and Kerber, 1990).

What about the psychoanalytic model of pathogenesis? Here again we find ample research evidence that it fits nicely within a natural science perspective. Some examples include research supporting the role of development on ADHD (Leuzinger-Bohleber, Canestri, and Target, 2010); in particular, developmental and trauma-causing deviations in affect-regulation play causal roles (Leuzinger-Bohleber, 2010). The deleterious impact of trauma on the development of mentalization leading to many disorders has been well documented (Fonagy, 2010), e.g., somatization disorders (Marty, 1968), depression (Leuzinger-Bohleber, 2015), ADHD (Sugarman, 2006), and borderline states (Fonagy, Steele, Steele, Leigh, Kennedy, Mattoon, and Target, 1995; Fonagy, Target, and Gergely, 2000). The above-mentioned research with projective tests has supported psychoanalytic explanations of several types of pathology, e.g., psychosis (Blatt and Ritzler, 1974; Blatt, Tuber, and Aurbach, 1980; Lerner, Sugarman, and Barbour, 1985), eating disorders (Sugarman, Quinlan, and Devenis, 1982), opiate addiction (Blatt, Wilber, Sugarman, and McDonald, 1984; Blatt, Berman, Bloom-Feshbach, Sugarman, Wilber, and

Kleber, 1984; Wilber, Rounsaville, Sugarman, Blatt, and Kleber, 1982), and borderline pathology (Hymowitz, Hunt, Carr, Hurt, and Spear, 1983; Lerner, Sugarman, and Gaughran, 1981; Lerner and Lerner, 1980; Singer, 1977; Spear, 1980). Attachment research has also supported the pathogenic importance of problematic early object relationships (Fonagy, 2001).

> There is general agreement that attachment security can serve as a protective factor against psychopathology, and that it is associated with a wide range of healthier personality variables such as lower anxiety (Collins & Read, 1990), less hostility, and greater ego resilience (Koback & Sceery, 1988), and greater ability to regulate affect through interpersonal relatedness (Simpson, et al., 1992; Vaillant, 1992). Insecure attachment appears to be a risk factor and is associated with such characteristics as a greater degree of depression (Armsden & Greenberg, 1987, anxiety, hostility, psychosomatic illness (Hazan & Shaver, 1990) and less ego resilience (Kobak & Sceery, 1988).
>
> (Fonagy, 2001, p. 33)

Is this support for psychoanalysis as a natural science also true for its model of mutative action? Here things become more complicated. Solms (2020) clearly believes that it, too, falls squarely within a natural science paradigm when he says that "psychoanalytic therapy achieves good outcomes" (p. 30). And, indeed, Shedler (2010) has demonstrated that this is clearly the case for psychoanalytic psychotherapy. To date, however, we do not find the same support for psychoanalysis proper because there have been significantly fewer outcome studies of it. Nonetheless, there have been some (Galatzer-Levy, Bachrach, Skolnikoff, and Waldron, 2000) and more are occurring (e.g. Leuzinger-Bohleber, Kallenbach, Bahrke, Kaufhold, Negele, Ernst, Keller, Fiedler, Hautzinger, and Beutel, 2020; Leuzinger-Bohleber, Kallenbach, and Schoett, 2016). Consequently, it seems reasonable to conclude that the efficacy of psychoanalytic mutative action can be studied from a natural science paradigm.

But the process of mutative action is more complicated than simply outcome. There are many psychoanalytic models of mutative action in our pluralistic world. Nonetheless, each model does emphasize its own conception of psychoanalytic process. In this way, the question becomes whether psychoanalytic process is best studied and understood from a natural science paradigm. Jiminez and Altimir (2020), in their optimistic attempt to answer in the affirmative, acknowledge that "traditional research strategies on psychoanalytic process have reached a dead end" (p. 59). Nonetheless, they hope that using methods derived from mother–infant research and an events paradigm approach will help them overcome this dead end. Solms (2020) believes that psychoanalytic process can be studied by explaining it as changing deeply automatized predictions that must be reconsolidated in working memory and moved out of solely non-declarative (permanently unconscious) memory.

He offers a model of reconsolidation using affects to access the meaning of symptoms. Others (Leuzinger-Bohleber, Kallenbach, and Schoett, 2016) also agree that psychoanalytic process can be considered within a natural science model.

But many question whether natural science addresses the centrality of subjective meaning in psychoanalytic process (Rothenberg, 2004).

> If there is a single overarching principle that governs our behavior in the analytic situation, it is that we attempt to understand our patient's individual, specific motivations, particularly as they are manifested in the analytic relationship, and to help the patient understand them. We deal, that is, with the specific contents of the patient's mind and the specific processes he or she uses to regulate them. Neuroscience clarifies the anatomical and physiological substrates from which these motivations arise. It may also say something about the general functioning of these motivations, but by its very nature it can say little about the *meaning* they have for an individual.
>
> (Pulver, 2003, p. 762, my italics)

Schafer suggests viewing the analytic process, instead, as allowing a set of histories to be retold from multiple perspectives as the analyst helps the patient to transform these narrative histories into new more complete, coherent, convincing ones that are better able to promote adaptation (Saks, 1999). His emphasis is on the narrative, not "objective" truths that are the "causes" of the patient's suffering. "What has been presented here amounts to a hermeneutic version of psychoanalysis. In this version, psychoanalysis is an interpretive discipline rather than a natural science. It deals in language and equivalents of language" (Schafer, 1983, p. 255). Spence (1982) also "elaborates and defends a conception of psychoanalysis as achieving, in its interpretations and constructions, primarily narrative truth as opposed to historical truth" (Saks, 1999, p. 66). This hermeneutic distinction between narrative and factual truth is crucial in challenging the idea that psychoanalysis is solely a natural science that cures by providing insight into what really happened or was imagined in the past.

> The linguistic and narrative aspects of an interpretation may well have priority over its historical truth, and we are making the somewhat heretical claim that an interpretation is effective because it gives the awkward happening a kind of linguistic and narrative closure, not because it can account for it in a purely *causal* sense. An interpretation satisfies because we are able to contain an unfinished piece of reality in a meaningful sentence; that is part of what we mean by finding its narrative home. The sentence acquires additional meaning when it meshes with other parts of the patient's life; it acquires narrative force by virtue of these connections

and adds narrative understanding to what is already known and understood. The power of language is such that simply putting something into words gives it a kind of authenticity; finding a narrative home for these words amplifies and expands the truth.

(Spence, 1982, p. 138, my italics)

At this point in our development, the best way to study and understand psychoanalytic process seems unsettled. It is important to acknowledge that neuroscience has advanced a great deal in the almost twenty years since Pulver wrote these ideas. Furthermore, there are other natural sciences like cognitive and developmental psychology that might adequately study it even if neuroscience cannot. On the other hand, it remains debatable whether the subjective meaning examined in the psychoanalytic process can ever be studied and explained deeply by the natural science paradigm. We must acknowledge the possibility that this model of psychoanalysis may best be studied from the perspective of a hermeneutic discipline. Narrative and meaning may be proven more important than historical or objective causation (Lichtenberg, Lachmann, and Fosshage, 2017).

Conclusion

Acknowledging that our field has certain dialectical tensions or ambiguities seems important in reducing the acrimonious, polemical pronouncements that characterize discussions about psychoanalytic education. Not recognizing that we have not yet grappled with defining our field prevents us from realizing that anxiety about it continues to disrupt and make psychoanalytic education unnecessarily rigid and authoritarian. Until we face that we are both a clinical profession and an academic discipline, we will avoid thoughtful study and debate about educational practices and priorities. Similarly, until we consider what sort of discipline we are, we will never agree on what our educational curriculum should be. Instead, we are likely to continue our battles over specific educational requirements and practices to avoid our internal anxiety that we do not really know what is best, or even effective. We cling to what we were taught by idealized teachers or supervisors because it feels too difficult and confusing to have to face certain existential ambiguities about our field. Ironically, we never learn that there is a lot of research data to support our basic epistemology. We might not have to choose between being a profession and a discipline if we engage these ambiguities and each other in reflective ways. Disagreements about simple and concrete educational practices like the training analysis or distance analysis simply distract us from the discussions necessary to move our field forward. We are at a crossroads as a field. It is time to engage in such discussions about our basic underlying tensions.

References

Ahumada, J.L. and Doria-Medina, R. (2010) New Orleans congress panel: what does conceptual research have to offer? In: M. Leuzinger-Bohleber, J. Canestri, and M. Target (editors) *Early Development and its Disturbances: Clinical, Conceptual, and Empirical Research on ADHD and Other Psychopathologies and its Epistemological Reflections*. London: Karnac, pp. 267–279.

Ainsworth, M.D.S. (1985) Attachments across the lifespan. *Bulletin of the New York Academy of Medicine*. 61: 792–812.

Ainsworth, M.D.S., Blehar, M.C., Waters, E., and Wall, S. (1978) *Patterns of Attachment: A Psychological Study of the Strange Situation*. Hillsdale, NJ: Lawrence Erlbaum.

Arlow, J.A. (1972) Some dilemmas in psychoanalytic education. *Journal of the American Psychoanalytic Association*. 20: 556–566.

Arlow, J.A. (2010) Unpublished papers of Jacob Arlow: comments on the psychoanalytic curriculum. *Bulletin of the Psychoanalytic Association of New York*. 48(2): 9–11.

Armsden, G.C. and Greenberg, M.T. (1987) The inventory of parent and peer attachment: individual differences and their relationship to psychological well-being in adolescence. *Journal of Youth and Adolescence*. 16: 427–454.

Auchincloss, E.L. and Michels, R. (2003) A reassessment of psychoanalytic education: controversies and changes. *International Journal of Psychoanalysis*. 84: 387–403.

Balint, M. (1948) On the psychoanalytic training system. *International Journal of Psychoanalysis*. 29: 163–173.

Bargh, J. and Chartrand, T. (1999) The unbearable automaticity of being. *American Psychologist*. 54: 462–479.

Beebe, B. and Lachmann, F.M. (1988) The contribution of mother–infant mutual influence to the origins of self- and object-representations. *Psychoanalytic Psychology*. 5: 305–337.

Beebe, B. and Lachmann, F.M. (1997) Mother–infant interaction structures and presymbolic self- and object-representations. *Psychoanalytic Dialogues*. 7: 113–182.

Bergmann, M.S. (2004) *Understanding Dissidence and Controversy in the History of Psychoanalysis*. New York: Other Press.

Bernardi, R. (2003) What kind of evidence makes the analyst change his or her theoretical and technical ideas? In: M. Leuzinger-Bohleber, A.U Dreher, and J. Canestri (editors). *Pluralism and Unity? Methods of Research in Psychoanalysis*. London: International Psychoanalytical Association, pp. 125–137.

Bernfeld, S. (1962) On psychoanalytic training. *Psychoanalytic Quarterly*. 31: 457–482.

Blatt, S.J. (1975) The validity of projective techniques and their research and clinical contributions. *Journal of Personality Assessment*. 39: 327–343.

Blatt, S.J. (1990) The Rorschach: a test of perception or an evaluation of representation. *Journal of Personality Assessment*. 55: 394–316.

Blatt, S.J. and Lerner, H.D. (1983) The psychological assessment of object representation. *Journal of Personality Assessment*. 47: 7–28.

Blatt, S.J. and Ritzler, B.A. (1974) Thought disorder and boundary disturbance in psychosis. *Journal of Clinical and Consulting Psychology.* 42: 370–381.

Blatt, S.J. and Sugarman, A. (1980) *An Object Relations Scale for the Thematic Apperception Test.* Unpublished research manual. New Haven, CT: Yale University.

Blatt, S.J., Brenneis, C.B., Schimek, S.G., and Glick, M. (1976) The normal and psychopathological impairment of the concept of the object on the Rorschach. *Journal of Abnormal Psychology.* 85: 364–373.

Blatt, S.J., Tuber, S.B., and Aurbach, J.S. (1980) Representation of interpersonal interactions on the Rorschach and level of psychopathology. *Journal of Personality Assessment.* 54: 711–728.

Blatt, S., Wilber, C., Sugarman, A., and McDonald, C. (1984) Psychodynamic theories of opiate addiction: new directions for research. *Clinical Psychology Review.* 4: 159–189.

Blatt, S., Berman, W., Bloom-Feshbach, S., Sugarman, A., Wilber, C., and Kleber, H. (1984) The psychological assessment of psychopathology in opiate addicts. *Journal of Nervous and Mental Disease.* 172: 156–165.

Britton, R. (2015) *Between Mind and Brain: Models of the Mind and Models in the Mind.* London: Karnac.

Collins, N.L. and Read, S.J. (1990) Adult attachment, working models and relationship quality in dating couples. *Journal of Personality and Social Psychology.* 58: 633–644.

De Litvan, M.A. (2007) Infant observation: a range of questions and challenges for contemporary psychoanalysis. *International Journal of Psychoanalysis.* 88: 713–773.

De Mijolla, A. (2003) Freud and psychoanalytic research: a brief historical overview. In: M. Leuzinger-Bohleber, A.U Dreher, and J. Canestri (editors). *Pluralism and Unity? Methods of Research in Psychoanalysis.* London: International Psychoanalytical Association, pp. 81–97.

Duarte Guimaraes Filho, P. (2009) Klinisch-konzeptuelle Forschung im Bereich des Aufbaus heutigen psychoanalytischen Wissens. In: M. Leuzinger-Bohleber, Canestri, and Target (editors) *Fruhe Entwicklungen und ihre Sturungen.* Frankfurt: Brandes & Apsel, pp. 237–252.

Emde, R.N. (1994) Individuality, context, and the search for meaning. *Child Development.* 65: 719–737.

Emde, R.N. (2020) Five advances in psychoanalytic thinking and their implications for outcome research. In: M. Leuzinger-Bohleber, M. Solms, and S.E. Arnold (editors). *Outcome Research and the Future of Psychoanalysis: Clinicians and Researchers in Dialogue.* London: Routledge, pp. 37–43.

Fonagy, P. (2001) *Attachment Theory and Psychoanalysis.* New York: Other Press.

Fonagy, P. (2010) Attachment, trauma, and psychoanalysis: where psychoanalysis meets neuroscience. In: Leuzinger-Bohleber, M., Canestri, J., and Target, M. (editors) *Early Development and its Disturbances: Clinical, Conceptual, and Empirical Research on ADHD and other Psychopathologies and its Epistemological Reflections.* London: Karnac, pp. 53–75.

Fonagy, P., Steele, M., Steele, H., Leigh, T., Kennedy, R., Mattoon, G., and Target, M. (1995) Attachment, the reflective self, and borderline states: the predictive specificity of the Adult Attachment Interview and pathological emotional development. In: S. Goldberg, R. Muir, and J. Kerr (editors) *Attachment Theory: Social, Developmental and Clinical Perspectives*. New York: Analytic Press, pp. 233–278.

Fonagy, P., Target, M., and Gergely, G. (2000) Attachment and borderline personality disorder: a theory and some evidence. *Psychiatric Clinics of North America*. 23: 103–122.

Fonagy, P., Gergely, G., Jurist, E.L., and Target, M. (2002) *Affect Regulation, Mentalization, and the Development of the Self*. New York: Other Press.

Freud, S. (1895) Project for a scientific psychology. *The Standard Edition of the Complete Psychological Works of Sigmund Freud*. I: 281–397.

Galatzer-Levy, R.M., Bachrach, H., Skolnikoff, A., and Waldron, S. (2000) *Does Psychoanalysis Work?* New Haven, CT: Yale University Press.

Gergely, G. and Watson, J. (1996) The social feedback theory of parental affect-mirroring. *International Journal of Psychoanalysis*. 77: 1181–1212.

Gill, M.M. and Holzman, P.S. (1976) *Psychology Versus Metapsychology: Psychoanalytic Essays in Memory of George S. Klein*. New York: International Universities Press.

Gilmore, K.J. and Meersand, P. (2014) *Normal Child and Adolescent Development: A Psychodynamic Primer*. Washington, DC: American Psychiatric Publishing.

Goodman, S. (1977) *Psychoanalytic Education and Research: The Current Situation and Future Possibilities*. New York: International Universities Press.

Green, A. (2003) The pluralism of sciences and psychoanalytic thinking. In: M. Leuzinger-Bohleber, A.U Dreher, and J. Canestri (editors) *Pluralism and Unity? Methods of Research in Psychoanalysis*. London: International Psychoanalytical Association, pp. 26–45.

Harder, D.W. (1979) The assessment of ambitious-narcissistic character style with three projective tests: the early memories, TAT, and the Rorschach. *Journal of Personality Assessment*. 43: 23–32.

Hartmann, H. (1964) *Essays on Ego Psychology: Selected Problems in Psychoanalytic Theory*. New York: International Universities Press.

Hartmann, H., Kris, E., and Loewenstein, R.M. (1964) *Papers on Psychoanalytic Psychology*. New York: International Universities Press.

Hatcher, R. and Krohn, A. (1980) Level of object representation and capacity for intensive psychotherapy with neurotics and borderlines. In: J.S. Kwawer, H.D. Lerner, P.M. Lerner, and A. Sugarman (editors). *Borderline Phenomena and the Rorschach Test*. New York: International Universities Press, pp. 299–320.

Hazan, C. and Shaver, P. (1990) Love and work: an attachment theoretical perspective. *Journal of Personality and Social Psychology*. 59: 270–280.

Holt, R.H. (1978) *Methods in Clinical Psychology: Vol. 1. Projective Assessment*. New York: Plenum.

Hymowitz, P., Hunt, H.F., Carr, A.C., Hurt, S.W., and Spear, W.E. (1983) The WAIS and the Rorschach tests in diagnosing borderline personality. *Journal of Personality Assessment*. 47: 588–596.

Jimenez, J.P. and Altimir, C. (2020) Developing an innovative, scientific, clinic-ally sensitive approach to investigate psychoanalytic process. In M. Leuzinger-Bohleber, M. Solms, and S.E. Arnold (editors). *Outcome Research and the Future of Psychoanalysis: Clinicians and Researchers in Dialogue*. London: Routledge, pp. 57–67.

Jurist, E.L. (2018) *Minding Emotions: Cultivating Mentalization in Psychotherapy*. New York: Guilford.

Jurist, E.L., Slade, A., and Bergner, S. (2008) (editors) *Mind to Mind: Infant Research, Neuroscience, and Psychoanalysis*. New York: Other Press.

Kachele, H. and Thoma, H. (2000) On the devaluation of the Eitingon-Freud model of psychoanalytic education. *International Journal of Psychoanalysis*. 81: 806–808.

Kernberg, O.F. (1986) Institutional problems of psychoanalytic education. *Journal of the American Psychoanalytic Association*. 34: 799–834.

Kernberg, O.F. (1996) Thirty methods to destroy the creativity of psychoanalytic candidates. *International Journal of Psychoanalysis*. 77: 1031–1040.

Kernberg, O.F. (2000) A concerned critique of psychoanalytic education. *International Journal of Psychoanalysis*. 81: 97–120.

Kernberg, O.F. and Michels, R. (2017) Thoughts on the present and future of psy-choanalysis. In: P. Zagermann (editor) *Psychoanalytic Education and Research: The Current Situation and Future Possibilities*. New York: International Universities Press, pp. 141–159.

Kirsner, D. (2000) *Unfree Associations: Inside Psychoanalytic Institutes*. London: Process Press.

Kirsner, D. (2017) The training analysis: still a roadblock in psychoanalytic educa-tion. In: P. Zagermann (editor). *The Future of Psychoanalysis: The Debate about the Training Analyst System*. London: Karnac, pp. 161–178.

Klein, G.S. (1976) *Psychoanalytic Theory: An Exploration of Essentials*. New York: International Universities Press.

Knight, R. (1953) The present status of organized psychoanalysis in the United States. *Journal of the American Psychoanalytic Association*. 1: 197–221.

Kobak, R. and Sceery, A. (1988) Attachment in late adolescence: working models, affect regulation and perceptions of self and others. *Child Development*. 59: 135–146.

Krohn, A. and Mayman, M. (1974) Object representations in dreams and projective tests. *Bulletin of the Menninger Clinic*. 38: 445–466.

Kwawer, J.S. (1980) Primitive interpersonal modes, borderline phenomena, and Rorschach content. In: J.S. Kwawer, H.D. Lerner, P.M. Lerner, and A. Sugarman (editors). *Borderline Phenomena and the Rorschach Test*. New York: International Universities Press, pp. 89–105.

Lerner, H.D., Sugarman, A., and Gaughran, J. (1981) Borderline and schizophrenic patients: a comparative study of defensive structure. *Journal of Nervous and Mental Disease*. 169: 705–711.

Lerner, H.D., Sugarman, A., and Barbour, C. (1985) Patterns of ego boundary disturb-ance in neurotic, borderline, and schizophrenic patients. *Psychoanalytic Psychology*. 2: 47–66.

Lerner, P.M. and Lerner, H.D. (1980) Rorschach assessment of primitive defenses in borderline personality structure. In: J.S. Kwawer, H.D. Lerner, P.M. Lerner, and A. Sugarman (editors). *Borderline Phenomena and the Rorschach Test.* New York: International Universities Press, pp. 257–274.

Leuzinger-Bohleber, M. (2010) Early affect regulation and its disturbances: approaching ADHD in a psychoanalysis with a child and an adult. In: Leuzinger-Bohleber, M., Canestri, J., and Target, M. (editors) *Early Development and its Disturbances: Clinical, Conceptual, and Empirical Research on ADHD and other Psychopathologies and its Epistemological Reflections.* London: Karnac, pp. 185–206.

Leuzinger-Bohleber, M. (2015) *Finding the Body in the Mind: Embodied Memories, Trauma, and Depression.* London: Karnac.

Leuzinger-Bohleber, M., Canestri, J., and Target, M. (2010) (editors) *Early Development and its Disturbances: Clinical, Conceptual, and Empirical Research on ADHD and other Psychopathologies and its Epistemological Reflections.* London: Karnac.

Leuzinger-Bohleber, M., Kallenbach, L., and Schoett, M.J. (2016) Pluralistic approaches to the study of process and outcome in psychoanalysis. The LAC depression study: a case in point. *Psychoanalytic Psychotherapy.* 30: 4–22.

Leuzinger-Bohleber, M., Arnold, S., and Solms, M. (2017) *The Unconscious: A Bridge between Psychoanalysis and Cognitive Neuroscience.* London: Routledge.

Leuzinger-Bohleber, M., Kallenbach, L., Bahrke, U., Kaufold, J., Negele, A., Ernst, M., Keller, W., Fiedler, G., Hautzinger, M., and Beutel, M.E. (2020) The LAC study: a comparative outcome study of psychoanalytic and cognitive-behavioral long-term therapies of chronic depressive patients. In: M. Leuzinger-Bohleber, M. Solms, and S.E. Arnold (editors). *Outcome Research and the Future of Psychoanalysis: Clinicians and Researchers in Dialogue.* London: Routledge, pp. 136–165.

Lewin, B.D. and Ross, H. (1960) *Psychoanalytic Education in the United States.* New York: Norton.

Lichtenberg, J.D., Lachmann, F.M., and Fosshage, J.L. (2017) *Narrative and Meaning: The Foundation of Mind, Creativity, and the Psychoanalytic Dialogue.* London: Routledge.

Loewenstein, R.M., Newman, L.M., Schur, M., and Solnit, A.J. (1966) *Psychoanalysis – A General Psychology: Essays in Honor of Heinz Hartmann.* New York: International Universities Press.

Main, M. and Solomon, J. (1990) Procedures for identifying infants as disorganized/disoriented during the Ainsworth Strange Situation. In: M. Greenberg, D. Cicchetti, and E.M. Cummings (editors). *Attachment During the Preschool Years: Theory, Research, and Intervention.* Chicago: University of Chicago Press, pp. 121–160.

Malcolm, J. (1980) *Psychoanalysis: The Impossible Profession.* New York: Vintage Books.

Marty, P. (1968) A major process of somatization: the progressive disorganization. *International Journal of Psychoanalysis.* 49: 246–249.

Mayes, L.C. and Cohen, D.J. (1996) Children's developing theory of mind. *Journal of the American Psychoanalytic Association.* 44: 117–142.

Mayes, L.C., Fonagy, P., and Target, M. (2007) (editors) *Developmental Science and Psychoanalysis: Integration and Innovation.* London: Karnac.

Mayman, M. (1963) Psychoanalytic study of the self-organization with psychological tests. In: B.T. Wigdor (editor) *Recent Advances in the Study of Behavior Changes: Proceedings of the Academic Assembly on Clinical Psychology*. Montreal: McGill University Press, pp. 37–117.

Mayman, M. (1967) Object representations and object relationships in Rorschach responses. *Journal of Projective Techniques*. 31: 17–25.

Mayman, M. (1968) Early memories and character structure. *Journal of Projective Techniques*. 32: 303–316.

Mayman, M. (1976) Psychoanalytic theory in retrospect and prospect. *Bulletin of the Menninger Clinic*. 40: 199–210.

Perdigao, G. (2020) On the APsaA–IPA relationship. *The American Psychoanalyst*. 54(2): 1–7.

Perron, R. (2003) What are we looking for? How? In: M. Leuzinger-Bohleber, A.U. Dreher, and J. Canestri (editors) *Pluralism and Unity? Methods of Research in Psychoanalysis*. London: International Psychoanalytical Association, pp. 97–109.

Perron, R. (2006) How to do research? Reply to Otto Kernberg. *International Journal of Psychoanalysis*. 87: 927–932.

Pulver, S.E. (2003) On the astonishing clinical irrelevance of neuroscience. *Journal of the American Psychoanalytic Association*. 51: 755–772.

Pyles, R. (2017) Still crazy after all these years. In: P. Zagermann (editor) *The Future of Psychoanalysis: The Debate about the Training Analyst System*. London: Karnac, pp. 221–259.

Rapaport, D. (1951) *Organization and Pathology of Thought: Selected Sources*. New York: Columbia University Press.

Rapaport, D. (1960) *The Structure of Psychoanalytic Theory: A Systemizing Attempt*. New York: International Universities Press.

Reeder, J. (2004) *Hate and Love in Psychoanalytic Institutions: The Dilemma of a Profession*. New York: Other Press.

Rees, E. (2007) Thinking about psychoanalytic curricula: an epistemological perspective. *Psychoanalytic Quarterly*. 76: 891–941.

Ricoeur, P. (1977) The question of proof in Freud's psychoanalytic writings. *Journal of the American Psychoanalytic Association*. 25: 835–871.

Rogawski, A.S. (1989) Education for psychoanalysts in the nineties. *Journal of the American Academy of Psychoanalysis*. 17: 173–180.

Rosenblatt, A.D. and Thickstun, J.T. (1977) *Modern Psychoanalytic Concepts in a General Psychology*. New York: International Universities Press.

Rothenberg, M.A. (2004) Down to cases: the ethical value of "non-scientificity" in dyadic psychoanalysis. *Journal of the American Psychoanalytic Association*. 52: 125–150.

Ryan, E. (1970). *Object Relationships and Ego Coping Styles in Early Memories*. Unpublished masters thesis. Ann Arbor: University of Michigan.

Saks, E. (1999) *Interpreting Interpretation: The Limits of Hermeneutic Psychoanalysis*. New Haven, CT: Yale University Press.

Sander, L. (1988) The event-structure of regulation in the neonate-caregiver system as a biological background for early organization of psychic structure. In: A. Goldberg (editor) *Frontiers in Self Psychology*. Hillsdale, NJ: Analytic Press, pp. 64–77.

Schafer, R. (1976) *A New Language for Psychoanalysis*. New Haven, CT: Yale University Press.

Schafer, R. (1983) *The Analytic Attitude*. New York: Basic Books.

Schore, A.N. (2019) *The Development of the Unconscious Mind*. New York. Norton.

Segal, H.G., Westen, D., Lohr, N.E., and Silk, K.R. (1993) Clinical assessment of object relations and social cognition using stories told to the Picture Arrangement subtest of the WAIS-R. *Journal of Personality Assessment*. 61: 58–80.

Shedler, J. (2010) The efficacy of psychodynamic psychotherapy. *American Psychologist*. 65: 98–109.

Sherwood, M. (1969) *The Logic of Explanation in Psychoanalysis*. New York: Academic Press.

Simpson, J.A., Rholes, W.S., and Nelligan, J.S. (1992) Support seeking and support giving within couples in an anxiety provoking situation: the role of attachment styles. *Journal of Personality and Social Psychology*. 60: 434–446.

Singer, M. (1977) The borderline diagnosis and psychological tests: review and research. In: P. Hartocollis (editor), *Borderline Personality Disorders: The Concept, the Syndrome, the Patient*. New York: International Universities Press, pp. 193–212.

Solms, M. (2000) Preliminaries for an integration of psychoanalysis and neuroscience. *Annual of Psychoanalysis*, 28: 179–200.

Solms, M. (2014) The primary concern of psychoanalysis. *Neuropsychoanalysis*. 16: 49–51.

Solms, M. (2020) The scientific basis of psychoanalysis: introductory remarks. In: M. Leuzinger-Bohleber, M. Solms, and S.E. Arnold (editors) *Outcome Research and the Future of Psychoanalysis: Clinicians and Researchers in Dialogue*. London: Routledge, pp. 26–34.

Spear, W.E. (1980) The psychological assessment of structural and thematic object representations in borderline and schizophrenic patients. In: J.S. Kwawer, H.D. Lerner, P.M. Lerner, and A. Sugarman (editors) *Borderline Phenomena and the Rorschach Test*. New York: International Universities Press, pp. 321–340.

Spear, W.E. and Sugarman, A. (1984) Dimensions of internalized object relations in borderline schizophrenic patients. *Psychoanalytic Psychology*. 1: 113–129.

Spence, D. (1982) *Narrative Truth and Historical Truth*. New York: Norton.

Sroufe, L. (1996) *Emotional Development: The Organization of Emotional Life in the Early Years*. New York: Cambridge University Press.

Sugarman, A. (2006) Panel report of Trauma and ADHD. *International Journal of Psychoanalysis*. 87: 237–241.

Sugarman, A. (2012) The reluctance to self-disclose: reflexive or reasoned. *Psychoanalytic Quarterly*. 81: 627–655.

Sugarman, A. (2018) The importance of promoting a sense of self-agency in child psychoanalysis. *Psychoanalytic Study of the Child*. 71: 108–122.

Sugarman, A. (2022) What does neuroscience offer psychoanalysis? Commentary on Solms's "revision of drive theory". *Journal of the American Psychoanalytic Association.* 70: page numbers forthcoming.

Sugarman, A., Quinlan, D., and Devenis, L. (1982) Ego boundary disturbance in anorexia nervosa: preliminary findings. *Journal of Personality Assessment.* 46: 455–461.

Trevarthen, C. (1979) Communication and cooperation in early infancy: a description of early intersubjectivity. In: M.M. Bullowa (editor). *Before Speech: The Beginning of Interpersonal Communication, I*, pp. 530–571. New York: Cambridge University Press.

Tronick, E. (2007) *The Neurobehavioral and Social-Emotional Development of Infants and Children.* New York: Norton.

Urist, J. (1977) The Rorschach Test and the assessment of object relations. *Journal of Personality Assessment.* 41: 3–9.

Vaillant, G.E. (1992) *Ego Mechanisms of Defense: A Guide for Clinicians and Researchers.* Washington, D.C.: American Psychiatric Association Press.

Vinocur de Fischbein, S. (2009) Pladoyer fur die interdisziplinare konzeptuelle und klinische Erforschung von Traumnarrativen. In: Leuzinger-Bohleber, M., Canestri, J., and Target, M. (editors) *Fruhe Entwicklungen und ihre Sturungen.* Frankfurt: Brandes & Apsel, pp. 252–285.

Waelder, R. (2007) The principle of multiple function: observations on over-determination. *Psychoanalytic Quarterly.* 76: 75–92.

Wallerstein, R.S. (1977) Psychoanalysis as a profession and psychoanalysis as a science: a stocktaking. In: S. Goodman (editor) *Psychoanalytic Education and Research: The Current Situation and Future Possibilities.* New York: International Universities Press, pp. 307–326.

Weinberger, J. and Stoycheva, V. (2019) *The Unconscious: Theory, Research, and Clinical Implications.* New York: Guilford.

Westen, D. (1991) Clinical assessment of object relations using the TAT. *Journal of Personality Assessment.* 56: 56–74.

Westen, D., Lohr, N., Silk, K., Gold, M.A., & Kerber, K. (1990) Object relations and social cognition in borderlines, depressives, and normal: a TAT analysis. *Psychological Assessment.* 2: 355–364.

Widlocher, D. (2003) Foreword. In: M. Leuzinger-Bohleber, A.U Dreher, and J. Canestri (editors) *Pluralism and Unity? Methods of Research in Psychoanalysis.* London: International Psychoanalytical Association, pp. xix–xxiv.

Wilber, C. Rounsaville, B., Sugarman, A., Blatt, J., and Kleber, H. (1982) Ego development in opiate addicts: an application of Loevinger's stage model. *Journal of Nervous and Mental Disease.* 170: 202–208.

Zagermann, P. (2017) (editor) *The Future of Psychoanalysis: The Debate about the Training Analyst System.* London: Karnac.

Chapter 17

Psychoanalytic institutes and their discontents

H. Shmuel Erlich

To write about the present state of the psychoanalytic institute is at the same time disheartening and pretentious. It is disheartening, perhaps even desperate, yet at the same time pretentious, for the same reason: so much has already been written and said, yet with precious little effect. The list of those who have looked at psychoanalytic education critically spans a psychoanalytic century and includes numerous illustrious names, too many to review and pay just tribute to.[1] In what follows, I will necessarily repeat, build upon, and hopefully elaborate points that need more attention.

Why then have I chosen this topic to write about? First, because it is a controversial issue, in certain ways the most controversial one we face. After a century of psychoanalytic training with the questions and discontents that have surrounded it, it seems we are at a crossroads that may prove decisive for the future of psychoanalytic training, and it is therefore only fitting for a volume devoted to such issues. Not less importantly, and as proper disclosure, I feel personally closely involved in and concerned about it. A major portion of my life has been spent teaching – at university, psychoanalytic institutes, reading seminars, and supervision of candidates. Beyond saying something about my person, however, it must point to my identification with the transmission of psychoanalysis. Perhaps no less pertinent is my involvement in the psychoanalytic educational enterprise at the institutional level – as chair of the Education Committee in my institute, and later of the IPA Education Committee, where, with my colleagues, I played a role in the IPA's recognition and ratification of the three models of training. Lastly, I have been involved in Tavistock-type group relations work and psychoanalytic-systemic organizational consultation for many years. It is an additional perspective that is relevant, and I believe can be of help in unravelling this complex historical issue.

The question I wish to address is this: Is the psychoanalytic institute discontent, and if so, what is the nature and what are the roots of this discontent? Obviously, the issue overlaps with questions about psychoanalytic education, which in turn have to do with how one becomes a psychoanalyst. It is

DOI: 10.4324/9781003340744-21

unavoidable, and I will undoubtedly occasionally broach on this issue, but my focus will be on the systemic issues involved and encountered by the psycho-analytic institute – the nature of its organization, the ways in which it defines and implements its primary task, and how it reviews and assesses its final product, i.e., the future generation of psychoanalysts. This last consideration was aptly put by the chair of our Education Committee, when, in a recent meeting about a training issue of a particular candidate, he asked: "And how will this affect the psychoanalyst he will be?"

Before approaching this task, some caveats need to be addressed. There is obviously no such thing as "the" psychoanalytic institute in any standardized and uniform sense. It is true that this may be said of all educational institutes – primary and secondary schools, colleges and universities. They each have their distinctive characteristics. Yet they are comparable in some ways: they must meet certain widely defined educational goals in formally tested and observ-able ways, and the achievements of their graduates are publicly observable. Is this equally true of psychoanalytic institutes? It seems the answer would be negative. Evaluation is often in serious trouble, and the achievements of the graduates of our institutes are for the most part measured by reputa-tion, a heady mix of social attribution, projections, transferences, and counter-transferences. This has to do with the ambiguity about the professional domain of psychoanalysis and the disagreements and diversity of perspectives about the domain of psychoanalytic knowledge (Auchincloss and Michels, 2003) on which I will elaborate later.

An organization or system is measured by the adequacy of the definition of its primary task and the degree to which it measures up to it in terms of its final product. Psychoanalytic institutes are sometimes regarded more as hallowed places where a mysterious process of transformation takes place. If we are willing to accept that the psychoanalytic institute is essentially an educational and training system, we need to examine its primary task, the means and methods to achieve it, and how well it is achieved in terms of its final product. Applying these criteria to the psychoanalytic institute, its historical development and present state, leads to the sad conclusion that it suffers of diffuseness and lack of clear definition and agreement about its primary task, as well as the transformative methods and operations to create its eventual output – an adequately trained psychoanalyst, capable of functioning autonomously and independently. Metaphorically and in indi-vidual developmental terms, one may say that following a difficult birth and a stormy childhood replete with childhood neuroses, the psychoanalytic institute at present possesses a diffuse identity and suffers from severe iden-tity crisis, which implies that it will be at risk in its adulthood, if it ever achieves it.

In what follows, I will address some of the factors that I see as having contributed to this systemic condition. As with any system, we need to look at its history, its inception, the dynamics marking its early and subsequent

development, its inputs and methods of transformation, and its final or eventual output. Clearly, these are my views on these points, and they are open to
criticism and disagreement.

The birth and inception of the psychoanalytic institute did not bode well
from the start. From its very inception, the Eitingon model did not try to rep-
licate Sigmund Freud's mode of practice, which was, after all, idiosyncratic.
Nor did it come full blown into existence: its development was gradual,
evolving in steps and stages, subject to considerable political pressures and
controversies (Schröter, 2002). The establishment of the first psychoanalytic
institute in Berlin quickly served as the prototype for the subsequent development and establishing of psychoanalytic institutes in other locations, and
to this day it is regarded as "the" mold for training, known as the Eitingon
model. In effect, the Berlin model was quite different from its subsequent
emulations. Its tri-partite structure included research, as well as a low-cost
polyclinic (Kächele and Thomä, 2000). Nevertheless, the founding of the
Berlin Institute signified the first step towards regulating and structuring
psychoanalytic training. Several facts are notable in this connection. In the
first place, it corresponded roughly with Freud's aim in creating the IPA:

> The formation of an official organization I considered necessary because
> I feared the abuses to which psychoanalysis would be subjected, once it
> should achieve popularity. I felt that there should be a place that could
> give the dictum: "With all this nonsense, analysis has nothing to do;
> this is not psychoanalysis." It was decided that at the meeting of the
> local groups which together formed the international organization,
> instruction should be given how psychoanalysis should be practiced,
> that physicians should be trained there and that the *local society should,
> in a way, stand sponsor for them.* It also appeared to me desirable that
> the adherents of psychoanalysis should meet for friendly intercourse and
> mutual support, inasmuch as *official science had pronounced its great ban
> and boycott against physicians and institutions practicing* psychoanalysis. This
> and nothing else I wished to attain by the founding of the "International
> Psychoanalytic Association." Perhaps it was more than could possibly be
> attained.
>
> (Freud, 1916, my emphasis)

The founding of the IPA was Freud's response for the rejection of psychoanalysis by the university, the embodiment of scientific recognition and establishment. As a countermeasure to this absence, "the local society should, *in
a way*, stand sponsor for them", i.e., provide the needed standardization and
certification. Freud's phrase "in a way" indicates that for him too, how this
should or would happen was vague and left unclear. To replace this "ban" and
rejection, the IPA took over the university-related function of validation and
standardization of training, and hence of certification.

The next step to remedy this situation was the establishment within the IPA of the International Training Committee in 1925 with Max Eitingon as its chair. The goal of standardizing and overseeing the training enterprise quickly foundered on emergent controversies, central in which was the issue of lay analysis (Freud, 1926) which nearly split the fledgling organization between its European and American components. The emergent issue was twofold: on the one hand, there was the question of input: *who is entitled to be trained?* On the other hand, was the issue of *who can be entrusted with the training*, or in other words, who can be a training analyst? The two issues are interrelated insofar as both represent the question of allocation of control, authority, and power, an issue intrinsic to all organizations, and also dangerously related to paranoiagenesis (Erlich, 2013).

Significant events in the inception and development of an organization typically tend to color and shape its subsequent development, and the above history and developmental traumas of the psychoanalytic institute demonstrate the fact that both issues are still with us today. The admission of candidates who are not qualified mental health practitioners is still unsettled in many institutes. It represents the conflict between adherence to professional and clinical standards of qualification for treatment as against the prospect of enriching psychoanalysis with contributions from non-clinical fields. The second issue, namely the selection and appointment of training analysts, is by far the most frequent cause for the strife, discontent, and animosity that characterize psychoanalytic institutes and societies and their proneness to inhouse fights and splitting.

The issue of the selection and appointment of training analysts needs further elaboration. While not its sole source, it plays a key role in the discontent of psychoanalytic institutions. A great deal has been said and written about this, seemingly to little avail, but it is important and pertinent to review it again. Since psychoanalysis developed outside the university, the nexus of knowledge and science, it had to deal with its mode of *transmission* independently, as Freud clearly saw and suggested. It thus had to devise systems of admission, of transformation through training, of qualifying and being certified, and of backing up, recognizing, and supporting its graduates. In other words, everything that is usually achieved through university education and the state's licensing based on it had to be invented and provided for, in a kind of semi-formal parallel track. This shadowy existence in a boundary region suits psychoanalysis well, since it fits perfectly with its essentially subversive nature (Erlich, 2013). But emergent pressures, both internal and external, reject and eschew this boundary existence in an understandable quest for recognition and respectability. Notably, where psychoanalysis has achieved this goal of respectability and recognition, as in the USA in the 50s and 60s of the previous century, it did not last and was followed by a serious and threatening decline. Nonetheless, as a profession, psychoanalysis still had to deal with the need to regulate its own training and transmission procedures.

Enter the training analyst system. It is essentially a sensible system, as any educational and training enterprise needs teachers and supervisors to carry out the transmission of knowledge and professional competence, and these persons must be sufficiently qualified to be entrusted with the task. Perhaps the initial intention was indeed just that, yet it turned out to be naïve and even destructive. The reasons and causes for this are multiple, and I will focus on two of them.

Unlike a university, the psychoanalytic institute is closely intertwined with the psychoanalytical society, even where structural differentiation is in place. Those selected and designated as training analysts form a differentiation within the psychoanalytic society, and as the poet aptly said, "Envy is the tax that all distinction must pay" (Emerson, 1909). The class differentiation of those who are selected to be training analysts cannot but create envy, and thus augment the troublesome proneness to the insidious effects of envy in psychoanalytic organizations (Erlich, 2016). As a distinct and distinguished class within the psychoanalytic organization, training analysts increasingly evolved into a powerful elite, imbued with control and authority, attracting envy and hostility, and serving as objects of idealization and aggression. In short, the very designation of a "superior," better-qualified group-within-a-group had to have a destructive impact on the wellbeing of the organization. Where the training analysis function was excluded, as in the French model, the issue around differentiation merely shifted to the status of those appointed as supervisors (Erlich and Erlich-Ginor, 2018). The Uruguayan model, which came into being as a revolt against the training analyst system and its usurpation of power, deals with this issue by defining working groups in several areas, including supervision and training analysis, thereby perhaps achieving a more egalitarian state of affairs.

The second reason for the complexity created by the training analyst system is that the primary definition of training analysts is the carrying out of the analysis of candidates (pertaining to the Eitingon and Uruguayan models). This primary function of the training analysts means that they are the immediate and profound objects of candidates' transferences. Whether intentionally or not, it ensures the suffusion and contamination of the psychoanalytic society with the unavoidable residues of these transferences, creating an unacknowledged, semi-conscious, and unconscious web of transferential residues that operate, often malignantly, within the society and its psychoanalytic institute. The institute is burdened with the weight of transference residues which come to life as adherence as well as opposition to theoretical positions, identifications and counter-identifications, loyalties and betrayals, love and hate, aggression and defenses against it.

A brief vignette may help demonstrate this burden. An analyst teaches a class in which he has an analysand. The candidate in question does not experience this as a problem, but other candidates are aghast at this "violation" and "disregard," which they do not express openly to the teacher but to the candidate. The teaching is burdened and undermined by these criticisms, objections, and righteous indignation about the "corruption of the transference" and "abuse" of the candidate. Since these attacks are not expressed openly, and the analyst learns of them in the analysis, she is unable to deal with it effectively.

This brief vignette illustrates the suffusion and undermining of the primary task of the institute, which is teaching and learning, both intellectually and emotionally, about psychoanalysis. It is malignant because it is impossible to address the issue since it does not come into the open, and the analysis where it finds expression (where it may express the candidate's repressed criticisms) is sacrosanct and confidential. Yet the candidates' criticism raises important issues about the nature and understanding of transference, its scope and place, the extent to which it is affected by real relationships, and so on, all of which could serve for learning, but the structural aspects render this impossible. Rather than being a learning opportunity, it will go down and be transmitted as a critical view of the particular training analyst and perhaps of the candidate as an object of abuse. It may, of course, be argued that all of this may have been averted if the analyst-teacher would have refused to teach the particular class because she has an analysand in it. While this is often the preferred solution, it perpetuates the problem by taking a one-sided view of transference and enacting it.

My point is that the inclusion of the training analysis in the candidate's formation as a significant component of the institute's training, as required by the Eitingon model, and at the same time entrusting it to a special class of analysts, suffuses the training and the institute with nearly impossible burdens, which directly affect and influence the institute's ability to pursue its primary task. Where the primary task cannot be accomplished in a good-enough manner, the institute's functioning is seriously compromised, it is bound to develop considerable difficulty, and it may eventually erupt in a destructive fashion.

So far, I have highlighted a few of the more significant issues that mark the history of the psychoanalytic institute, its inception and early developmental stages, the controversies it had to face regarding selection and admission of candidates (its systemic input), the evolution of the training analysis and how it shaped its processes of transformation and functioning, and how all of these affected its primary task. There is an array of related issues that stem from this, such as the ubiquitous difficulties encountered around selection and admission of candidates, and issues around monitoring their progress in a constructive, non-persecutory, and non-infantilizing manner. These issues are greatly influenced and shaped by socio-cultural factors, economic conditions, as well as national and geographical heritage and characteristics. They are issues which the institute must face and deal with, but they are peripheral. They are not intrinsic to the institute's structure and dynamics, as a system created to ensure the transmission of psychoanalysis through training and education. I will therefore not elaborate on them, although they certainly deserve careful consideration.

An additional issue that is essential to the process of transformation is the curriculum offered by the psychoanalytic institute. This issue is especially poignant because of the current plurality of psychoanalytic approaches. It may be stated in an oversimplified way as the proportion of seminar time allotted to learning Freud's writings as against providing space for a great many subsequent and contemporary authors. Admittedly, it is virtually impossible to discuss this issue without touching on and revealing one's ideal representation of psychoanalysis, what it needs and should be and become. The curriculum is thus another intrinsically controversial issue, dredging up intergenerational conflicts and confrontations, loyalties and divergences (which are also related to the above issue of the training analysis), and imbued with emotional investments and passions (Busch, 2020). My personal view is akin to Thomä and Kächele's statement, that "an analyst is necessarily born into a Jewish genealogy and acquires his professional identity through identification with Freud's work" (2020, p. 19). The identification with Freud's *work* (as against his person), its appreciative as well as critical study and evaluation, is the unique and defining characteristic of psychoanalysis, which sets it apart from other theories and therapies, no matter how efficacious they may be. It serves to internalize the understanding that psychoanalysis is more than a form of therapy, that it is a fundamental and comprehensive theory of mental functioning and a scientific, ethical, and philosophical view of man and humanity.

To strike a balance between teaching Freud and subsequent developments and authors is a difficult issue, and institutes vary considerably in its resolution. The balance struck is often influenced more by emotional and political factors than by educational considerations. For example, teaching Freud may be resisted or opposed because it is seen as representing psychoanalytical orthodoxy, or as being passé and at most of historical interest; the decision to put the emphasis on post-Freudian authors and approaches is seen as bringing psychoanalysis up to date and more in line with present practices, supposedly thus rendering it more attractive and palatable. Again, it may also be influenced by the theoretical position of one's training analyst, whether pro or con. Or it may represent the political situation the society is in at the time.

Whatever the overt or underlying influences may be, they have in common the question mentioned above: What sort of psychoanalyst do we want to see coming out of the institute's training program? This nagging question is directly related to the issue of the *output* or final product of the institute as a system, which I will shortly address. I want to point out that while the question is called for, it implies a constricted view of the candidate as future analyst. Candidates are not a malleable substance, and their development usually continues long after qualification. While the institute plays a major role in shaping their identity, it is but one powerful factor among many others. Precisely because of this, it is important to provide candidates with a strong footing in Freud's writings, not to make them orthodox Freudians (which is rather doubtful nowadays) but to provide them with a sound psychoanalytic foundation that will serve them in their future development, wherever it may take them.

An important caveat about teaching Freud: Who teaches it, from what perspective, and with what goal in mind is of absolute importance (Busch, 2020). Beyond deep knowledge of the material, teaching Freud requires an educational posture meaningfully identified with the subject matter, while at the same time sufficiently removed and open to questioning and critical comments, as well as the willingness to integrate it with present views.

The last aspect of the training institute we need to consider is its final product or output. Two distinct yet interrelated issues are involved: evaluation of the transformative process the candidates are undergoing, and the quality of the psychoanalysts the institute produces.

Institutes vary greatly in how they evaluate the candidates' progress. The depth of penetration and intensity of involvement of evaluation methods and processes are far from uniform. Some institutes engage closely with the candidate and follow a concerned, hands-on procedure. Others are satisfied with periodic meetings at points of transition in the course of training. Some do not apply regular or built-in evaluation and are content to assign the evaluation of the candidate's progress entirely to the supervisors. A few require periodic written material to be used in evaluation. This variety underscores the fact that, systemically speaking, psychoanalytic institutes have a serious problem with evaluation – not only of candidates, but of themselves.

In most systems (including educational ones) evaluation is a way to monitor, assess, and learn about the quality of the product, and through this, about the state and quality of the system, its strengths and weaknesses. This sort of evaluation is almost entirely absent in psychoanalytic institutes. It may even be said that psychoanalytic institutes *as systems* do not wish to know how well they are performing their task. In no way does this imply that members and officers of the organization are indifferent to this. To the contrary, and as the above-mentioned question of the chair of the Education Committee ("And how will this affect the psychoanalyst he will be?") demonstrates, there may be deep concerns about it. The fact is, however, that *as a system*, this function is not in place in any meaningful or rigorous way. The distinction is instructive, as it demonstrates again the difference between individual and even group feelings and views, and the systemic level that behaves differently.

Evaluation of the individual candidate's progress is typically entrusted to the supervisors. There is no question that the supervisor is in the best position to monitor and evaluate the candidate's development, perhaps even to assess the critical question of what kind of psychoanalyst she or he will be. Yet, although this assertion is sensible and well founded, it turns out in practice to be problematic and disappointing. Yet it is not because the supervisor does not see the candidate clearly, or because he or she has not formed an opinion about him. In the great majority of cases the supervisor does evaluate the candidate and has a reliable picture of him. The problem is in communicating and sharing this evaluation and making it known, even if only to the Education Committee.

There are many reasons for this difficulty, some of which touch on the issues already mentioned, and others that arise separately (Erlich and Erlich-Ginor, 2018). Let us consider some of the more salient points.

The growing and current psychoanalytic "pluralism" concerning the goals and nature of psychoanalytic theory and treatment makes it extremely difficult to judge any technique or intervention without getting into theoretical controversy. Such controversies often involve the gap between conflict-based theories and deficit-based ones, the place and role of the analyst in the treatment, the extent of his/her participation, self-revelation, the need for a maternal as against paternal stance, the readiness or reticence about being a bad object, etc. The pluralism regarding the technique and goal of psychoanalytic treatment reflects the theoretical pluralism and the numerous "schools" and orientations. It is greatly influenced by the psychoanalytic personality that is chosen as an object of identification and idealization, whether one's training analyst, supervisor, or a theoretical figure. The theoretical pluralism has created a situation in which every approach is on equal footing with all others, since there is no way to demonstrate convincingly the advantages or disadvantages of one over the other. The pluralism of theory and training models makes it very difficult to relate to the work of a candidate in any "objective" fashion. It creates confusion, controversy, and competition for both candidates and supervisors, and undermines the authority of training and education committees. It makes it impossible to define the objectives of psychoanalytic training beyond vague generalities, like "to develop a psychoanalytic attitude" that cannot be defined (Cabaniss, 2008).

The group dynamics that ensue are marked by *Basic Assumption (BA)* functioning (Bion, 1961). The ideological positions underpinning the different approaches turn them into systems of belief, invoking "truths," rather than theoretical models. It fosters the formation of "schools," especially if a particular approach becomes identified with a charismatic leader. The result is a *BA Dependency* group that is devoutly dependent upon a cherished and emulated leader. Grandiose messianic fantasies of healing and even of creating a better world may be around, representing the *BA Pairing*. Having to defend a given ideological position against real or imagined attacks and derision generates aggression which is projected and becomes persecutory. This *BA Fight-Flight* is transmitted to the candidates and perpetuated through them, becoming a vicious cycle.

A further source of difficulty stems from factors inherent in the psychoanalytic stance and identity. We spend years training people not to be judgmental, to prefer exploration and understanding to evaluative judgments, especially if these will influence real-life decisions. It is very difficult for the same people to be asked to change their skin and perform evaluations, which have become antithetical and taboo to them. In this connection (of adhering to a psycho-analytic stance), it is instructive that when a problem emerges about a candidate, the solution that is typically offered is for him to have more analysis. While analysis is valuable in combatting personal issues and deficiencies, it is magical to think it can enhance skills.

Finally, the supervisor's position is seriously troubled by the problematics, touched on above, which envelop the training analyst role. Appointment to training analyst is often understood as a badge of status in the psychoanalytic society, the achievement of an honorable position of seniority and respectability, rather than as a *role* and *function* to be fulfilled on behalf of an institute. It is sometimes unclear whether a supervisor is acting on behalf of his/her institute or conducting a private affair. Where supervisors regard the supervision as an intimate confidential pairing that must be protected, similarly to an analysis, they are reluctant to admit a "third" into it, whether in the form of the Education Committee or an exchange with other supervisors. Obviously, such a stance and understanding of the supervisor's role hinders any kind of evaluation.

I have attempted to pull together some of the complex contributing factors to what I described as the present discontent of the psychoanalytic institute. I offered the view of the psychoanalytic institute as an educational and training system, like other such systems, and at the same time unique because of its history and development. Its uniqueness stems from the historical evolution of psychoanalysis, and how it shaped its internal structures and roles. My major focus was on the ways this has obfuscated the institute's primary task, its definition and implementation, and especially the way it has affected the function of evaluation.

In view of these rather critical observations, it would only be fair to ask if this means that we need to give up and reject the structures and methodologies that define the psychoanalytic institute at present. My answer to this would be both yes and no. There are some factors that we can and need to reconsider; there are other, unknown, latent processes that we can only guess how they may contribute and influence the institute's future.

I think that Wallerstein's question, "One psychoanalysis or many?" has been answered. Psychoanalysis in the twenty-first century is an irreversible conglomeration of views, insights, and conceptualizations of the mind and the human condition. There is much richness in this as well as confusion, and one must find one's own way and footing. But I do not think of it as eclecticism, which regards all parts as equally suited to choose from, but rather in terms of Bolognini's (2007) metaphor, as the relationship with one's family tree, the figures and intergenerational influences within it. One's relationships with different generations and figures is permeated by different degrees of closeness, affinity, and passion. Yet one may sometimes be surprised to discover unexpected closeness and meaning with a relative who was previously distant or shunned. It also implies that investing a particular figure exclusively with all of one's passion and idealization may well mean a narcissistic relationship that eschews the reality and complexity of being part of the family. Freud, in this metaphor, is the grandfather who established the family and gave it life, and all subsequent relationships begin and are intertwined with him.

The psychoanalytic pluralism is here to stay, and it needs to become a source of enrichment rather than divisiveness and controversy, even if admittedly some theories represent the opposite of others. In this regard, it is of utmost importance to remember that none of our theories, Freud's included, are "truths." A theory is a map of reality, and a map need not be confused with the real terrain (Erlich, 2020). Maps provide a means of orientation, especially in new and unknown territories, and different maps focus on different aspects of the terrain. Unlike the physical sciences, there is little that can be established about the mind either by experiment or by psychoanalysis, a point Freud reiterated repeatedly. Clinical "evidence" is always subject to interpretation and cannot provide proof.

What does this imply for the possible future direction of the psychoanalytic institute? Obviously, the institute must be open to and entertain diversity and pluralism, but this may easily degenerate into eclecticism. That is why I see the serious study of Freud's writings as a must basis for any psychoanalyst, as in Thomä and Kächele's (2020) definition quoted above. It needs to be the *foundation and core* around which one's *psychoanalytic* identity is formed and forged. I emphasize *psychoanalytic* as distinguished from *psychotherapeutic* identity, because there is an important difference between the two that can only be appreciated and understood by starting from Freud.

Beyond the indispensable study of Freud's writings, the institute needs to provide a wide-ranging background about the matrices from which the mind develops and is shaped. The narrow, clinically focused version of the tri-partite model of psychoanalytic education (personal analysis, supervised cases, theoretical courses) should be revised, expanded, and revitalized. Most of those who seek psychoanalytic training nowadays come to it relatively late and with considerable clinical expertise, and the institute's efforts are often directed towards helping them to unlearn some of the therapeutic skills they have acquired.

Expanding the curriculum to include non-clinical areas signals a return to the roots of the psychoanalytic institute. Freud argued that ideally, alongside other subjects,

> analytic instruction would include branches of knowledge ... [such as] the history of civilization, mythology, the psychology of religion and the science of literature. Unless he is well at home in these subjects, an analyst can make nothing of a large amount of his material.

(1926, p. 245)

As already noted, the prototype of the Berlin Institute's tri-partite model was quite different than its subsequent emulations, and included teaching, treatment, and research. The idea seems to have been the creation of a "minor university," as Simmel put it in his 10-Year Report of the Institute (DPG, 1930, p. 11). This ambition foundered on the rocks of the Nazis' rise to power and the subsequent persecution and outlawing of psychoanalysis, but also, and in no small measure, due to the wish/need to establish psychoanalysis as a profession, perhaps following the medical model, which has not been achieved universally.

A present-day view of the future direction for the psychoanalytic institute would greatly expand its scope and horizons. It would include up-to-date areas of knowledge from the life sciences and neuro-psychoanalysis beside pertinent literature, history, anthropology, and mythology. This will necessitate the inclusion of non-psychoanalysts as experts in these areas, which would be of real benefit in reducing the mutual antagonism and gap between psychoanalysis and related university areas.

I am not suggesting a reduction of the clinical-theoretical aspects, but their reorganization: rather than studying each post-Freudian theoretician separately (Klein, Bion, Winnicott, Kohut, etc.) as is often the case, to teach their contributions around specific subject matters, which would highlight their similarities and differences and the value of their advances, while reducing redundancy. Ideally, a low-cost clinic would be affiliated with the institute (this used to be the case in my society, and is present-day practice in some, e.g., the British Psychoanalytic Society).

A foreseeable objection to this proposal is that it is grandiose, overly ambitious, and utopian. Perhaps. It surely would need much more work and thoughtful consideration than what I have briefly outlined. But if we seriously take account of the current discontent of the psychoanalytic institute, we need to ask ourselves where it is heading in its present form. As the cry of a "crisis" of psychoanalysis is sounded in different places, and with some societies not growing and others suffering of attrition, it is safe to assume that at least some of this malaise is related to the psychoanalytic institute. The institute is, among its other functions, a window, perhaps a showcase, to the world. Its attractiveness or lack of it plays a major role in the future of psychoanalysis. Perhaps such a revamping and facelifting as I have suggested may enhance its attractiveness for the young and future generations.

Note

1 A much-abbreviated sample of such contributions includes: Auchincloss and Michels (2003), Conchi (2009), Eisold (1994; 2003; 2004; 2017), Kernberg (1986; 1996; 2000; 2006; 2007; 2010; 2011), Kerberg et al. (2012), Kernberg and Michels (2016); Kirsner (2001; 2010).

References

Auchincloss, E. and Michels, R. (2003) A reassessment of psychoanalytic education. *International Journal of Psychoanalysis.* 84: 387–403.

Bion, W.R. (1961) *Experiences in Group.* London: Tavistock Publications.

Bolognini, S. (2007) Freud's objects. Plurality and complexity in the analyst's inner world and in his "working Self". *Rivista di Psicoanalisi,* 2007. 1: 179–195. (English version: *Italian Psychoanalytic Annual,* 2008. 2: 43–57.)

Busch, F. (2020) The troubling problems of knowledge in psychoanalytic institutes. *International Journal of Controversial Discussions.* 2: 3–26.

Cabaniss, D.L. (2008) Becoming a school: developing learning objectives for psychoanalytic education. *Psychoanalytic Inquiry.* 28: 262–277.

Conchi, M. (2009) A prescription for ideal training. *Contemporary Psychoanalysis.* 45: 394–405.

Deutsche Psychoanalytische Gesellschaft (DPG) (1930) *10 Jahre Berliner Psychoanalytisches Institut.* Vienna: Internationaler Psychoanalytischer Verlag.

Eisold, K. (1994) The intolerance of diversity in psychoanalytic institutes. *International Journal of Psychoanalysis.* 75: 785–800.

Eisold, K. (2003) Toward a psychoanalytic politics. *Journal of the American Psychoanalysis Association.* 51: 301–321.

Eisold, K. (2004) Psychoanalytic training: the "faculty system". *Psychoanalytic Inquiry.* 24: 51–70.

Eisold, K. (2017) What's wrong with analytic training? *Contemporary Psychoanalysis.* 53: 280–287.

Emerson, R.W. (1909) *Journals of Ralph Waldo Emerson.* Boston: Houghton Mifflin.

Erlich, H.S. (2013) *The Couch in the Marketplace: Psychoanalysis and Social Reality.* London: Karnac.

Erlich, H.S. (2016) Envy and its vicissitudes in psychoanalytic organizations. Paper presented at the EPF Annual Conference, Berlin, 19 March 2016.

Erlich, H.S. (2020) Psychoanalysis as the Tower of Babel. *International Journal of Controversial Discussions.* 2: 84–94.

Erlich, H.S. and Erlich-Ginor, M. (2018) Who is afraid of psychoanalytic evaluation? *International Journal of Psychoanalysis.* 99(5): 1129–1143.

Freud, S. (1916) The history of the psychoanalytic movement. *Psychoanalytic Review.* 3: 406–454.

Freud, S. (1926) The question of lay analysis. *The Standard Edition of the Complete Psychological Works of Sigmund Freud.* 20: 177–258.

Kächele, H. and Thomä, H. (2000) On the devaluation of the Eitingon-Freud model of psychoanalytic education. *International Journal of Psychoanalysis.* 81: 806–808.

Kernberg, O.F. (1986) Institutional Problems of Psychoanalytic Education. *Journal of the American Psychoanalysis Association.* 34: 799–834.

Kernberg, O.F. (1996) Thirty methods to destroy the creativity of psychoanalytic candidates. *International Journal of Psychoanalysis.* 77: 1031–1040.

Kernberg, O.F. (2000) A concerned critique of psychoanalytic education. *International Journal of Psychoanalysis.* 81: 97–120.

Kernberg, O.F. (2006) The coming changes in psychoanalytic education: Part I. *International Journal of Psychoanalysis.* 87: 1649–1673.

Kernberg, O.F. (2007) The coming changes in psychoanalytic education: Part II. *International Journal of Psychoanalysis.* 88: 183–202.

Kernberg, O.F. (2010) A new organization of psychoanalytic education. *Psychoanalytic Review.* 97: 997–1020.

Kernberg, O.F. (2011) Psychoanalysis and the university: a difficult relationship. *International Journal of Psychoanalysis.* 92: 609–622.

Kernberg, O.F. and Michels, R. (2016) Thoughts on the present and future of psychoanalytic education. *Journal of the American Psychoanalysis Association.* 64: 477–493.

Kernberg, O.F., Cabaniss, D., Auchincloss, E., Glick, R., and Roose, S. (2012) Three problematic assumptions about psychoanalytic education: a brief communication. *Journal of the American Psychoanalysis Association.* 60: 97–102.

Kirsner, D. (2001) The future of psychoanalytic institutes. *Psychoanalytic Psychology.* 18: 195–212.

Kirsner, D. (2010) Training analysis: the shibboleth of psychoanalytic education. *Psychoanalytic Review,* 97: 971–995.

Schröter, M. (2002) Max Eitingon and the struggle to establish an international standard for psychoanalytic training (1925–1929). *International Journal of Psychoanalysis.* 83: 875–893.

Thomä, H. and Kächele, H. (2020) *Psychoanalytic Therapy Vol. 1: Principles.* Gießen, Germany: Psychosozial-Verlag.

Chapter 18

A perspective from Buenos Aires

Abel Fainstein

Each generation faces the challenge of defining the epochal crossroads for our discipline and from there being able to think about the policies of psychoanalysis, the training of new generations of psychoanalysts, and the institutions most suitable for carrying them out.

Being something particular to each part of the world and of each culture, I will endeavor to do this from the perspective of my practice in Buenos Aires, Argentina, and several decades of institutional work, including the Argentine Psychoanalytic Association (APA), the Psychoanalytic Federation of Latin America (FEPAL), the International Psychoanalytic Association (IPA), the Argentine School of Psychotherapy for Graduates (AAPG), and the University of Salvador (USAL).

I propose to define these crossroads by considering the following points:

1. What to call psychoanalysis and its relationship with other disciplines such as philosophy, psychiatry, psychology, neurosciences, literature, art, sociology, politics, bioethics, ecology, etc.
2. How to build a "psychoanalysis for tomorrow" with a contemporary disciplinary matrix: Freudian, complex, pluralistic, and based on what Andre Green (2010) considers in germ in Freudian work, that is, the complex thought described by Edgar Morin (2005).[1]
3. The most adequate training for new generations of psychoanalysts on the basis that there is no "one" training, much less an ideal one. How to achieve the most suitable models and train for a "possible psycho-analysis", avoiding nostalgic posturing. Long treatments, consisting of four or five weekly sessions on the couch, generally for patients with neur-otic functioning, and disregarding different cultures, theories, societies, etc., today are not synonymous with psychoanalysis.
4. How to demystify the idea of the unique, of the uniform as absolute forms, and how to promote a policy based on a work ethic and groupings (Goldstein, 2011).

DOI: 10.4324/9781003340744-22

5. How to work with a plurality of theories and models, on the "limit" (Trias, 1991 as cited by Glocer Fiorini L. 2015), as well as with other disciplines, respecting their particular singularity, and avoiding integrations that simplify their complexity.

6. The somewhat inclusive relationship between psychoanalysis and psychotherapy and its interaction with psychiatry.

7. How to avoid isolation from today's world, addressing issues such as violence, marginalization, exclusion, and uncertainty that are part of our everyday lives. How to respect their hyper-complexity and from there rethink our theories and our clinic.

8. How to interact with the universities while respecting their particular discourses. In this way, to summon the incipient transferences of the younger generations and to attain accreditation for formation and academic research.

9. How to counteract the implications of identification through transference in the structure of societies and training: the harmful effects of mass psychology.

10. Bearing in mind that we are unable to avoid what psychoanalysis teaches us in terms of parricide and filicide, how to address the aging of members, while the younger generations are being drawn toward other institutions.

Being, as I said, something epochal and characteristic of our psychoanalytic culture and social conditions, I will try to establish my position concerning each of these points. This is only to provide a reference for our development and eventually serve for thinking about them in other contexts.

Inclusion and exclusion, openness and confinement, preservation and subversion, orthodoxy and heresy are typical institutional oscillations and, at best, alternate cyclically, hence, the importance of institutional policies to regulate them in order to neutralize regressive and dominating movements by certain power groups that lead to exclusion, confinement, and/or conservatism.

Psychoanalysis has been part of Western culture for more than 100 years, and interest in it is growing each day in the Orient. Similarly, its presence is expanding throughout culture in general, in art, politics, education, sociology, and so forth. Moreover, together with the expansion of what we know as the psychoanalytic method, its application has extended to non-neurotic psychic functioning.

We observe, however, at least in our setting, that the practice, according to the canons of what has been called the cure type, is in decline.

Having to define what is psychoanalysis, or what it is not, invites us to consider at least two possible pathways: a broader one that accepts different conceptions, and another that limits to the fullest what can be considered psychoanalysis while excluding everything else from of its field.

This invites us to return to Wallerstein's question about one or many psychoanalyses; defining its future and possible crossroads depends largely on this question. My experience and the results of articulating this plurality in our midst, to which I will refer later, makes me lean toward many and in debate.

I agree with Pontalis that psychoanalysis is essentially a migratory discipline, moving from one language, one culture, and one knowledge to another. It is in this migratory capacity, its openness toward the encounter with the other, the doubt and the uncertainty, that the heart of the analytic experience lies.

I also agree with Ludwig Fleck (1927), a Hungarian chemist and contemporary of Freud, paraphrased by Arnold Richards (2017), regarding "the politics of exclusion": groupthink within a collective can coalesce into an increasingly canonical similarity, resisting new and innovative ideas, and expelling those with divergent ones. However, multiple perspectives and new voices communicating in open exchange function as an antidote to such attraction and, I would add, neutralize endogamy, as well as what Irene Ruggiero defined as "narcissistic degeneration of the mechanisms of filiation" (Ruggiero, as cited in Marion, 2020).

Considering that the structure and function of institutions and institutes, as well as their relationship with the academic world, are strongly connected with each of these options, and based on my experience and that of other authors, I will develop a few premises that make the policies of psychoanalysis more suitable for facing these crossroads.

The debate between Rachel Blass (2010) and Lewis Aron (2010) about the former's 2010 article, both published in the *IJPA*, is a good starting point for thinking about and establishing positions on this matter.

I agree with Blass that the risk of generating impoverishing exclusions should not impede the exercise of defining what we mean by psychoanalysis. But this, I add, on the condition of having what García Badaracco (2010) called open-mindedness toward the new, the different, and to what is on the border, to maintain the vitality of psychoanalysis.

I agree with Aron, however, that appealing to the truth, the essence, or the nature of psychoanalysis, as an antidote to postmodern relativism, as expressed by Blass, does not help, and we should be warned.

Psychoanalysis and its practice are intimately linked to its sociocultural, political, and economic context and theoretical models of the psychoanalyst. Today, the foundation of our discipline, the unconscious, has many theorizations that lead to very different practices. This being the case, from the intradisciplinary and contextual perspective, it is difficult to think of one psychoanalysis, and we need to work on this diversity and its possible articulations.

Away from the initial threats to undermine this diversity, which required the expulsion of those who dissented, we must now address it. The role of unconscious dynamics and infantile sexuality are no longer at the center of discussion among those who recognize themselves as psychoanalysts. Although some hierarchize the analytic encounter, it seems difficult to conceive of it in practice without the contribution of the drives.

The limiting effects of restrictive positions can be seen in what happened with the theories of Melanie Klein and the English school in the 1970s when continuation with Freudian theory was discussed. The same occurred among us years later with regards to ego psychology, and now with regards to relational psychoanalysis, which is questioned by some as non-psychoanalytical.

Although Lacan was not naive, and by deepening his differences in the clinic, he was perhaps seeking his marginalization from the IPA, his developments reached an unforeseen expansion in many parts of the world. In addition to their shaping the practice of his followers, they enrich that of many of us who do not consider ourselves "Lacanian." In recent years, his contributions have been studied and transmitted with interest, especially in IPA societies in Latin America, and we know that the almost universal acceptance that psychoanalysis has today in the world of culture at large, as well as in academic settings, has been especially benefitted by his contributions and by that of some of his followers.

In short, the diversity of models, theories, and practices that fortunately we have today, the different models of the unconscious, and the many psychoanalyses require work on their differences in an attempt to account for the hyper-complexity of our field. Restrictions or exclusions only impoverish its development and, as I said, in some cases, threaten its practice, especially in the field of health.

This is not a potential risk today. This is what is already happening in countries where psychoanalysts are reporting that they have only one or two patients in analysis, and the institutes of psychoanalysis have only one or two applicants per year, and sometimes none at all. There is also the added difficulty of supervising cases when the settings for suitable treatments are severely limited.

In this context, I consider that a sufficiently broad umbrella, based on the conviction that there are unconscious dynamics, and highlighting the effects of the practice, the efficacy of the transference encounter with an analyst in its multiple variants, and possible neutrality, can harbor necessary diversity. Drives, which for some seemed to be explicitly relegated, are, in my opinion, unavoidable, even for understanding the efficacy of the analytic relationship if we focus our practice on them.

The importance of the other in the intra-subjective field seems to have been accentuated at the expense of approaches centered on the instinctual and the intra-psychic. Sexualization, conceived by many as coming from the other, erases differences between the internal and the external. Freud already spoke of the individual and the social in his developments.

At the risk of simplifying the panorama of psychoanalysis in Buenos Aires, I will include references to its very important development. My only purpose is to show its power and vitality, a product, among other things, of the wide theoretical, clinical, and community frontiers and permanent intra-, inter-, and transdisciplinary work. This is what I propose as a way to approach the crossroads described above.

Psychoanalysis has been expanding in Buenos Aires since the 1950s, to the point of becoming one of its "world capitals." This can be seen by the large number of practitioners, schools, groups, and students of psychology. This is also seen in the presence of psychoanalysis in the study plans of psychology and medicine, in educational practices starting from early childhood, and in public hospitals and private practices within the mental health field. As well, many medical specialties, such as pediatrics, gynecology, dermatology, and others, where the study of the doctor–patient relationship and the pathogenesis and treatment of different conditions are strongly influenced by psychoanalysis in its different variants.

Local psychoanalytic production is followed with interest throughout the Latin American region. Authors such as J. Ahumada, M. and W. Baranger, J. Bleger, H. Bleichmar, A. Cabral, H. Etchegoyen, H. Faimberg, L. Grinberg, J. García Badaracco, L. Glocer Fiorini, M. Goldstein, L. Hornstein, L. Kancyper, D. Liberman, R. Losso, J. Maldonado, N. Marucco, R. Rubinstein, J. Tesone, and J. Ulnik have been translated, and are followed with interest in other parts of the world.

Although there is considerable consensus regarding the specificity of psychoanalysis and its particular contributions to the dynamically based psychotherapeutic practice, it is thought of as a continuum of more or less rich alloys of "pure gold." They are clearly differentiated from the practices unrelated to unconscious dynamics, which rely on suggestion or cognitive-behavioral techniques. We agree with Juan Francisco Jordán in that pure gold only serves to be safely kept within bank vaults, yet cannot be used; while it accumulates in those conditions, many become impoverished.

Although with very differing pay, an analyst in Buenos Aires would only exceptionally say that they have two or three patients in analysis. We have said that this occurs where psychoanalysis is only considered as such if practiced in four or five weekly sessions, on the couch, and especially with neurotic functioning. Broadening the definition allows for the inclusion of many possible practices in different alloys of pure gold.

As I stated above, following many years of the unanimous requirement of four or five weekly sessions to be considered psychoanalysis, this has not been the case over the last two or three decades. Psychoanalysis is no longer defined by the frequency of sessions or the cure type setting. This has not only allowed its practice to be developed in private settings, but also in public hospitals and health centers, with a variable frequency of sessions, and sometimes at no charge or at very accessible fees. Let us recall that Freud's idea was to extend treatment to less-favored social classes.

Psychoanalysts work many hours in treatments at a greater or lesser number of sessions, although with an increasing predominance of low weekly frequency. We work with adults, adolescents, and children in individual, couple, and family treatments, in all cases, of psychoanalytic orientation with different alloys of pure gold. Additionally, we treat serious patients as a team with psychiatrists. The analyst's training is not alien to how psychoanalytic their practice is, hence the importance of stimulating it by including this diversity beyond the "cure type." Limiting it to the latter, although its implementation may be difficult, makes the practice challenging to sustain and, as I said, keeps new generations away from the institutes that require it.

The growing interest in what is called off-the-couch psychoanalysis and the different community approaches to it in education, health, law, and organizations are testimony to the richness of Freudian contribution, provided that it be put to practice.

The twenty-eight colleagues who started training in 2021 at the Argentine Psychoanalytic Association, almost doubling the average of recent years, are part of this auspicious reality, based on a broad perspective of psychoanalytic practice.

Among the member societies of the IPA are the Argentine Psychoanalytic Association (APA) founded in 1942, the Buenos Aires Psychoanalytic Association (ABdeBA), and the Argentine Society of Psychoanalysis (SAP). With approximately 1,500 members among them, there are approximately 200 members between three societies and one study group in the cities of Cordoba, Mendoza, Rosario, and San Luis, all of which are located several hundred kilometers outside of Buenos Aires.

To these approximately 1,700 members and several hundred colleagues in training within the IPA, there are several institutions, many of which were inspired by some of their members, carrying out scientific and training programs of a pluralistic nature. These include, among others, the well-known Argentine School of Psychotherapy for Graduates (AAPG) and the Colegio de Psicoanalistas that offer psychoanalytic training.

In recent decades there has been a strong development of societies defining themselves as "Lacanian," beginning with the Freudian School of Argentina (EFA), the Freudian School of Buenos Aires (EFBA), the School of Lacanian Orientation (EOL), which belongs to the World Association of Psychoanalysis, the local branch of the World Association of Lacanian Forums, and several dozen smaller groups that are assembled together in the Lacanian Convergence for Freudian Psychoanalysis. There are also several schools of psychoanalysis in public hospitals, which are tuition-free. All of the above, in a more or less formal way, draw many of the thousands of graduates that the psychology undergraduate degree programs have. As I have said, the orientation of the majority of these degree programs, especially in the public universities, is Lacanian.

The preference of the new generations for university and hospital training, while less systematized, requires the analyst's analysis, clinical theoretical studies, and case supervision, in what Fernando Ulloa (2000) called the "Virtual Institution". This, as in other parts of the world, leads to the aging of the population of the IPA institutions, and if this tendency persists, we will be facing a crossroads in the future.

Several masters and doctoral degree programs have been added in both IPA and Lacanian institutions over the last twenty years, due to the search for academic recognition that the institutions generally do not offer, but that the new generations require, especially those who are dedicated to teaching.

The university, in addition to offering the ideal space for favoring the first transferences to undergraduate students and recent graduates, is by nature a space for intra-, inter-, and transdisciplinary development and exchange.

While some psychoanalytic institutions have opted for a university format, others prefer to maintain their specificity and instead associate with universities to develop study programs. Although the formats are to be evaluated in the coming years, in our experience, psychoanalytic training is not conducive to the design of university regulations, operating structures, programs, or professor appointments, which is why in the Argentine Psychoanalytic Association, I strongly supported partnering with the Salvador University. Several dozen graduates from both programs demonstrate its vitality.

Although it is difficult to quantify, it is assumed that there are thousands of health professionals with psychoanalytically oriented practices. Some speak of more than 30,000. Although it is hard to specify the number of active members in this group, which defines itself as "Lacanian," this orientation brings together several thousand practitioners of psychoanalysis in its scientific activities and congresses.

The IPA institutions, unlike in other countries, even in the region, include important groups of colleagues who recognize themselves as Freudo-Lacanian, or directly Lacanian, in relation to the theories they sustain. Their practices mobilize interesting debates within their societies.

In addition to the *Journal of Psychoanalysis of the Argentine Psychoanalytic Association*, which has published several annual issues without pause since 1943, there are now a dozen well-known printed and virtual journals from many of the aforementioned institutions. Worth mentioning is *Psychoanalysis in the Hospital*, published by psychoanalytic practitioners working in this setting and who are Lacanian in orientation.

Moreover, there is a strong presence in the culture at large as well as in the media, including online journals such as *La Epoca* and *Art Out*, published by the Argentine Psychoanalytic Association, *Lacaniana*, from the Escuela de Orientación Lacaniana, *Topía*, and *De inconcientes*.

Additionally, several colleagues, such as V. Galli, R. Soriano, and H. Persano, had been appointed state and city mental health directors, and M. Aguinis served as a state cultural director under democratically elected governments after 1983. As well, psychoanalysts frequently chair mental health clinics at state and private hospitals.

The international perspective on local psychoanalysis is one of surprise and admiration for the enthusiasm that is perceived with regards to our discipline. As I said before, and as in a few countries, being in or having been in analysis is socially valued, and across all social classes there is a strong acceptance of some kind of psychoanalytic psychotherapy, either publicly or privately.

As a result, a high percentage of middle- and upper-middle-class intellectuals are or have been in analysis; it is very common to have had some kind of a psychotherapeutic experience.

At the same time, the media seek our opinions daily on the most diverse range of topics. Film, theater, literature, visual arts, politics, sociology, etc. are deeply influenced by psychoanalysis.

It is common to read interviews with psychoanalysts in widely circulating newspapers or magazines, including presidents of the IPA or other international organizations. When our colleague Virginia Ungar was elected president of the IPA, a photograph of her appeared on the front page of the local press.

All of the above is the result of the extraordinary work initiated by the pioneers of our movement in the 1940s, 50s, and 60s. Celes Cárcamo, Angel Garma, Marie Langer, Enrique Pichon Riviere, Arnaldo Rascovsky, and others taught in the universities and hospitals, and they spoke to public opinion while founding the APA, in 1942. This was an extremely strong psychoanalytic group that trained analysts following the criteria of IPA. Years later, J. Bleger, D. Liberman, L. Ostrov, J. Abuchaem, F. Ulloa, J. García Badaracco, and others carried out important work in both public and private universities. This work continues to this day by colleagues such as J.J. Calzetta, J. Canteros, R. Doria Medina, V. Galli, R. Losso, H. Persano, S. Quiroga, C. Raznoszczyk Schejtman, L. Ricón, J. Tenconi, C. Tkach, J. Ulnik, R. Urribarri, A. Wald, and M.T. Reyes, among others.

The broad field of development of practices is not foreign to a productive interaction between what is known as Freudian psychoanalysis and that of its followers, or classical in its multiple variants and Lacanian psychoanalysis.

The challenge we have faced at the beginning of the twenty-first century has been to sustain this development, especially its practice in the field of health.

There being multiple options for training today, it is difficult to continue being one of the options searched for by new generations of analysts. Working together with psychiatrists, especially with the younger ones, who are strongly influenced by the neurosciences and critiques of psychoanalysis have proven to be a fruitful path at this crossroads.

Considering the breadth of what has been described about the practice, to continue with formative models created almost a hundred years ago is, in the words of Madeleine Baranger (2003), "scandalous."

Accepting that there is more than one psychoanalysis and theories and training models, as well as opening up to discussion with other disciplines, with the only safeguard of maintaining its specificity, have proven to be useful in engaging younger generations while, at the same time, bringing up to date those who are not so young. Articulation with philosophy, history, art, and the neurosciences notably enriches this field, which disputes pluralistic perspectives such as those of the IPA institutions and those derived from them, as well as perspectives dedicated almost exclusively to Lacanian psychoanalysis.

In recent years, I have expressed that nothing guarantees a priori the result of an analysis, therefore the training. It can only be evaluated a posteriori, and we must think of the best ways to do this. Supervisions, institutional debate among colleagues (Bolognini, 2014), written production, clinical exercises, and participation in original devices, such as the working parties, allow for this. Surely there will be other methods in the future and these need to be promoted in societies and institutes.

I think that the "subversive character of psychoanalysis" (personal communication of S. Frisch) and the "mysterious attraction of the dynamics of the unconscious" (idem of F. Ylander) will sustain new generations of analysts. Those who want to motivate them must be able to maintain these premises.

Piera Aulagnier (2005) stated that models are required to keep from falling *into anarchy and absolute irresponsibility, oligarchy*, or even autocracy.

I agree with Jaime Szpilka (2002) that the unconscious needs institutions to shelter it. At the same time, however, it runs the risk of being crushed by them for its survival. This tension is inevitable, and the effectiveness of institutions in the transmission of psychoanalysis depends on their management. Oftentimes, the confluence of knowledge and power has harmful consequences, especially within small groups. In this same vein, Willy Baranger (1987) described the paradox of becoming too institutionalized and no longer being psychoanalytic, or renouncing all formal criteria and ceasing to be an institution.

The importance of favoring singular paths that avoid mass psychology and standardized curricula as much as possible, as well as the possibility of being able to permanently work on the theoretical and clinical practices of its members, make for the ongoing training of analysts. Unfortunately, this is not what happens in most societies and institutes. We agree with Aulagnier (2005) in the irony that unfortunately, knowledge about the transference of its members is diluted when the latter acts on the very fabric of its analytic society.

Finally, I agree with Madeleine Baranger (2003) in that to fulfill its mission, a psychoanalytic institution must function in consonance with the specifics of psychoanalysis, not neglect its evolution, and take into account epochal conditions.

This implies:

- instituting as a permanent action rather than crystalizing institutions, therefore preventing bureaucratization and dogmatism;
- taking into account that no single theory can provide for the complexity of its field of study; working with a plurality of theories seems to be the most appropriate way for its scientific development;
- the training provided, while it must fulfill its commitment to the essence of Freudian discovery, that is, the unconscious, should accept this same plurality in terms of the practices it sustains;
- a necessary contextualization of psychoanalysis in the whole of science and culture through a space for intra-, inter- and transdisciplinary dialogue;
- a necessary presence in undergraduate and graduate university courses;
- a strong insertion into culture, society, and the community with outreach policies aimed toward each of these areas;
- a democratic administration with alternation in its freely elected leadership; and
- methods that prevent or neutralize the phenomena derived from the psychology of the masses, based especially on hierarchizing the complete independence of the analysis of its members from the institution and its powers.

While at the recently inaugurated Berlin Institute, Franz Alexander (1985) recalled the Freudian objections to preventing the new discipline from being systematized, thus crystalized, early on. Angel Garma (1959), one of the pioneers in Buenos Aires, proposed greater freedom for individuals and groups in the associations, within a single unit. The reform carried out in 1974 in the Argentine Psychoanalytic Association included Garma's proposal of only a few compulsory courses, curricular freedom and choice of professors, preventing excessive work, remunerating professors, developing knowledge about infancy, obtaining adequate gratitude, and spreading psychoanalysis in the community. The effects of this persist to this day in the training model and in the societal structure.

Almost forty years later, Kernberg (1996) referred to the many ways in which the creativity of candidates is hindered. For him, while psychoanalysis is said to be a combination of art and science, the institutional structures correspond more to a combination of technical school and theological seminary than to a university or art school. In the same vein, Kirsner (2004) referred extensively to the risks of basing the policies of psychoanalysis on difficult to implement standards instead of on ones of insertion into the culture, the community, and the university. He described the inconvenience of insular and restrictive policies versus more open and inclusive ones. For this Australian academic, the rise of psychoanalysis outside the IPA, in countries such as Argentina, Brazil, and France, is linked to its intimate relationship with culture and the university.

Summary

I have presented the crossroads, which, in my opinion, psychoanalysis is facing today in our context, as well as my views on the possible policies of psycho-analysis in the face of these crossroads.

By showing the power and vitality of psychoanalysis in Buenos Aires, I tried to exemplify the results of having broad theoretical, clinical, and community frontiers, as well as permanent intra-, inter-, and transdisciplinary work. This is what I propose as a way to approach the crossroads described above.

Note

1 Complex thinking (Morin, 2005), from the Latin complexus, supposes that which is woven together. Complexity expresses the impossibility of defining what surrounds us in a simple way. It approaches knowledge in its conditions of pro-duction, emergence, and practice. This process ceases to be linear, simple, and irreversible for it to develop in a critical and reflexive way. The world is not only made up of relationships, but also of realities endowed with a certain autonomy. It also presupposes a recursive causality: effects are necessary for the process that generates them.

The inclusion of heterogeneous constituents requires complex methods and assumes the inexistence of a neutral observer.

Originating in the natural sciences, it has extended to all domains of know-ledge as it emerges from the social and because the predictability of the course of human communities is not possible. This is about the self-eco-organizing rela-tionship of the object with respect to its ecosystem as well as linking it to the context of contexts, the planetary context.

References

Alexander, F. (1985) *On forme des psychanalystes: Rapport original sur les dix ans de l'Institut Psychanalytique de Berlin 1920–1930*. Paris: Denoël.

Aron, L. (2010) On: Responding to Rachel Blass' article Affirming "That's not psycho-analysis!" On the value of the politically incorrect act of attempting to define the limits of our field. *International Journal of Psychoanalysis*, 91(5), 1279–1280.

Aulagnier, P. (2005) *Un intérprete en busca de sentido* (2nd edition). Buenos Aires: Siglo XXI.

Baranger, W. (1987) Mesa Redonda del Claustro de Candidatos de la APA del 25/6/85. In: *En Vicisitudes del análisis didáctico*. Nueva Librería.

Baranger, M. (2003) Formación psicoanalítica: la reforma del '74, treinta años después. *Revista de Psicoanálisis*. 60(4): 1043–1050.

Baranger, W., Picollo, A., Paulucci, O. and Martínez Luque, E. (1987) Vicisitudes del análisis didáctico. Mesa Redonda del Claustro de Candidatos de la APA del 25/6/85. *Teoría, clínica, transmisión, psicoanálisis* (pp. 301–321). Buenos Aires: Nueva Librería.

Blass, R. (2010) On: The comments of Emanuel Berman, Lewis Aron, Yoram Hazan and Steven Stern. *International Journal of Psychoanalysis*. 91(5): 1285–1287.

Bolognini, S. (2014) Towards a "Quadripartite model"? *IPA Newsletter*, May. www. psihoanalitiki-ipa.si/files/Bolognini-Towards.pdf

Freud, S. (1978) *Obras Completas*. Buenos Aires: Amorrortu Editores.

García Badaracco, J. (2010) Sobre la "mente cerrada". *Revista de Psicoanálisis*. 67(1/2): 19–35.

Garma, A. (1959) Cómo mejorar las relaciones entre psicoanalistas. *Revista de Psicoanálisis*. 16(4): 362–367.

Glocer Fiorini, L. (2015) *La diferencia sexual en debate: cuerpos, deseos y ficciones*. Buenos Aires: Lugar.

Goldstein, M. (2011) La nostalgia del absoluto en la institución psicoanalítica. *Psicoanálisis y el hospital*. 20(40): 85–93.

Green, A. (2010) *El pensamiento clínico*. Buenos Aires: Amorrortu.

Kernberg, O. (1996) Thirty methods to destroy the creativity of psychoanalytical candidates. *International Journal of Psychoanalysis*. 77: 1031–1034.

Kirsner, D. (2004) Psychoanalysis and its discontents. *Psychoanalytic Psychology*. XXI: 339–352.

Marion, P. (2020) In F. Busch (Ed.), *Dear candidate: Analysts from around the world offer personal reflections on psychoanalytic training, education, and the profession* (pp. 27–31). London: Routledge.

Morin, E. (2005) *Introducción al pensamiento complejo*. Barcelona: Gedisa.

Richards, A. (2017) Sociology and psychoanalysis: The development of scientific knowledge by Jews in the Hasburg Empire – Freud, Brill and Fleck. In: A. Lynch (Ed.), *Psychoanalysis: Perspectives on thought collectives: More selected papers by Arnold Richards*, volume 2 (pp. 27–48). New York: IPBooks.

Szpilka, J. (2002) Sobre los cambios en APA en 1974: a Madeleine Baranger, Willy Baranger y Jorge Mom, que fueron el verdadero espíritu del cambio de 1974 en APA. In: A. Varios (Ed.), *60 Años de Psicoanálisis en la Argentina. Pasado. Presente. Futuro* (pp. 170–179). Buenos Aires: Lumen.

Ulloa, F. (2000) Mi experiencia con la institución psicoanalítica. *Acheronta*. 11: 222–224.

Part IV

New directions

Chapter 19

The self as mental agent
Explorations of a long-neglected concept

Werner Bohleber

Preliminary remarks

All analysts who work with traumatized patients know the problem that certain stimuli can cause memories of the trauma to suddenly intrude into consciousness again, paralyzing the ego and creating a dissociated state of consciousness.[1] These intrusions are experienced as completely overwhelming, to which the ego passively surrenders. The question of how a traumatically paralyzed ego can regain a sense of inner activity poses a complicated treatment problem. Therapeutically, it is a matter for the patient to regain what in contemporary research is called the "agency of the self."

For quite some time I have been concerned with the fact that the psychoanalytic theory of structure and representation cannot adequately capture the inner capacity for self-reflection, i.e., to be able to engage in dialogue with oneself. Anthropologically, the essential defining characteristic of the human being is his self-reflexivity. Its peculiarity lies in the fact that in it the individual self "accomplishes a kind of inner pluralization" and can relate itself back to this pluralization (Claessens, 1970). Hans Loewald (1980) speaks here of "duality" and of a splitting of mental processes "by which an inner encounter arises" (p. 168). This splitting constitutes the "process-structure of the ego," through which self-reflection and self-knowledge are made possible. For Loewald, the "thrust of psychoanalysis" lies in these "higher forms of reflective memory" (ibid., p. 171).

There is a close connection between self-agency and self-reflection. In order to understand how we can reflect on ourselves, we need to get a view of a self that can act as a mental agent towards itself. In my chapter, I will discuss and try to clarify these characteristics of the self from different perspectives and research approaches. I would like to begin with a brief overview of the conceptions of the self in psychoanalysis that have been developed so far.

DOI: 10.4324/9781003340744-24

The concept of the self in psychoanalysis

The psychoanalytic literature on the concept of the self reveals considerable confusion, which does not always make it easy to find one's way through the various conceptions. Freud used the concept of the ego both for the whole person and for a psychic substructure. He never cleared up this ambiguity, but always maintained the inner tension of his concept of the ego (Laplanche and Pontalis, 1973). It was then Heinz Hartmann (1950) who separated the two aspects of the ego and introduced the concept of the self. He sought to solve the conceptual problems of fitting into the structural model by introducing the notion of "self-representation" and thus assigning the self as a concept of experience to the structure of the ego. Psychoanalytic discussions have been working on these conceptual problems for decades. I would like to refer to the contributions of Edith Jacobson, Otto Kernberg, John Gedo and W.W. Meissner. With Heinz Kohut there emerged conceptions of the self that left the structural model behind. Kohut postulated the self on the one hand as an experiential concept and as the place of subjective experience, and on the other hand as a structural concept and as the core of personality. The cohesive self is the source of agency, self-esteem, and a sense of continuity. As a bipolar self, it is characterized by a tension between the pursuit of actualization and one's self-ideals. British object relations theories, for their part, focused attention on a self as a counterpart of the object. Donald Winnicott, with his work on the development of the child self, occupies a central position in this regard.

The more recent intersubjective approaches emphasize the development of the self in the intersubjective matrix. There is no self or subject by itself; it becomes a self only through an other. Against purely psychological constructions of the self, e.g., as a "narrative self," other authors emphasize that the self has an independent core that emerges from its own biologically based primary activity and becomes a source of the sense of self. A radical position was taken by relational analysts who denied that there is a unitary self at all. They conceive of multiple multiform selves that emerge from different self–object situations. The idea of a unified self is seen here as an illusion of our mind, which fills gaps with this idea and creates connections between the particular selves.

My brief overview of psychoanalytic conceptions of the self was intended to focus attention on the fact that in them an essential characteristic of the human self is only mentioned in passing or not at all, namely its dual structure, which makes it possible for humans to reflect on themselves as mental agents in the first place.

The dual structure of the self

When man reflects on himself, he steps out of the experiencing self – phenomenologically speaking – and goes to a meta-level in order to reconsider what he has experienced and to take himself as an object. This fundamental split in the inner constitution of the self has long been a topic of philosophy. This split creates the ability of man to transcend himself, and thus to see himself quasi from the outside and to be able to reflect on himself. In psychology and in the social sciences, William James (1890) and next to him Charles Cooley and George Herbert Mead are the classics of such a dual concept of self. James distinguished two aspects: the self as subject, the "I" as pure experience, and the self as empirical object, the "me". The "I" is the active agent that constructs the "me", i.e., the mental representations of the self, and has a unifying function. Mead (1934) further developed this approach of James. The "I" can only realize itself through identification with the social others (its significant others) and thus come to its "me," i.e., to the representations of itself.

In psychoanalysis, the "I" as the holistic agent that can keep the self-process going was neglected for a long time. Freud made a remarkable reflection on this in the "New Introductory Lectures" from 1932:

> We wish to make the ego the matter of our enquiry, our very own ego. But is that possible? After all, the ego is in its very essence a subject; how can it be made into an object? Well, there is no doubt that it can be. The ego can take itself as an object, can treat itself like other objects, can observe itself, criticize itself, and do Heaven knows what with itself. In this, one part of the ego is setting itself over against the rest. So the ego can be split; it splits itself during a number of its functions – temporarily at least. Its parts can come together again afterwards. That is not exactly a novelty, though it may perhaps be putting an unusual emphasis on what is generally known.

Freud was not further interested in the self-reflexive function that the ego possesses through its ability to split, but his reflection aimed to introduce the superego into the train of thought: a superego as the part of the ego that develops into its own agency and rises above the ego.

Richard Sterba (1934) made similar observations at the International Psychoanalytic Congress in Wiesbaden in 1932, but drew different conclusions from Freud. He sought to make the reflexive potency that the ego possesses through its capacity for dissociation fruitful for the analytic process. His concept of therapeutic dissociation (splitting) of the ego later became widely known. The special feature of therapeutic work consists in the "shifting of [a] subject's consciousness" (p. 121) from the stream of the experiencing and affect-occupied ego to "islands of intellectual contemplation" (p. 125), on which a "self-contemplation" (p. 125) becomes possible. The condition for being able to effectively establish such a standpoint of contemplation lies in a positive transference of the patient. At the end of his paper Sterba refers to Johann Gottfried Herder and sums up:

Perhaps I may say in conclusion that the therapeutic dissociation of the ego in analysis is merely an extension, into new fields, of that self-contemplation which from all time has been regarded as the most essential trait of man in distinction to other living beings.

(1934, p. 72)

Sterba thus implicitly refers to a philosophical-anthropological discussion that took place in the 1920s about the relationship between nature and spirit in humans. In a similar way, Robert Waelder had already spoken in 1930 in his paper "The principle of multiple function" (1936a/2007) of the fact that – anthropologically seen – the superego is the "domain of the human being; it is the element through which man in his experience steps beyond himself and looks at himself as the object" (2007, p. 91). In his essay on the problem of freedom in psychoanalysis (1934) he took up Sterba's thoughts.

Freedom in its most general sense seems to us to consist in a man appearing not to be tied down to his biological situation and to his environment, to the hic et nunc of his actual existence, but appearing to be able on occasion to pass beyond the actualities of his perceptual relations, to rise above himself and to objectify his standpoint of the moment.

(1936, p. 90)

Taking up a position above one's own ego opens up an objectivation of one's self for the human being, which Waelder distinguishes from superego's critical-punitive function as a comprehensive "formal function of the superego" (1936b, p. 92) and which he sought to locate in the structural model as a "structural task" even above the superego (1937, p. 137).[2]

These tentative attempts to create a place for self-reflection in the conceptual framework of psychoanalysis, however, came to a standstill due to the forced emigration of the analysts by the Nazi regime. With the exception of Lacan's "je" and "moi", there was no longer any theoretical effort to take a closer look at this dual self and its function as a mental agent. First infant research and then neuroscience opened up a new view of the functions of self-agency and self-reflection with their studies.

The development of the self as an agent

For Louis Sander (2008), self-regulation is a basic function of all biological organisms. The mother–infant system also moves forward toward a regulating equilibrium. In the process, patterns of interaction emerge that become consolidated and refined. They create a familiar, recurring event structure and establish in the infant regularly occurring configurations of expectancy to re-establish need-satisfying situations. By regulating and satisfying the infant's states, the mother ensures that there arises in the infant a sense of directly influencing and directing his own state in the desired direction, thus creating in the infant a sense of being the author of the desired states. But because this experience of agency is intersubjectively induced, a certain "indistinctness" is inherent in the infant's perception of who the agent is. Here, a second fact comes to his aid. After the infant's needs have been satisfied, a period of so-called "disengagement" regularly occurs in the mother–infant system, during which the infant is awake and can engage in his endogenously arising motivations and interests, such as watching his mother, playing with his fingers, or moving a mobile. For Sander, this activity is an "alternative" that stands by to support and extend emergent agency. These two forms of regulation of self-states provide the infant and later the toddler with a growing "sense of individual agency" (2008, p. 287). Sander emphasizes that this development, however, depends essentially on the child's actions being recognized and acknowledged as its own self by the mother.

Infant research has explored other developmental processes that contribute to the formation of a sense of self-agency. I can only outline a few of them. The visual-motor system becomes functional very early and enables the infant to actively interact with the primary object and to determine the beginning as well as the end of eye contact. With her vocal and mimic expressions, the mother mirrors the infant's affective behavior, creating a pleasurable interactive and imitative back-and-forth. This characteristic turn-taking structure of the interaction sequences provide the infant with a basic sense of agency (Beebe et al., 2003; Knox, 2011), which is then further reinforced by the inevitable small episodes of "disruption and repair" (Tronick and Cohn, 1989). These early interactions with the affective facial play integrated into them are internalized by the infant and the sense of agency becomes an essential resource of the implicit unconscious. A very own sense of an active self is formed, provided with a basic affective tint, which also originates from the intersubjective exchange between mother and child.[3]

Peter Fonagy and his research group (Fonagy et al., 2002) have examined important stages in the emergence of a mental self. Drawing on the social biofeedback theory of developmental researchers Gergely and Watson, they formulate a theory of mentalization based on stages of a developing sense of agency. They explicitly break with the previous psychoanalytic tradition, which for far too long had been in the shadow of Cartesian traditions and had assumed that the experience of mental agency is innately given. Fonagy et al. no longer define the self from its representations, but they place themselves in the tradition of William James with his distinction of the "I" as the active agent and the "me" as representational aspects of the self. They are arguing that mental agency can be seen as a developing or constructed capacity. Self-reflection is thus considered as an evolutionary achievement of man, which has evolved out of the primary object relations (2002, p. 5). Fonagy et al.'s theory of mentalization is based on the assumption that infants have an innate sensitivity to contingencies. Therefore, an infant can establish a relationship between his physical reaction and processes that follow it and feel himself to be an actor. Crucial to this is the temporal factor. If the temporal difference between the two events is too great, there is no contingency perception, i.e., the two events do not belong together. The mother's affect-mirroring takes advantage of this contingency mechanism.[4] The baby does not initially have conscious access to the internal indicators of its emotional state. It is at the mercy of its states and cannot represent them. The mother must read and interpret its behavioral expressions. She does this by speaking with a raised but variable pitch of voice and accompanying it with facial expressions to match. In doing so, the mother provides an empathic reflection of her child's emotional state immediately. Due to the temporally contingent immediacy of this "marked" reaction of the mother, the infant associates the perceived emotional expression with itself, as if it were its author. He or she decouples the emotion expression from the mother and internalizes it as a protosymbolic representation of his or her own emotional state. On this, the infant and then the child gradually builds "second-order representations" which provide him with the cognitive means to actively attribute his inner states to his own self and thus to be able to regulate them himself.

These second-order representations are not a direct state description of reality, but an interpretation. Firth and Firth (2003) have broken down the significance of this in more detail. In order to mentally express an experienced state, its representation is detached (decoupled) from it. Such decoupling is the basic process of mentalization. The causative reality is thereby transcended, so that a reflexive distance arises, which then also makes it possible to detach oneself even further from the immediate reality and to be able to think and fantasize one's own ideas, intentions, and desires without a connection to it. The self is therefore not only able to rise above reality and thereby represent it, but it can also still rise above its own representations, i.e., re-represent them on a meta-level, a process that forms the starting point for the emergence of a reflexive mentality.

I cannot here further present the developmental phases of the transformation of the self into a mental agent described by Fonagy et al. and other researchers. My aim was to show, through the developmental research, how basically anchored in the human sense of self is the sense of one's own agency and a reflexive mentality.

Contribution of neurobiology to the conception of an "embodied" self

To begin with, I would like to describe a self-observation. If my own self is in a cognitive and affective balance, I am able to perceive an affective basic feeling of it that cannot be put into words. It is a comprehensive basic feeling of the self, not clearly delineated, anchored in the body, which provides me with the continuity of my self-experience. Against its background, the ongoing specific self-feelings are formed in each case, without the basic self-feeling being lost. This fact points to a duality of the self, which some authors call its paradoxical nature (Emde, 1988; Modell, 1993): On the one hand, the self is a structure mediating continuity and therefore must be continuous; on the other hand, it is a constantly changing consciousness.

Highly interesting findings about this two-part structure of our sense of self come from the neurosciences. Besides Jaap Panksepp's research on the "core self," it is above all the work of Antonio Damasio that is of importance here. He has elaborated a neurobiological theory of the self and presented it in a phenomenological language. According to this, the brain constructs consciousness by generating a self-process within an awake mind, the elementary level of which is the so-called proto-self (2010, p. 180). The proto-self, which is located in the upper level of the brain stem, contains the spontaneous feelings of the living body (primordial feelings), which as background feelings provide continuity and give the person "a rock-solid, wordless affirmation that I am alive" (ibid., p. 185). When the proto-self enters into interactions with objects it "must be raised and made to stand out" from this basic affective experience and enter a connection with the events that arise from it. That is, it enters into relationship with the cortex, as that part of the brain that represents the object or experience present at the moment. The self thereby functions like a "protagonist" who has an "agency" and appropriates the objects as its "own property." This protagonist-core-self must not be imagined as a substance, but it is a constantly pulsating process that modifies the proto-self into a core self through "its moment-to-moment engagement as caused by any object being perceived" (ibid., p. 202). Because this is the only way to ensure that object-related feelings can arise in the face of the large number of objects that interact with the organism. In brief, Damasio conceptualizes the self in its paradoxical duality as an affective and constancy mediating basic core and as an active, constantly "online" pulsating process that appropriates objects. At the same time, this self generates a "feeling that I have agency relative to the objects and that the actions being carried out by my body are commanded by my mind" (ibid., p. 185). Mark Solms (2013) has formulated the consequences of the findings of neuroscience for psychoanalysis, revising the Freudian structural model and turning it on its head. Freud, too, had succumbed to the "corticocentric fallacy" that the cortex was the seat of consciousness. As Panksepp and Damasio have shown, the "affective primary self" (ibid., p. 16) that generates consciousness is anchored in ancient brain structures. The self is therefore first a bodily self. Solms recognizes in this self the Freudian id. As "background subject" it forms the "inner self." It is a pure affective consciousness, which, however, can only become aware of itself when it connects with images that are laid out in cortical memory as learned representations. For Solms, the ego is also a learned representation and forms the "external self." In itself, the ego is unconscious. Only when it is occupied with consciousness by the id can we think and act with it as an "I." For Solms, the superego is the "abstractive self" and thus the "reflexive scaffolding" with which we can reflect on ourselves. Solms thus conceives of a self that, with its "constant 'presence' of feeling," is the basic background subject of all cognition and becomes aware of itself as an acting subject through representational processes. The self can then transcend these processes once again in order to be able to reflexively consider itself. Solms thus confirms the considerations of Robert Waelder, who sought to locate self-reflection even "above" the known functions of the superego.

Like infant research, neurobiological research with its own categories also describes the duality of the self as a constant background feeling and as a simultaneously acting protagonist who forms a representational core self through connection with objects and acquires the capacity for reflexive transcendence through processes of re-representation. I would now like to move on to psychoanalytic conceptions of the self, which in turn attempt to theoretically map this duality of the self.

Donald Winnicott's theory of the self

Jan Abram emphasizes that Winnicott's work can rightly be considered a theory of the self (2007, p. 5ff). While much of his work has been widely received, the same cannot be said of his theory of the self. Winnicott assumes, as we know, an absolute dependence of the infant. In order for a sense of self to form, it is of central importance that the mother adapts sufficiently well and contingently to her child and his needs, thereby promoting in him a sense that it is he himself who satisfies his hunger. According to Abram, this illusory act can be described roughly as "I cry, and the food comes" (ibid., p. 8). Winnicott emphasizes that every infant brings a "creative potential" as an "innate predisposition,"[5] which, through a reliable contingent supply, sets in motion the omnipotent illusion that she has created the object and she has made "a personal contribution" (ibid., p. 8). It is a first experience of agency, reinforced by the spontaneous gestures the infant makes during periods of undisturbed attention. Through their innumerable repetitions, "a True Self begins to have life through the strength given to the infant's weak ego by the mother's implementation of the infant's omnipotent expressions" (1960/1965, p. 145). For Winnicott, the spontaneous gesture is the true self in action, but it must not be understood in purely psychological terms; it is also fed by the vitality of the bodily tissues, by the sensing of heart activity, breathing, and other bodily functions. Her progressive cognitive development gradually enables the infant to come to recognize the illusory element in her experience of omnipotence and to transfer it to play and fantasy (1960/1965, p. 146). The more the child develops and the more he succeeds in distinguishing between "me" and "not-me," the more the adaptability of the self to social situations is also required. To capture this fact theoretically, Winnicott introduces a split between a true and a false self.

In his clinical practice, Winnicott encountered a wide range of healthy and pathological manifestations of the two selves and their interaction. The false self is the part that is turned outward in connection with the world. Through its "compliance," it can adapt and seek conditions "which will make it possible for the True Self to come into its own" and to preserve its creativity and spontaneity through participation in cultural experience (1960/1965, p. 143). The true self, in turn, has the function of always challenging the social realizations of the false self, especially when, rather than seeking genuine compromise, it tends toward conformity. If the degree of split between them is pathologically high, we find a split-off compliant false self that hides the true self in such a way that it no longer has access to it. With a low and healthy degree of split, both remain in contact with each other. In a later writing (1963/1965) Winnicott specifies what he means by the "intimacy" of the true self. It is his core, an "incommunicado" private self. "Although healthy persons communicate ... the other fact is equally true, that each individual is an isolate, permanently non-communicating, permanently unknown, in fact unfound" (ibid., p. 187). This "non-communicating central self" is silent to the outside world, but it has a kind of communication with itself that is "like the music of the spheres, absolutely personal. It belongs to being alive" (ibid., p. 102). Winnicott's terms here capture an aspect of the self that I sought to describe above as a comprehensive basic affective sense of self with its affective tint emanating from early interactions with the primary object.

Winnicott's conception of a self split into a true and a false self has an implicit normative character through which social realization is always suspected of being conformist and thereby betraying the true self. The relationship between the two selves also corresponds more to a "one-way influence," in which the false self loses the ability to mediate a creative feedback to the true self that can originate from social realization. In self-agency, as Winnicott understands it, the remnants of an omnipotent sense of self are preserved. I consider this an important finding that helps us to understand why, in life-threatening and traumatic situations, remnants of a sense of omnipotence can be reactivated, keeping the sense of agency from collapsing. The self is thus protected against a cascade of feelings of helplessness and panic that would otherwise plunge it into helpless passivity.

Arnold Modell's theory of the self

Starting with Donald Winnicott and drawing on William James, Arnold Modell has expanded his theory of the self over decades (1993; 2003; 2008). For him, the self is an agent superior to all other mental structures, which he grounds in psychobiology. The self is dependent on social recognition, but not entirely, for a part of it can become autonomous and free itself from dependence on social recognition. Referring to Winnicott's "true self," Modell also calls this aspect the "private self." Conceptually, he locates it in states

of "non-being-in-relation" that form a "private space" in which the experience of the self is its very own, which cannot be communicated. This private self derives its power not only from its involvement in social structures,
but also essentially from its inner contact with its basic affective core, which
Modell anchors not only in relational experiences of early childhood, but also
in the biological core self described by neuroscience. In it, the capacity for
autonomy finds its firm ground, which does not allow the self to become
wholly dependent on social recognition. This psychobiological matrix enables
the self to be a coherent and continuity-providing entity. But it also has a present structure, making it an ephemeral entity that changes from moment to
moment. This paradox of the self needs to be explained. In theories of the self,
we find quite different solutions to this problem. Modell bases his solution
on Gerald Edelman's neurobiological theory. According to Edelman, evolution has endowed the human self with a neural scheme of past, present, and
future. This enables it to keep its distance from the inputs of the immediate
present and to be able "to be free of the tyranny of ongoing events in real
time" (Modell, 1993, p. 71). Through this distance, the self gains the ability
to commute with its agency between the present and the past, to become self-
aware, and to create new meanings and expand the old ones. In this way, self-
agency provides the self with the ability to remain in the flow of the moment
while ensuring its coherence and continuity.

But let us return to Modell's conception of a private self. With this concept,
he has brought a self-experience to the fore that had been widely neglected
in psychoanalysis – with the exception of Winnicott. With a self whose
autonomy is based on an inner biologically anchored affective core experience,
Modell on the one hand defends himself against a totalizing claim of common
theories of intersubjectivity; on the other hand he exposes himself to the
danger of hypostatizing the autonomy of the private self. This is a problem
that also arises in Winnicott's conception of the "true self." Autonomy of the
self is more than just our very own basic affective feeling. For in its autonomy
the self is always related to something social from which it is set apart. The
private self must also take the "detour" via the other, otherwise it remains an
empty consciousness.

The mental agency and the associative reflexive self

I would like to begin by using a phenomenological description to show
how our mental activity unfolds in psychic space and how it is thereby
connected to a sensorimotor sensation. As human beings, we are able to enter
an inner meta-level and immerse ourselves in the world of our ideas, to let
our thoughts wander, to follow them, to observe associations, to think about
them, and to let them affect us in their meaning. But thoughts can also break
in quite suddenly. If we want to gain clarity about conflictual constellations,
we look for and draw on related scenarios and weigh them up against each

other. Gaining new meanings involves an emotional movement that creates space in an existing psychological constriction and expands the self. There is much to suggest that space is a basic condition of our psyche. An example: a traumatized patient reacted to an upcoming minor eye surgery with panic. After my interpretation that she was experiencing the eye operation as a repetition of her childhood trauma, the panic disappeared. As a 3-year-old she had had a traumatizing eye surgery for strabismus. Now she could distinguish past and present again and told me of a feeling that a clamp had been loosened inside her. She no longer felt constricted by her fear but expanded inwardly.

My descriptions of mental activity sought to bring up a specific aspect of our "embodied" selves that I would like to explore further. Daniel Stern (2010) has described "forms of vitality" inherent in all human forms of expression. Leuzinger-Bohleber (2016) show that the self is constantly being actively constructed in a dynamic interaction of the body with its environment. For Lakoff and Johnson (1999), the mind is inherently embodied and perceptual and motor systems play a foundational role in our own concept definition and in rational inference. Our conceptual reasoning is neither disembodied nor abstract nor modality-neutral. "Abstract reasoning in general exploits the sensory-motor system" (Gallese and Lakoff, 2005, p. 473). In this way, mental agency is directly grounded in physical agency. I find these theses fascinating, because our thinking self is not only active and creative, but also feels a sensory-motor drive to wander through the mental space that opens up within it. In this, a basic anthropological movement unfolds, for the self as an actor must "divest" (entäußern) itself into the world of its objects (take on social roles) and, through a reflexive turning back to itself and to its world of representations, reassure itself of its own coherence and continuity. It is a process that is indispensable, but never comes to an end, because the double structure of the self implies that "I" and "me" can never become completely identical. Man can never fully catch up with himself, i.e., never fully understand himself. In psychoanalysis, Erikson and other authors have attempted to conceptualize central aspects of this situation of self-doubling and self-"divesting"(Selbstentäußerung) with the concept of identity (cf. Bohleber, 2010).

The traumatized dissociative self

Trauma always affects the core of the self and alters the psychobiological balance. Henry Krystal (1988) has described in detail the direct effects of the traumatic situation on the individual. He had treated Holocaust survivors and derived a general model of a traumatic state from their extreme traumatization. Whereas for Freud helplessness was at the center of the traumatic experience, Krystal sought to describe this state more precisely. If a danger is understood as inevitable and inescapable, this leads to an inner capitulation and a self-surrender of the affected person. This surrender sets in motion a traumatic process. The affective reactions are paralyzed and numbed, a circumstance that is initially experienced as a relief because the unbearable painful affects disappear. But giving oneself up has fatal consequences: there is a progressive blocking of mental functions, such as memory, imagination, associations, problem solving, etc. The person falls into a trance state. This blocks all initiatives of the self that could serve its self-assertion. Krystal emphasizes the lethal potential inherent in this process of self-surrender, because if the traumatic situation continues, it leads to the shutting down of all self-preserving initiatives. His clinical experience showed Krystal that in people who were able to maintain their activity, even if it was limited to thinking, planning, or fantasizing, the impact of the trauma was limited and the traumatic process could be brought to a halt (1988, p. 232). However, if the initiative and thus the self-agency breaks down, an inexorable progression towards a so-called "robot-state" begins with a far-reaching shut-off of psychic functions. If this traumatic process continued in concentration camp inmates, it could lead to a suppression of all vitality and to "psychogenic death."

I have presented Krystal's findings on extreme traumatization in such detail because they give an impression of the central importance of self-agency for the health and survival of the traumatized person. In most severe traumatizations, the onset of the traumatic process can be stopped earlier than in the case of the former concentration camp inmates studied by Krystal. However, the massive effects on the core of the self remain. Wilson, Friedman, and Lindy (2001) have treated people with other traumas, and they describe the consequences of trauma for psyche and organism as follows:

> Trauma impacts the psychic core – the very soul – of the survivor and generates a search for meaning as to why the event had to happen. A state of 'dispiritedness' may cause a profound questioning of existence and force belief systems to change ... The alteration of psychoformative processes may lead to a decentering of the self, a loss of groundedness and of a sense of sameness and continuity ... In extreme cases, a radical discontinuity may occur in ego identity, leaving scars to the inner agency of the psyche.
>
> (Wilson et al., 2001, p. 30)

Finally, I would like to deal with these "scars" that trauma leaves on the agency of the self. Today, in trauma research, not only the immediate experience of the traumatic event with its impact is the focus of interest, but more and more the memories with their intrusive and increasingly persistent character have been assigned an essential significance for the biological and psychological consequences. The excessive arousal of the traumatic situation overwhelms and paralyzes the integrative functions of memory, causing the self to lose its memory-forming power. Therefore, because of its overwhelming affectivity and fragmentary structure, it cannot provide the memories with autobiographical meaning through associative connections and thus consolidate them. The memories become isolated from the rest of the stream of consciousness.

In individuals who are severely traumatized and develop post-traumatic stress disorder, the traumatic memories do not lose their intensity or their intrusive power, but the intrusions become chronic. The suddenness of their breaking into consciousness is increasingly experienced as a pure overwhelming and thus acquires a re-traumatizing character. Often it is only fragments of these memories that break in, with visual and sensory impressions dominating over verbal-narrative elements. They may be released by multiple triggers that need not be directly related to the traumatic event. They often remain unconscious, so that the intrusion occurs suddenly and as if "out of the blue."

This suddenness has a frightening and paralyzing character and catapults the self into a dissociated state of consciousness and self-alienation. It feels itself placed in a passive state, loses its flexibility, and experiences itself subjected to the dominance of the intruding memory. Active reflection on what the meaning of it all might be is unsuccessful. Self-reflection has lost all power; it has become stereotyped, repetitive useless thinking that is going around in circles. The psychic space is constricted. It takes a longer time for the weakened self to free itself from this state. Sometimes it is a dream that can release the self from the traumatic helplessness and bring back the inner familiar sense of self. Or it is experiencing one's own activity from other areas of life that make the inner sense of agency accessible again. After a patient recovered this active state, he described it thus: He experienced his regained agency like a protective cloak for his naked self, because it would keep the dissociative paralyzing state away and would calm the fear of renewed intrusion.

This analysis of traumatic breakdowns gives us an indication of how essential agency is as an active protection for a self that otherwise feels powerless and helpless. The metaphor of the protective cloak points to the psycho-structural protective and defensive function afforded to the sense of self-agency. In normal life we are not aware of this, our self-agency is intact, and with its help we can cope with what we encounter from outside and from inside.

Conclusion

One of the essential goals of analytic treatment is known to be the promotion of self-knowledge through self-reflection. It can be advanced through identification with the analytic method. Although psychoanalysis has intensively explored the pathology of self-knowledge through making the unconscious conscious in the analytic relationship, it has long presupposed the function of the self as a mental agent or implicitly incorporated it into the ego without identifying the capacity for self-reflection as a special ego function.

From birth, self-agency is the constituent feature of the sense of self. Given the split of the self into "I" and "me," the agency of the self is the means by which mental contents and representations can be reflexively thought through and integrated. I have gathered various aspects that characterize the self as a mental agent. They can serve as approaches or building blocks for a future conception of the self in which agency will occupy a central place.

Notes

1 This chapter is reprinted by permission from Springer Nature, Forum der Psychoanalyse, 38: 17–32, Das Selbst als mentaler Akteur. Ein vernachlässigtes Konzept der Psychoanalyse. Copyright: the author, 2022.
2 In his 1960 book *Basic Theory of Psychoanalysis*, Waelder presents the same ideas in some more detail.
3 Daniel Stern (1985/2000) characterizes this early developmental phase as an "emergent self," which then develops further into a "core self," whose fundamental invariant is the sense of its own agency.
4 Jean Knox (2011) points out that this explicit emphasis on the role of the contingency mechanism and the marking of affect expression by the mother does not sufficiently take into account the research on implicit turn-taking behaviors that shape an interpersonal behavioral unconscious.
5 Sander calls this potential a "primary endogenous activity" (see above).

References

Abram, J. (2007) *The Language of Winnicott. A Dictionary of Winnicott's Use of Words*, 2nd edition. London/New York: Routledge.
Beebe, B., Rustin, J., Sorter, D., and Knoblauch, S. (2003) An expanded view of intersubjectivity in infancy and its application to psychoanalysis. *Psychoanalytic Dialogues*. 13: 805–841.
Bohleber, W. (2010) *Destructiveness, Intersubjectivity, and Trauma: The Identity Crisis of Modern Psychoanalysis*. London: Karnac.
Claessens, D. (1970) *Instinkt, Psyche, Geltung. Zur Legitimation menschlichen Verhaltens*, 2nd edition. Köln und Opladen: Westdeutscher Verlag.
Damasio, A. (2010) *Self Comes to Mind: Constructing the Conscious Brain*. London: Vintage Books.
Emde, R. (1988) Development terminable and interminable – I. Innate and motivational factors from infancy. *International Journal of Psychoanalysis*. 69: 23–42.
Fonagy, P., Gergeley, G., Jurist, E., and Target, M. (2002) *Affect Regulation, Mentalization, and the Development of the Self*. New York: Other Press.
Freud, S. (1933) New introductory letters in psychoanalysis. *The Standard Edition of the Complete Psychological Works of Sigmund Freud*. 22: 3–182.
Frith, U. and Frith, C.D. (2003) Development and neurophysiology of mentalizing. *Philosophical Transactions of the Royal Society B*. 358: 459–473.
Gallese, V. and Lakoff, G. (2005) The brain's concepts: the role of the sensory-motor system in conceptual knowledge. *Cognitive Neuropsychology*. 22: 455–479.

Hartmann, H. (1950) *Essays on Ego Psychology. Selected Problems in Psychoanalytic Theory*. New York: International Universities Press.

James, W. (1890) *Principles of Psychology*. New York: Henry Holt.

Knox, J. (2011) *Self-Agency in Psychotherapy: Attachment, Autonomy, and Intimacy*. New York/London: Norton.

Krystal, H. (1988) *Integration and Self-Healing: Affect, Trauma, Alexithymia*. Hillsdale: The Analytic Press.

Lakoff, G. and Johnson, M. (1999) *Philosophy in the Flesh*. New York: Basic Books.

Laplanche, J. and Pontalis, J.B. (1973) *The Language of Psychoanalysis*. London: Hogarth Press.

Leuzinger-Bohleber, M. (2016) Enactments in transference: embodiment, trauma and depression. What have psychoanalysis and the neurosciences to offer to each other. In: Weigel, S. and Scharbert, G. (editors). *A Neuro-Psychoanalytical Dialogue for Bridging Freud and the Neurosciences*. Wiesbaden: Springer, pp. 33–46.

Loewald, H. (1980) *Papers on Psychoanalysis*. New Haven/London: Yale University Press.

Mead, G.H. (1934) *Mind, Self and Society: From the Standpoint of a Social Behaviorist*. Chicago: Chicago University Press

Modell, A.H. (1993) *The Private Self*. Cambridge/London: Harvard University Press.

Modell, A.H. (2003) *Imagination and the Meaningful Brain*. Cambridge MA/London: The MIT Press.

Modell, A.H. (2008) Horse and rider revisited: the dynamic unconscious and the self as agent. *Contemporary Psychoanalysis*. 44: 351–366.

Sander, L.W. (2008) *Living Systems, Evolving Consciousness, and the Emerging Person*. New York: Routledge.

Solms, M. (2013) The conscious id. *Neuropsychoanalysis*. 15: 5–19.

Sterba, R. (1934) The fate of the ego in analytic therapy. *International Journal of Psychoanalysis*. 15: 117–126.

Stern, D. (1985) *The Interpersonal World of the Infant*, 2nd edition. New York: Basic Books.

Stern, D. (2010) *Forms of Vitality: Exploring Dynamic Experience in Psychology, the Arts, Psychotherapy, and Development*. Oxford: Oxford University Press.

Tronick, E. and Cohn, J. (1989) Infant–mother face-to-face interaction: age and gender differences in coordination and the occurrence of miscoordination. *Child Development*. 60: 85–92.

Waelder, R. (1936a) The principle of multiple function: observations on over-determination. *Psychoanalytic Quarterly*. 76: 75–92.

Waelder, R. (1936b) The problem of freedom in psycho-analysis and the problem of reality-testing. *International Journal of Psychoanalysis*. 17: 89–108.

Waelder, R. (1960) *Basic Theory of Psychoanalysis*. New York: International Universities Press.

Wilson, J., Friedman, M., and Lindy J. (editors) (2001) *Treating Psychological Traumas & PTSD*. New York and London: Guilford Press.

Winnicott, D.W. (1965) *The Maturational Processes and the Facilitating Environment: Studies in the Theory of Emotional Development*. London: Hogarth Press.

Chapter 20

Another perspective on dreams
The dream as an experience

Stefano Bolognini

In the last 20 years, especially in the wake of Bion's exploration, a substantial part of psychoanalytic scientific work has been concerned with the oneiric aspects of wakefulness, highlighting how much of a "dream" (in a broad and analogical sense) there is in the multi-layered complexity of consciousness and, ultimately, bringing further elements to the vision of an Ego far less master in its own house than commonly believed.

In this chapter I intend instead to consider not so much the equivalents of dreaming in wakefulness, but a function only occasionally performed by dreaming in the psychic life of the human being, and yet so valuable and important as to constitute a separate chapter, worthy of being explored in turn and valued as it deserves for its potential impact on people's lives.

I am referring to the function of the dream to enable the subject to have new experiences, with mutational passages generated by favorable, occasional internal unconscious agreements between Ego, Superego, and Id, which in turn make possible a different and innovative experience of the Self, understood here not as a representational area of the Self, but as an experiential area that the noetic levels of the Ego may or may not recognize in a more or less complete way, and that the subject however comes to experience unexpectedly, but effectively, right in the dream.

The theme is not new in psychoanalysis, and to tell the truth it evokes even before a number of mythological and literary references that would easily lead to sliding towards the seductive register of magic, omnipotence, and idealization of the dream itself: the dream inspired by the gods, the revelatory or premonitory dream, the fruit and at the same time the engine of a superhuman sapientiality, and even at the risk of an analytical overestimation, pointed out surprisingly by Freud himself when in *Observations on the Theory and Practice of the Interpretation of Dreams* (1923), he warned the analysts themselves about the danger of idealizing "*a mysterious unconscious*," to the point of stating: "*One forgets too often that a dream is mostly a thought like all the others*" (p. 424, vol. OSF; p. 112, vol. 19 SE).

This is not the point of view of the present chapter, aimed far more modestly at exploring occasional intrapsychic meteorologies and conjunctures

DOI: 10.4324/9781003340744-25

that result in transformative dream productions precisely because they are intensely experiential in themselves.

My goal, however, is to highlight and enhance these events, so that the analyst can understand them and use them as rare opportunities, without ignoring them, without misunderstanding them, and above all without ruining them with know-it-all technical ignorance by favoring premature interpretations.

These favorable intrapsychic meteorologies and conjunctures allow a subjective experience of the Self in a condition of softening or even partial suspension of the unconscious defensive Ego, without at the same time – always at an unconscious level – a Superegoic persecutory intervention intervening to transform the ongoing experience into a nightmare.

The regime of greater benignity of these privileged deep meteorologies seems to involve less recourse to the work of masking, shifting and condensing scenarios, object representations, and events: ultimately, many of these dreams seem to open a direct door to access and to experience something of the Self condition, without too much subterfuge or cryptic and labyrinthine convolutions to decipher.

Of course, this transformation, which is most often connected to the transferential/countertransferential events of the process and to the developments of the analytic relationship, cannot be decided programmatically; in fact, it is made more accessible by complex and sometimes inconspicuous micro-operations of remediation of the patient's inner world, which changes not only by endogenous evolutionary drive, but also, as we know, by the effect of interactions with the analyst.

Accurate and sensitive monitoring of this process can enable contemporary analysts to competently "read" the continuity between the deep phantasmatic relation, the world of internal objects, the past, the "here and now," the "outside of here and now," and the potential future of the "all times." I reiterate as fundamental the fact that the analyst knows how to appreciate the richness and fertility of these developments, distinguishing physiology from pathology with sufficient clarity.

The analyst's function of being able to perceive, witness, and at least partially share the atmosphere and meaning of these experiential experiences is decisive (Busch, 2007; Poland, 2000).

Beyond the fulfillment of desire

In his book *Dreams that Turn the Page*, Jean-Michel Quinodoz (2001), exploring the area of dreams that worry patients because they give representation to anxieties or problems that they do not want to contact and that they fear as signs of worsening, while showing instead an advancement in analytical work, also lists a series of childhood dreams reported by Freud that show unequivocally at work the function of desire fulfillment.

These are famous dreams in the history of psychoanalysis: children who in a dream eat strawberries or eggs that during the day have been or will be rationed to them for various reasons; others who make trips to the lake or acrobatic climbs that are impractical for them in reality, and so on. "The common element in these children's dreams is obvious. They all fulfill desires that have arisen during the day and remained unfulfilled. They are simple and clear wish fulfillments." In these notes I explore instead, deliberately, an area that extends beyond simple wish fulfillment. I would call it an experiential area of perspective-opening and evolutionary testing, not set up hallucinatorily and substitutionally to appease a desire or need, but effective in producing change.

Effective deep dreaming

In a very detailed study, the result of his research on dreaming started in 1953, Dement and Vaughan (1999) confirmed that the dream in its most significant form and with the greatest experiential function is the one that occurs during REM phase; moreover, the predominant mental activity in REM dreams is the one most charged with affective images, while in most NREM dreams the prevailing mode (although not the only one) is the secondary process.

This researcher, like others, not only confirms how the recovery of deep sleep is essential for the reintegrative function of brain tissue (which is in agreement with the well-known fact that subjects who suffer from insomnia have a greater fatigue and irritability during the day as well as a greater performance deficit), but joins the line of those who have extended the potential function of the dream to the area of creative problem solving, such as, e.g., Cohen and Cox (1975), who pointed out that the dream can be a process aimed not only at representation, but also at the resolution of emotional and even intellectual problems, through specific functional steps.

In a study now considered a classic, these two researchers administered to several subjects an experience of failure in a task before they fell asleep. Those who included this experience in their dreams were better the next day and were more able to successfully confront the task failed the night before, compared to those who had not dreamed it. The authors also wondered whether the subjects who were able to dream that situation were basically in better shape than the others.

In fact, the list of contributions on the topic of "not only representation and not only wish fulfillment" is very long.

Maeder (1912) of a dream *"function ludique,"* as a preparatory exercise to subsequent operations in external reality; Grinberg et al. (1967), describing the "elaborative" dreams of the phases of integration, have shown the growing reparative capacity of the patient, who begins to know how to take care of himself; Garma (1970) has outlined a "broad thinking" during dreams, thinking of an archaic type strongly visual, but in which there are judgments, reflections, criticisms, and other mental processes of the same type as those of the waking; the theoretical line that starts from Winnicott and arrives to Bollas has valued the experiential dimension of the dream; De Moncheaux (1978) has hypothesized a reintegrative function of the dream with respect to trauma; Matte Blanco (1981) has re-examined a possible aspect of displacement, in the dream, as a sometimes creative opening towards new places, times, and possible representations, and condensation as an attempt to integrate different space-time categories.

Levin (1990) reports that an increase in REM sleep and dreaming seems to be related to the "ability to use imagination effectively, to follow divergent [creative] thinking, and holistic problem-solving" (p. 37).

Along the same lines, Kramer (1993), who addressed the effects of dream activity on mood regulation function, summarizing data from other research, notes, "Dreaming well at night, which happens about 60% of the time, is the result of progressive, sequential, and figurative problem-solving activity that takes place throughout the night" (p. 187).

Nothing surprising, after all, to us analysts, who have long cultivated a view of creativity as the effect of a fortunate combination and virtuous alternation between primary and secondary processes.

And since here I intend to focus the research mainly on the effective aspects of the dream related to a lived experience "true even if not real" (Bolognini, 2008; 2017), I would like to point out a unique clinical note of the same Dement (op. cit.) which reports the technical progress of a golfer: he, after repeated failures in an attempt – in waking state – to improve his setting in the execution of certain shots, was then able to successfully change his mode of grip on the golf club following a dream in which he was able to effectively experience the appropriate change of attitude.

Fosshage (1997; 2006) emphasized more than others the general synthetic function of the primary process, but also underlined how in the dream, through high-intensity sensorial and visual images, it emphasizes and enhances the affective coloring of the experience. For this author, clinical evidence of the developmental function of mental activity that takes place during dreaming occurs when for the first time a new psychological configuration, or change, emerges in a dream that cannot be traced back to alert mental activity and that suggests to him the idea of a "functional efficacy of dreams."

"A patient, for example, may dream of asserting himself for the first time to a critical father. The emergence in the dream of a new configuration suggests that the person with his dream activity produces change or, at least, promotes development."

It is evident how these observations by Fosshage go far beyond the simple concept of wish fulfillment.

On the level of technique, he recommends two things:

1. Very careful listening to the patient's subjective experience during the dream.
2. Analytic inquiry should tend to broaden the patient's experience of the dream, if the patient does not proceed spontaneously in this direction. For example, "What did you feel when such and such a thing happened in the dream? What did you feel?" (in his opinion, general questions such as "What do you associate with the dream?" or "What does this dream mean to you?" tend to be too open-ended and undefined, and often induce an intellectualized and affectless approach to the dream).

According to Fosshage, focusing all attention on the "experience" of the dream can advantageously neutralize the patient's often defensive interpretation of the waking dream, which can be in marked contrast to its metaphorical and thematic structure. On the other hand, a shared exploration, based on conscious resonance, corroborates the dream experience and confirms to the patient the vividness and significance of his dream experience.

To sum up: the experiential side of the dream can allow, sometimes, operations of knowledge of potentialities of the Self that until that moment had not been contacted and experienced, and creates a special psychic condition that allows human beings, even in retrospect, to feel the representations of the dream as "true," even if not "real" (Bolognini, 2000). This feeling of experiential "truth" of the dream is not infrequently transmitted also to the analyst, to whom the dream is narrated, and puts him in turn in a condition to share in vivo the experience of the patient; this condition of "joint dreaming," or reverie, allows one to dream undreamed dreams and interrupted nightmares (Ogden, 1997). However, Ogden focuses primarily on joint dreaming in session. In the clinical materials I will present, I will refer first of all to the power of dreaming as an experience in itself for the patient, then transmissible also to the analyst if the latter has the ability to dream together with the patient in reverie (Bolognini, 2008).

I intend to emphasize the integrative aspects of the dream experience by taking up here the inspired digression of André Green during the discussion that took place at a conference on dreams in 2005 (Lucca):

Experience is more than language, it is that movement that is determined within and that makes it possible to say that something happens. We do not know what, but something happens. The fact that something happens may have something to do with integrative experience and above all with the surprise in front of what happens. There it is, there I think about it! Here I am thinking back to this or that event! There! I think of her in this or that way!

The two clinical excerpts I will present concern two different setting situations (the first patient is in analytic psychotherapy; the second has been in analysis for many years).

The element of continuity between the two cases is precisely constituted by the quite similar experiential value of some of their dream events, with unexpected effects, in both cases, of an effective integrative ulteriority.

Clinical case: Carlo

For some years now I have been seeing in analytical psychotherapy, two sessions a week, a patient, whom I will call Carlo, who lives at a great distance from my city, and who despite this is very constant and assiduous in the work we are doing.

He comes to me to work on wounds that have never healed, but here I will avoid reporting biographical elements, which are dramatically significant, in order to focus on a specific event pertinent to the theme.

He is a man about 55; he has been married for 25 years; he leads a regular life; he does some things periodically with his wife (trips, cinema); he is an intelligent, honest person, able to think independently and endowed with original and positive qualities.

As I said, he had a life full of extremely tragic and traumatic events, from which he was able to emerge with tenacity and courage and that he can tell in full, without reticence, even if sometimes with a touch of excessive nonchalance, which from the beginning I felt oriented more towards a partial emotional avoidance than to manic defenses, in fact not present in him in a significant way. Over time, I was able to discover that more than a true avoidance, behind that nonchalance was hidden a sort of accepted, resigned normality of not being able to afford to share with anyone the painful and disturbing emotions related to his personal traumas (especially early losses of various family members in highly dramatic circumstances).

When, over time, Carlo became progressively more familiar with our encounters, the analyst's attitude of recognizing and above all sharing something of those profound experiences (of course, in the two different perspectives and proportions of those who, like him, carry those experiences violently stamped inside, and those who instead experience them there and then, through countertransferential resonance) caused him some initial hesitation; but then it became evident that Carlo was able to use those possibilities, and indeed he benefited greatly from them, as he recognized.

I can say that from the very beginning I enjoyed meeting him, that I appreciated his qualities, and that I felt an instinctive human sympathy for him. He also inspired in me a sense of respect, because he was an intellectually honest person, who did not tell his story with narcissistic self-deceptions.

His relationship with his wife had been very pleasant at first, though never passionate (as it had been with previous girlfriends); over time it had become rather ritualistic, polite, and even mutually solicitous, but not warm. He had never cheated on her, nor had he ever had feelings of possible betrayal on her part, but they both no longer felt desire, and had not had sexual intimacy for years; he gave me the impression that they lived like two brothers.

Since he was a physically healthy individual and capable of contact and exchange, I wondered how he could live – precisely – in a regime of abstinence like a monk, devoting himself to some hobbies in his free time, in a regime perhaps suspended between removal and sublimation.

Once, when I explicitly asked him how he lived that regime, he said that it was not pleasant but that he could not do otherwise: he did not intend to leave his wife, theirs was a relationship of mutual support and he was used to it; and once again images of two little brothers, in need of supporting each other, came to my mind.

For biographical reasons of both of them it made sense, but that is not the ground I want to go into here. I just want to describe Carlo's arrival at the session on a spring day (a few months ago), a completely different arrival than usual.

Always discreet, attentive, and punctual, this time the patient rang five minutes early, and it was immediately clear that he had not realized it. He appeared dazed and radiant at the same time, with an expression of almost happiness – quite unusual for him, who mostly showed a somewhat sad and ironic expression towards life, with that partial self-protective distancing that was his usual attitude, and which was not there at all in this case. The nonchalance was gone.

I immediately understood that he was driven by a strong desire to tell me something: after a few seconds he explained to me that towards morning he had had a dream, an extraordinary dream that he not only remembered very well, but that was still pervading him, and that he could not understand how real it had been when he dreamed it, and still at that moment, as if he were partly immersed in it.

The dream was simple and powerful: he was in loving intimacy, sentimental and physical, with a young woman who was attractive but also deeply affectionate with him; and this situation had lasted for a long time – at least in his subjective experience – and above all it seemed real, he felt it was real … somehow it WAS real!

The pleasant daze that prolonged in his waking state was accompanied in him by a sort of happy gratitude towards the event, which Carlo described to me very well and managed to convey to me, to the point that in a certain sense I found nothing strange in it: he was describing to me a beautiful human experience, which he deeply needed.

Due to a combination of factors, in his inner world he seemed to have managed to "find" a moment of benign agreement between his internal instances: the censorship devices had not been triggered, there had been no depressing or masking oneiric work, the representational function had worked at its best, and the experiential immersion in the dream had taken place with a vividness, a livability, and a preserved continuity between unconscious, pre-conscious, and consciousness that Carlo had never been able to afford, at least on the basis of what I had been able to observe in my years of work with him.

A happy conjuncture in the intrapsychic meteorology, some new kind of occasional agreement between his internal objects seemed to have accom-panied and made possible that experience, which showed no signs of mania or paroxysmal eroticization: the patient's Central Ego (Fairbairn, 1944) was well aware of the novelty and "non concrete reality" of that dream event, but remained tolerant, and willing in turn not to attack, remove, or deny the experienced condition.

I was surprised by my own experience during that session: I felt that I understood quite well what my patient was experiencing; I was – as they say – happy for him, because I felt that he really needed to contact both the object of desire and the parts of himself that had long been excluded from that possibility. I thought that the most useful thing, at that moment, was not to inform the patient's Ego about its internal dynamics, but to assist the patient and share from a close and respectful, but also recognizable, position that experience of something true, very true, in which the Ego and the Superego, at last, had given space not only to representation, but to the well-integrated experience of a deep need of the Self.

On the one hand, I felt like a parent happily witnessing emotional (and exciting, for those who witness it) growth.

On the other hand, I also felt spontaneous to explore with my thoughts and with a fantastic representation the underlying continuity, so little logical and so much psychological, that we analysts know and practice every day in session: the continuity of the deep life of patients with aspects of the analytic relationship, the transformative situation that, through transferential regres-sion, but not only, can reopen the games where they were closed in the past.

I will not dwell here on the multiple aspects of deep connection with the object/analyst and with the previous work that had made that passage possible.

I will focus my attention on the sense of truth characteristic of certain dreams, to say that it goes beyond *figurabilité* (Botella, 2007) – it is not limited to giving representation: it is a moment of further integration, in which without confusion between the "real" and the "true" (Carlo knew very well that what he dreamed was not real, it was not hallucinated at all) potential aspects of the Self can come into play and develop, being experienced, precisely, as true.

Nd clinical case: Pietro

From the undifferentiated amphibian to the lion

Pietro is an architect in his 30s, intelligent, studious, and of good moral character.

He is not a very disturbed patient, but (quite a rare case, nowadays!) a mild neurotic with some obsessive traits and a strong sexual inhibition; despite living with his girlfriend Margherita, he retains some infantile aspects that suggest a sort of protracted latency.

He asked for analysis because of a sense of inadequacy in the developments of his life, both in his life in a couple and professionally, and he has been willingly committed from the beginning, developing a confident transference – without idealization – that seems to confirm an overall positive primary experience in the basic relationship with the object.

The father figure is not particularly devalued but seems faded: the father is described as a decent, good person, but succumbs to his own mother.

During his training, Pietro – in spite of a brilliant curriculum of studies – has taken care to rely on figures who are not particularly incisive, who have put him in a position to learn what is necessary to carry out his work technically, but who have not inspired to him any particular evolutionary thrust.

Professionally, he carries on a small-scale routine, not daring to venture into more challenging waters.

At home he depends a lot on his partner, with whom he gets along well but to whom he "relies" with a certain passivity, in a relationship that resembles that of mother–son; to me he seems immersed in a rather regressive symbiosis, in which he also basks a bit. Sexual activity is scarce, "on demand," even if he does not mind at all, but usually he does not "think about it."

He brings a dream, in the second year of analysis, which testifies to a change that has been taking place for some time now:

P: Doctor, today I want to tell you about a dream, from last night. With Margherita and another couple of friends we went to visit a natural park. From a terrace/bar I see a natural lake (I notice that he repeats "natural"), full of fish, very beautiful. But in this kind of aquatic zoo there are also small hippos with outer shells like rhinos, and sea turtles.

Suddenly a very large lion appears, chased by those animals, who try to kill him. He fights furiously, but they try to drown him underwater! (Pietro is very agitated: he seems to be reliving the dream "from inside" as he tells it, and he makes me participate in the drama of the scene.) I feel pity and anxiety: I'm rooting for him, but it won't be easy for him to be saved. They weigh on him, they push him under, he struggles, it's a fierce fight! I woke up all agitated.

A (IMPRESSED AND THOUGHTFUL): Yes, you make me feel that there is a very fierce battle going on inside you: between those very primitive and amphibious animals, linked to the aquatic environment, and the lion, a more evolved and prouder animal, that they are trying to pull down.

P (VERY CONCENTRATED): In a certain sense it was the struggle between two different worlds, between two ways of being, I would almost say ...

between two civilizations (pause; we are both reflecting, as if we were reviewing the scene in play-back).

At this point, something comes to mind that apparently doesn't have much to do with it, but after a short while it turns out to be anything but insignificant, so I propose it directly:

A.: Yesterday you were talking about your idea of sending your project for the underpass to the bus station, to the competition announced by the Municipality, and then – vice versa – of the opposite tendency to give up and go to sleep; how did it end up?

P (WITH IMMEDIATE OPENING): A very hard struggle, Doctor! I'd write three lines, then I'd be ashamed of what I'd written and turn on the TV; then I'd turn it off, start writing again, and so on. (PAUSE) After all, that's what I've been doing for years: nothing could be easier than avoiding commitment and danger, letting yourself go into the arms of mommy-TV.

A: while to take part in the contest … you need the courage of a lion!

P (LAUGHS; THEN BECOMES SERIOUS AGAIN): Yes, but Doctor, I can assure you that the dream struggle was really scary! (again impressed) … luckily I was safe on the terrace.

A: You see the internal struggles from the terrace/analysis: you are relatively safe, but you cannot avoid getting both scared and excited.

The session continued with associations about the lion and other animals.

Pietro is experiencing an intense conflict between the inertial tendency to keep himself sleepy amphibiously fusional (he has spent years sprawled out on the couch at home reading and watching television, avoiding many aspects of life), and the push towards developing a more individuated, energetic, and adult masculine identity.

Sometimes he also attacks me (and there then the lion is me, like a father to be "pulled down," castrated, and neutralized), but more often he uses me as a guide.

What interests me is that he now integrates well the feeling and the understanding, the "seeing" of things from the "terrace/bar"/analysis and the "feeling involved" in the struggle; that he connects the oneiric reality to the diurnal one (the castration anxieties reactivated by the idea of the project for the competition), putting the Central Ego to work as well, after the intense experience of the dream and the states of the Self experienced in it.

Next session

P: We are in session, in the stone house in my original mountain village. I see everything from below: your desk, your …

I told you about the fact that I felt belittled by my father: then you stood up and showed me a picture with four photos and a title: "THE

PSYCHOSEXUAL DEVELOPMENT OF MAN." In the last picture there is a penis in erection. You were cheerful, in a good mood about your own business, and I am happy for this unconventional way of your using photos in the session.

A (DECIDED): You explain to me that you want to be helped to see yourself clearly, to be able to represent your development here in analysis (= the four photos/four sessions), to be able to portray yourself as more "lion-like" (= the photo with the erect penis); and you feel that in order to help you, I have to be a little "higher" than you (as a personal development: the desk higher, etc.), even at the cost of some idealization, and that it is good that I am in good shape ("in a good mood for your business"). (pause) But what comes to mind about being "belittled by your father"?

P: I had a great dedication to him as a child, and I felt that he loved me. But once, in front of the town bar, he introduced me to a gentleman as "MY BAMBOCCETTO" (a dialect expression, equivalent to "MY BABY"): it made me feel like a clumsy, awkward child, even though it was, after all, an affectionate expression. I was 6 years old, it hurt my pride a lot, I felt humiliated, and I felt anger. Even when I was a teenager: he denied me the use of his car, fearing that something might happen to me, and we had some very hard fights; but there was nothing to be done. After graduation and after his death, I had the money for a car, but not the courage. As you know, I only got my driver's license a year ago.

A (PENSIVE): Without a driver's license, you would have felt like a toothless lion!

P (LAUGHING, AND RECOVERING): Eh, eh! Today I got home at 2 p.m. Margherita said to me: "Are you hungry?" "Yes." While she was heating up the pizza, she set the table. "No" – I said – "today I feel like eating standing up: American style!" And Margherita: "Ah, how I like you when you're a big animal!" ... and she didn't know about the dream!!! ... It made me laugh.

I feel I share a sense of smugness (partly out of concordant, Ego syntonic countertransference with him, and partly out of complementary, paternal equivalent countertransference), and I shut up.

I think Pietro is getting tougher and smarter, toughening up.

I could tell him that he feels less of a "*bamboccetto*/baby," but I feel that would be redundant and all too attuned: better not to overdo the celebrations. Instead, I want to see which way his associations take.

P: In the dream you Doctor had an unconventional but useful attitude. I'm reminded of that episode a few months ago when Engineer X sent me that separate, beautiful, seductive client of his to the studio for a project. Sexual fantasies came to me, and I also felt a certain attraction; shame and guilt, I felt like a pig, and I thought I should change jobs (actually I was put in such a way that I considered myself a pig even if I was interested in beautiful girls on the street). I struggled with those thoughts. I was so relieved to talk about it here.

The patient is also integrating, along with more evolved sexual drives, a partial pregenital component of phallic narcissism, which is nonetheless important for the cohesive reinforcement of masculine identity: a healthy and necessary component, of which he was lacking.

To be grateful to the analyst for the help received is certainly not "childish," but I feel I should neither emphasize nor confirm the acknowledgements that come out of his preconscious: his genitality is still forming, and his "erection" (the "eating standing up, American style") is still experimental.

The patient's communication contains, in my opinion, a precise warning to the analyst: not to infantilize him too much, not to analytically "stay on top of him too much" (as his loving parents did on another level), and to be there when he is really needed.

In these sessions, I see a feeling of healthy pride appearing in a nascent state, a sense of the masculine Self that is beginning to assert itself and to which I intend to give space, without behaving like an apprehensive, overprotective, and overly incumbent parent.

It seems to me, however, that the process of rediscovery and integration of the partial drive and narcissistic components is proceeding, and I would also ascribe to this my countertransferential experience, more and more often marked by a certain satisfaction, as when I see one of my grandchildren kick the ball and score a goal.

One could also reasonably object that this dream represents the realisation of a wish of the patient: that of becoming capable of an opportune adult "erective" style, which he had lacked until then.

This is certainly true, but the accent in this sequence falls on the experiential aspect, exactly as in the case of the golfer described by Dement: in both cases there is not only the hallucinatory substitution of an unpleasant reality with a more satisfying one, but a learning by experience takes place within the dream itself.

The dream of the lion and the anti-evolutionary hippopotamuses helped us not only because it figuratively described the terms of the conflict, allowing us to decipher its meaning and dynamics, but also because it was a powerful dream, transformative precisely because it was strongly experiential, to the point of being shareable during its telling, as if we had both seen a film in the same movie theater.

Conclusions

The purpose of these notes, which do not aspire to present entirely new concepts, is therefore to help one to recognize, experience, understand, appreciate, and – when possible – use analytically certain dreams that are the result of privileged conjunctions of the intrapsychic coexistence and cooperation of the internal agencies, as well as of the patient and the analyst in their joint work, to the point of allowing the patient to live experiences that integrate and broaden contact with his Self.

It is always exciting to see a person attempt, dare, try, and experience something new, even if his or her proceeding is initially conflicting, uncertain, and hesitant.

In a certain sense, when faced with the emotional narration of certain dreams, it is a matter of encouraging in the patient the birth of a sensitive and aesthetic internal structure, and not only an investigative one.

References

Bolognini, S. (editor) (2000) *Il sogno cent'anni dopo (The Dream 100 Years after)*. Turin: Boringhieri.

Bolognini, S. (2008) *Secret Passages. The Theory and Technique of the Interpsychic Relations*. London: IPA New Library, Routledge.

Bolognini, S. (2017) La mentalità artistica (The artistic mentality). In *Arte e psicoanalisi: il respiro della creatività*, edited by G. De Giorgio. Milan: Franco Angeli.

Busch, F. (2007) An optimistic turn. *Psychoanalytic Quarterly*. 76: 609–615.

Cohen, D. and Cox, C. (1975) Neuroticism in the sleep laboratory: implications for representational and adaptive properties of dreaming. *Journal of Abnormal Psychology*. 84: 91–108.

De Moncheaux, C. (1978) Dreaming and the organizing function of the ego. *International Journal of Psychoanalysis*. 59: 443–453.

Dement, W.C. and Vaughan, C.L. (1999) *The Promise of Sleep*. New York: Bantam Doubleday Dell Publishing Group.

Fairbairn, R. (1944) Endopsychic structure considered in terms of object-relationships. *International Journal of Psychoanalysis*. 25: 70–92.

Fosshage, J.L. (1997) The organizing function of dream mentation. *Contemporary Psychoanalyisis*. 33(3), 429–458.

Fosshage, J.L. (2006) Lavorare con i sogni. Alcune considerazioni di base per un approfondimento (XIV Forum IFPS Roma 2006).

Freud, S. (1923) Observations on the theory and practice of the interpretation of dreams. 19: 112.

Garma, A. (1970) *Nuevas aportaciones al psicoanálisis de los sueños*. Buenos Aires: Paidós.

Grinberg, L. (1967) Función del soñar y clasificación clinica de los sueños en el proceso analitico. *Revista de Psicoanalisis*. 24: 749–789.

Kramer, M. (1993) The selective mood regulatory function of dreaming: an update and revision. In: *The Functions of Dreaming*, edited by A. Moffitt. Albany, NY: State University Press of New York.

Levin, R. (1990) Psychoanalytic theories on the function of dreaming: a review of the empirical dream research. In: J. Masling (editor), *Empirical Studies of Psychoanalytic Theories*, Vol. 3, pp. 1–53. Chicago: Analytic Press, Inc.

Maeder, A. (1912) Über die Funktion des Traumes. *Jahrbuch fur Psychoanalitische und Psychopathologische Forschungen.* 4: 692.

Matte Blanco, I. (1981) *The Unconscious as Infinite Sets: An Essay in Bi-Logic.* London: Karnac.

Ogden, T. (1997) Reverie and interpretation. *Psychoanalysis Quarterly.* 66(4): 567595.

Poland, W.S. (2000) The analyst's witnessing and otherness. *Journal of the American Psychoanalytic Association.* 48: 17–34.

Quinodoz, J.M. (2001) *Les Reves qui tournent une page – réves d'intégration a contenu paradoxal regressif.* Paris: PUF.

Chapter 21

Intersections between the feminine and the infantile

Virginia Ungar

Receiving the invitation to write about "Psychoanalysis at the Crossroads" has provided the stimulus to reflect on a topic that evokes the image of a central hub from which many paths diverge. To begin, one must choose one of these paths.

Donald Meltzer once said that all psychoanalytic work is, to some extent, autobiographical. And it is in that regard that I will involve myself in this writing.

Crossroads alludes to intersections that imply encounters. These could be encounters between lines, spaces, or elements of a different nature. Of course, they could also be encounters between people. The notion of the encounter is crucial in psychoanalysis, although perhaps there is no theoretical conceptualization that reflects its importance in our profession. I see this book as paving the way in that direction.

As analysts, our work is based on both encounters and, of course, disagreements. Without going into too much detail, from the moment of birth it is about encounters, the encounter of the newborn with the world, which in Meltzer's terms is the encounter with the mother, who in turn represents the beauty of the world (Meltzer, 1988).

What else does analysis involve? It is the encounter between two people wherein, if everything proceeds naturally, transference is initiated, and from there the process develops with all its vicissitudes.

Encounters and disagreements take place in a time and space and, especially, in a context, in a culture.

This has never been clearer than during the COVID-19 pandemic, which provoked a humanitarian crisis of as yet unknown proportions. It affected our lives and our relationships, and it also laid bare the enormous inequalities that exist in the world in terms of health, education, access to employment and a decent life. It revealed the fragility of humans, of our own limits, and we were forced to live with uncertainty, which we have always lived with but managed very well to deny it.

DOI: 10.4324/9781003340744-26

As with any crisis, it has brought out the positive impulses of solidarity as well as those of destructiveness. On the positive side, a connection was forged with reality and the social responsibility of care and of getting vaccinated. However, denialism also emerged, along with movements that reject otherness and encourage xenophobia, racism, and different expressions of violence.

Speaking of the autobiographical, the invitation to write for this book has led me to think about the past six years of my life since I was elected to the position of IPA president in 2015 and, more specifically, about my experience during the period from July 2015 to July 2017.

At that time, just being the first woman in history to preside over the International Psychoanalytical Association raised a bit of a stir, as well as many questions as to why it took until 2015 for a woman to be elected when the IPA had been founded in 1910. This, together with the experience of managing an organization with almost 13,000 members and 5,500 analysts in training, has made me reflect and study issues that I was not previously accustomed to thinking about.

These issues include, first of all, the condition of women today and the subject of sexual and gender diversities. COWAP's invitations to their plenary sessions at its congresses and to its conferences and publications helped me learn more about these issues, which led me to delve deeper into other subjects, such as authority, power, and leadership, and their relationship to gender. And so, the theme of the first congress held under our Latin American tenure emerged naturally and, after discussing it with Sergio Nick, we decided on the title *The Feminine*. As you know, the London Congress was extremely successful, with 2,500 attendees and lively debates.

For our second congress, we chose the theme of *The Infantile*, which continues the task of trying to conceptualize terms that were part of our psychoanalytic vocabulary but had yet to be given their own due.

The July 2021 congress was a real challenge because we had to switch to an online format, but it was very stimulating and received a large number of participants, more than 1,800 attendees who overcame the geographical distances and differences in time zones and languages.

At this time, I think it may be interesting to try to place myself at the intersection of the two themes as embedded in the experience of leading an institution such as the IPA. I know that this will also help me process both the experiences of the past years and the end of my stewardship.

To begin, when we refer to the Feminine in psychoanalysis, we cannot cast aside the much-discussed Freudian ideas about womanhood, not just in terms of the phallocentrism but also the non-representation of the female genitalia or, in other words, what can be represented is the absence, the lack thereof. Melanie Klein followed another path with her proposal of the early Oedipus complex, that of the unconscious notion of the vagina in the child, a firm commitment to the relationship with the interior of the mother's body and that of a rather fierce early feminine superego. This brief mention of these now classic perspectives of psychoanalysis cannot fail to include Lacan's oft-quoted aphorism "the woman does not exist." Without going into further discussion, it reveals the difficulty of considering the Feminine as a universal and the need to situate it in the singularity of each woman.

Of course, there are many very important contributions in our field that have provided the basis for further studies on femininity, as well as for the studies on gender that emerged years later.

While acknowledging that this is too constrained a space for an adequate discussion, I do want to mention that it has been exciting to reread Marie Langer's *Maternidad y sexo* (*Motherhood and Sexuality*) (Langer, 1951), first published in 1951, and in which she opens a surprising space for debating issues such as femininity, maternity, what she terms the disorders "of fertilization," as well as pregnancy, childbirth, and breastfeeding. From the opening chapter, her arguments on "women and their current conflict" are striking; she provides a historical overview of the place of woman in society and poses questions that continue to be valid today, 70 years after its publication. For example, just two of the issues she covers in the first chapter involve women and work and the question as to whether maternity is indisputable.

For the London Congress, I proposed holding a panel in tribute to Marie Langer. The proposal was accepted by the IPA in Health Committee – one of the components of the IPA in the Community structure – and her daughter Ana, who is an internationally recognized women's health specialist, joined us. There came further tributes and documentaries, one of which I recommend in particular, directed by Lily Ford (2020), shown this year at a University College of London Congress in which I participated virtually as a panelist. The documentary was produced within the framework of the *Hidden Persuaders* project, led by Daniel Pick at Birkbeck, University of London. I am pleased to share with you that, entirely independently of the event, in 2021, the project obtained the First Prize of the IPA in the Community Award, in the category of Culture.

Now, if we go beyond the boundaries of psychoanalysis and into other fields, it is also difficult not to consider the Feminine as opposite in a binarism that Simone de Beauvoir already questioned with great lucidity in 1949, in the prologue of *The Second Sex* (de Beauvoir, 1949). In order to place the Feminine in opposition to the universal masculine polarization can take several forms. Linking the position to binarism creates an illusion since, being dichotomous, the categories are mutually exclusive.

It is also usual for there to be an easy slide into the maternal function, home to the receptive. These functions-scenarios of "the Feminine" are ultimately non-exclusive when we think of them as broader, non-dichotomous categories. That is, as present beyond the woman herself, so as to reinforce the idea that the feminine unfolds in multiple scenarios. "The Feminine" can even be reappropriated precisely from otherness and understood as present beyond women, in the singularity of each individual.

In November 2018, I was invited to give a presentation and participate in a round table at the COWAP Congress in Los Angeles, USA, entitled "Facing Misogyny: The Dialectic between the Internal and External Glass Ceiling."

That invitation led to my research into the concept of the "glass ceiling," a term originally coined within the social sciences and, specifically, within feminist economics. The glass ceiling is that invisible barrier that prevents women from rising to the same positions as men. There is no explicit reason for its existence – it is determined by social relations and by subjective preconceptions rooted in the collective unconscious that, when accompanied by concrete legislation and ontologically verifiable evidence (the fact that fewer women occupy managerial positions), lead to a vicious circle of self-justification: women do not access certain spaces because "it is not in our nature."

The glass ceiling is, to be redundant, the crystallization of a falsely justified social asymmetry that has both concrete and social consequences because it is so rooted in the individuality of each subject as part of their unconscious belief system.

On the other hand, the glass ceiling operates through such subtle mechanisms that it is constantly absorbed by our subjectivities, thus generating a second space of limitation within our internal setting. Our internal glass ceiling is our own shuttering of our desires, the thought that there are certain things that we cannot even desire, or the alteration of our own desires so as to adapt ourselves to a hegemonic model of a woman in a state of submission.

The theme of desire was reflected in COWAP's 2019 Congress, entitled "What Do Women Want Today?" Held in Washington, D.C., the event served as an important stimulus for delving into issues such as authority, power, and their relationship with gender, since a question that often arises is whether there are particularities in relation to gender when it comes to management.

The question of what women want today led me to another question, one that Kristeva asked during her talk at the 2019 London Congress, when she took up what she called the *enigmatic* question that Freud posed to Marie Bonaparte: "What does a woman want?", "*Was will das Weib?*" And immediately, she clarified the question is not about desire (*Wunsch*) but want (*Wollen*). For Kristeva, this is the pillar of choice in an ethical life. She then clarified that "the elusive ('what does she want?') points to the relationship of the *feminine* to the *ideals* of life and to *life itself*, which is inseparable from cultural ideals" (Kristeva, 2019).

The issue **is not** what a woman wants, it is not about *desire* but *want*, which for Kristeva is the crux of an ethical position. She also wondered whether Freud would not have pursued an ethical refounding through the Feminine, and stated that the biopolitics of modernity still forces this enigmatic question on us.

Today, as posed by Kristeva, it is possible to ask the question; in the past, there was no place for women to ask it. Now, a woman can ask herself several questions; first of all, if she wants to be a woman, but also, if she wants to be a wife, if she wants to be a mother. At the time Freud formulated his famous question, there was no place to even ask it.

This historic question for psychoanalysis seems to have been raised in an analysis session with Marie Bonaparte, who was taking notes when her analyst, none other than Sigmund Freud, said: "The great unanswered question which I myself have not been able to answer despite my thirty years of study of the female soul is the following: What does a woman want?"

We could say Freud located the question in the abstract: What does a woman want? Today, with the time that has elapsed and the enormous cultural and social changes that have occurred, we can talk about what women want. Furthermore, women want different and unique things; we do not all want the same thing.

In addition, I can imagine how a teenage girl from my own country may respond if I asked her this question today: "What kind of question is this?" she would say. "It would never occur to me to ask a question in those terms. Women are first and foremost people."

But beyond this era-defining question and the viewpoint of young women who are in favor of abandoning binarism, I believe that an initial response would be that women want equality, parity.

Although feminism has done and continues to do great work and women's movements have initiated a new way of doing politics, we cannot deny that women today do not have equal access or equal opportunities, nor is their unpaid work in the domestic sphere recognized. Nor can we deny that violence against women in its most aberrant forms, such as femicide, continues to increase.

These are the voices that continue to be heard, and they must continue to speak out as they can; today, much more so because of what cyberspace allows. In any case, I must emphasize that although it is the women's collective that has made it possible for us to be heard, the scope of psychoanalytic work lies with singularities.

This is the nature of our task; it is essentially singular. But this singularity is always constituted in relation to a context that this person inhabits. The exteriority is always plural.

Freud posed his question in a context in which the collective was essentially the family; there were no other collectives like those of women's movements today.

I would now like to add another possible response, that perhaps must precede the previous response, which is that women want to be heard. This is the only way to understand the massive movements that have emerged like a collective cry, first by women, and now by women, men, adolescents, and children.

We must be aware that we are preceded by a history full of silences: forced silences and silenced voices.

Mary Beard's book, *Women and Power*, published in 2017, helped me understand this point. It is a manifesto in which the author provides a historical overview of the mechanisms to silence women that are so deeply rooted in Western culture.

She traces the origins of this mandate to keep women silent to the story of one woman, at the very beginning of Western literary tradition, who appears in Homer's *Odyssey*, written almost three thousand years ago. As we know, the epic recounts the adventures of Ulysses on his journey home at the end of the Trojan War, while Penelope awaits his return. It is also the story of Telemachus, their son. In Book 1 of the poem, Penelope descends from her private chambers to the palace hall and finds a bard singing a tale of the vicissitudes of men returning home from war to a group of her suitors. She does not like the song and asks him to sing something more cheerful, to which her son Telemachus responds, "Mother, go back to the house and tend to your own tasks, to spinning and weaving ... Speaking is a matter for men, for all men, but for myself in particular, as I am the master of this house." Penelope retires to her quarters.

Beard takes this fragment of the *Odyssey* as the first written evidence in Western culture that women's voices must be silenced in the public sphere. She goes further, saying that what emerges is the idea that a man must learn to control public discourse and silence women as part of his becoming a man.

I would now like to expand the response to that historic question: women want equal access to positions of power. This is an issue that merits in-depth studies since, in my opinion, it is not just about the individual struggle of one or several women seeking to gain access to positions of authority – and to maintain them – in spite of all the negatives it stirs up. For evidence, all one needs to do is turn to the studies that monitor the varying degrees of misogynistic reactions on social media during an electoral campaign. In terms of its construction, the exercise of power continues to have a masculine focus. Since the current model for exercising power is one of domination, we must deconstruct it, as it comes from times when women were not even considered in its exercise.

From this perspective, it is interesting to think that there was a time in which, to his female patients who arrived with symptoms of hysterical conversion and who had no voice to be heard, Freud offered the possibility to "associate freely and speak about what comes to mind." He allowed them to talk, and their symptoms subsided.

For a woman to occupy a position of power today requires a great responsibility and enormous commitment. We can all agree that gender is socially constructed. And as Judith Butler already proposed, this construction emerges from a performative process.

Butler stated in an interview that the occupation of public spaces in relation to women's movements is also performative as a construction of power, and she presents it as an indispensable task of our time if we want to achieve changes in the world (Butler, 2019).

The issue of women and their exclusion from spaces of power has a long history in which the darkest and most terrible experiences are in the background and must always be taken into account; I need only mention the hunting and burning of witches as one example, as has been immortalized in Arthur Miller's *The Crucible*.

This is such a gripping topic; however, I set out to explore the intersection of the Feminine and the Infantile and, once again, it is Julia Kristeva who helped me along that path. I remember clearly that during her opening address for the 2019 conference she referred to the Feminine as transformative and something that is neither *innate* nor *acquired*, but the tireless *conquest* of the two phases of the unfinished Oedipus. She pointed out something important, which is that the vivacity of the Feminine can either diversify or succumb to the trials of the merciless socio-historical reality.

She also referred to the fact that in our era, women are at once an *emerging force*, with all its upheavals of values and identities, and, at the same time, an *irreducible otherness*, an object of desire, fear, and envy, of oppression and exploitation, of abuse and exclusion.

I will not repeat here all of the ideas she presented, but I confess she gave me much to think about after the Congress, based on her clear psychoanalytic opinion anchored in the deepest Freudian tradition and in a metapsychology that is linked to her openness to philosophy and other disciplines such as semiotics, in which she is a central figure.

Let's move onto the Infantile, which was discussed in detail at the last IPA Congress, where I participated in a discussion group entitled "The Forces of the Infantile in Feminine Leadership." I found the word "forces" to be a very appropriate way to refer to the Infantile.

That is how I understand the Infantile, as a force that is alive within us and is the source of our creativity, of our capacity to be amazed and to be open to new things. During the Congress, Florence Guignard defined it as a basic structure of the human mind that is alive and active in all of us throughout our lives.

Her central idea is that the Infantile is alive and is also a dynamic and constantly changing process. In her book *The Infantile in Psychoanalytic Practice Today* (2022), she sets out to study in detail the place of the Infantile in the analytic relationship. She begins her argument from the impact that a patient's Infantile has on the analyst's Infantile as it allows a connection with the most primitive part of the patient, enabling analysis through a process that is both identificatory and relational.

Her line of thought is familiar to me since my own theoretical framework is Kleinian and post-Kleinian; I am a child analyst and have practiced and taught Esther Bick's *Infant Observation Method*.

I also base myself on Meltzer's ideas; he was my teacher and already in 1967, in *The Psycho-Analytical Process*, he referred to the analytic method as follows: "The relationship is, of course, transference and countertransference, the unconscious and infantile functions of the minds of the patient and of the analyst" (1967, p. 20).

Meltzer also said, in Chapter 6 of *Claustrum*, that "the most satisfactory answer to the question, "Why do you seek analysis?" would be, "Because I need to gather together my needs for infantile transference so that there may be some possibility of working conflicts through instead of repeatedly enacting them" (1992, p. 97).

To conclude, I would like to return to my initial proposal of linking the Feminine and the Infantile in an attempt to understand some of the characteristics of the Feminine in the task of leadership.

The Feminine as a transformative power, together with the Infantile as a living and constantly changing force linked to the creativity of each and every one of us, provides support to the "forces" to which I have referred above.

Like any process of subjectivation, it will play out in relation to the historical-social context of each era. Although our own era is not that of the beginning of the last century, we must recognize the vulnerable position women have had and still have in our society in terms of the inequality of opportunities in the labor market.

In addition, psychoanalysts have a gap in our political-institutional education that coexists with a certain socially widespread, anti-political common sense that questions political activity and observes professional politicians (as well as those who make decisions, participate, and lead in institutions) with distrust. Thus, anyone with political-institutional aspirations, on any scale, raises suspicion. Questions are asked, such as: "Since when have they been interested in politics?" "What will they get out of it?" And, best of all, "Why are they getting involved in all this, if they are one of the good ones?"

Beyond this common social perception, the conduct of psychoanalytic institutions must be considered and reconsidered. It is in times of crisis that the ability to lead an institution is put to the test. This is when both solidarity and the components that are most destructive, inhospitable, and intolerant to difference emerge, with the latter leading to violence.

This is when two qualities become necessary: the ethical position of being faithful to one's own principles (to always be oneself) and the flexibility to make the changes necessary to confront the crisis.

It is at these moments that I recall Max Weber's extraordinary lecture (1919), "Politics as a vocation." In it, the German sociologist meditates on the virtues of the politician and singles out three in particular: their passion, sense of responsibility, and prudence.

When we consider political undertakings in light of this discussion, his words are more than current. Passion, like positivity, is dedication to a cause. Weber says that it is passion for a cause that makes us men, and here we should add women if we are to include the gender perspective. In fact, today, it makes us complex human beings.

However, passion is not enough. Responsibility to a cause is what guides political action, and it is prudence that ultimately shapes political subjectivity. In times like ours, when it is necessary to reconsider the conditions for the exercise of our profession and the meaning of institutions, nothing seems more certain. Or can we perhaps imagine and build new territories of psychoanalysis, for example, without passion, responsibility, and prudence?

References

Beard, M. (2017) *Women and Power. A Manifesto*. Mary Beard Publications.

Butler, J., Cano, V., and Fernández Cordero, L. (2019) *Vidas en lucha. Conversaciones*. Buenos Aires: Katz Editores.

De Beauvoir, S. (1949) *El segundo sexo*. Buenos Aires: Debolsillo Contemporánea, Penguin Random House. (Thurman, J. (editor) (2011) The Second Sex. New York: Random House.)

Ford, L. (2020) Chasing the revolution. Marie Langer, Psychoanalysis and Society. Documentary film, Hidden Persuaders project, Birkbeck University of London, UK.

Guignard, F. (2022) *The Infantile in Psychoanalytic Practice Today*. London: Routledge.

Kristeva, J. (2019) Prelude to an ethics of the feminine. Opening lecture given at the 51st IPA Congress, 24 July, London, United Kingdom.

Langer, M. (1951) *Maternidad y sexo*. México: Paidós. (*Motherhood and Sexuality*. New York: Guilford Press, 1992.)

Meltzer, D. (1967) *The Psychoanalytical Process*. Perth: Clunie Press.

Meltzer, D. (1988) *The Apprehension of Beauty*. Perth: Clunie Press.

Meltzer, D. (1992) *The Claustrum. An Investigation of Claustrophobic Phenomena*. London: Roland Harris Educational Trust.

Weber, M. (1918) Politics as a vocation. Originally a speech given at Munich University. *Essays in Sociology*, pp 77–128. New York: Oxford University Press.

Index

Note: Page numbers in *italic* denote figures and in **bold** denote tables, end of chapter notes are denoted by a letter n between page number and note number.